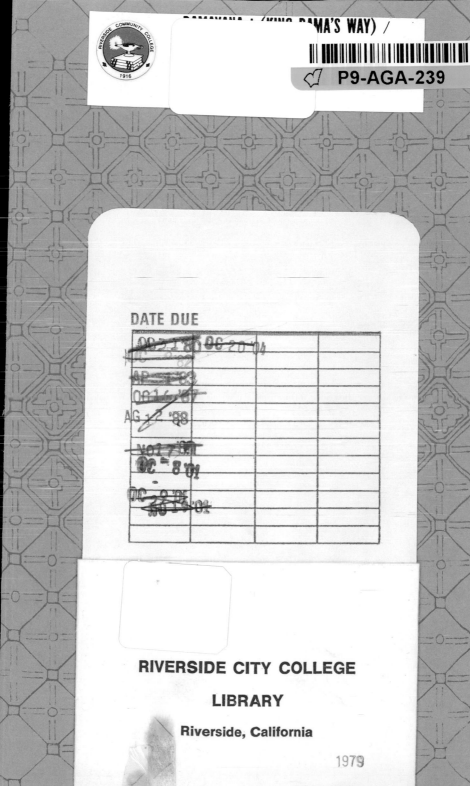

Ramayana

KING RAMA'S WAY

Valmiki's *Ramayana*
told in English prose by
William Buck

Ramayana

by William Buck

with an introduction by
B. A. van Nooten
illustrated by Shirley Triest

University of California Press
Berkeley · Los Angeles · London

For Paul, my son

University of California Press
Berkeley and Los Angeles, California
University of California Press, Ltd.
London, England
Copyright © 1976, by
The Regents of the University of California
ISBN 0-520-02016-2
Library of Congress Catalog Card Number: 78-153549
Printed in the United States of America

contents

Publisher's Preface   ix
Introduction   xiii
List of Characters   xxv

PART ONE.
The Prince of Ayodhya   1

Born as a Man   3
The Thorn in the World's Side   19
Taste This Water   48
The Two Wishes   60
Lord of the Wild Trees   85
Bharata Returns   110
The Sandals   122

PART TWO.
Sita's Rescue   137

Dandaka Forest   138
The Golden Deer   162
Hanuman!   176
The Search   200
Hanuman's Jump   219

v

Here I Am   242
The New Moon   258
The Building of the Bridge   278
The Siege of Lanka   293
The Invisible Warrior   308
Ravana and Time   325

PART THREE.
The Dharma Wheel   355

Here's Love!   356
The Wonderful Return   374
In What Dream?   389
Farewell Again, My Lady and
My King   404

List of Illustrations

Map . . . , xxiii

Then one cloudy Winter's day . . . , 4
Garuda shrieked and screamed . . . , 26
He bound Indra in illusion . . . , 46
. . . it broke in two above the grip . . . , 54
"What can I do even if I wanted?", 66
"I would go and give that statue a good kick", 90
. . . then he took him away . . . , 108
. . . but the crow returned., 128
. . . before the serpents knew he had even come in., 152
"I am too old and tired to talk anymore", 172
Hanuman saw the glorious sun rise . . . , 186
He withdrew a scroll from his robes . . . , 212
Hanuman stood on the hilltop . . . , 224
"Forget him!" yelled Ravana., 244
Ravana looked at Hanuman with twenty eyes., 260
They quickly ran out onto Rama's bridge . . . , 276
Hanuman jumped hard and high at Kumbhakarna., 304
. . . the scent of those herbs spread over the battlefield . . . , 314
. . . like the petals of a graceful flower . . . , 336

vii

"For you from the dead King",   350

. . . and drew up Rama holding Sita . . . ,   372

Sita was entranced.,   400

. . . "took her only child . . . ,   416

. . . first in through the water.,   428

. . . in fine little letters . . . ,   432

publisher's preface

In 1955 William Buck discovered an elaborate nineteenth-century edition of *The Sacred Song of the Lord, the Bhagavad-Gita of Lord Krishna* in a state library in Carson City, Nevada. Captivated by this find, he plunged into a study of Indian literature which has resulted in this rendering of *Ramayana*, a retelling of *Mahabharata*, and an unfinished manuscript of *Harivamsa*—unfinished because of his death in 1970 at the age of 37.

His discovery of the *Bhagavad-Gita* moved Mr. Buck to read the *Mahabharata*, and he would be satisfied with nothing less than a full translation. An 11-volume set was then being reprinted in India, and in his determination he subsidized the reprinting when it became apparent that the publisher had insufficient funds to complete the task.

Midway through his reading, Mr. Buck decided the *Ramayana* and *Mahabharata* should be rewritten for a modern English-speaking audience. In his own words, "*Mahabharata* was about 5,000 pages, and *Ramayana* much shorter. When I read these translations I thought how nice to tell the story so it wouldn't be so hard to read. We talk about all the repetition and digression of the originals, but as you read all that endless impossible prose a very definite character comes to each actor in the story, and the land and times are most clearly shown. I wanted to transfer this story to a readable book."

To this end, William Buck began years of reading and rereading the translations, studying Sanskrit, planning, and writing. One of his approaches was to decipher and list all the elaborate appellatives used in place of names for heroes and gods and kings and princesses in the original text. He then used the qualities of these appellatives to describe the characters in his own renderings and thus preserve their mood and meanings. He read all available English versions of the two great epics, but said of them, "I have never seen any versions of either story in English that were not mere outlines, or incomplete, except for the two literal translations." He always kept in mind that the epics were originally sung, and reading aloud from both the original translations and Buck's own work became part of the Buck family life.

William Buck's vision of his task was firm, and he had the balanced form of each epic clearly in his mind as he worked. In his words, "It is always apparent just what is the thread of the story and what are later interpolations. It is stuffed with preachments, treatises of special interests, doctrines of later caste systems, long passages of theological dogma, but these are in chunks, and only slow the story." His goal was to tell the tales in such a way that the modern reader would not be discouraged from knowing and loving them as he did. He wanted to convey the spirit, the truth, of the epics.

In answer to a critic of his manuscripts he replied, "I've made many changes and combinations in both books, but I wish to have them considered as stories which they are, rather than as examples of technically accurate scholarship, which I told you they weren't. One thing however is true. Read the stories and you get the real spirit of the original once you're done, and if they're entertaining that's all I ask." And in another letter: "*Ramayana* is one of the world's most popular stories, and it is part of its own tradition to be re-told in different times and places, as I have done."

That was his aim—to make it possible for contemporary

readers to know the *Ramayana* in terms meaningful for modern times, as well as in terms of its origins. Of the finished manuscripts he wrote, "My method in writing both *Mahabharata* and *Ramayana* was to begin with a literal translation from which to extract the story, and then to tell that story in an interesting way that would preserve the spirit and flavor of the original. My motive is therefore that of the storyteller. I'm not trying to prove anything and I have made my own changes to tell the story better. Here are two great stories just waiting for people to read them. Based on the words of ancient songs, I have written books. I tried to make them interesting to read. I don't think you will find many other books like them."

introduction

by B. A. van Nooten

Few authors in world literature can lay claim to having inspired as many poets and dramatists, and to having transmitted moral and ethical values to as vast and receptive an audience in nations living thousands of miles apart and with radically different languages and cultures, as the obscure, almost legendary composer of the Sanskrit *Ramayana*, a poet known to us as Valmiki.

Valmiki probably lived somewhere in northeast India, where much of the action of the story takes place. Legends make him a reformed robber converted to a virtuous life by a saint, but from the one and only literary work that remains of him we recognize him as a poetic genius, a man of refined and aesthetic sense and a pure instinct for moral living. The *Ramayana* (literally "Rama's Way") is one of the two great epics of India, the other being the *Mahabharata*. It is a long epic, some 25,000 verses in extent, and tells a story of courtly intrigue, heroic renunciation, fierce battles, and the triumph of good over evil. Prince Rama of Ayodhya is the hero. He is born into a noble family of rulers, but treacherous machinations of his stepmother force him to abdicate his claim to the throne of Ayodhya in favor of his half-brother, Bharata. Rama himself withdraws into the forest for thirteen years accom-

xiii

panied by his faithful wife Sita and his devoted half-brother, Lakshmana. Here they move in a strange world, part mythical, part spiritual, populated by gentle, God-seeking sages, but also by grim ogres and vicious demons who try to disturb Rama's tranquil life and thwart his noble intentions. In that world, a conflict develops between on the one hand the righteous Rama, a scion of the illustrious ancient solar dynasty, and on the other hand the legions of the dark, the Rakshasas or demons with ugly, menacing, repulsive forms who stalk the forest in search of mischief. Thanks to Rama's gallantry, he, Sita, and Lakshmana overcome the demonic powers until a great calamity befalls them: faithful Sita is abducted by the monstrous demon king Ravana. He flies with her to Lanka, his capital, but she never yields to him, reminding him steadfastly of her vow to Rama, her one and only lord.

Meanwhile Rama and Lakshamana search frantically for signs of life from Sita, going from one witness to another to learn of her whereabouts. Finally, they ally themselves with an army of talking monkeys and bears under the generalship of the mighty monkey Hanuman. The animals discover the place where Sita is kept prisoner, an island not far from India, probably prosperous Lanka, now known as Ceylon, or Sri Lanka. Hanuman with a tremendous bound leaps across and visits Sita. After setting fire to the city he returns to Rama who decides to rescue his wife by force. Thousands upon thousands of monkeys help to build a causeway across to the island, the remains of which are still visible—or so tradition goes. A frightful battle ensues. Hosts of monkeys and demons are slaughtered, the heroes use not only conventional weapons, but also divinely inspired arms and magic tricks. The demons can change shape at will by virtue of their maya, or magical power, and often succeed in deceiving the heroes. Rama and his allies perform feats of incredible fortitude, lifting up huge rocks and even mountains and suffering injuries beyond comprehension. In the end, as can be expected, the good are victorious and it is at this point that Rama discovers his divine antecedents. He is an incarnation of the great god Vishnu who has come on earth to save mankind from oppression by demonic forces.

Rama and Sita return to the capital of their country, Ayodhya, where Rama is crowned king. For many years their rule is glorious but then evil tongues spread rumors about Sita's abduction by Ravana long ago. Was she really as pure as she professed to be? Had the handsome Ravana really never touched her? In deep sorrow Rama asks Sita to leave for the forest and never to come back. No just ruler can live under a cloud of immoral conduct, even if it is no more than suspected misbehavior. Sita goes to the forest and gives birth to Rama's two children, Kusa and Lava. The great poet-sage Valmiki takes care of them and in time teaches them the great story of Rama's exploits, the *Ramayana*.

About the *Ramayana*'s date little can be said with certainty. It is a major work in the Hindu tradition but this tradition concerned itself very little with exact historical chronology. Roughly, and mainly by virtue of external and linguistic evidence, we accept a period of a few hundred years between 200 B.C. and A.D. 200 as a likely date for its composition. It probably grew fairly gradually, with the beginning and the end of the story being added on at the end of that period. So the story of Sita's second rejection by Rama as well as the incident of her being swallowed up by the earth are later additions. It is safe to say that Valmiki (if he really was the composer) drew upon a number of popular Rama folk tales for his epic which he wove together into a great frame story, together with numerous exotic and fabulous incidents. The conventional techniques of Sanskrit narrative are found here also: the use of narrators at various stages, the descriptions of nature to suggest the mood of the action, occasional divine interventions, and so on. It is, therefore, a traditional Indian literary work, but its impact on the people of India has been no less than phenomenal. It has inspired the themes for hundreds of major and minor literary works and plays. For two thousand years, down to the present day, Rama's exploits are celebrated in religious festivals, temple ceremonies, public holidays, and private ceremonies. Places where Rama walked are now famous as places of pilgrimage where thousands of Hindus flock every year. People in the villages tell their children the story of Rama, as we tell our children fairy tales. People in the cities can watch cinematic adaptations of Rama episodes and read abbreviated forms of its narrative in pocketbook editions. Rama has been transformed into an object of devotion and Rama worship is still a powerful religious force. The last words of the famous statesman Mohandas Gandhi were "Ram-ram," before he died from an assassin's bullet.

What can this popularity be attributed to? Among several factors, perhaps the most important is the characterization of the *Ramayana*. It is a work of exemplars, of models of good behavior which people in distress and frustration, when doubts assail them, can follow and imitate with beneficial results. We have Rama, the noble and virtuous prince whose supreme heroism lies not so much in the fact that he conquers his enemies, but in the fact that he stoically and dispassionately endures the greatest hardships, including rejection and calumny on the part of his nearest family. Sita too is a non-heroine: she is the constant victim of fate but all through her tribulations she remains faithful to her husband and does what he wants. She has become a model that pious Hindu women attempt to copy down to the present day. In these days of female emancipation these are unpopular sentiments in the West, but there is a perspective on life in which this model of behavior is as certain a way to liberation as the staunchest rebellion— and many Hindus have that perspective.

For many Indians, especially those who worship God as Vishnu, the *Ramayana* is mainly a religious poem describing the *avatara* (incarnation) of God on earth, his struggles with the powers of evil and his victory. The incarnation is often unaware of his divine role, but his actions are always noble, his regard of his fellowmen gracious and kind, his patience and forbearance of other people's slights exemplary—until he is faced with the embodiment of real wickedness, the devil incarnate. Then his righteous ire is aroused and his determination to eradicate and kill the evil powers cannot be stopped. For many in the audience listening to *Rama's Way*, that constitutes the essential story. But even those who are not particularly religiously oriented appreciate the *Ramayana* as a fascinating tale of adventure, heroism, exciting plots, and frightful monsters. It lends itself to bombastic portrayals in art and sculpture. For instance, the scene of thousands upon thousands of frantic monkeys clashing in combat with hordes of sinister-looking demons was portrayed on the wall reliefs of the Cambodian temple of Angkor Wat and in the Ketjak dance in Bali. There are romantic and emotional scenes, too, such as Rama's pathetic departure for the forest with Sita and his brother. The sorrow Rama feels when faithful Sita has been abducted is hard to forget. The scene of Sita's suffering in Ravana's palace in Lanka, in the midst of his spiteful, haughty wives who constantly pressure her to yield to their lord, is a touching example of her unswerving conjugal faith.

The question may be raised whether the great battle in the *Ramayana* represents an historic event. It is hard to answer. We can only speculate, as others have done, that the poem is based on a battle of great antiquity. The oldest Aryans, the ancestors of the Nordic people in India today, descended from the Iranian plateau into India some time in the middle of the second millennium B.C. They met speakers of Dravidian languages who now mainly live in South India. That meeting ultimately led to a fusion of the Dravidian and Aryan cultures in North India which at present has a largely homogeneous population. But the Aryan influence came into the south at a much later date, perhaps around the time that the Rama stories appeared. So speculation goes that the *Ramayana* represents a glorified account of this excursion of the Aryans into southern India with Rama as the Aryan cultural hero, and the Rakshasas of Lanka, as well as the monkeys and bears, the less developed races encountered by the Aryans.

This theory is highly speculative and probably false. As more archaeological evidence is uncovered we find that there have been flourishing civilizations in southern India for al-

xvii

most as long as in northern India. It is, therefore, not correct to believe that the *Ramayana* is a poeticized account of the Aryan inroads into South India. It is similarly incorrect to think of the figures of the bears and the monkeys somehow as contemptuous designations of uncivilized tribesmen. On the contrary, they are respected and even venerated creatures who embody qualities of strength, persistence, and enthusiasm, with a characteristic trust in their human leaders, which is often moving to observe. Without resentment and with blind faith they hurl themselves into battle and almost certain death because they believe the superior human creatures know what they are doing. To see in them portrayals of human beings is a matter of interpretation, not of fact. They are monkeys and bears capable of communicating with people; they are not caricatures of human beings.

As was stated earlier, the *Ramayana* has had a vast distribution over the countries of Southeast Asia bordering on the Indian Ocean and the Pacific. Burma, Cambodia, Thailand, Indonesia, and even the Philippines, to name only a few, are places where the Rama story was introduced and where it was accepted by the people and incorporated into their own cultures. In the course of this assimilation changes were oftentimes made, some deliberate, some unconscious. Sometimes the court poet of a local raja would celebrate his patron's greatness by picturing him as Rama, the hero, the conqueror of the world. He would fabricate a few scenes, omit a few others, and so compose a new Rama story. The geographical names were often changed to agree with the features of the locale, but the reverse also happened. In Indonesia, for instance, mountains like Brama, Sumeru, and rivers like Serayu still attest to the ancient influence of the Hindu epics. But the literary works, in addition, often had a popular version that was passed down by word of mouth, by professional storytellers, or just by merchants and travelers. In these popular versions the influence of local customs is often much more evident, and it is sometimes even difficult to discern the original Rama-Sita plot in amongst the incidental local stories.

Such is the case, for instance, with the recently discovered Philippine Rama story.

Against the background of this cultural adaptation of the *Ramayana* we should view William Buck's translation. It is not really a translation but more of a rewriting of the *Ramayana*, using as source material the published English translations. For translations of the *Ramayana* into English do exist, but none so far is very satisfactory, either from a scholarly, or from a literary point of view. William Buck's adaptation is an extraordinary accomplishment. He was neither a scholar nor a well-known author, and though he retells the Rama story with many variations of detail, he has succeeded in capturing the most important characteristics of the *Ramayana*: the simple religious tone that pervades the Indian original. We find in this rendering of the work the same awe of divine creation, the same wonder and unquestioning belief in the interrelation of natural and supernatural events that have appealed to millions of people who in the past two thousand years have listened to the recitation and reenactment of the Rama story. In the minds of many people who hear the *Ramayana* a mystery is being presented, and slowly, erratically, parts of the mystery unfold. If we are fortunate, we get occasional glimpses of a higher, purer reality that holds out hope for those enmeshed in the sorry state of mundane existence. Again and again this revelation causes us to read and rethink the epic in order to experience again this joy of discovery. The struggle between good and evil is on our behalf and Rama is our hero.

It is pointless to enumerate all the places where Buck's *Ramayana* differs from the original, but a few of the more important differences should be mentioned. One of the most striking concerns Sita's reunion with Rama at the end of the battle, when she is brought before him in the crowning moment of triumph after a nightmarish war. One expects Rama to receive her graciously and tenderly back into his royal household and so, indeed, he acts in the story recounted by Buck. But in the Indian *Ramayana* there is no such happy episode. Here Rama haughtily rebuffs Sita when she appears

xix

before him led by Lakshmana. He believes that her honor has been compromised in Lanka and that she is unfit to become a queen. In despair Sita threatens to immolate herself in a fire that Lakshmana has lit at her request, but as if by magic, the God of Fire rises out of the pyre and refuses to burn her. He chides Rama and then the two are reunited. Buck has omitted this controversial episode and instead, has the Fire God lead Sita to Rama. Also, at that time Buck produces a stone letter sent by Ravana posthumously to Rama announcing his reconciliation. The Sanskrit *Ramayana* has no such incident.

The *Ramayana* epitomizes the spirit of ancient India with its vague but grand concepts of moral rectitude and its consequences for a person's fate. Both Rama and Sita are portrayed as following their *dharma*, a term meaning "personal duty," as well as "law, eternal law" and personified as the God of Justice. Adherence to *dharma* secures for oneself a more agreeable position in the next life one is to lead. The concepts of reincarnation and *karma*, the inexorable law of retribution for evil deeds and reward for unselfish behavior, dominate the lives of the people and semi-divine creatures that roam the earth. As in the *Mahabharata*, another Indian epic, gods sometimes interact with human beings. They are powerful, immortal, but not omnipotent. Vishnu who is usually represented in sculpture with a discus, mace, conchshell and lotus in his four hands, a mighty god who wields great power over the fate of mankind, is nevertheless compelled by the magic energy of a sage like Narada to yield his emblems of divinity. Likewise, the great god Indra was defeated by the demonic Ravana and his son. By performing ascetic practices (Sanskrit *tapas* which also means "heat"), a human being can cause Indra's throne to heat up, forcing him to grant a wish. In this way men and women can assert their will over gods.

Rama's Way tacitly assumes that we are aware of some of the conventions of Sanskrit mythology and literature. The world as we see it is the product of a long evolutionary cycle, subdivided into four world ages (*yugas*). In the first, mankind is perfect and *dharma* "righteous behavior" goes on four feet.

In the second *yuga* it loses a quarter of its power and mankind becomes less perfect. In the third, another quarter is lost and in the present fourth *yuga*, or Kali-yuga, misfortune, calamity and moral degradation are rampant. The world ages are named after the four throws recognized in the Indian dice game: Krita, Dvapara, Treta, Kali. The *Ramayana* takes place in the Treta-yuga. In each yuga the Brahmans constitute the upper caste of four classes of society. The three upper castes are regarded as the "twice-born" in the society they live in, once naturally and once when they receive the sacred thread. The sacred thread is given by a priest to the young boy of the family at a solemn ceremony which takes place before puberty. It is worn next to the skin over the right shoulder. Girls do not receive a sacred thread.

In other places in this work we meet up with literary clichés and conventions. Ascetics, for instance, usually wear their hair flattened down without ornamentations, in contrast to city people and royalty who groom and style their hair. Rama before entering the forest also adopts the matted hairdo of the wandering mendicant, but when he leads the army into Lanka he gives up the wanderer's life and lets his hair flow free, again. Another convention is that mountains used to fly around freely until Indra shot their wings off. Hence Mainaka Hill is said to have possessed wings. Also certain practices are sometimes mentioned which have no correspondence in our literature. Smelling somebody's hair, for instance, is a common manifestation of affection.

At times Buck has inserted some Sanskrit terms by way of *mantras*, "magical spells" endowed with supernatural power. They are not really meaningful expressions so their translation has been omitted. For instance, the terms *rakshama* and *yakshama* (Sanskrit *rakshyaamah* 'we shall protect,' *yakshyaamah* 'we shall sacrifice' p. 20) are simplified etymologies for the words *rakṣasa-* and *yakṣa-*, semi-divine beings. The word *yamam* (p. 48) means something like 'may I restrain, control' and is a convenient etymology for the name of the God of Death, Yama.

The main sequence of events in the Indian original and in Buck's rendition is the same, except that in Buck's version the story begins ten thousand years after the war, when Rama's children Kusa and Lava, unbeknownst to their father, have learnt the story of his battle from Valmiki and are reciting it in the Naimisha forest. The original *Ramayana* begins in the city of Ayodhya with the events leading up to Rama's birth. Valmiki was called the Adikavi, or "first poet" of Sanskrit literature and some of his remarkable talent shines forth in this English rendering. The reader will find pleasure in reading it aloud to himself or to others. In that way he may experience the fascination the epic has held for so many people for such a long time.

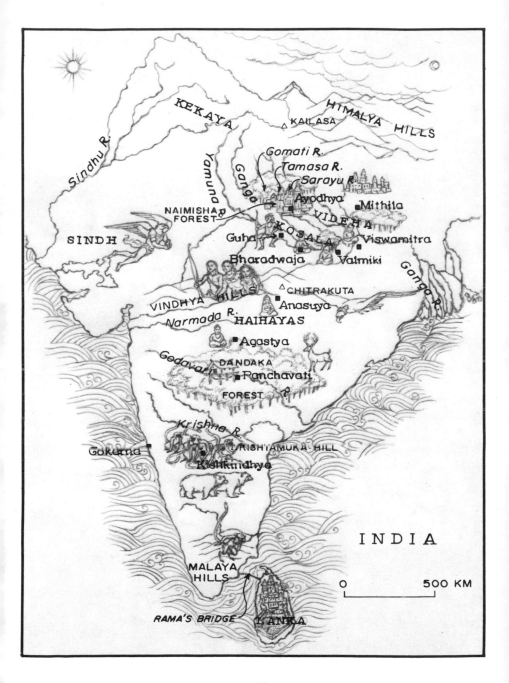

KEKAYA

HIMALYA HILLS

KAILASA

Sindhu R.

Yamuna

Ganga

Gomati R.

Tamasa R.

Sarayu R.

Ayodhya

Mithila

NAIMISHA FOREST

KOSALA

VIDEHA

SINDH

Guha

Viswamitra

Bharadwaja

Valmiki

Ganga R.

VINDHYA HILLS

CHITRAKUTA

Anasuya

Narmada R.

HAIHAYAS

Godavari

Agastya

DANDAKA

Panchavati

FOREST

Krishna R.

RISHYAMUKA HILL

Gokarna

Kishkindhya

INDIA

MALAYA
HILLS

0   500 KM

RAMA'S BRIDGE

LANKA

list of characters

AGASTYA. The forest saint who gave Rama a bow and arrow.

AGNI. The fire god.

AHALYA. The most beautiful woman ever created.

AIRAVATA. Indra's elephant.

ANUSUYA. Atri's wife, who gave Sita ornaments in the forest.

ANGADA. The monkey prince.

ANJANA. Hanuman's mother.

ARJUNA OF A THOUSAND ARMS. The Haihaya king.

ARUNA. Charioteer of the sun.

ASWAPATI. Kaikeyi's father, the Kekaya king.

ATRI. A saint dwelling near the Vindhya mountains.

BHARADWAJA. A hermit of the woods who received Rama; he lived on to become the father of Drona.

BHARATA. Dasaratha's son and Rama's brother; no relation to the namesake of the Kurus.

BRAHMA. Grandfather and Creator of the worlds.

CHANDRA. The Moon.
CHITRARATHA. The Gandharva king, lord of heaven's musicians.
DADHICA. An ancient warrior, revived by Indra.
DADHIMUKHA. A monkey, keeper of Sugriva's Honey Park
DASARATHA. Rama's father.
DEVI. Shiva's consort.
DUNDHUVI. A giant buffalo.
DURVASAS. A grim ascetic.

GARUDA. King of Birds, ridden by Narayana.
GAUTAMA. A sage, Ahalya's husband.
GUHA. The hunter king.

HANUMAN. The monkey, Son of the Wind.
HEMA. An Apsarasa, Queen Mandodari's mother.
HIMAVAN. The Lord of the Himalya, Devi's father.

ILVALA. A cannibal.
INDRA. The Rain God, King of heaven.
INDRAJIT. Ravana's son.
INDRANI. Indra's wife.

JAMBAVAN. King of the Bears.
JAMBUMALI. Prahasta's son.
JANAKA. The Videha King, Sita's father.
JATAYU. The Dandaka vulture King.

KADRU. One of Kashyapa's wives, mother of the snakes.
KAIKASI. Sumali's daughter and wife of Nishrava.
KAIKEYI. Bharata's mother.
KALA. Time.
KAMA. The god of love. He is bodiless.
KASHYAPA. An ancient sage.
KAUSALYA. Rama's mother.

KHARA. Demon commander of Dandaka Forest.
KUMBHAKARNA. Ravana's giant brother.
KUSA. Rama's elder son.

LAKSHMANA. Rama's brother, Sumitra's son.
LAKSHMI. The goddess of good fortune and Narayana's consort.
LAVA. Rama's younger son.

MAINAKA. A live, golden submarine mountain.
MALI. One of the three demons for whom Lanka was built.
MALYAVAN. Mali's brother.
MANDAKARNI. A sage dwelling in a lake.
MANDODARI. Queen of Lanka.
MANIBHADRA. The Yaksha king.
MANTHARA. Kaikeyi's old nurse.
MARICHA. The demon who became a golden deer.
MATALI. India's charioteer.
MATANGA. The saint who lived by Rishyamukha Hill.
MAYA THE
ASURA. The divine artist of illusion, a magician.
MAYAVI. Dundhuvi's son.
MEGHANADA. Indrajit's birth name.

NALA. The monkey who built Rama's bridge to Lanka.
NALAKUBARA. Son of the god of wealth.
NANDIN. Shiva's white bull.
NARADA. A heavenly sage born from Brahma's mind.
NARAYANA. The great god Vishnu who preserves the three worlds.

PARVATI. A name of Devi.
PRAHASTA. Ravana's general.

PULASTYA. One of Brahma's sons. He impregnates Trinavindu's daughter.
PULOMA. Indrani's father.
PUSHPAKA. A huge aerial chariot.

RAHU. The Asura whose living head, cut off at the neck, causes the eclipse of sun and moon by swallowing them in the sky.
RAMA.
RAMBHA. A lovely nymph.
RAVANA. The demon king.
RIKSHARAJA. The first monkey. He changes sex.
RUMA. Sugriva's wife, queen of Kishkindha.

SAMPATI. Jatayu's brother.
SAMUDRA. Ocean.
SARANA. Demon spy of Ravana.
SARASWATI. Goddess of speech.
SARDULA. Demon spy of Ravana.
SATRUGHNA. Rama's brother, Sumitra's son.
SAUNAKA. Who hears the story.
SAUTI. The storyteller.
SAVARI. A female hermit, friendly to Rama.
SHIVA. The great god whose third eye will burn the universe.
SINHIKA. A female monster.
SITA. Rama's wife.
SUBAHU. A demon killed by Lakshmana.
SUGRIVA. The monkey king.
SUKA. Ravana's minister.
SUKESA. Father of Mali, Sumali and Malyavan.
SUKRA. Indrajit's preceptor.
SUMALI. The third of the three Rakshasas who first lived in Lanka.
SUMANTRA. The royal charioteer of Ayodhya.
SUMITRA. Mother of Satrughna and Lakshmana.
SURABHI. The cow of plenty.

xxviii

SURPANAKHA.	Ravana's sister.
SURYA.	The Sun.
SWAYAMPRABHA.	An enchantress.
TARA.	Wife of the monkey king Vali.
TRIJATA.	The Rakshasi who befriended Sita.
TRINAVINDU.	Father of a nymph.
TUMBURU.	A Gandharva.
UCCHAIHSRAVAS.	A famous horse.
VAISHRAVANA.	The treasure king.
VAJRA-DANSHTRA.	Thunder-Tooth.
VALAKHILYAS.	Benign little deities floating in the air.
VALI.	Sugriva's brother.
VALMIKI.	Who invented poetry.
VARUNA.	God of the waters and guardian of the west and of the worlds undersea.
VASISHTHA.	Dasaratha's priest.
VASUKI.	King of Serpents.
VATAPI.	A cannibal in the Vindhya mountains.
VAYU.	The wind god.
VIBHISHANA.	Ravana's brother.
VIDYUJ-JIHVA.	Lightning-Tongue.
VINATA.	One of Kashyapa's wives, mother of Garuda.
VIRADHA.	A long-armed monster.
VISHNU.	The great god Narayana, pervading the universe, moving in the waters, preserving and restoring life.
VISWAKARMAN.	Heavenly architect and lord of the arts.
VISWAMITRA.	Who took Rama to protect him in the forest.
YAMA.	God of death.
YUDHAJIT.	Bharata's uncle, prince of Kekaya and Kaikeyi's brother.

Oh Man, I am the demon warrior Indrajit, hard to see. I fight invisibly, hidden by enchantment from your sight. I attack behind the wild winds of evil thought; I put out many lights left unguarded. I know you, and good deeds done in life are your only shield when you must die and go alone past me to another world. You may hide at night from the Sun, but never from your own heart—where lives Lord Narayana. The entire worlds are watching your deeds, and therefore forgiveness is Dharma.

Valmiki the Poet looked down into water held cupped in his hand and saw into the past. Before he looked, he thought the world was sweet poison. Men seemed to be living in lies, not knowing where their ways went. The days seemed made of ignorance and doubt, and cast from deception and illusion. But in the water he saw—a dream, a chance, and a great adventure. Valmiki trusted the True and forgot the rest; he found the whole universe like a bright jewel set firm in forgiving and held fast by love.

Widen your heart. Abandon anger. Believe me, your few days are numbered; make one fast choice now and no second!

Come, clear your heart and quickly walk with me into Brahma, while there is time.

part one

the prince of ayodhya

Om!
I bow to Lord Narayana,
To Lady Lakshmi of Good Fortune,
To Hanuman the best of monkeys,
And to Saraswati,
The Goddess of words and stories:
JAYA!
Victory!

BORN AS A MAN

Sauti the story teller told this tale to his friend Saunaka in Naimisha Forest. Bending with humility he finished the wonderful *Mahabharata* in the evening, and the next morning Saunaka asked, "Lotus-eyed Sauti, who was that monkey Hanuman who met Bhima in the Hills, and who stayed in Arjuna's war-flag while he fought? What is that story of Rama, which keeps Hanuman alive so long as it is told by men on Earth?"

Sauti answered, "That story is *Ramayana*, a tale of romance and love and of wild adventure, the very crest-jewel of poetry and a legend of the times and worlds of old. Arjuna the Pandava is gone, and Fire took away his bow, but somewhere Time waits to rearm him. So Time is beyond Fire, but *Ramayana* is beyond Time. Rama's days have long gone past; I do not believe there ever existed before, or will ever exist again such days in the world we know . . . . "

Saunaka said, "Tell me again an old story."

Sauti said, "Rama ruled the Earth for eleven thousand years. He gave a year-long festival in this very Naimisha Forest. All of this land was in his kingdom then; one age of the world ago; long, long ago; long before now, and far in the past. Rama was King from the center of the world to the four Oceans' shores."

Saunaka said, "I never tire of listening, I am never satisfied. If you know more stories tell them to me."

"Yes," answered Sauti. "If you would hear it, listen to *Ramayana* as it happened."

3

Then one cloudy Winter's day . . .

Listen, my friend—

I love this *Ramayana*. We live now in the third age of Time, and Rama lived in the second age of the world. *Ramayana* has long been standing above other stories; you must look up to find it. Valmiki the Poet put the deeds of Rama into musical verses; he clothed them in the sound of singing. Before *Ramayana* there was no poetry on Earth.

As a young man, Valmiki searched through the world seeking open friendship and happiness and hope, and finding none of these he went alone into the empty forest where no man lived, to a spot near where the Tamasa river flows into Ganga. There he sat for years without moving, so still that white ants built an anthill over him. There Valmiki sat inside that anthill for thousands of years with only his eyes showing out, trying to find the True, his hands folded and his mind lost in contemplation.

Then one cloudy winter's day, at noon, the heavenly sage Narada, the inventor of music, born from Brahma's mind, flew from heaven to Valmiki and said, "Come out! Help me!"

"It's too cold," answered Valmiki. "Away with the worlds, where a little pleasure costs a lot of pain. Don't make trouble."

"Would I ever? See how Life goes by, with every creature doing what follows his nature." Narada knelt and looked in Valmiki's eyes. "Master, what can I say to you?"

Valmiki said, "Just name me one honest man and I'll move."

"Rama!" said Narada. "Come out of there!"

"Who is Rama?"

"Rama rules as King in Ayodhya. He is born in the Solar race and a descendant of the Sun; he is brave and gentle and firm in fight. By Rama's command his adorable Queen Sita is being brought here into the forest on a chariot, and though she suspects nothing yet, here she will be left abandoned. Unless you comfort her she will drown herself in Ganga and kill as well her unborn sons by Rama."

"What did she do wrong?" asked Valmiki.

"Nothing," said Narada. "Sita is innocent and blameless.

5

She has lived as Rama's Queen for nearly ten thousand years; before that, Rama saved her from great danger by wondrous and incredible deeds. And now behold one of the terrors of kingship, that Rama must let her go because his people talk against her. Get up, save her life, and let her live here with you and your companions; and make in measured words the song of Rama, and teach it to Rama's two sons."

"I have no companions here," said Valmiki.

"You have now. Coming here, I sang a friend-gathering song. Valmiki, I've seen other skies than these, other worlds, and other friends. People are counting on you . . . and I can hear the chariot from Ayodhya approaching across Ganga."

Valmiki said, "I have no skill in any craft, even in words."

"There stops the chariot! Right now—here they come across Ganga in a boat, or will you also give way and forsake Sita too from fear of other people? *See!* She has discovered she is lost, and the boat is launched back without her. Oh hurry— there the sunlight comes from behind the dark clouds—there Ganga the River Goddess begins unseen to whisper spells over Sita and makes her swift-flowing waters seem a warm safe home. *Act now, Valmiki; call out and the rest must follow.*"

Valmiki stood up and broke free out of that hard anthill. Suddenly he saw all around him many houses of hermits and their families, young trees carefully watered, a retreat cleared from the forest. Four boys ran up to him from the river and cried "The wife of some great warrior weeps by Ganga. She is fair as a Goddess fallen from heaven all bewildered, all alone, never seen before, with child, and with small gifts from the city tied within a silk cloth beside her. Go to her, welcome her, protect her . . . ."

Valmiki ran to Sita on the riverbank. "Sita, stay here in my hermitage, you have found here your father's house in a for- eign land, we will care for you as our daughter." And seeing Sita he thought, "What a fine fair woman, how beautiful!"

Quickly the hermit wives surrounded Sita and took her to their homes. Narada had gone. Valmiki went alone to the clear Ganga waterside and bathed. He washed away the anthill dust and peeled grey bark from a tree and made new fresh clothes.

Then he sat back resting against a stone. He watched two small white waterbirds in a tree nearby. The male bird was singing to his mate when before Valmiki's eyes an arrow hit him, and the little bird fell from the limb. He thrashed on the ground an instant and then lay dead, and blood drops stained his feathers.

Heartbroken the dead bird's mate cried—*Your long feathers! Your tuneful songs!*

A bird-hunter came from the forest holding a bow. Valmiki's heart was pounding and he cursed the killer—

You will find no rest for the long years of Eternity,
For you killed a bird in love and unsuspecting.

❧

One look at Valmiki and the hunter ran for his life, but fever already burned in his blood; he died that day. Valmiki turned back to his hermitage thinking, "This is truly how I remember the ways of the world." Then he thought, "Those words I cursed him with make a verse, and that verse could be sung to music."

For days the words ran through Valmiki's mind. Whatever he seemed to be doing he was really thinking of his verse. On the fourth day after Sita's rescue, Lord Brahma the creator of the worlds appeared in Valmiki's new retreat. He looked like an old man with red skin and white hair, with four arms, with four faces around one head, holding in his hands a ladle and a rosary, a waterpot and a holy book.

Valmiki greeted Brahma, "Sit by me," and taking water from a pitcher he washed Brahma's feet, and gave him other water to drink. But after that, even sitting there with the Grandfather of all the Universe watching him, still Valmiki remembered only the two waterbirds and thought to himself, "What a crime! There was not one bite of meat on that little bird! What use is a world run all wrong without a grain of mercy in it?"

7

Those thoughts were as clear to Brahma as if Valmiki had been shouting in his ear. Brahma said, "So, by a river, the world's first verse has been born from pity, and love and compassion for a tiny bird has made you a poet. Use your discovery to tell Rama's story, and your verses will defeat Time. As you make your poem, Rama's life will be revealed to you, and no word of yours will be untrue."

Lord Brahma returned to his heaven, far above the changing heavens of Indra and the gods, riding on his chariot drawn by white swans and snow geese. Valmiki sat every day facing East on a grass mat. He held a little water cupped in his hands, and looking down into it he clearly saw Rama and Sita. He saw them move, he heard them talk and laugh. He saw all Rama's life happen within the water; he held the past world in his palm; and part by part he made *Ramayana* delightful to the ear, pleasing to the mind, and a true happiness to the heart.

Not many months after Valmiki began his poetry, Sita's twin sons were born. Valmiki named them Kusa and Lava. They grew up resembling their father Rama as the Moon's reflection resembles the Moon himself. Kusa and Lava were handsome as Kama the Love God disarmed by pleasure. All the hermit women loved them, and watched those two boys instead of offering worship to the gods.

As Valmiki composed *Ramayana*, and as Kusa and Lava grew old enough to learn, he taught it to them by memory. When they were twelve years old Valmiki had brought his story nearly up to the present, and Kusa and Lava knew every foot of it, and sang *Ramayana* to a lute and a drum, like Gandharvas, the heavenly musicians.

That year King Rama held a year's celebration in Naimisha Forest along the river Gomati. At home, Kusa and Lava re hearsed their song. Deer listened from the wood and birds from the trees. They practiced long, and many forest men came to listen. After each day they brought Kusa and Lava gifts and presents—a waterjar, a bark-cloth shirt, a deerskin, some thread, a grass belt, red cloth, an axe, a cord to tie firewood, a cooking pot, and wild food they had gathered.

Then they all went to Rama's festival. People had come there from all over the world. Valmiki kept Sita hidden, but he sent Kusa and Lava to sing *Ramayana* in a clearing. When they started to sing the other business of the festival stopped. They held their hearers motionless. For a year they sang some of *Ramayana* every morning, and never told their names. Everyone gathered round them. Every day King Rama came to listen. He looked long at his two sons he had never seen and wondered who they were, and beside Rama stood a golden statue of Sita, for Rama loved her though he had sent her away.

Kusa and Lava began, "We sing a song of kingly fame—Oh Listen . . . ."

      ✦   ✦   ✦

Rama, free your mind from malice and ill will; this is Valmiki's song.

On the banks of the Sarayu river is Fair Ayodhya, the royal capital of Kosala. She is a fabled city, famed among men, twelve leagues long and ten wide, with Sala trees, filled with grain and gold. Heaven is fair, Ayodhya is fairer; Heaven is cool in summer, but the Kosala hills are better.

Majesty, when your father Dasaratha was alive he ruled from the tall white Ayodhya palace built atop a rising hill; he was Lord of the Earth and the Lord of Men; he was a solar King bright as the noonday Sun. In those bright days now gone by forever, the gods from the air saw Kosala to be clear as a mirror, with no least touch of evil to make any black shadow over the land. The Kosalas were well-fed and healthy, the Sarayu was filled with boats, every cow's horns were covered with rings of silver and bands of gold. Every man could keep what he had in peace and gain what more he wanted.

The young people wore elegant clothes, and life was joyful among the gardens and in the pleasure-parks. Three- and seven-storied mansions lined the wide straight streets. The Kosalas had no enemies and Ayodhya was unconquerable. Flowers grew all over. Long-tusked elephants walked the streets wearing bells on their necks. There were rows of full shops with open doors, pale white palaces, and lordly trees; rattling chariots drove by and there was music; foreign caravans came bringing merchants and rich tribute from lesser kings.

Fair Ayodhya was filled with warriors, like a mountain cave filled with lions; her warriors were impatient and deadly to foes. Each man of them could alone defeat ten thousand chariots, but no one came against them. They kept the city safe and tried to right whatever wrongs they could discover. Dasaratha's ministers were loyal and wise, able to find hidden motives and fight with words, cautious, never binding themselves to a lie, acting by their word, and sending out spies to report what took place in all the world.

Fair Ayodhya was a matchlessly brilliant city with lots of food and wood and water. But though Dasaratha was an old man, sixty thousand years old, he had no son to inherit his kingdom. He called his priest Vasishtha and said, "Brahmana, I always long for a son. I can find no happiness without him, therefore make a sacrifice with fire, to please the gods."

Vasishtha said, "Excellent. Well done. You will have sons after your own heart."

Dasaratha told his charioteer Sumantra *Arrange for this*. He went to his three Queens and said, "We will have sons," and hearing those sweet words their faces shone like lotus flowers opening out after the long cold winter's end.

Sumantra piled provisions by the Sarayu and Vasishtha chose a day whose ruling stars were fortunate. After his morning bath King Dasaratha on that day watched Vasishtha light the holy fires by the river. Vasishtha began then to sing spellbinding mantras, he reached out for a flat wooden ladle and dipped it into clear liquid butter, and he started to pour the offering into the sacrificial fire—*Indra King of heaven, Come*.

❧

In heaven above, Indra turned and sighed and hissed like an angry snake. His fine robes were burnt and torn, his face and chest were covered with dried blood. He was angry; he heard Vasishtha's call and it made him still angrier.

Indra looked about his heaven. It was a hopeless ruin. The once beautiful heavenly garden Nandana was uprooted, crushed and buried beneath soot and cinders. Heaven's long golden street was littered with slain Gandharvas, with Apsarasas, the dancing women of heaven, lying killed, and with the corpses of Rakshasa demons. The high stately pleasure-palaces were razed to broken stones and tiles. The heavenly stream of Ganga ran red with blood. Exhausted thunders and broken lightnings lay underfoot, drawn Rakshasa swords were already rusting in the river, lingering fires and smoke ate smoldering holes in heaven's high walls, the charred Gate of the Gods lay split and wrenched from its heavy posts.

Indra had just fought the Battle of Heaven. He had proudly stood up against the Demon King Ravana. He alone had not submitted with his people to the Rakshasas. He had fought back hard and lost, he had been captured and released and now stood again in heaven.

Now Indra's eyes filled with tears. He ground his teeth and clenched his fists; then reaching down he seized a chunk of

11

shattered adamant and flew with it up to Brahma's high heaven beyond change. He stood there before Brahma's palace, and with tremendous force threw the stone right through the beautiful gold and jade bars of the biggest window. Guards ran out with spears and swords. But when they saw Indra they hung down their heads in shame and motioned him to enter.

Brahma sat on a lotus throne of sandalwood in a room at the end of a long hall and through a doorway set three steps beyond the end of the Universe.

Indra entered. "You are to blame! It's your fault, all of it!"

"Alas," said Brahma, "it is *my* loss that ever I created any of you."

"Ravana the Ten-headed Rakshasa King has wantonly slain my people!" said Indra. "His son Indrajit captured me fighting invisibly, then soon freed me for some reason."

"I arranged that."

Indra frowned. "And you have also arranged it so that no one in heaven can kill Ravana! You set him over us all. He asked and you granted it—*look what you've done, you old*—" But the last word couldn't come out of Indra's throat. Whatever word he thought of, none was strong enough to tell his feelings, so he couldn't speak.

"*An old fool!*" he said at last. "Why? Why? Just tell me *why* you grant boons to demons?"

"O Indra, it was but an elusive impulse."

"This time you've made a monster invulnerable. Ravana is the disgrace of all Creation and a reproach to the worlds. How can we withstand him when even the gods cannot kill him? Are we to live under evil?"

Though he already knew, Brahma asked, "Where are the other gods?"

Indra replied, "Agni the Fire God heats the stoves in Ravana's kitchens; the rains do his washing; Vayu the Wind sweeps the yards of Lanka; Varuna Lord of Waters supplies the wines for Ravana's court; the Sun lights Ravana's halls and the Moon his gardens . . . so great is the power of fear!"

12

"Oh Indra, look again."

Indra looked down at Earth and Lanka. "Why, those forms are false! The others have escaped . . . ."

Brahma held out a silver bowl of Soma wine and Indra swiftly drank it down. Then he sighed again, but smiling. Brahma too drank, and looked carefully at Indra.

"God of Rain," said Brahma, "let the pain go. Where is Viswakarman the Architect of heaven?"

"He is always by himself somewhere," said Indra.

"Put him back to work. Rebuild heaven."

Indra squeezed his arms. "Besides all the rest, Ravana himself enjoys the food men sacrifice to us gods, and basks in all our smoke. Destroyed are the gardens in heaven that once made my eyes happy and my heart sing. Now there is no song heard, and I fear even to go down to the sacrifice of the Ayodhya King Dasaratha."

Brahma said, "Remember how to speak the old language with me . . . Ravana is careless . . . he has long been careless. *Stop your suffering and raise your head.* Dasaratha will reach his desire. Four sons will be his. Take the Kosala King's offerings and no one will stop you. Keep out of Ravana's sight and be patient. Do not fight him again and how can you be defeated? Think before and not after you act."

Indra's weariness was gone. He said, "Like the poor Earth, my heavens themselves are now proved flawed and fleeting, fast-dying and stricken by devilish demons. Have a care for my world! I am Lord of the Gods. I am not weak like a mere man, I am Indra of a Hundred Sacrifices, Destroyer of Cities, Indra of the Thunder-Hand, Lord of Paradise, Lord of Lightnings! And a demon beast overcame *me*—"

"Indra, be ashamed! Be silent!" Brahma refilled their Soma bowls. "What can I do? I can never lie, and I do not know every answer."

Indra asked, "Who knows then?"

"Go to Narayana," said Brahma. "Only Narayana knows, or maybe he doesn't. But for myself, where can I find the end,

13

where the beginning, where the middle of all this? Ask Nara-
yana—*How was Ravana careless?*—then obey the mantras of
Vasishtha."

❦

Indra went to Narayana, the Lord Vishnu, the Soul of the Uni-
verse. Narayana sat watching Indra approach. Indra pressed
together his hands, touched his brow, and bent his head
low to Narayana's feet. "Searcher of Hearts, I bow to you,
namas. I have still faith in the Good Law of Dharma." In-
dra looked up past Narayana's wide dark chest crossed by a
neckchain of sapphires, up into the great god's joyful black
eyes wide as lotus petals.

Narayana in his yellow saffron summer robes smiled down
at Indra. "Yes, a good enough fight," said Narayana. "No fear,
Lord of Gods."

"How shall we bring down Ravana?" asked Indra. "Because
of Brahma's boon is the Demon King strong, and for no other
cause of his own. Help me, you are my only refuge, there is no
other for me. *I will gather my storms again and attack Lanka, give me
your permission to fight Ravana once more!*"

"Never!" said Narayana. "Don't you understand that Brah-
ma's words are always true? Do not falsify the three spheres
of life. I would not have let you fight in the first place, though
you were right to resist and Ravana was wrong. Ravana
asked Brahma—*Let me be unslayable by every creature of Heaven
and of the underworlds.* And Brahma promised—*So be it.* That
boon is unbreakable, yet will I cause Ravana's death. That
is the truth. Only ask me . . . ."

"Ah," said Indra, "from disdain Ravana did not mention
men or animals, and took no safeguard against them. He eats
men; they are his food and why should he fear them? Lord, on
Earth life resembles Hell again. We need you again. Look at
us, see us, and bless us. For the good of all the worlds, Lord
Narayana, accept birth as a man."

"I already have."

Waves of happiness washed over Indra. "Dark blue Narayana clad in yellow, become four. Put aside the shell trumpet, the razor-edged chakra, the lotus and mace you hold in your four hands. Empty your dark hands; descend into the borrowed and fanciful world of men, desperate and glittering. Become Dasaratha's four sons born of blood and seed. Take your Goddess Lakshmi and let her be your mortal wife."

"We will go down," said Narayana.

"Lord, kill him, kill Ravana forever. I hate that proud and pampered Rakshasa. Favor me and curse him; give to Death his faces torn apart; dry away our fear as the Sun dries morning dew."

"I will," said Narayana. "Listen, Vasishtha begins to call you to Earth with songs, to Ayodhya by the sleepy Sarayu."

❧

The melted butter from Vasishtha's ladle fell into the flames. Vasishtha sang—*Indra be my bridge from high to low, do my bidding, obey me . . . .*

The tongues of fire danced, and Indra came unseen in the sky, free again and feasting on smoke. Vasishtha sang—*Narayana, we take your protection. Leave your home a moment, draw near, come to us . . . .*

Vasishtha threw flowers in the fire and quickly stepped back to stand beside King Dasaratha. They heard a ringing loud noise, a fierce clang of metal; but saw nothing.

"What was that?" asked the old King.

"The sharp discus drops," said Vasishtha.

They heard a crash like a falling tree and Vasishtha said, "The huge mace is fallen." There was a hollow rolling sound. "The shell is down." They caught the sudden scent of lotuses.

Then a giant black man rose from the flames in a stream of smoke and a burning shower of sparks. He stepped out from the fire and frowned and glared with menace at the King, but Dasaratha faced him unmoved. The giant wore crimson, his whole body was covered with dark lion's hair, his belt was a bowstring, his palms were marked with thunder-signs and the soles of his feet with wheels. He had a thick glossy beard and

15

long black hair on his head. He had the yellow eyes of a tiger and held out a steaming golden bowl like the Sun with a silver cover.

Dasaratha took the bowl in his hands. The black giant said, "Feed this to your wives, it will bring you sons." The fire crackled and the black man vanished.

Inside the bowl was rice cooked with milk and sweetened with sugar. Vasishtha walked three times round the fire in right-turning circles. Dasaratha felt like a poor man who has found a treasure undreamt of, like a man rich in happiness, like a lost voyager finding the way home.

✥

Dasaratha went to the inner rooms of his palace. All the servants of his three Queens were smiling; their faces lighted the rooms as the sky is flooded with the lovely beams and rays of the autumn Moon.

Dasaratha gave the gleaming bowl to his first wife, Kausalya, and said, "Eat half of it." When Kausalya had eaten half the rice he gave his second wife Sumitra half of what remained. He gave his youngest wife Kaikeyi half of what Sumitra had left. He thought a moment, and gave all the rest to Sumitra again.

A year later on the ninth day of spring Rama was first born to Kausalya. Later that same day Bharata was born to Kaikeyi; then still later Sumitra bore two sons, Lakshmana and Satrughna. Their father lit their birth-fires in jars of Earth; he named them on the eleventh day of their lives, and the Kosalas danced in the streets and rang all the temple bells.

Rama grew to be his father's favorite son. Rama was not tall and not short. He had more energy than the Sun and a deep voice. He had colorful green eyes; his skin was cool soft green and so smooth even dust would not cling to him; his wavy hair was dark green; he walked like a lion; the soles of his feet were flat and marked with royal Dharma-wheels. There was no hollow between his shoulder blades on his back; his arms were long and reached to his knees; he had forty identical

16

white teeth all shaped like pomegranate seeds; his thumbs bore the four lines of knowledge where they joined his hands. He had high shoulders like a lion, and a graceful brow, a broad chest, three folds in his neck at the base of his throat like the spirals on a shell. He had deep collarbones and a long tongue, a sharp nose, heavy jaws and the eyelashes of a bull. His breath was lotus-scented. Of all men only Rama was born knowing his own heart.

Lakshmana was Rama's second self; he was Rama's own life walking beside him. He always kept Rama company, and served him in everything before himself. Lakshmana was of golden skin and measureless strength, his eyes were blue as wildflowers and his straight hair was golden-brown. Lakshmana would not sleep without Rama near him nor eat unless Rama shared his food. When Rama went riding on horseback, there rode Lakshmana behind him holding a bow.

Prince Bharata was born with red skin, rosy eyes and scarlet lips and fiery hair red as flame. His brother Satrughna had dark blue skin and black eyes and black hair. And in the same way that his twin Lakshmana was drawn to Rama, Satrughna accompanied Bharata everywhere and thought Bharata dearer than his own life itself.

❧

When the four princes were sixteen years old the recluse Viswamitra came to Kosala in the spring. The frontier guards sent word to Ayodhya and King Dasaratha met him there on foot outside the city. The King held flowers and water, grass and rice, and said, "Welcome to you, brahmana. I hope your journey to me went well."

Viswamitra answered, "I hope your land here is peaceful and your kingdom rich. Are all your friends well? Are your warriors obedient to you and defiant to your enemies? I hope your foes are dead and that you keep well the duties of a King."

They walked together into Ayodhya. The priest Vasishtha met them and said, "Viswamitra, you arrive here like summer rain, like the recovery of something lost, like bright dawn after night. By our good fortune we have gained your company. Today our births have borne fruit and our lives gained their goals."

When they were seated in the palace Dasaratha said to Viswamitra, "Why have you come? Whatever you want I will gladly give you."

"Promise me," said Viswamitra.

"I promise."

Viswamitra said, "Majesty, that promise becomes you alone. No one else would make it. The pathless forest where I live has become a courtyard of evil and no longer is there any safety from the Rakshasas of the monstrous Demon King Ravana."

the thorn in the world's side

Where I have been there is no light
From any Sun; we have no Moon nor Stars,
No lightnings like these, much less any of this Fire.

There I must light up all around me.
By my sight all is illumined.

Here I am born again to kill the Evil,
And like a black she-leopard going with me in my shadow
Never does Victory leave my side:
One; one only and no second!

Viswamitra said, "King, for years I have tried to complete a sacrifice in the solitary forest. I do nothing wrong and leave nothing out. I never daydream, and my work is absolutely without lapses or holes. The most learned Rakshasa could surely detect no entrance, yet when I speak a blessing I hear the heavy tread of countless running feet in the air above me and see no one. Just when I am to make the offering and end the rites, flesh and gore fall on my altar. My waterjars break untouched, my figwood ladles warp and groan and my fires go out."

Dasaratha said, "How have Rakshasas overcome Brahma power? Where are the gods who should protect you?"

Viswamitra replied, "Majesty, we are living in the second age of the world, and the quarter part of Virtue has now died among men. These are faded days and Dharma declines. In the first age food came by wishing and grew from Earth without tending. No one wept, nor was cruel, nor hurt another; and there were not many gods then among different men but only one.

19

"This age began with the first slaughter and sacrifice of an innocent animal to some lower god; men started to take action to gain objects and rewards; they gave no more gifts free just for the giving, except rarely, more and more rarely as years pass. This is a time of scene-shifting and contrivance; men no longer live as long; there are all about us arguments and objections and ambushes and devious cunning, deceitful sorcery and craft and fraud and guile and trickery and lies and many devices. King, against Ravana's Rakshasas there is no help in the forest and no help from the gods."

"I pity those living after us," said Dasaratha. "Who is Ravana?"

"He is King of Lanka," said Viswamitra," a piece of grit in the world's eye to make her weep. Ravana has conquered Heaven and Hell. His brutal helpers hunger for me. They fly fast and change shapes at will; they love eating hermits; they feed on harmless men and consume creatures like Death himself."

Listen, Majesty—

By the light of very ancient history you will learn how the three worlds have fallen prey to the inhuman race of the Night-Wanderers. You will hear what the hateful demon Ravana has done.

At the last beginning of Time as at every beginning, Brahma the Creator of the Worlds was reborn from a lotus. That flower grew from the navel of Lord Narayana as he slept afloat on the waters, lying on the white coils of the endless serpent Sesha. Brahma saw water everywhere and he grew anxious lest it be stolen. So out of water he made four guardians; two mated couples male and female.

Those four people said, "We are hungry and thirsty."

Brahma told them, "Watch this water, don't let a drop of it get lost."

One couple answered him, "*Rakshama,* we will protect it."

The other pair said, "*Yakshama,* we shall worship it."

20

Those couples were the first Rakshasas and the first Yakshas. Narayana then carefully rescued the Earth from under water. Brahma somehow made the five elements; he fashioned the worlds and made food and other races.

The Rakshasa couple lived on Earth. That Rakshasi was pregnant; she was filled with child as a raincloud is filled with water by the sea. Majesty, Rakshasis conceive and give birth all in one day. She went alone to a deserted hillside and bore a son, then she left the baby demon there abandoned. She forgot him and hurried back to her husband, and her newborn child put his fist in his mouth and cried slowly.

Just then above that hill in the sky Lord Shiva was riding with Devi on the back of Nandin the white brahma bull. Devi heard the faint little cries; she looked down and saw the helpless baby, and she sent the great god Shiva down onto the hill.

The terrible Lord Shiva bent over that child, picked him up and held him gently. Shiva Lord of the destruction preceding creation wore a tiger's skin still dripping blood, the holy thread over his shoulder was a mottled serpent; he had in his hair the crescent Moon; he was in form a pale white man with white ashes in his hair and his throat was blue, and on his brow was his deadly third eye closed. He gave that baby his mother's age and to please Devi gave him the power of flight; and these gifts stayed with the Rakshasa race, and their children grow to their mother's age the day they're born.

That Rakshasa was Sukesa. He was charming and polite, and welcome everywhere. He married the daughter of a Gandharva, and her company made him happy. He had three sons and named them Mali, Sumali and Malyavan.

Those three young Rakshasas wanted a better place to live. They wanted their earthly homes to be beautiful. They flew to heaven to Viswakarman the heavenly architect. They found him forging an iron axe with a steel hammer, pounding away while sparks flew burning holes in his leather clothes.

Viswakarman was surrounded by tall clay jars of waters and oils for tempering blades. His anvils and firepits and bellows and dirty charcoal bags cluttered the room; long

21

leather belts and running wheels and whining wooden gears went rattling overhead in confusion; round the rafters hung thunderbolts to be sharpened and spare axles and chariot chains; underfoot were metal cuttings and pointed scrap and curly shavings; the light was bad; acid fumes and coal dust filled the hot air; and clamor and din never ceased in his workshop.

Malyavan drew near and said in a loud voice, "Dear Lord of Arts . . . ."

Viswakarman stopped hammering, but his furnaces still roared and the gears ground on. He yelled back—*Is it made of metal?*

Malyavan shouted, "A home . . . beauty . . . for us . . . somewhere quiet . . . ."

Viswakarman ran his grimy hand over his sweaty brow and brushed some filings out of his hair. He gestured toward a back door—*Come follow me.*

He led the three Rakshasa brothers through that door into a quiet room, light and clean, ideal for an artist. The goddesses and wives of heaven came to welcome Viswakarman warm glad smiles and cool drinks. And Viswakarman no longer looked like a metalsmith. Just by going through the door he had changed into a beautiful sensitive workman wearing airy clothes and remote from care.

Now Malyavan could speak. "Prince of Artists, you have made the gods' flying chariots; you have put speed into the legs of horses; you have given the strong their strength; you have made husband and wife the one for the other from before their birth, and those who love the gods got that love from you. When your daughter married the Sun and found him too bright you put him on your lathe and shaved him down a bit. What is there you cannot create or model?"

The goddesses gave Viswakarman garlands and loving looks, and he asked Malyavan, "What shall I build for you?"

"Build us a home grand as the Halls of Shiva, with high painted ceilings, rich in ornaments and flowered gardens."

22

Viswakarman smiled. "I hear that Shiva lives in a drafty hut that every moment threatens to collapse on him."

Malyavan fell at Viswakarman's feet. "Oh, we are truly ignorant and poor. Make us a fine city, a fortress where we may live."

Viswakarman answered, "On Earth the Isle of Lanka in the southern sea is vacant. I will build Lanka City there for you, on the brow of Trikuta Hill rising to the clouds, somewhere not far below the highest of his three summits."

Before their eyes Viswakarman changed again. He became all-seeing and had on every side eyes and faces and arms. From his back came the two great wide wings by which he fashions all forms and shapes, fanning the air and blowing them into life.

Viswakarman took a staff, went outside and struck the ground of heaven hard. A golden city arose; there was Beautiful Lanka of golden walls. "Can you live there?" asked Viswakarman.

"We will live in her as the gods live in heaven," said Malyavan. "How skillful, what an admirable artist you are!"

The city vanished. Viswakarman said, "If you like the plan of it I will make it real. First I must cut the trees and mine the gold and shape the stones."

"Have you no helpers for that?"

Viswakarman turned on him. "Of course not, are you mad? When the master carpenter no longer goes out into the forests to choose his own tree, when he no longer cuts it down himself and saws his own boards then say farewell to the arts!"

❧

So Beautiful Lanka was built. The race of Rakshasas flourished under Sukesa's three sons. Sukesa himself lived with his wife in a Gandharva house on the slopes of Himalya until he died, a courtly old demon kind to all.

But as they increased in number there was not room for every Rakshasa to live in Lanka. Some left the others and

23

prowled roaming through the forests across the sea to the north, and there began to eat the raw flesh of men, as they do now, striking by night. They would murder the gentle teachers in their retreats and avoid the well-armed tribes of hunters, as though picking only the easy ripe fruit from a tree.

In those days the heavenly sage Narada sat in the sky trying to play a song of music on his lute of tortoise-shell and yellow wood. When he was in a good mood he was unreasonable, irritable and cross and wondrously disagreeable; and interruptions infuriated him. He could not even tune the lute-strings, for horrible cries rising from Earth's forests filled his ears. Narada set aside his lute and soared down, and in Dandaka Forest he stood angrily before the first demon he saw and said, "Be quiet or else!"

The Rakshasa said, "Oh Man you are my dinner now."

"I am no man, I live in heaven and . . . ." The Rakshasa had swallowed him whole. But Narada was hot as a barrel of embers. The demon spat him out and still his stomach burned.

Narada glared at him. "Your peaceful days are gone! *I will sing such a song . . . .*"

Narada flew back to his lute.

> *For I will play in your despite,*
> *And I will make the wrongs all right.*
> *For I will do, what pleases me . . . .*

He perfectly tuned his lute with shaking hands, and sitting inside a cloud high above Dandaka Forest he sang—*Dark blue Narayana and black Rakshasas!*

❧

The awful dark shadow of the giant shell-trumpet Panchajanya fell over Lanka; the water-born king of shells roared. Narayana came on the bird Garuda in armor bright as a thousand suns!

Sentries ran to Malyavan and the brave Night-Wanderers rose into the sky. Their chariots and elephants came racing

24

through the air; their fast-flying graceful war-horses, red and white and pale blue, milled and pawed the sky. Garuda flew to the attack. Narayana was hidden by swarms of demon arrows hard-hitting, true-flying and thirsty.

> *He has disappeared; listen, he is lost.*
> *He is lost, but do I hear*
> *A crying bowstring! Do I hear*
> *Fear to the demons!*

The demon horses stumbled. The noise of Narayana's bow turned their elephants to stone; they fell from the sky and broke. Wildly swung the war-flags, blood poured in rivers, Lanka was measured by corpse-lengths. Narayana beheaded Mali. Sumali and Malyavan fled wounded and burning in grief down to safety in the underworlds beneath the sea, through a door under Ocean.

Garuda shrieked and screamed and turned in the air like a hurricane. Narayana's arrows flew, white-hot flights of arrows humming, piercing Dandaka Forest, raining down into Lanka. The Rakshasa pride was fallen; their heroes were dead; the southern sea was stained; the Forest ran red with Rakshasa blood. The demons fled like the clouds of doom driven before the black wind of the End of the Worlds. Their jeweled necklaces and earrings fell over Lanka Island, their dark bodies covered the waves.

Narada set down his lute. No living Rakshasa remained on Earth. Lanka City was empty.

❧

So, Majesty, were the demons driven away once long ago, but they hoarded their possessions and hopes far underground in the Naga Kingdoms and watched for some chance to return.

Pulastya was one of Brahma's Mind-born sons, one of the inspired forefathers of life. He lived on a lonely hill of the Himalyas, alone, looking out over the lowlands. He felt no

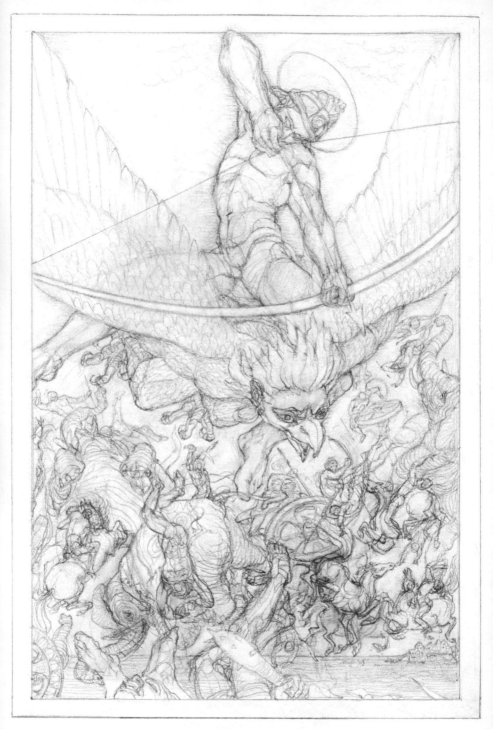

Garuda shrieked and screamed . . .

need to be busy; he watched the world go by; he was in love with the quiet of the high hills, with the pines and the deodars, with Himalya rising to heaven.

That same hill was a favorite playground for Apsarasas and Naga girls, who ran about singing and laughing together with the daughters of the local hermits. When they disturbed him for the hundred-and-eighth time Pulastya told them, "If I ever see any girl playing around here any more she will become pregnant!"

Fearing that they stayed away. But the daughter of the hermit Trinavindu had not heard this curse. The very next day she came looking round Pulastya's home for her friends. She came into his sight as he was singing; he only glanced at her but she turned pale and ran to her father.

Trinavindu said, "Why are you no longer a maid?"

She wrung her hands. "Nothing happened, I was walking alone."

Trinavindu centered his mind and in an instant he knew the answer. He led her back to Pulastya and said, "Take this girl as alms from me, for your happiness."

Pulastya accepted her. Their son was Vishrava. Vishrava married a brahmana's daughter and when his son was born he called him Vaishravana.

Vaishravana was a happy child, good-spirited and friendly. He stayed on his grandfather's hillside smiling away, greeting the days like new friends. So happily did he live that he forgot to eat or drink, and for a thousand years he even forgot to breathe.

When he did that, in heaven Indra's marble throne grew hot. Lord Brahma had to come down and ask Vaishravana what he would like to have or to be.

"I want to be always generous," answered Vaishravana, and Brahma made him Lord of Treasures and Riches and Wealth. The Treasure Lord took the Yakshas of the hill-lakes who loved water for his treasure-keepers and made their king Manibhadra his friend. And from Brahma he also received the huge aerial mind-driven chariot Pushpaka made by Viswakarman in heaven, that could fly with horses or without them and was big as a small city, and all covered with flowers. And further, Vaishravana got immortality and all the wealth of the three worlds and kingdom over kings.

But Brahma gave him nowhere to live. Vaishravana asked his father what to do, and Vishrava sent him to deserted Lanka. The Yakshas carried the treasures of the worlds across the southern sea or rode over the waters in Pushpaka chariot. Vaishravana made Beautiful Lanka his home, and from time to time he would return to Himalya to visit his parents, floating along by himself on rays of light.

❧

In the netherworlds of the Nagas Malyavan and Sumali were still alive. Looking up through the saltwater of the southern sea, from beneath a crevice in the ocean floor they saw Vaishravana taking his riches to Lanka. Malyavan didn't mind, but when Sumali saw Vaishravana's wealth gleaming and casting brilliant lights even on the floor of the sea he was hit by envy. Unhappiness fell on him and he asked questions and learned all about the birth of the Treasure King.

Sumali told his daughter Kaikasi, "Go to Vishrava and get sons like that!" She cast down her eyes, but fearing to disobey her father she went to the Hills.

She stood before Vishrava scuffing the ground with her toe. He looked at her and she said, "I am Kaikasi, read the rest for yourself."

Vishrava took her for his second wife, and when she gave birth it was to four Rakshasas, three sons and a daughter. First-born was Ravana. Ravana had ten hideous heads and twenty arms; he was blacker than a heap of soot and fit to horrify the Universe; he had two fangs curving up from each mouth and coppery lips and twenty red eyes. When he was born every dog in the world howled as loud as he could and chased his tail madly turning left in circles.

Next was born the giant Kumbhakarna with ears shaped like the big earthen waterjars that stand higher than a man's waist, and he grew up in one day to stand taller than a high house. Then the frightful girl Surpanakha was born, and last of all was born Vibhishana the good demon.

Not long after their birth, Ravana and Vibhishana saw the Treasure Lord come home on one of his visits. Ravana became sad that he had no such brilliance himself. Then Ravana made the colossal Kumbhakarna stay home and not wander over Earth eating saints, and in that wide mountain forest the three brothers sat contemplating the absolute immensity of Life. In contemplation they entered Eternity.

And at the end of every thousand years, Ravana cut off one of his heads and threw it into fire as a sacrifice, until nine of his heads were gone and but one day remained before he would cut the last one. That day was passing. Ten thousand years and Ravana's life were about to end together.

Ravana held the knife to his throat, when Brahma appeared and said, "Stop! Ask me a boon at once!"

"I am glad that I please you," said Ravana.

"Please me!" said Brahma. "Your will is dreadful, too strong to be neglected; like a bad disease I must treat it. Your pains make me hurt. Ask!"

"May I be unslayable and never defeated by the gods or any one from any heaven, by Hell's devils or Asuras or demon spirits, by underworld serpents or Yakshas or Rakshasas."

"Granted!" said Brahma quickly. He gave Ravana back his burnt heads better looking than before. They rose living from the ashes and settled on Ravana's necks. Ravana smiled and smoothed down his black moustaches.

Brahma told Vibhishana, "Ask."

"May I never forget Dharma in peril or in pleasure, in comfort or in distraction."

Brahma said, "Yes; and you will be immortal on Earth and exempt from death or oblivion; and my truth knows no turning."

Lord Brahma turned to Kumbhakarna, but the Wind came to him invisibly and whispered, "Grandfather, give him nothing. He has already eaten seven Apsarasas and ten Gandharvas

29

and many saints; he blunders about ruining peace and happiness. Consider what he did with no boons, and with them he will eat everyone."

Brahma thought, "Saraswati white Goddess of Speech, for a moment capture the words of Kumbhakarna." She entered the giant's throat and Brahma said aloud, "Kumbhakarna, quickly ask and quick be given."

Kumbhakarna answered, "What I really want is to sleep for half a year after every day I have to spend awake in this stupid world." He no sooner spoke than he fell over into a deep sleep.

❧

Then did Sumali come from under Earth. He embraced Ravana and said, "Now why fear? No god, not even Narayana can hurt us. Lead us back to Lanka as before!"

Ravana sent Sumali to Lanka, and the old Rakshasa told Vaishravana, "Go, this is our city."

Again the Treasure Lord asked his father what to do. Vishrava said, "Don't fight your own brother. Leave Lanka as you found her, move your treasure, live on Kailasa Hill north of these Himalyas, live on Silver Mountain." So Vaishravana became the Guardian God of the North, one of the four Guardians of the world's four directions.

Ravana moved into Lanka, and the millions of Rakshasas who had multiplied in exile underground came there with their families and animals. Old Malyavan stood blinking and smiling on Lanka's sunny beach, happy and proud of Ravana. Rakshasas went over the lands again, dark as thunderclouds, with earrings of bright gleams of gold.

One day Ravana was walking alone through the forests on the side of Trikuta Hill by his city. There he met the Asura Maya standing under the trees, holding hands with a beautiful fair-skinned girl. The Asuras are the former gods of old; they are from before.

Ravana asked, "Who are you and whose is this fawn-eyed girl?"

Maya smiled. "I am Maya, a poor artist struggling to sur-

30

vive. She is my daughter Mandodari; Hema the Apsarasa is her mother. I lived happily in love with Hema for a thousand years, but then just after Mandodari's birth her mother left us on some affair of the gods. Now in the sorrow of separation we live in grief in our humble home; we wander sadly in our golden palace; through tearful eyes we watch the stars at night; we languish long on diamond stairways; we sigh by silver curtains and fountains of nectar; and in our ten thousand empty rooms we hear from the trees outside the moaning of our singing wind-harps strung with glass and there we cry."

"I am Ravana and your servant," said the Demon King.

"You must be a warrior." Maya sounded more cheerful. "In all truth, my boy, a daughter's father must choose between misery and dishonor. I spend all my time watching her. She has got to be given away. I have to get rid of her. Long is the way, for someone must marry Mandodari, but no one comes to ask for her. Her youth is passing. She is artless and innocent, but who knows *who* may ask for her? Unmarried she puts all our ancestors in uncertainty. Ravana, you are a handsome fellow, your face quite striking, your arms very original, your faults surely not worth mentioning . . . we go out walking, but always I must bring her back home again, like carrying my own illusion home with me . . . ."

Ravana said, "Brahma himself is my great-grandfather and I am King of Lanka."

"Fascinating!" said Maya. "Charming! Take her, My Lord, take the daughter of Maya the Master of all Arts and Skill."

❧

So Ravana wed the golden-skinned Daughter of Illusion. He lit a fire and married her. And days later, there stood before Ravana his full-grown son Meghanada, like fire released from hiding in fuel, set free to burn. Meghanada had a voice like a cloud full of thunder. He changed his form and appearance at will; if he had a true form only his mother Mandodari knew what it was.

Then from the Himalyan hillside Ravana and Vibhishana

31

carried Kumbhakarna to Lanka as he slept, and Ravana had built over him a huge mansion of one big room like a shed. He chose the demon Prahasta as his General, and Prahasta gathered soldiers into an army. Then the Demon King threw ten arms around his son and the other ten round his General, and they began to fly off with countless soldiers to rape the worlds for days at a time.

They would make many raids into the Himalya hills and there like the Wind they broke down trees and tore the orchards and pavilions set along the paths to heaven. Gandharvas and Apsarasas visiting on Earth were captured and eaten, men were devoured, Ravana stole fair maidens of every race for his warriors in Lanka; and then refugees ran to Vaishravana on Mount Kailasa.

Vaishravana sent a Yaksha to see Ravana in Lanka. The Yaksha said, "The noble Treasure King hears of your bestial attacks on the innocent and asks you to remember right and wrong and not to dishonor your family. He tells you—*Stop, brother, for I live near heaven and I hear the gods wish for your destruction and seek ways to kill you.*"

Ravana smiled. "My jewel-bellied brother!" He drew a sword and killed the Yaksha. He sent him to the kitchen to be roasted and served,and his bones made into broth.

And when they had eaten, Ravana and Prahasta rose into the sky. They darted north over the sea and flew over cities and streams and plains, racing to silver Kailasa.

Manibhadra the Yaksha King saw them come and ran to stand in the gate of the Treasure Palace. Ravana yelled at him, "Surrender or die!"

"Where's our messenger?" asked Manibhadra.

"He's dead. In the soup!" cried General Prahasta.

Vaishravana heard that from inside his palace and called out a window, "That does it! Kill my brother!"

Yakshas poured out the palace windows. Manibhadra flew over the walls like a hawk, followed by whirling flame-crested Yakshas spinning in the air, filled with the energy they had stolen from careless treasure-lovers in the big cities of men, and crying their war-cries—*Yes. No. I don't want. Let me have. More!*

Prahasta killed a thousand of them and Ravana got the rest. But Manibhadra remained under the gateway arch of gold. His green eyes were shining; his blue hair was tied with strings of white blossoms; his lavender skin was steaming. He was very strong; he frowned and stamped his feet; he waved his powerful arms and glanced from his eye-corners. He pulled the palace gate from its stout hinges and flattened Prahasta with it. He grinned and sailed through the air at Ravana, and hit him with his fist from above so hard the mountain shook. Manibhadra drove Ravana right down into the ground like a post, turned and saw Prahasta trying to get free, and with a magic wave of his hand put fear of loss and hope of gain into Prahasta's heart in exactly equal parts and so paralyzed him.

But where is the straight fair fighting of the Yakshas and where are the tricks of illusion that Rakshasas use? Ravana blinded Manibhadra with darkness and hit the Yaksha King on the head with a steel mace, so hard that ever after Manibhadra's skull was dented in on the side.

Manibhadra fell unconscious. The nine invisible treasures sent their spirits to carry him to safety. Vaishravana came sadly out from his palace and told Ravana, "We surrender. You have conquered our world and destroyed our friendship. Take what you want, for nothing now will ever more be freely given you. I won't fight you any more . . . you may take me for a coward, afraid to do wrong."

Ravana pried Prahasta out from under the gate-leaf and from his brother he took the giant aerial chariot Pushpaka. All by itself the chariot rose into the sky, and riding there with Prahasta Ravana left for Lanka thinking himself master of all and everyone.

Indra came down from his Heaven and said to Vaishravana, "Your slain Yakshas are flying through my sky. Ravana is your brother, but now I turn my face from him, I curse him forever."

Vaishravana shook his head in wonder. "He will not stop!"

"If not, he will *be* stopped," said Indra. "He'll be *crushed!*"

Vaishravana sighed. "In ignorance he drinks poison, in confusion he refuses the antidote. He plans in detail his own ruin and wastes all his strength. Straight-speaking people cannot even talk at all with one so outrageous and treacherous. I could not even talk with him here . . . ."

❧

As they flew south in Pushpaka, Ravana and Prahasta saw a golden reed forest held in nets of sunlight on a mountainside, a woodland of bamboos and canes. They were taken by the sight and turned the chariot for a closer look, when all at once Pushpaka came to a jarring halt and stuck there immovable in the sky.

Prahasta groaned, "This thing won't work, there's always something wrong with everything."

But then they saw Nandin, Shiva's white bull, grazing below them. Nandin looked up and changed his shape. He became a yellowy-brown dwarf and rose to stand in the air near them, his ugly head shaven, his limbs too short for his body, his chest like a barrel. First he just looked. Then he sniffed, then he growled under his breath, then in a lordly tone he said, "Turn and go, turn and go, Ravana. Shiva sports here with Devi, no one can approach the Wood of Reeds, no one can ever pass me."

When Ravana saw that badly dressed midget looking down his nose at him he yelled—*Who is this Shiva?* Ravana jumped down onto the foot of the mountain, but there before him was that same little Nandin. This time he was leaning on a stick and wearing the red face of a monkey.

Ravana had to laugh. He threw back his heads and laughed as loud as all the thunders ever made rolling together over heaven. But Nandin spoke quietly, "Demon King, you may frolic and mock my face, but animals looking like me will destroy you. I could finish you off right now, easy as talking, but your own deeds will kill you, not me."

34

Ravana snorted, "Little cow, I'll uproot this bump of dirt! How dares Shiva play here like some special king with no fear of me?" Ravana grabbed the hill and shook it like a rag. All Shiva's twisted goblins and speckled imps and tiny gnomes and ghosts rolled tumbling down from above. On the hilltop Parvati the Himalya's daughter trembled and caught hold of her Lord Shiva.

Shiva pressed his big toe gently on the ground, and that mountain struck his stony roots right through the Earth round Ravana, and bars of stone held the Demon King a prisoner. Ravana pushed and fought to get free but the strength of his twenty arms was nothing.

Then Ravana began to sing from his prison under the mountain's foot, and on the summit Shiva listened from afar with Devi on his lap. The great Lord Shiva smiled; those were good songs. Shiva sat on a bench, one leg bent under him and the other touching Earth, holding Devi, holding a trident, wearing rags and snakes, drinking wine and eating ganja, his hair adorned with the streak of the Moon. Ravana kept singing and years passed by as though they were moments.

For the beauty of his songs Shiva set Ravana free. By that time Prahasta had recovered somewhat, and they returned to Lanka in the immense stolen chariot. But Ravana could not remain content. As soon as he had rested a little he again set out with Prahasta on Pushpaka, this time to overthrow the kingdoms of men.

❧

Ravana stood on the chariot with his General under a royal white umbrella of a hundred ribs of gold and went from city to city, seeking war. But all the kings had heard of him and thought Ravana invincible. They all said—*We are conquered*—until working his way north Ravana reached the capital of the Haihaya people.

That was the city of King Arjuna of the Thousand Arms. King Arjuna had ruled there for eight-four thousand years when Ravana landed by the city walls and sent in the message—*Surrender or die!*

Four of the gods were in the city. When they heard Ravana had arrived they took the disguises of animals. Indra became a peacock, Yama the Death Lord turned into a crow, Vaishravana became a lizard and Varuna the King Under Waves chose a swan.

King Arjuna was out, but his old war minister came to the gate. He spit out some red betel juice, leaned back on his heels, looked way up at Ravana and said, "Ah how fine it is to rule the world just by saying you do! Great Hero, we blink our eyes in flattery and worship; we praise you for defeating your own brother. But we don't know what to do. We have never heard words of challenge like yours except when we say them to others in conquest. Our King is not here, but he bathes in the Narmada River with his wives."

Ravana went after King Arjuna. The gods within the city dropped out of their disguises, but still those four living animals were standing there.

Indra said, "Peacock, you will never have to fear snakes. Your tail will no longer be plain blue, but will have a hundred iridescent eyes, and when the rain falls you will dance with joy remembering our friendship."

Yama said, "Crow, you will never die unless you're killed. In famine you will eat before the hungry men. The only person to watch out for is someone walking alone down the road past your tree, who bends over and picks up a throwing stone."

In those days swans had blue wingtips and their breasts were green as tender grass. Varuna said, "Swan, become the happiest of birds, swim white and peaceful on the water near me."

Vaishravana the Treasure Lord said, "Lizard, I am pleased with you, you will be golden-gleaming, your head will shine with gold."

In the Vindhya Hills Ravana brought his chariot down to Earth by the Narmada river racing gladly to the western sea.

36

He decided to worship Shiva before he fought, and broke flowery boughs from the white and gold blossom trees and carefully set them out by the water. Ravana then bathed and splashed in the river like an elephant, then put on a clean white robe and got ready to sing. He held his twenty hands pressed together two by two. His ten heads fanned out, his heavy earrings swayed, he bent his weight over and stood on one foot in the sand.

Downstream aways, King Arjuna was showing off for his wives. With his thousand arms he dammed up the Narmada. The water rose in waves and flowed backwards; it came up to Ravana's knee and washed away his every flower.

"That must be Arjuna," said Ravana. "I'll handle this man alone." He walked downriver, and saw the Haihaya King, an immovable hill of a man with arms outstretched, red-eyed with wines, his long hair afloat on the water. Two soldiers came and saluted Ravana. "Your Majesty, our King is drunk and plays with his women. Be our welcome guest until morning and then fight him."

But Prahasta came running up, barging through the trees bringing Ravana his steel war-mace, and then King Arjuna cocked his ears. King Arjuna stepped out of the river and the waters surged away. He didn't waste any time. He picked up a golden club five hundred hands long and hit Ravana. The club broke against Ravana's chest, bits of burning gold went shooting through the air; and Ravana wept, and backed away four steps and sat down.

Arjuna put down his club and picked up Ravana. He held the Demon King squirming in a fifty-arm grip, and roared like a tiger clawing down a deer, so loud that Ravana's grandfather Pulastya could hear it in the Himalya Hills.

Pulastya went to save Ravana. King Arjuna welcomed him, "Now my poor river is better than heaven, for here and not there do I meet you."

Pulastya said, "Majesty, Ravana is hard to bind as the Wind but you have done it. Now his glories are yours. Be satisfied, free him for me."

37

King Arjuna said not a word but set Ravana free at once. Ravana went shamefully back to his chariot and drove aimlessly away in disgrace.

As he and Prahasta passed over a deserted forest somewhere, they happened to see the heavenly sage Narada riding by on a cloud. Narada came close to them and said in midair, "Ravana, you are unslayable even by gods, and men are mortal; they are already dead, so fight a worthy enemy."

"Who?"

"Men are made of straw," said Narada. "They are worthless and frail and contemptible, their brief lives are loans that must be soon repaid. They are Death's subjects, Yama the Death Lord rules them; therefore conquer Yama."

Ravana's faces brightened. He forgot his defeat and felt as good as ever. Narada said, "But how could even you go while living to the Land of Death?"

Ravana said, "Consider it done!" He pointed Pushpaka to the south. That flowery chariot picked up speed and shot past the southern horizon and dipped down into Yama's kingdom like a rain of jewels.

❧

There was the Vaitarani River running with blood; down there were steep black barren hills, the death-wind moaning, hot sands and shrieks from the darkness. Prahasta flew away in fear and Ravana was alone. And in the ghastly flaring light of Hell Ravana saw a corpse shrouded in brown sitting on the wasted ground and looking at him, grinning at him like a skull, his yellow skin streaked with cremation ashes and cemetery dust, skin like leather stretched taut, bones all showing. There were red fires in his dried and sunken eyes, and when he breathed it sounded like the death-rattle of the dying.

That person looked at Ravana and said, "Do not enter here like a dog, Rakshasa King!"

The sword-bladed trees of Hell rang in the wind. Ravana narrowed his eyes and said, "Where is Yama the God of Death?"

38

"What do you want with him?"

Ravana said, "I have taken him for my lasting enemy and I take you for the same whoever you are."

The seeming corpse replied, "Demon King, seek for Death among the living and not here. These black hills are the frontiers of Hell, Hell that burns with the fire of deeds done wrong. With the fire of acts, Ravana, is Heaven brilliant and Hell aflame. Do you believe in Hell, or will you play the fool in my presence, until it is too late, until you begin to learn but it is all too late . . . cringing and whimpering and all too late . . . ."

"Who are you then?"

The corpse laughed a dusty laugh. He pointed with his wrinkled bony hand. "Yama is that way. Oh Ravana, be gone, I am Kala . . . I am Time . . . I am Time . . . ." And there he changed, and became a fair young man, wearing fresh flowers and smiling with all his life before him; and the sights and sounds of Hell became those of a love-park on the fair countryside of Earth.

While Ravana was talking to Time, Narada flew to Yama, who was sitting at home. The Death King turned his head to see him with his immovable eyes and said, "Narada, why do I see you here? You are too fond of strife and trouble."

"Listen," said Narada, "Ravana comes to vanquish you."

"Does he?"

Suddenly before Yama stood Death, Death who wears many faces, Death who makes nothing of all this world, standing with many rods and maces in his arms. Narada shivered and Death watched him.

"Sad it is," said Yama gently, "to have an enemy like this Death. Therefore try to make him your friend; you have met before, and come to you he must, once more at least. I have partly veiled him. Do right, Narada, tune your lutes and cease to meddle in the wonderful universe."

Death spoke to Yama, "Let me go. Great warriors in strong armor fail and fall before me like bridges of beautiful sand. I can dissolve anything; it takes no strength of mine."

Yama said quietly, "Stay still, Oh Death. The very Sun, my father, does not boast of his power; in fact, he manages to be silent."

"My dear Master, release me . . . ."

"Hide them, my friend, hide those scepters and rods."

"My patient Lord . . . ."

"Not yet. I walk to meetings slowly and on foot, I do not run."

"Let me but touch him . . . ."

"*Yamam!* I restrain you!" Yama raised his green hand, and Death vanished.

Then Ravana came and bowed to Yama. "Death Lord, surrender to me."

"I surrender to you," said Yama kindly, "until you call for me some day."

Yama also disappeared. Ravana turned to Narada. "See, I rule over the Death Lord. Who dares deny I am the Emperor of every wide world?"

"Who dares deny it?" said Narada. "If you have the time, sit down, I'll tell you their names."

"What need?" smiled Ravana. "I will visit my devoted subjects for myself."

Ravana found General Prahasta hiding somewhere and the two of them returned to Lanka. This time, there Ravana collected a small Rakshasa army of three million demons, put them all on Pushpaka chariot, and with his son Meghanada beside him drove to the Naga worlds of the underground serpents, the luxurious underworlds far more delightful to every sense than heaven. They stopped by a palace of columns and pillars lit up by brilliant gems, brighter than if it stood in sunlight.

That was the home of Vasuki the King of the Serpent Tribes. By the doorway hung a plow for delving Earth and a pestle for grinding ores. Vasuki came out to see who was there, in form a man from the waist up, a snake below, dressed in purple, wearing a white shell necklace and a tall tapering crown of white waxy flowers. He hated to see strangers in his home; he scowled and looked around as though he had entered another's cave by mistake.

Oh Dasaratha, the hooded serpents of the underground are hard to frighten; they do not threaten very easily, never knowing when to fear. Vasuki advanced to within striking distance, joined his hands together and said, "Why Ravana, you didn't bring enough demons here with you, go get some more, you can hardly even trouble my sleep with these toy devils!"

"Surrender to me," said Ravana.

Vasuki answered him, "I rule the Nagas, but we are all the people of the Water King Varuna, our Lord Undersea. See him. I hope this is bad news to you!"

"Little worm, where is he?"

Then Vasuki turned himself entirely into a venomous snake. He spread flat his hood and swayed slowly from side to side. *Weaknessss to you, Ravana, ssspare me your sneersss . . . .* Vasuki's flat glittery head was weaving back and forth; his glassy round eyes were fixed on Ravana and never blinking, first one eye and then the other, their irises yellowy and their pupils round and black, round black circles, eyes that held . . . .

"We will burn you like fire," said Vasuki, "we will burn you to the bones, here your life is worthless to ussss . . . our Lord Varuna has left his white palace running with streams. He is in Brahma's highest heaven hearing songs."

"Tell him to give up and I won't harm him."

"Oh I will tell *that* to Varuna!" Vasuki straightened himself out and flew away like an arrow. When he returned he was riding with Brahma, calmly coiled in the corner of Brahma's swan-chariot, no longer angry.

Brahma said, "Varuna who embraces Earth with his seas and oceans must surrender to you every kingdom below the lands and under waves. Ravana, how have you lost all the goodwill, all the love and kindness that is the heart's release?"

41

Ravana bowed his ten heads and sighed. Brahma was gone; Vasuki was gone; everyone was dying; no deed was worth doing; old age was dry and brittle.

Behind him Ravana heard a dry cough. He turned. There was Time, standing behind him, letting his shriveled shadow fall over the Demon King.

❦

Ravana drove Pushpaka back into daylight, and still with his army he rose up into the sky to the home of the Sun. Fast as the chariot flew it was a long trip. It was twilight when Ravana arrived. He could see the rays of Surya the Sun shining out from cracks between the stones of his palace. He could smell heat, hot iron and baking stone; he saw the one-wheeled golden chariot just returned, the seven white horses harnessed still with serpents; he saw a sky-road with no support, a long road and no turning, a going forward with no help.

When Ravana stopped his car there was a great silence. Then a gatekeeper came from the palace, crossed the fields of air with his hair burning and his fingers covered with hot copper gloves. He said, "As you wish, Ravana, as you wish."

Ravana took that for a surrender. He set a new course for the lovely bright mansions of the Moon, eighty thousand leagues above Earth in outer space. It was truly cold there, cold as winter's Moon in the clear frosty night high in the hills. Cold mists turned slowly over dark lakes in the distance; stark black trees broke leafless from the barren ground. There were white freezing glaciers creeping closer. Ravana saw only cold desolation, cold ice, cold stars; and felt a brittleness like glass in the air.

A star spirit appeared, casting a thin shadow behind him from the bright glory of his beaming face. "Lord of Lanka, what lunacy is this? Do not oppress my Lord Chandra the Moon, the silver King of Stars, for he wishes well to all. Consider this your home . . . stay here with us forever . . . ."

Ravana saw General Prahasta already looking over his shoulder for the way home, and said quickly, "I accept your surrender." Pushpaka chariot went back down toward Earth and the air was warmer. Ravana smiled at his son Meghanada, "Nothing to it!" They turned again, rose in a different way, and came to the gate of Indra's heaven. Ravana looked in at the immortal celestial city of Amaravati built along the heavenly Ganga river. He said, "This won't take a moment," and got out of the car.

A five-crested Gandharva, some musician of heaven, stood leaning by the Gate of the Gods. Ravana went up to him and said, "Summon your Master Indra to admit his defeat."

"Who?"

"Your Master Indra."

"Do *what*?" smiled the Gandharva.

Ravana drew his curving sword. "Who do you think you are?"

"I am Chitraratha the Gandharva King, the Lord of Music, and I don't run errands for dirty black spiders!"

Ravana swung at him with his sword and missed. Suddenly in Chitraratha's hand was a long Gandharva wand shimmering and waving. Ravana had a terrible sword; but Chitraratha's wand was tough and supple and springy like a riding whip, gay and colored, cut from the edge of a rainbow, so slender that twenty hands were no guard against it, and it sang and whistled when it cut the air.

"Get out of our sky!" Chitraratha jabbed Ravana in the stomach and struck him across the fingers so hard that he dropped his sword. Chitraratha flew away and the massive Gates of Heaven slammed closed behind him. The latch shot home, the bar fell, the bolt was drawn through and the lock snapped shut. Ravana heard Chitraratha singing a war-song, he heard thunders mutter and the iron wheels of war-chariots turning and heavenly horses running in armor. From behind heaven's pale adamant walls Ravana could see the flashes of lightnings, and flying sparks of fire tossed in the winds. The ground quaked as heavy thunderstones rolled into place, and shook beneath the feet of elephants. Storms were gathering in the air.

43

Ravana yelled, "I will plunge my arms into these dishwater gods!" And inside the walls Chitraratha flew to Indra and said, "I hope you know what you're doing."

"Never fear at any time!" Indra drew his silver sword and the day grew brighter. He drank some of his Soma. "I shade the sun himself with rain! Find some shelter for the dancing girls and the quiet spirits."

"They won't leave you," said Chitraratha. "Give me some of that juice." He drank Indra's Soma bowl dry in one swallow. "The beautiful Apsarasas, those gems of women, refuse to go, but stand armed with bows and brazen knives. The silent writers will not run and hide now; they prepare to tell their tales in someone else's blood for a change."

"Well done!" said Indra. "I don't care what *anybody* says, never will I take orders from that overbearing monster Ravana, that evil fraud—look out!"

The old Rakshasa Sumali came charging headlong at them over the wall, throwing out maces and arrows like flagstaffs, chopping down the Gandharvas in his path and heading straight for Indra. Indra took a diamond thunder, made in six points like two tridents set one at each end of a short rod; he gripped it at the middle, took aim and threw it. No person but Indra may bear the touch of a thrown thunderbolt. It hit Sumali and left no trace of him; he was blasted into blazing light.

❦

Dasaratha, so began the Battle of Heaven, a year before your four sons' births. Fatal weapons of every virtue clashed in the air; the walls fell; the warriors of heaven gave way, sinking, embracing each other, falling like a river cliff undercut.

Ravana knew they had won already, and he raised the flag of Lanka, pure cloth-of-gold. But too soon. The storm gods tore it away. They hit the demons with power like a tidal wave, like the summer rains beating down, like the lightnings streaming from the clouds, like herds of elephants stampeding downhill. They hit the demons hard as the death of a friend.

44

The Rakshasas were a mountain of dark blue ore crumbling and the wild winds sang through their spears.

Then Meghanada brought black darkness by illusion and blinded gods and demons all but himself. In that bewilderment the old Asura chief Puloma came to save his daughter Indrani the Queen of Heaven. Puloma came darkly dressed, darkly adorned, darkly glancing. He plowed untouched through the demons and took Indrani down to his home under sea, and he also took brave Chitraratha with him to sing to comfort her.

Still the storm gods searched blindly for Ravana. Airavata, Indra's white elephant, swung his trunk and flapped out his ears, he stuck out his tail and charged at a terrible speed trumpeting and tossing his head and guided by scent. He collided with Ravana and with his four tusks threw him down on his back. Ravana lay with armor torn and drenched with rains, bruised by thunders and burnt by snapping lightnings, battered by the whirlwinds filled with the fragments of war; and across Ravana's breast ran four deep bleeding wounds and Airavata stood over him calling in rage and challenging all Hell to War.

Meghanada thought—*Father's dead!* He bound Indra in illusion, then invisibly he approached Ravana and shouted, "Are you alive? I have Indra captive!"

Those words ended Ravana's pain. Every might and power went out of the storms. Then followed by Ravana and all the demons still alive, Meghanada carried Indra still bound to Lanka, threw him prisoner into a dungeon, locked him in and kept the key.

Brahma came to Lanka. He said to Ravana's son, "Now call yourself Indrajit, Indra's Conqueror. Free him and take something from me in return."

Indrajit answered, "Immortality."

"Prince, I cannot give that gift to you, if you have asked for it."

Indrajit said, "Grandfather of the Worlds, when Ravana is in danger may I call up with offerings from the fire altar a war

45

He bound Indra in illusion . . .

chariot drawn by four tigers that moves at will; while I ride on it may I be charmed to win any battle against any creature; and may no one but other Rakshasas see me when I wish to fight invisible."

"I give all that," said Brahma. Indrajit held out the dungeon key but Lord Brahma will never touch a weapon. By thought Brahma first removed from Indra's mind all despair and fear. He sent the idea—*I am free*—and so annihilated the jail walls.

◈ ◈ ◈

"Now throughout the forests Rakshasas cruelly torment us like men in Hell," said Viswamitra. "You have heard what evil has befallen Earth and all the worlds. At night the demons yell to one another—*I am Narayana! I am the Moon! I am Everything!* These are their more meek and modest boasts, what can I say of their serious praise and sincere drunken flatteries? The Night-Wanderers strut and swagger and pull apart Dharma. Out there, Dasaratha, beyond these walls of Ayodhya demons range over the worlds like the winds. Two of them especially cross me. So I have come to Fair Ayodhya I must have a warrior. I need Rama to kill them"

"My child!" said the King.

"I will not use up any of my hard-won merit to curse demons," said Viswamitra. "I have come for Rama. It must be Rama. I will cover him with blessings and fame, though he wears still a boy's long side-locks, though he is but sixteen."

Dasaratha said, "After living through sixty thousand long years, in my old age have I at last gained a son. How can you take a tender child, my firstborn son, and lead him to Death?"

"Very well," said Viswamitra, "break your promise. And if you are doing right may you be happy!"

Vasishtha said, "Brahmana keep your temper; King, keep your word. Observe the defects of this world and do not add to them."

47

taste this water

Mother Earth laughed—

I quake: the Cities of Men downfall.
Yet these Kings, these mortal puppets
Are willing to admit they own me!

Viswamitra said, "Majesty, when I am tired in the evening, Desire and Wrath whom the gods cannot tame come bowing to me and gladly rub my feet. When I ask anything, that command is valuable. Whoever finds the chance to obey me is in my debt."

"Take Rama and his brother Lakshmana," said Dasaratha. He called for Rama and Lakshmana and told them, "Arm yourselves and serve this brahmana."

"Do not fear for your sons," said Viswamitra." I have not run from demons in fear; but the retreat of a strong man is like the silent drawing back of a fist to strike a blow!"

The old King held his two sons. He embraced them, and smelled the hair on the crowns of their heads. They were still round-faced children and so young. But Rama and Lakshmana expertly put on their bows and quivers, donned their swords and archer's gloves like men; the King smiled then, and felt no more grief for their going.

Viswamitra led the two boys from the city. Just outside the white walls of Fair Ayodhya they stopped by the Sarayu River. There Viswamitra sat by the water and said, "Princes of Ayodhya, because Ravana overlooked men I have things to teach you; I have places to guide you, therefore become my students."

48

Rama and Lakshmana shed their weapons, and they each gathered and brought to Viswamitra a bundle of firewood sticks, as one does when first meeting his preceptor. Then in a hermit's cup made from half a coconut shell Viswamitra dipped up some water and told Rama, "Take this cup and drink it down. Drink it all at once or you will never finish it, and it will do no good." Rama drank it. Viswamitra taught him two mantras, one for strength and one for more strength. He refilled his cup and did the same for Lakshmana. He taught them both how to rightly time and correctly speak the words.

"These are two spells of Power; they are the daughters of Brahma," said Viswamitra. "Say them and you gain wisdom and good fortune; even when you are asleep or distracted, no enemy can surprise you; tiredness or thirst or illness or hunger cannot get to you; you can easily find the answer to any uncertainty, solve any secret, end any argument, reach the True. These are great words, they are Brahma's own."

They went on; they all three slept the night on leaves and grass. In the morning Viswamitra sang to the Sun and bathed; they followed Sarayu downstream and that afternoon approached the deep roar and thunder of the meeting of the waters of Sarayu and Ganga, in Angadesha Forest, where every tree was thousands of years old.

That night Viswamitra taught heavenly weapons to Rama, beginning with the dread Brahma weapon and working down. They sat in the dark. Rama said the controlling mantras and one by one the weapons appeared before him. He touched each one and said, "Return when I remember you." Some weapons had celestial shapes, some were like live coals, some were smoke, some looked like great suns and moons. They went turning round Rama and vanished.

The next morning some hermits took Rama and Lakshmana and Viswamitra across the holy River Ganga on a raft, and before noon they were at Viswamitra's retreat, a lonely hut of canes and branches. The brahmana unpacked his traveling fire and put a bowl of flames from it onto his sloping altar.

"Now I will begin," said Viswamitra. "Stand here. Protect

49

me for six days and nights, then on the seventh day be more alert, especially toward night as the sacrifice draws to an end, and once I begin I will not speak." He fell silent. Mentally he called Agni the Fire Lord; mentally he presented him a place to sit, asked about his journey, mentally offered him water on which flowers floated.

On the seventh evening Viswamitra put a handful of jewels and colored rice all mixed together onto his altar, and a few flowers. He lit some incense and laid out green and white grass stalks and a bowl of liquid butter.

Then out of nowhere, like two black clouds the Rakshasas Maricha and Subahu swept in over the treetops, and on Viswamitra's altar the fire flickered in terror. Rama took three aiming steps backwards, for about the distance of a staff, and he shot three arrows at Maricha. The three arrows came together and struck Maricha's heart all as one. But they did not kill him; their force carried him through the air for hundreds of leagues and dumped him unconscious into the far western sea.

Lakshmana killed Subahu with one shot. At full dark the sacrifice was finished, and Viswamitra said, "This wood is clear of demons, that was my desire." He looked at Rama. "Prince, they were off guard. This time it was light and easy for you, but many hard things are easy to begin . . . If ever again you meet Rakshasas, do not move your mark, do not spare them from kindness again."

Viswamitra said, "I dislike lowlands. I was here only to do this rite, now come with me part way back to my home in the Hills, where my sister is a river. For in the Videha kingdom of King Janaka, the Husband of Earth, there is a bow no one can bend. They say it's Shiva's bow. It hangs within a box in the smoke of aloeswood, decked with flowers. Rama, you must see that bow."

When they reached the Videha land, walking by easy stages, the tigers and serpents of Angadesha who had escorted Viswamitra turned back as an army will disperse when the King enters his palace from a journey, knowing their friend

50

was safe in Janaka's country. The hills were rising and the rivers ran swift and cold. Not far from Mithila, the capital of Videha, Viswamitra stopped a little way off the road, and there in a grove of trees Rama saw an ancient crumbling stone wall overgrown with vines. The wall trembled when the dust from Rama's feet touched it, and it seemed to be almost alive.

"Where are we?" asked Rama.

"This is the empty retreat of Gautama," answered Viswamitra, "and for long it lies under his wrathful curse."

Listen, my Prince—

Using his mind, Brahma created some creatures called Men, all the same in color and speech, all absolutely identical. Then he created the same number of females for them, but this time he gave all of the beauty to just one woman and named her Ahalya.

Indra saw her, but before he could speak to her the hermit Gautama married Ahalya and lived with her here, while Indra waited and watched for his chance. Finally he took Gautama's form while he was away from home bathing one day, and made love to Ahalya. She was not fooled by his disguise, but she consented out of curiosity.

And after, Indra hurried to leave. He was almost out of sight when Gautama appeared in wet clothes and saw him.

> *To man and woman,*
> *Forbearance is a becoming ornament;*
> *Very hard to do—*
> *Hardest of all, to forgive a god.*

Indra lost his male sex; and since that curse of Gautama the rule of no Indra is secure, the role of Indra is impermanent. Indra fled to Agni. He hid inside a firepit that was within a förge that was inside a furnace. In the presence of Fire Indra said, "Oh I took from Gautama the power that threatened heaven, his merit is gone by my stirring his anger to cursing. All for the work of the gods, for *your* sake am I cursed!"

51

Agni replied, "Barely escaped alive, and already the bad is changing to good in your story! I restore your male sex."

Agni went to the dead Fathers and said, "I am Fire; only Fire can eat anything pure or impure; I am Fire burning."

The shadowy souls replied, "Take the impurity. Burn away from the sacrificial rams those fleshly parts. We take the rest; we will take pure watery offerings clean as a new life, tranquil as a lake deep and cool."

And so today in black smoke those male parts of rams are lifted by Agni to heaven when we offer burnt food to our Fathers, and Indra feeds on them and they restore him. Here on this spot Gautama told his wife, "Beauty alone caused this. No longer will you be the one fair woman in the universe." He took her beauty and scattered it to others, he took so much beauty from Ahalya that she became invisible, and her spirit lives concealed by boughs and leaves somewhere by that stone wall.

Ahalya said, "We have no neighbors. He looked just like you." Gautama could not retract his words but he could limit them. He made an end for his curse in the future, "When Rama comes to this grove you are free."

◈   ◈   ◈

"His curse expires as I speak," continued Viswamitra," so enter there this ruined hermitage, and deliver the divinely beautiful Ahalya."

Rama went in. There was a shower of marigolds out of the blue sky and they heard Gandharva music. Ahalya came gradually again into sight by the old wall, as beautiful then as ever, like the Sun rising reflected in rippling water, and like the Sun she could not be looked at too closely or too long. Rama saw Viswamitra waving—*Come away;* and at the same time Ahalya the Beautiful swept her arm gracefully to one side—*Sit as my guest.*

Rama went and sat by her a moment. Ahalya pressed her right hand over his heart and smiled—*From the Ancient World.* Then Rama rose and rejoined Viswamitra and Lakshmana.

They all walked three times around Ahalya, keeping her on their right, and they left her there behind them, sitting among golden flowers. When they had gone on aways they looked back and saw a beautiful halo of all colors brilliant and shining through the trees, and saw Gautama in a flying chariot return for her.

Soon they saw Mithila, a city of castles and spires, and they found King Janaka coming to meet them. He brought cool water to Viswamitra. "Blessed are we, brahmana. Obliged and well-favored are we with your visit. But why have you led young warriors by this back trail to my city?"

"These are the Ayodhya princes Rama and Lakshmana," said Viswamitra. "They are eager to see your bow."

"Long since did Shiva give me that heavenly bow," said the King. "To bend Shiva's Bow is the dowry of my daughter Sita, whose mother is Prithivi, the goddess Earth."

Rama asked, "How could that be, Majesty?"

Janaka answered, "Rama, this land, this kingdom, all this wide world under the curving blue sky belongs to Mother Earth and to no one else. Only in a flight of the mind, only in a dream is all this worldly land called a kingdom. Fourteen years ago I was plowing in a clearing beyond the city, when turning back I found her lying in the furrow I had just made; I found Sita. As a golden-skinned baby she rose from her mother Earth and sat throwing handfuls of dust over her feet. I consider her a treasure well-found, well-revealed. She is a delight for my fields and hills. And Sita is beautiful, a girl more lovely than any garden, half divine and unmarried."

Rama said, "We are curious to see the strength of your bow."

King Janaka called an order, and five strong men with great difficulty brought Shiva's Bow out from its own house in Mithila, drawing it along on an eight-wheeled cart, that held the bow protected within a long iron case covered with flowers.

"You must understand," said Janaka, "that Sita has the final consent. Others have come; none could even lift this bow. I

53

. . . it broke in two above the grip . . .

passed them by, I have used this jewel of a bow as my raft to cross the sea of fourteen years. Now you have come. It is sad for me, but it is time for her to marry, and I am a poor man about to spend his last coin."

Janaka's minister came and said, "Here it is, Majesty, show it if you think it worth showing."

Janaka said, "Rama, open the box."

Rama raised the lid. Sandalwood dust and incense ash fell off from it in a powdery cloud. Rama looked and thought, "This bow is beyond men. But playfully first let me just touch it." He touched it. "Perhaps I can try to hold it . . . ."

All the Videha men had come out of the city and were watching. Rama balanced the bow and lifted it. He strung it. Then he drew it so strongly that it broke in two above the grip, with a noise so loud that everyone watching fell down, except Rama and Lakshmana, Viswamitra and King Janaka.

Janaka shook his head. "Who would have believed?" He helped his minister to rise. "Ask Sita."

The minister rubbed his ears. "She has seen him from her high window and touched him with her eyes and fallen in love with him already."

❧

Janaka sent a fast-riding herald to invite King Dasaratha to the wedding. The herald came to Fair Ayodhya and said, "Let the Videha King free himself from his promise. Strength is Sita's dowry, so let Rama marry her, and come with me to Mithila, and bring your priest Vasishtha."

Dasaratha replied, "Justly is Janaka King. A gift from a superior must be accepted."

"Janaka's brother has also three daughters. If you are willing let Lakshmana marry, bring Satrughna and Bharata and let them marry."

Dasaratha said, "Excellent, take gold, take silver."

The charioteer Sumantra arrayed the army and loaded fat pack elephants with presents. King Dasaratha carried the four birth-fires of his sons onto his chariot, and seven days after

55

Rama had broken Shiva's Bow he reached Mithila. A plowed royal field of furrows cut across the road, and King and soldiers stopped, and Vasishtha went ahead alone, stepping carefully through the new-plowed land.

Vasishtha found Janaka and said, "The Ayodhya king has come, we await your commands."

Janaka asked, "I wonder, who is the warder there who makes you wait? Who follows rules when entering his own house?"

"Earth herself cuts across our way," said Vasishtha.

"So it begins. We will marry them outdoors, in that field, good fortune to you."

Viswamitra joined Vasishtha. The two brahmanas built up with shovels a wide altar of Earth. Over that they strung from poles an awning thatched of grass. They built a fire of buttered sticks in a clay bowl, lit it and set it on the altar; they set out flowers and golden spoons, waterpots painted with colors and trays spread with ripe grain, shells and incense burners, cups and vases, and saucers spread with colored parched wheat, and a bronze bell-metal milking jar filled with milk and honey for the gods, and put down carpets to stand on.

Rama and Lakshmana came out from Mithila; Dasaratha and his four sons stood by the altar. Then Janaka came striding over his field, smiling, leading four maidens like flames of fire. Three of them were lovely. But the most beautiful was Sita, Sita the Star of Beauty born from Earth.

Sita was a fair young girl. Her dark eyes were like the eyes of a doe, her lips were full, her long dark hair was falling down her back clear to her ankles and it was fragrant from being scented over incense smoke. She had a red brow-mark and lines of red and white sandalwood paste on her arms; the soles of her feet were dyed red with lac; she wore crimson robes and silver veils light as air, belts of embroidery and fine chains swaying as she walked, jeweled diadems and bell anklets, new barley shoots behind her ear, bridal garlands of jasmine, and seven strands of pearls around her neck and falling over her full round breasts. But who describes Sita? All this was forgotten when she looked at you. When she smiled, what else existed?

As his wedding gift, King Janaka tied into Sita's hair over her forehead a round pearl on a leaf of gold. He had brought out her birth-fire and now poured it into one earthen bowl with Rama's. He led Rama and Sita to the altar under the awning and stood them near the mingled fire.

There were no pretentious brahmana priests in Videha. Long before had Janaka got rid of them. First they told him he needed them to make offerings to the little gods, so Janaka broke all the statues of the lesser gods. Then the priests said that anything a man did for himself trying to find the True was wrong and useless and only they knew all the answers. Janaka didn't argue. He put a hearty curse on them, their heads fell off and their brittle bones were stolen by thieves.

So King Janaka himself married Rama to Sita. He said, *Ramachandra, Rama like the Moon, take Sita as your companion in the living of your life. Look at her, never see enough of her, cherish her with the eyes of love. Sita, love him well forever, walk with him as his wife and follow him like his own shadow forever. I marry you.*

Janaka brought together Rama's hand and Sita's, green and gold touching. He poured water over them—*So overflows my happiness.* Then Rama led Sita away, a new-married man.

Sita knew that she and Rama were destined lovers for all time past, will be so for all future to come. She rejoiced to meet him again after long separation. She saw Rama closely for the first time and thought, "He is surely Kama the Love God . . . yet Kama has no body . . . he can't be seen and Rama can . . . ."

Before Fire for a witness Rama's three brothers were also married, taking their brides' hands. Round the field the Videhas blew shells and rang bells with loud hard mallets and beat their drums and sang.

The next day Dasaratha said, "Janaka, best of men, let my sons' wives come home with them to Ayodhya."

"Farewell," said the Videha King.

Viswamitra was also leaving. He said to Janaka, "I will go on uphill."

"Keep climbing higher," said Janaka. "Do you have a shield?"

"I'm not a soldier," said Viswamitra.

"No matter," said Janaka. "Take Dharma for your shield, brahmana. Have you a sword?"

"What sword?"

"Take Truth."

❦

To each of the four brides Janaka gave two great Videha wolf-dogs, an elephant and sixteen horses, a basket of gold beads and four deerskins, two fine yellow woolen blankets and an entire chariot full of turquoise from the Hills. Janaka told Sita, "Her father protects a maid, but once she is wed, she must ever take the safety of her Lord. You leave me now, but never your mother Earth." He embraced his only child; he held her gently in his hard strong hands that were rough from a long lifetime of plowing and planting and reaping. Then Sita got on an elephant with Rama and they rode off to Kosala. Janaka followed walking behind for a short way and turned back to Mithila.

The Kosalas met Dasaratha and his sons a day's journey from Ayodhya. Along the city streets people waited, eager to see the brides. And in the high white royal palace overlooking Fair Ayodhya the three Queens welcomed the brides with every enjoyable object; happiest of all to see them was the youngest Queen, the joyful slender-waisted Kaikeyi. The four princesses first put flowers at the Ayodhya shrine, then they bowed to those who deserved it, then they went away alone with their husbands.

Rama and Sita lived in Rama's black stone Palace of the Moon, and twelve years went by in Ayodhya. Little by little Dasaratha turned over the work of the kingdom to Rama.

Rama's nature was quiet and free. He didn't give good advice and tell others what he thought best and show them

58

their mistakes. He knew when to save and when to spend. He could judge men finely and keep his own counsel. He could read hearts. He knew his own faults better than the failings of others. He could speak well and reason in a chain of eloquent words. Half a benefit was more to him than a hundred injuries. Bad accidents never happened near him. He could speak every language and was an expert archer who shot golden arrows; and he didn't believe that what he preferred from himself was always best for everyone else.

Rama was kind and courteous and never ill. To harsh words he returned no blame. He was warmhearted and generous and a real friend to all. He tried living right and found it easier than he'd thought. He collected the King's taxes so that over half the people didn't really mind paying him. He was a remarkable prince and every Kosala loved him except for five or six fools. He was hospitable and he spoke first to every guest in welcome words. He was a quiet strong man; he could bend iron in his hands or fix a bird's broken wing. He would not scold the whole world nor take to task the universe, and so his pleasure and his anger never went for nothing.

Rama would not work very long without a holiday; he wouldn't walk far without stopping to greet a friend, nor speak long without smiling. His entertainments and dances were the best in the world. He loved Sita well; he lived his life for the sake of her being a part of it. He would often find a new gift for his friends. He did not fear to pass a whole day without work. Whatever he did, he ennobled it by how he did it. Rama's way was noble.

HERE ENDS THE
BOOK OF THE BOYHOOD OF RAMA.
HIS YOUTH IS PAST.
THE AYODHYA BOOK BEGINS.

59

the two wishes

You saved my life;
I love you;
Ask me twice for anything!

Wide grey mountain eyes flecked with gold,
Lined with black and innocent—
And now tears!
Oh King, be careful!

After Rama and Sita had been married for twelve years, in the spring Queen Kaikeyi's brother Yudhajit, Bharata's uncle, came riding to Fair Ayodhya from the hill kingdom of Kekaya and told Prince Bharata, "Your grandfather King Aswapati, the Lord of Horses, wants to see you, for he is now an old man who has never seen his grandson."

Dasaratha gave permission, and Bharata with his brother Satrughna left on a chariot for the Hills with Yudhajit. While they were gone Dasaratha all at once felt he had enough of kingdom, and more than anything wanted to see Rama rule. He thought, "Why die first? Let me see him on my throne from here on Earth, not looking down from heaven."

He called the Kosala Council—the lesser Kings and the governors, provincial noblemen and the brave heroes, the wise and the learned and the Kosala judges whose just and certain eyesight was reason. They assembled and sat in a half-circle looking up at Dasaratha on his throne.

Dasaratha said, "I have grown very old, I have reached great age. The one thing remaining for me to do on Earth in this life is to make my son Rama a King, if you will approve that. I give you gifts, I welcome you. Tell me what you think of my son Rama. The opinions of disinterested men are different from the beliefs of a father, and the Truth may sometimes come out like Fire from friction between the two."

The assembly cheered; they gave the full-throated Kosala lion-roar and shook the palace. They said, "Make the coronation ceremonies! Of all the princes among men Rama is best! Make him our King in the morning!"

But Dasaratha said in anger, "Be still! You wish for Rama as soon as you hear my desire. While I still rule why do you wish for another King?"

For the briefest moment the chiefs and warriors talked together, then Sumantra the charioteer rose to speak for all of them. "We say this, Majesty—let your son Rama ride the huge white elephant; let us see his face beneath the white umbrella. Some men rule themselves; we Kosalas are ruled by excellent kings. Dasaratha, you follow the Dharma-path walked by your ancestors, and thoughtless of your own happiness you protect us. We know you, we have seen you teach to Rama all royal skill, we want you to see your son made King. Give away your duties and rest without burdens now, for old age has fallen on your mortal body and Time approaches you. If we deserve happiness give us Rama wearing the crown of many good talents. We love to see Rama. When he looks at us our doubts vanish and our debts are paid. I have seen Rama riding by the fields and as a father enquiring after his well-loved sons, he will ask the teachers—*Do your students obey you?* He will ask the preceptors of arms—*Do your students never walk without their weapons?*"

Dasaratha said, "Do not let a father's fondness deceive an entire kingdom."

"We won't!" said Sumantra. "Follow your own heart's true feelings, Majesty. Those true feelings are one with right Dharma. No one ever born can govern Kosala better than Rama, or better care for Fair Ayodhya and look after her. Our women young and old pray to their gods morning and night for good fortune to Rama. Why ask for anything else? While Rama lives here what can go wrong? He knows all our names. He would gladly spare us all his time if we would take it. He asks of our shops, and wishes well to our sons, to our fires, to our wives and animals. I, Sumantra the Charioteer, have seen him weep at our sorrows; *I* saw him laugh with us at our festivals."

"Are these your reasons?" asked Dasaratha.

"The one reason," replied Sumantra, "is that if Rama says something to me I can believe it." Sumantra sat down. All the men in that court audience raised their hands palms touching to their heads, and King Dasaratha looked out on those joined hands as though looking at a pond covered with unopened lotus buds.

Vasishtha then rose and said, "Majesty, though Bharata and Satrughna are still in Kekaya, yet tonight begins a rare and fortunate meeting of the Moon and stars that lasts but one day. Let me install Rama as our King tomorrow for the happiness of all the world."

Dasaratha sat upon his throne, very old, his hair white, his beard white, his robes white, resembling some father-god, his life nearly parted and gone. He blinked his eyes and tears fell down his face. "My people, I am very happy. My influence with you is very great."

❦

Dasaratha dismissed the assembly and told Sumantra, "Give this twice-born Vasishtha whatever he needs and bring Rama to me in my private rooms."

From his window Dasaratha saw Rama quickly climbing the palace steps, Rama his son, like his own image in a mirror seen rightly adorned with youth. Rama entered and knelt and bowed low to his father. "I am Rama, Majesty."

Dasaratha reached down, held Rama's hands and raised him up. "Oh Rama, no longer bow to me. You are now *my* King. Listen—for many nights have I dreamt of stars falling to the ground in daylight with terror and noise. The region round my star of life is invaded by fatal planets and my Death, I think, rushes swiftly at me. So my thoughts have changed and left this world, for ever-changing is the mind of man. Rama, to me the sight of you on the Ayodhya throne will be cool rain coming after summer's life-draining heat. Tomorrow while our groves blossom take this Kosala as your inheritance. I have in my lifetime given to the gods hundreds of offerings and sacrifices and so paid my debt to them; I have studied and passed on what I learned that was not secret and so satisfied my teachers; I have fathered sons and so paid off my ancestors; I have given gifts to brahmanas and to other men and made them happy, and they have no claim on me; and by enjoying a good life I have pleased and paid my debts to myself. All are paid. I will rule no longer."

Rama said, "But sir, warriors can't take gifts, rule on, Majesty."

Dasaratha smiled. "My son, I command you, tonight keep fast and silent watch till dawn, and let your friends guard you well—many things can go wrong, in the dark night before a King is made." The old King sighed, and rubbed his hand over his eyes. "Rama, I have had . . . strange, many strange visions . . . . I don't know, I cannot be sure, but beyond Ayodhya people await you; they will offer you things that are really yours already. These things . . . take them, no fear of breaking Dharma to you!"

Rama went to his mother Kausalya. She was at her altar, wearing new white silk and bright bracelets, offering water to the gods. The other Queens were there with her. Kausalya said, "Rama, Rama, I am so happy! Always I wanted to see this day."

Sumitra said, "You will be the Best of Kings."

Kaikeyi kissed him. "Now your father will not have to work so hard; he will have more time for just living and finding joy with me, with all of us." She smiled. "I would like to see the King as free as any of his common people, able to lie in the parks when he will, free to come and go and let the busy world just pass him by."

Vasishtha then came for Rama. Rama's three mothers blessed him, and Vasishtha led him to his own palace. When Rama and Sita had bathed that evening, and said their twilight prayers, Vasishtha threw strong mantras over them, and left them seated on grass on the bare floor and sworn to stay wakeful, not to speak, not to eat. Then Vasishtha made his way out of Rama's black palace past the warriors, past the old men softly singing spells to the stars, past the guard of tribesmen, out into the noisy crowded streets of Ayodhya.

So it was that Fair Ayodhya seen from the rooftops became a blossom of colors unfolding, a stream of lights swimming, a lake of stars in motion. The Royal Master of the Revels smiled and put on his vests and medals, his key and chain and furry hat, and unlocked the doorway to the palace wines, and gave out drinks of kindly kingly cheer. The streets were sprinkled with flowers and water. The taverns were full. The beautiful courtesans threw their great houses open to all. Grand officers in steel armor and helmets and silver shoes, wearing silks alive with colors, wearing leather gauntlet gloves and black belts and long swords were in the royal palace and the courtyards of the King helping Sumantra make everything ready. The Ayodhya marketplace was impassable. Music and cheerful noise poured out into all the streets from all the houses. The lame broke their crutches and danced; sick people got up out of bed; misers gave away gold; the King's kitchen served out free food, butter and roasts and steaming rice; and the young women came out walking by the flower stalls in their best clothes, armed with Love's arrows shot from the glances of their eyes and impatient for the next night when the celebration would really begin.

〰

As evening came, as the lamps set on branching crystal trees lighted the roads and crossings of Ayodhya, Manthara the hunchback, Kaikeyi's old serving woman, climbed limping up the outside stairs of the royal palace white as another Moon and tall as Himalya. Manthara herself came from Kekaya; she was Queen Kaikeyi's old family nurse, a sin-seeking hag, sour and malicious and cruel, bent and twisted in her heart.

Like an old furtive turtle she blinked and peered down through the hanging gardens at the festive city. She entered the palace and saw a passing serving girl wearing a new bangle. Manthara grabbed and punched her and screeched, "Where did you steal those diamonds?"

The girl backed against the wall. "Kaikeyi made us presents, dear Manthara."

"Eh? What? Never!"

"Oh happy Manthara, tomorrow Rama will be our King!"

Manthara's face crumpled and collapsed like a hill of poor worthless stone knocked apart in an earthquake. She ran to Kaikeyi and yelled, "Get up! Get up! Here comes the high tide of misfortune!"

Kaikeyi was lying on her back eating mangoes. Her eyes had dark outer corners that nearly touched her ears. She laughed like a girl and threw a sack of rubies at Manthara. "Don't spoil our night with gloom."

Manthara caught the rubies and threw them down. "Oh Queen" she whined, "the brighter the light the blacker the shadows! Here comes enduring destruction! Danger, evil, loss and grief . . . Rama will be King!"

"I know." Kaikeyi tossed her a bigger bunch of gems. "Take them for your reward for welcome news, and if you can't be happy be quiet."

Manthara frowned, her brow was like a cliff of folded stones. "Tell your son Bharata never to return. Think of him now as an orphan in hiding."

Kaikeyi leaned upon her elbow. "You're still angry. After twenty years you cannot forgive gentle Rama for once shooting a play-arrow at your hump."

"Don't you know your lazy days are over?" said Manthara. "Rama's mother will be almight around here. How do you think she really feels about you?"

"All I know is I like her fine," said Kaikeyi. "Just what do you mean anyway?"

"Kausalya will soon have you as her slave. All will look

"*What can I do even if I wanted?*"

down on you. And with your fall I will fall as well, because I am so loyal."

Kaikeyi said, "Rama is just as dear to me as my own son Bharata. Ever since Rama was a child you have tried to lay on him your own vices, which are indeed truly large enough for more than two."

"Take the measure of your enemies and destroy them while you can," said Manthara. "You can be Mistress of the World. Or a slave, take your choice."

"What can I do even if I wanted?"

"Make Dasaratha install Bharata as King. Use your two wishes. Or do you still remember, how once as a young man Dasaratha entered as the gods' ally into their war against the Asuras of drought?"

"That's when I drove his sky-chariot and saved his life," said Kaikeyi.

"It was you who told me all I know of this," said Manthara, "and from friendship to you I have not forgotten it. He promised you two wishes and you answered—*My joy is great enough that you still live. What do I want but your love from you My Lord? Keep the two gifts till I ask.*"

Kaikeyi looked at an old white scar across the heel of her right hand, the sign of a deep cut, just missing her wrist. "Oh, he was badly wounded, Manthara, and the wheel came nearly off the chariot way up in the sky, and he was badly bleeding . . . . I had his blood all over me . . ." Kaikeyi sighed and her eyes were far away, she was seeing again the past. "Alright, I'll ask him to give Ayodhya to Bharata."

Manthara said, "You must banish Rama to the forest with the second wish. Send him away for fourteen years, then he will no longer be the people's favorite, or otherwise he will kill Bharata to recover the throne!"

"My son, Oh my Bharata!" Kaikeyi burst into tears, seeing in her mind Bharata's corpse, his skin blanched by poison, on his face a frozen dead smile; her son killed by treachery.

Oh King Rama, our Master Valmiki looking down into the past world held in his hand, looking into the water saw Time

67

cast his shadow over Kaikeyi's heart, a sight hard to watch. The dancing feet of Ayodhya stopped dead.

❦

Kaikeyi the youngest Queen of Ayodhya! Her breathing tightened and her palms perspired; her soul was all dark; her heart pounded and Anger pressed his mask over her beautiful face. She hastened to take wrong for right, turned the wrong way like a doe running to the trap where her fawn is tied. "I had not understood, Manthara, the plot against me. You are bent but beautiful, you are curved as a flower bowing to the wind. Take ornaments and your beauty will challenge the Moon's.

Kaikeyi ran to the palace anger-room, slammed the door and locked it behind her. She broke off her strands of pearls. She lay in the dark thrashing her arms on the bare stone floor, tearing her clothes and screaming—*I want to die!*

It was a little before dawn. Servants awoke Dasaratha. The King came quickly down the halls, into the women's rooms, to the anger-room door. That chamber had but one brass-bound iron door, no windows, little air, no light unless one were brought in—and inside Kaikeyi lay amid her broken pearls and flowers and jewels, feeding her evil, panting and weeping from her puffy eyes, turning down the corners of her mouth, an Apsarasa fallen for the sake of love from heaven and abandoned to despair on the Himalya hillside by her lover.

Dasaratha was old, but he easily shattered that door by one stroke of one hand. He looked around for some enemy, his face flaming in wrath, his breath hot like a Naga's. Taking a lantern he entered the room, he saw Kaikeyi lying like one illusion spread out to capture another, and pain crossed his face, and the jewelry broken on the floor glittered like stars in the sky.

"Who does you hurt? Who shall mourn?" said Dasaratha. "Arise, I am the King of Kings in this world, all the land that lies in sunlight is mine."

Kaikeyi sobbed, "No, this is way beyond you."

68

Dasaratha said, "I can do anything. I have physicians well-paid to wait for times like these; let them see you. I tell you, I am the King! I can fearlessly please or displease anyone. I can disgrace my friends, reward the undeserving, punish the innocent or promote fools to high rank. I can raise up a poor man or lower a rich one to poverty. I can seize wealth and contribute it to charity and pay for priests to pray for me!"

"But this is too high a price to ask of you, Majesty," said Kaikeyi. "It was wrong of me to do this, forgive me and think no more of it. I fear, I am shamed I came here."

Dasaratha grew very proud. *"My Lady, what is it? What do you want?"*

"I want my two wishes."

"Take them, whatever you want."

"Make Bharata King and not Rama. Send Rama to the forest for fourteen years."

"Change your mind, Kaikeyi."

"Do both these things for me now. Grant me my two wishes."

"I give what you ask," said Dasaratha. He looked at Kaikeyi as though she were a stranger to him. "I will honor your wishes. Why are you uneasy as if you had done some wrong in taking what is yours? You have asked me to redeem your promises from a Solar King, you will not be cheated by me, promises must be true. Yet you have put me and all Earth in ill-humor. I am a stag facing a tigress, a snake held within a charmed circle."

"Then you'll do it?" asked Kaikeyi.

"My one thought," said the King, "is but to see Rama once more before he goes away, for his departure will kill me. Kaikeyi, if you somehow married Death himself you would soon be his widow, I think you would kill anyone!"

Then the charioteer Sumantra came and approached the anger-room. "Majesty, Night has fled before the morning's light, and the wakening Earth filled with life awaits you."

Dasaratha turned on Sumantra in rage. *"Charioteer, this hound from Hell, this bitch betrays me!"* Sumantra stepped back in fear of his life. "Sumantra, from happiness I slept but lightly till I was summoned here. But this Kaikeyi changes her love as often as lightning changes her path, she severs affections like a sharp knife, and in doing wrong she is swifter than an arrow. *I curse her!* Let this carnal Queen fall to damnation; let her spend the rest of her life in dread of the next world!"

"What?"

Dasaratha could not at first speak more, he was choked by the mist of grief in his throat, by the fumes of wrath. Then he said, "At once bring Rama here."

Rama came with Lakshmana, stood at the anger-doorway and said, "Victory to you, Father."

Dasaratha faintly said, "Oh Rama."

Rama waited but the King said no more. Kaikeyi spoke, "Gentle Rama, let Bharata become our King, and instead of the throne of Ayodhya, take a hermit's life in the vast forests for fourteen years."

Rama said, "Bharata or myself, we are much the same. But without the King's command I cannot come or go a single step."

"But these are my two promises!" said Kaikeyi.

"That is between you two," said Rama. "You had no need to use them, I would have gone at your wish. But why does Dasaratha breathe so slowly, and stand silently weeping, staring at the floor?"

"Rama, have I done right?" asked Kaikeyi.

"If you say you have, you have; I will believe you. But Mother, I cannot leave the King in sorrow."

"He will soon recover. Hurry and go."

Rama bowed to his father. "Sir, I am Rama."

Dasaratha whispered, "Child, I am insane; therefore confine me and become the King."

"I would never make you lose your faith and honesty," said Rama. "I will go today out from Ayodhya for fourteen years. I will return to say farewell before I leave." Rama rose to his feet and said to Kaikeyi, "Dasaratha never takes back, never fails to carry out what he has once spoken. Mother, I am like my father, trust me, have no fear."

❦

Rama walked away. He looked just the same as ever, but Lakshmana was stunned and followed him in a daze. They went through the palace and Rama greeted his friends as always, he did not look wishfully at the throne nor did he turn his eyes from it. The clear Moon is handsome, and slipping behind a cloud or waning he is still good to see.

Rama went to his mother's rooms. Kausalya was in tears, she saw him and said, "Were you never born I would have but the one sorrow of barrenness. Do what you want, you don't have to obey him. Stay with me, hide here in my room for fourteen years."

Lakshmana then spoke, "Even the King hopes Rama will refuse! But a wrong thrown at Rama seems to bring out no anger in him; it is like a seed thrown on stone."

Kausalya sat on a golden couch and said, "Sit by me, Rama."

Rama only touched the gold frame and stayed standing. "I need a seat of grass, I'm a hermit of the forest now, I want no softness."

"I sinned greatly in another life," said Kausalya. "Surely I kept children from their mothers. My son, my heart is iron for it does not tear; there is no room for me in the Land of Death, for Yama will not lead me from life though I desire to go."

Lakshmana looked round the room and said, "Queen, the King is a slimy old fish who eats his own brood. Why allow him to put us all in another's power? Wait, I will just go kill my father, I will not stand this." Lakshmana waved his golden arms.

Rama looked at him. "Oh Lakshmana."

Lakshmana went on. "Brother, leave everything to me. Go on with your business, when I unleash my strength the entire population of the three worlds cannot obstruct you." He

71

started for the door. "My hands are for killing, how has he ruled so long?"

Rama held him back and turned him around. "Be still, or you may yet see seeds sprout on stones, Lakshmana!"

"I am also your parent," said Kausalya. "Rama, I command you to stay. Or else I will die, for you are dear to me, and the King makes war on me as well. Do what you want, Rama!"

"I'll go, Mother."

"Do that," she said, "and Kosala is ruined, I am dead, your father's life and fame are gone, and out of all of us only Kaikeyi and Bharata will be happy. You will fall into Hell for killing your mother!"

"Have you seen Death's face," said Rama, "have you seen Hell that you will talk of it so lightly and use it for your blame? Kaikeyi was always carefree; this deed is nothing like her, and it is truly not her doing to sadden the King. I wait patiently for you to open your eyes and see. No man is always the same. Worry and care waylay us all. Kings will misrule one day and bring justice to all the next. Singers will fall into the pit of helpless misery for no cause, and then may sing their happiest songs. Men may take anger against all in the world and from that rage do great kindness and fashion wonders of beauty. People who think they care for nothing at all have saved more lives than they ever knew, yet believe themselves alone, and unloved."

Lakshmana said, "I must go with you."

Rama said, "Lakshmana, I bind you with an oath of the cruel Kshatriya Dharma, as with chains, to go with me and protect me."

"I promise."

"Queen Kausalya, I bind you with an oath of Love's Dharma, as with happiness, to remain by your husband as a warrior's wife among your enemies."

"I promise," said the Queen. "I bless you for your journey, both of you, and whoever shall go with you, and whoever shall help you and welcome you."

Rama said, "Wait for my return. Wait for me, everything will be all right."

❧

Rama went alone to Sita and said, "The time will quickly pass, you will soon see me return."

She answered softly, "It is very strange, My Lord, that you alone among all men in the world have not heard that a wife and her husband are one."

"There is no happiness in the forest," said Rama. "There is danger. Lions roar and keep pitiless watch from the mouths of their hill-caves, waterfalls crash and pain the ears, and so the wood is full of misery."

"Surely your fortune is also mine," said Sita.

"Enraged elephants in their fury trample men to death."

"Kings in cities execute their faithful friends at any hour, day or night."

"There is little to eat but windfallen fruit and white roots."

"I will eat after you have taken your share of them."

"There is no water, vines shut out the Sun, at night there are but hard beds of leaves."

"I will gather flowers."

"Creeping serpents slither across the trails and swim crookedly in the rivers awaiting prey."

"The wayfarer will see flocks of colored birds fly and disappear into shady trees."

"There is always hunger and darkness and great fear," said Rama. "Scorpions sting and poison the blood; there is fever in the air, fires rage uncontrolled; there are no dear friends nearby, and so the wood is full of misery."

"It is Ayodhya that would be the widerness for me without you," said Sita. "Your bow is no decoration, your knife is not for wood-chopping, your arrows are not toys, but keep me from your arguments. We will be together. The water will be nectar, the thistles silk, the raw hides many-colored blankets. I'll be no burden. Rama, I depend on you. I cannot be cast

73

away like water left in a cup. Dear Rama, I am the humble dust at your feet, perfectly happy. How will you avoid me?"

"Then come," smiled Rama. "You love me and I love you, what more is there? Without delay give away all our possessions that we won't take with us, and get ready to go."

❧

Sumantra the charioteer found the priest Vasishtha in the silent street and said, "Brahmana, the world is without support, it is gone to Hell. The old Kshatriya Dharma is vanished forever. Sorrow will kill the King, shackled by lust to a vile prostitute posing as our Queen."

Vasishtha said, "Truly I find the world much the same as ever."

"Hear Ayodhya, silent with blame!"

"Let go anger, abandon violence," said Vasishtha. "Don't you know anything? Rama is the Sun of the Sun, the fame of fame. He goes with Sita, he goes with Lakshmi, he goes with victory."

"Ah no," said Sumantra. "Clever speakers feign piety to deceive and tell others of Dharma in rich tones, but there was a time . . . ."

"Clever profiteers also feign foreign wars to deceive the simple and all paid liars are not priests," said Vasishtha. "Traitors make a show of righteousness and holding knives behind their backs they plead for peace. But my place is to calm, to avoid, to soften, to look before walking and take thought before speaking. Men must have laws, sometimes hard to follow, but harder to find once lost. Dasaratha will die, so let him die in peace, for your life too must end one day. Give up war's desires. Throw out fear of fearful things. An hour of separation cannot be avoided. Let the King die alone in a room as an elephant badly wounded by a lion goes to die in peace."

"The gods are blind. Brahmana, how will Rama who never knew misfortune live in bark rags and eat bad food?"

74

"Sita will cherish him. He will eat well and live well. Cease to judge men by their outsides. Store the coronation supplies for Bharata, as you gathered them for Rama. Time alone causes change. Kaikeyi loved Rama. She never cared for government but only for Dasaratha. With her he would relax, she never forced him into anything, but gave him love and let him forget that he was different from any other man. Time makes her press relentlessly for Rama's exile with harsh words. She was easy-going. And why has she never used these wishes before? What is beyond understanding—that is Destiny."

"Destiny?" said Sumantra. "That is a poor frail thing, where all is lost because a good hour passes and the stars who care nothing for us are not in their right places. Who is Time to turn his back on *us*? Are we not *men*? But now soon Earth will be a widow, the King will die."

"Time is hidden from you, charioteer. You can only see his work, not him."

"I'll not believe that, brahmana. When I meet a roadblock I break it!"

"Destiny is unthinkable, how can you regret it?" asked Vasishtha.

❦

The Kosalas came pushing through the streets again, crowding their way to Rama's palace—*Throw down your inventions and your plows, go see Sita, she gives away riches. End your hard work to feed your little children!*

Vasishtha and Sumantra followed the crowd, but when they arrived all the clothes and jewels and horses and elephants and chariots were gone, and Sita had given the palace itself to her servants, to live in on full salary till their return.

Rama was there and Vasishtha asked him, "What do I get? I am idle but I love good things, that's the mark of my high birth."

Rama pointed to a long pasture filled with grazing cows that

75

ran from the side of his house to the river. "Sita has emptied every room here," he said. He gave Vasishtha a short heavy staff. "Those cows are all I have left, and they are yours as far as you can throw over them."

Vasishtha took the rod, stood in the yard, quickly tightened his robe round his waist and hurled the staff. It went sailing far over every cow and fell clear on the other side of the Sarayu.

Then Vasishtha smiling held up his two hands palms outwards and let his arms fall in circles to his sides. All fell silent. Rama and Sita and Lakshmana drew near. Vasishtha knelt in the sunlight with the others kneeling round him and said—*Life is short.*

"Truly it is! Rama, now no one sings your praises to wake you, no chariot will clear a way before you, no servants will run ahead to build a resting place, and also no one any longer plots against you.

"Rama, Sita, Lakshmana. For your safety I give the gods flowers and smoke and praise. I place you as travelers in the care of the holy mountains and the sacred trees large and small, in care of the birds and the Sun and Moon, the air, the day and the night, the lakes and islands; and let them all lend you their strength. I throw seeds into the fires for the Guardians of the world's directions and ask them to stop the breath of all who are hostile to you. I throw flowers up into the air and make my blessings fall—*No fear, no grief, and follow me.*

"Depart from us encircled and protected by the heavens and the sky, and served by creatures moving or immobile, by the planets and stars and by Mother Earth. Return when the trees blossom again for the fourteenth time. As much as I can, I turn aside from you all hurt and harm from horned beasts and every injury from flesh-eating animals . . . . May the every prayer said in the forests by the holy men crown your way with good fortune."

"Rama, Sita, Lakshmana!" Vasishtha dropped over their heads grains of colored rice. *Sorrow flees from you.*

Vasishtha stood over them. "Go wherever you like. I will

see you return. And on that day, when Rama is in royal robes I will gaze at you, my face will shine with joy!"

❧

Then Rama went to the King's palace to say goodbye to his father and Sumantra fell into stride beside him. They went down the palace halls. There the weeping Revel Master took off his finery. He shut the wine-vault doors and locked them closed and barred them; he sat there dressed in forest clothes, like an old hermit. He threw away the key and could see no joy; he sat not in a palace but in a death-waiting house, he was a pilgrim come to die at some holy place in one of the little stone-built rooms.

Sumantra sighed and shook his head. "So! See revealed the poverty of gentleness, that cannot help you who always use it. Rama, be forgiving while it's peacetime, but when people come against you, you'll only win by force. Reason must at last resort to power, and compassion is feeble, it is weak, it trembles."

Rama stopped walking. "Did you then want me very much for your King?"

"You know I'm right!" said Sumantra.

"No, only truly angry," said Rama.

"I will kill Kaikeyi cleanly, a warrior's way, for she has murdered my King!"

Rama said, "I thought you were a real fighter, not just an edgy old man who kills women, boasting beforehand of his sins to come."

"Has that bleating ass Vasishtha stolen your manhood?" asked Sumantra. "Why listen to his pretended talk of Time and Fate? What real man meekly bows to Destiny?"

"Rama does."

"Then you have a man's form and a woman's deeds! You've spent all your courage. Prince, pay Fate no regard, do not believe in good and evil!"

Rama said, "Rust will come to bright things, fire will burn

our homes, blight will consume our grain, all these are sendings from Fate."

Sumantra caught Rama and banged him up against the wall. "Little green Rama, how dare you adore Time while your King still lives? I will go see Dasaratha now, and you will wait, and you will not tell me any more talk!" Then instantly he released Rama and fell to his knees. "I take you for my King, Rama."

"Must you see him? Rise, my charioteer. With more abuse must you burn him, though I forbid it?"

"I can't take wrong orders from anyone," said Sumantra. "Majesty, listen. You have little anger now, but if you ever have don't hide it in your own heart; let it fall on your foes lest your heart burst! I won't hurt that whore. I prefer your company for one moment to the wealth of all creation. But in my mind burns a summer wildfire of grief inflamed by the hot gale winds of your departure, fed by my inflammable tears, kindled by my remembrance, and smoking black."

"Never match strength with me," said Rama. "You do not have to drive over your friends and injure them. Go ahead, I permit you."

Rama looked away, and Sumantra went to the anger room, where Dasaratha paced back and forth, and Kaikeyi sat frozen in a corner. Sumantra said, "Desire bites hard, Dasaratha! Break your shameful fetters, let this hour never pass, let Rama never leave. Don't obey this woman, she has no whit of decency."

Dasaratha only said, "Those were my promises, Sumantra."

Sumantra said, "You're far astray; my hurt is that you call it Dharma that you follow. I've known you all my life— and *now* I must regret it, for I am of honest ways and I am yours."

"I have nearly finished my life," said Dasaratha. "Will you not stand as my friend for only a few days more? Better I died yesterday, for I must drive Lakshmi of good fortune out from my city. Do not take away from me the closest friendship that I ever had, and the best regard in which I was ever held. I deserve from you a better end to life than that."

"I will not take them away," said Sumantra, "That I will never do. Give me your leave; may I be the one to drive Rama to the forest if he must go. I had great anger against you, but it's gone."

Dasaratha said, "You may take him. You are Sumantra the best charioteer, the best driver ever born in all this world, this world where there is but one right road, where the directions and the ways are hard to see, hard to find, hard to remember."

❧

Sumantra went to get his chariot ready, and Rama went in to see his father. Dasaratha stood pressing his hands together, sighing, shaking his head in dismay. Dasaratha said, "My son, Sumantra is really a peaceful, sober man, happy to sit with me and remember our past wars and our ancient battles for the gods. He is right, I am degraded. By a petty promise I have broken a greater law in a fit of madness. I have violated fair combat and chosen lingering murder. Am I not a cowardly assassin, Rama?"

"Not to me," said Rama, "never to me. I can tell an enemy in the form of a friend—you are my father and no foe of mine. Will I disobey you and judge your commands because your motive may be desire? As though it were on a wheel, whatever we see of happiness and sorrow all turns round Fate. Fear and bravery, freedom and bondage, birth and death, love and anger all pivot on Time's wheel-hub. Wise men may give up long hard training all in an instant, things well-begun may be hindered by unthought-of accidents, all from Time. The Father is the Master. You gave me my life. So end Kaikeyi's alarm and find peace. Drive out bad feelings as you banish me, I will see you free from debt when I return. One must keep promises or not make them.'

"I think that is no longer true," said Dasaratha.

Rama said, "If I disobey you, no other good deed, no wealth, no power will restore my good name. Keep your word

79

and preserve the three worlds, keep us safe. For every broken promise breaks away a little Dharma, and every break of Dharma brings closer the day the worlds too must break apart. When Dharma is altogether gone the three worlds will end; they will be destroyed once more. If man breaks his word, why should the stars above keep their promises not to fall? Why should Fire not burn us all or Ocean not leap his shores and drown us?"

"That is all true," said Dasaratha. "Oh Rama, if you doubt something be careful, for when you once speak you are bound! Never threaten harm to an enemy; just hit him hard!"

Rama said, "I ask you something."

"Ask anything."

"Earth Lord, it is only noble to be good. Do right, while you can. Change your curse on Kaikeyi."

"Then let her spend but the wink of an eye damned in Hell, for I cannot withdraw my words completely, or I would, Rama, I would do anything for you."

"Never curse her again."

"For now, for all the future I'll speak no bad to her."

"Love Bharata."

"I love."

"Let Sita go with me."

"Once given as your wife, she is yours even after death. The shade of your feet is better for her than a palace roof alone or a home in heaven. You are Lord to her, I will not sin more by preventing her."

"Let Lakshmana protect us."

"I let him."

"Goodbye, my father."

"But do not go today; stay with me tonight and leave to-morrow."

"I said I would go today. I will hold your feet after fourteen years. Farewell, father."

"Farewell, Rama."

Lakshmana came in. "Great King, Maharaja, rule for a thousand years, and farewell."

"Farewell, Lakshmana."

Sita entered. "My house is now the forest. Farewell my Father."

"Farewell, Sita. *All is lost! All is lost!*"

❧

Rama and Lakshmana and Sita met Vasishtha by a small back door to the palace. Rama and Lakshmana first put on their impenetrable armor all of gold, and Lakshmana put on a black hide belt with a gold-handled belt-knife. Then over that they put on the two pieces of soft dyed barkcloth worn by ascetics, tied on belts of grass, put on forest sandals. And Vasishtha said, "Rama, never forget the weapons you learned from Viswamitra."

Sita held some bark clothes, cast down her eyes and asked Vasishtha, "Brahmana, how do hermits dress in these?"

"A knot by the waist," said Vasishtha, "but throw those down. Wear your silks and ornaments, Kaikeyi had not her eye on you, and the wishes say nothing of this."

Then Sumantra drove up on the royal chariot, a four-horse war-car rattling with noise. He said, "Prince Rama, I feel better now. I will drive you from the city, but the streets seem near impassable. Ornaments clash as the women strike their breasts, and the men cry—*Who ever exiles his own son?* Rama, they consider empty the life of anyone who will not see you leave, at whom you will not look as you go. They consider banishment the reward of virtue for every man now; they set at nothing the world's comforts and the highest joys of heaven if they can but see you. The Kosalas cannot withdraw their minds from you, they will rush after you like thirsty travelers sighting water in the desert. All the forest guides prepare to lead; your wrestling partners, all your friends, all the merchants and their women, all the little children and the dreadful warriors of Ayodhya—now all of us will follow you!"

"But why?" asked Rama. "What have I to do with a following? I'm leaving Ayodhya, how can I take her people? Who keeps attached to an elephant rope once the animal himself is free?"

Sumantra smiled. "But this will be a great departure indeed,

81

more than was bargained for! Your people, they call themselves. They leave garden and field, they carry everything out from their homes and now dig up their buried treasures, and load all onto carts, and go out the gates, and line the roads."

"Not now," said Rama. "Can't you tell them? Charioteer, there may some day be a time, when all may follow me—ask them to wait."

"But you depart!"

"No, not now, later I may truly depart."

"They say it must be today. From this day forth will Ayodhya be vacant, her dusty yards unswept, her cattle gone, her flags torn down, her wells dry, her fires dead. Broken things abandoned will clutter her streets, and these broad ways will be the paths where wild cats and owls roam. Rats will crawl and cunning snakes will slither from hole to hole. Nevermore will any offerings be made from here to heaven; the temples of Fair Ayodhya will be without their garlands, without their images, abandoned by the gods, and ominous. So they say, Rama, so they say."

"What can I do? I give them all to Bharata, he won't harm them."

"No King ever yet gave the free Kosala men to anyone," said Sumantra.

"How can they think to live?"

"All our stores of food have been loaded onto wagons. In the forest the Kosalas will kill deer and elephants; they will drink wild honey, and see many rivers, and drive the lions back here into Ayodhya's ruins. They will forget this city, and again forget her, and at last never speak, never dream of her. The Kosalas will make new fields, cut the grass and plant grain. They will leave behind the golden coins and silver bars in the treasury, let Bharata have them; we have better; we have all our hopes . . . there can be no kingdom where you are not King . . . you'll see the forest flourish into a city, or we will wander homeless with you!"

Rama looked at Vasishtha. "Brahmana, help me! Fair Ayodhya is my city, don't let me hear in the forest that she has died of shame. You must somehow prevent them."

82

Vasishtha said, "Let them do what they want today and they will be tired tomorrow. Rama, the people's outcries last seven days, no longer. If I have ever said anything wrong to you from familiarity, or given you offense through ignorance, forgive me. Rama, I salute you, I bless you."

Vasishtha turned to Sita and said, "You do not forsake your Lord in misfortune, I salute you, I bless you!"

He told Lakshmana, "Prince, this design of yours to serve Rama is already a great blessing to you, a great good fortune, your high wide way to heaven. You follow him, I salute you, I bless you."

Then the brahmana Vasishtha embraced Sumantra the Charioteer. *So there is still one good heart in the Kosala Kingdom! I see honor, I see again that proud warriors' Dharma of kindliness and bravery and gladly casting off the body on the battlefield of war. I see fairness and skill and courage once more! That is the Kshatriya Dharma that I remember. It is good to see, old man, good to see!*

❦

Lakshmana put Rama's fire inside a bowl in a corner of the chariot. Sumantra put bows and arrows on board, and under the driver's seat in front he put a hoe and a root-gathering basket bound in goathide. Vasishtha helped Sita get on the car; the two princes climbed up; Sumantra got on and the exile began.

Sumantra held the reins. The four horses raised their heads, the chariot trembled, it seemed to come alive. Sumantra said, "Go."

The red horses ran. They were out of the back palace courtyard, through the palace gates, and racing wildly down the street to the southern gate of Ayodhya. Then Dasaratha cried down from a palace balcony behind them—*Stop! Stay!*

"Go faster," said Rama. "Later say you did not hear him."

Too late, Dasaratha rushed from the palace. Too late he repented. He covered his face with his hands; he could not endure the sight of that fleeing chariot. *Stop them!*

Sumantra told his horses, in a voice not loud, "Go on, run, go on."

The gate guards heard the King. Sumantra came too fast at them; there was no time to close the gate but they swiftly formed ranks to block the car.

Sumantra bent over and took up a war-whip, a whip for striking men not horses. "Hang on, Sita!" His white hair streamed out straight back from his head in the wind of flight. Again Sumantra drove with his warrior behind him, alone against a hostile army, ready to fight anyone. Sumantra was never easy to stop. The red horses never slowed, never broke stride. There came the gate, the hooves and wheels thundered, the gateway rattled like dice.

Sumantra flailed his whip to this side and that. He hit back the Kosalas from the street,then with blows and lashes, holding his breath in anger he struck down forty rows of guards, and in terrible confusion broke free through the gate. The chariot dashed away from Fair Ayodhya over the narrow Kosala road going south in the evening.

Wind-driven black clouds swept the vault of heaven like ocean waves and covered the sky. Along the road the tall trees sounded in the wind, and in the trees the still birds did not fly to seek their food, but sang piteously begging some help against disaster.

Suddenly the rapid raging river Tamasa threw her dark waves across the road to forbid Sumantra. By the riverside the charioteer uncoupled the tired horses, and when they had rolled in the dust he bathed them and made them drink. He fed them grass while Lakshmana built a fire in the high wind, and while the many people following from Ayodhya drew near in the night.

lord of the wild trees

It is not strange to me nor wonderful that Indra should downpour rain, or the thousand-rayed Sun banish darkness from heaven, or the Moon bathe the clear Night in his rays, or that a good friend like you should bring me delight, or that whatever is graceful should be harbored within you.

In the windy night the old men of Ayodhya first arrived where Rama was and said, "We so commanded the dark Tamasa River and she obeyed us. Like her, we throw ourselves at your feet. Friend Rama, we beg you to return. We put down in the dust our shaking heads, our hair white as cranes."

Rama replied, "You are old in years and honored in wisdom, and the merits of your good deeds are great. But you must take all this water away from my path. I uphold the King's word, and you cannot use the streams of Earth against Earth's own Lord."

"Oh Rama, we told the fleet horses not to go on. They have ears and know our prayer." The old men reached out and touched Rama, and gazed at him in the firelight, drinking him in with their sight. "In all justice you must be carried into Ayodhya and not away from her."

"What cause for sorrow here?" asked Rama. "Bharata will be a strong and gentle King. You will do me good if you return and cheer my father."

The old men said, "Oh Rama, look back, see the fires that walk following you on the shoulders of loyal Kosala men, see by their glare those umbrellas still open, tossed by the wind, that will give you shade when it is day once more."

Rama sighed and said no more to them. He went to Lakshmana and said, "With you by my side near me I am easy about

85

Sita's protection. My brother, tonight I will fast and drink only water. From now on, do not let your mind dwell long on our past happiness."

Lakshmana made a bed of branches and leaves, and there Rama and Sita slept that night. Lakshmana and Sumantra sat by Tamasa's shore among the trees growing from the water, talking softly together about Rama until just before the first hint of dawn.

Then Rama in his sleep felt the air change, he felt Night depart and awoke. He saw the Kosalas who had followed him still asleep all around. He quietly awakened Sita and told Sumantra, "I must deliver these men from their own misfortune. If we can escape they will have to go home where they will recover, I cannot drag them after me into my exile."

Sumantra went to his chariot and without a sound pulled it by hand out from the sleepers. By a small noise he summoned the four horses and harnessed them. He drove his three passengers down the midstream of the river, and after awhile let them out across the river to wait near a forest track, and filled the chariot with stones. Then returning through the water to the Tamasa camp he drove ashore right near where he had entered the river and went back toward Ayodhya. And finally as he went, he threw out the stones one by one, and the lightened chariot gradually left no path on the hard earth.

Then he told the horses, "Run." There was not one little branch broken where he passed; those red horses had years before pulled a flying chariot through the air, and leaving no hoof-marks was not difficult for them. They stirred no fallen leaf and made no sound, and swiftly Sumantra circled back through the forest, again crossed Tamasa, and met Rama before any Kosala had awakened.

For a moment Sumantra faced the chariot north to invoke good fortune and a successful journey. And Rama stood facing Ayodhya and touching his hands together he said, "Best of cities, I will see you again, the gods guard you well."

Sumantra said, "Quickly get on." They drove away from Fair Ayodhya to the lands of the southwest. The forest track soon joined the south road. The countryside of Kosala stretched out away in the distance; far as the eye could see the round trees rose from the flat plains. All day they rode through the kingdom of Kosala stopping only for noonday prayers. The villages and the fields grew fewer and farther between, then in the late afternoon there were no more settlements. They saw no more white cattle and no houses or ponds—only the forest closing in on them. Their road began to fail. It turned into a cowpath and then vanished. They were crossing the southern boundary of Kosala. At dusk Sumantra stopped the chariot by the Ganga River flowing from heaven through Shiva's hair; Rama got down with the others, and they walked a little way and stood under a huge ancient spreading nut tree.

❧

That tree marked the Kingdom of the Far Forest and the realm of Guha the Hunter King. Rama and Sita, Lakshmana and Sumantra all bathed in the beautiful Ganges, where bathing a man may wash off the sins from his heart as he takes the dirt from his skin, and both come out clean.

Then as they stood in wet clothes under the trees of the Secret Forest, they heard whistles from the wood and looked in their direction. They saw nothing and when they looked back they saw Guha come to welcome them.

Guha was a little thin brown man, short, with soft brown eyes, with a beard of a few hairs and a pure white grin. He was painted and tattooed with red and blue lines and wore a short black bearskin skirt for his only clothes. He had on a necklace of tiger teeth and a belt of deer hooves laced on a thong, musical anklets of claws and pieces of ivory and black wood tied together, bone earrings, armbands of braided grass and bright spotted beans and stone beads cut with corners. In his curly hair were feathers, red and yellow and green and white and black. Hung from his belt were a magic rattle of bone rings and shells, a horn of honey, a bird noose of vine and a worn bamboo case that held tiny poisoned wooden darts. He was Rama's friend.

Guha ran to Rama, and Rama embraced him in a hug hard enough to crush a bear, and the savage King pounded Rama's back with friendly stunning blows, and laughed like a child.

"Oh Rama, Rama! Now you are an outcast like me!"

"You! You look more outlandish than I remembered you!" laughed Rama. Guha whistled and hunter-men came out of the trees bearing wooden trays of hot steaming food.

"Eat!" cried Guha. He threw himself on Lakshmana and thumped Sumantra. He smiled at Sita and spread down a blanket for her and his men put down the food and drink. "Princess," he said, "I know your mother well and I have known Rama since he was a boy."

"How glad I am to find a friend at last," said Sita. She smiled. "We meet you here!"

"That smile is all my payment," said Guha. "Queen, take food. Tell me what I can give you. Listen—demons fear me, men fear me, dear friends dare not come near me when I am out of sorts, and here on my own ground, in my own forest I can defeat any army ever created."

Sita said, "Oh Guha, we have had such a bad time!"

"Eat! Eat! Today is over. In Ayodhya men are driven raving mad by too many laws and rules. Freedom for me! I am a man of action, I heard what happened and never mind."

"How did you meet Rama before today?"

"A chase led me once to Ayodhya, and there I met Rama and Lakshmana, and though they were city boys I cared for their friendship. While they grew into men I met them again many times among the trees outside the city. I taught them forest lore and hunting. Lakshmana learned well." Guha smiled. "But Rama I could never teach to hunt."

Now the silent dark men of the greenwood came and made a fire under the great nut tree. They all sat around it and ate from banana leaves and drank from horns. There was meat and fish and sugar-bread, small sweet wild fruit and eggs and strong blossom-wines. Rama had fasted one night looking forward to happiness; he had fasted a second night looking back on a sad day. Now he ate thinking of nothing; he breathed in the clean air and the firelight lit up his face with golden light.

When they finished Guha put a necklace of pink seashells over Sita's head. "I adopt you into my people," he said. "You are in my family, for your heart is free."

Sita laid her head on Rama's shoulder. One of Guha's men said something in the whistling bird-language, and Rama carried her to the bed they had made for him. Sumantra relaxed and lay on his back looking up at all the stars of heaven through the trees; then he was asleep and Guha's people covered him with many thin blankets.

Guha lit up a fat cigar of sandalwood dust and nutmeg powder all rolled in long leaves and held together with goat butter. He leaned back against the tree and puffed smoke and looked at Lakshmana. Guha said, "Bows in hand we will watch over them through the dark night by Ganga. Oh child, we have made a soft bed for you also, lie down and rest. I am used to being awake at all hours but you deserve comfort."

Lakshmana closed his eyes and crunched a candied apple in his teeth. "King of the Wilderness, with Rama asleep on the ground and in misfortune what use would be my comfort?" He sighed. "I remember when you would come near to Ayodhya in happy days . . . ."

"Then I challenge you to a drinking contest," said Guha.

Lakshmana threw his bark back off his shoulder. "I accept." Lakshmana chose two horns and tried to make sure that each held the same amount. They seemed to, and he filled them with wine.

Guha carefully lined up five full wine jugs in a row and took one horn from Lakshmana. His men left more wood for the fire and retired into the shadows of the night as if into nowhere. "Prince, do not worry over the future," said Guha, "or try to outguess fortune, for it is hard enough to know what one is doing at the moment right now. I will tell you a story."

Listen, Lakshmana—

A busybody cannot sleep in peace if he knows of one man free to do as he will; he cannot tolerate someone who likes to

"I would go and give that statue a good kick"

live alone, in his own way. Did you never wonder how I got to Ayodhya, the one time I've ever been inside a city?

Your father's priest Vasishtha decided to reform me and my people. He sent some brahmanas over the border into my forest, and by Ganga they set up a stone image of Shiva, under the branches of this very nut tree twenty years ago.

Many men are all talk and no deeds, all words and no wisdom, and what they don't know of they think does not exist. Those pious brahmanas lived in fancy tents not far from here. Morning and evening they brought flowers and offered food to that stone Shiva and praised him. I met them and gave them a good welcome and some little presents of gold birds and nine-headed snakes of lead. But I told them—*I worship only God, and God is a tree.* And every night when I returned from hunting I would go and give that statue a good kick.

Then the rains came. The forest floor was an ocean of mud, and Ganga rose in flood and forced those brahmanas away to high ground. They left Shiva all alone half underwater for days at a time. Yet every night, even when I had to wade over logs, when I was exhausted, when I was hungry or sick, every night I went happily up to that senseless block of stone and kicked it.

Shortly after the rains, one night when I was going home very late I arrived here at the time of the animals' drinking. A lean wolf-pack greeted me. Their shiny eyes were hungry, the rains had starved them. My arrows were all gone. I had no fire to frighten them. They kept me from the statue, but though I could have outrun them and gone home I climbed this old tree. I held onto a limb and thought, "One way or another, before this night is over I must kick that rock."

So I waited in the tree above Shiva. I had not eaten all day, so I tried to eat the green nuts on the tree, but they were so bitter I could not even swallow one bite but spit it out. That annoyed me a little bit, and the wolves round Shiva's statue snapped up at me with sharp white teeth trying in vain to reach me, but I waited for my chance to kick Shiva.

I had no food, there was no place to sleep, the night turned cold and the dew fell. The wolves would not go, and I shivered in the moonlight so hard that leaves and dewdrops and bitter green nuts fell all over the statue. Finally at dawn the wolves ran when my people came tracking me, but the night had passed. I had failed to greet Shiva as he deserved, and I was so passionately angry that I chased the brahmanas back to Ayodhya where they hid behind Vasishtha's skirts.

Dasaratha met me there. I told him, "I will adore only the holy trees!" He took my hand and made me a King. I already ruled this whole forest, but until then I was but a common man!

When I got back here, Lakshmana, Shiva's image was gone somewhere else and I forgot about it. I went on hunting and eating and drinking until one afternoon I felt ill. A little green bird sat near me unafraid, and I died in my hut after a short attack of fatal fever.

Yama's messengers came to get me, four ruffians holding snarling dogs on chains. With contempt they tore my soul from my dead body, bound me in a noose and started south with me to Yama's world, all done in an instant. I could imagine my reception. As a soul I was no bigger than a thumb, but still I struggled violently. But that death-noose could not slip loose even in a dream.

Then as we came round a narrow turn in the forest path, a small mean-looking dwarf stood in the way. He fixed his round brown eyes on Yama's bullies. He snorted and said, "Unknot that noose! Give over Guha's soul to me, he is not to die yet."

The death-spirits laughed. "He is *already* dead! Stand aside, we will leave you now!"

"Try it and I'll block you. I am Nandin the peaceful guardian of the wild. By Shiva's order release him."

"This is his *death*, you little runt!"

"Liars," said Nandin. "You are but thieves, it is not time for him to die."

"What did you call us?"

"Have a kindness to the small and the weak," said Nandin. "I beg you to let him go—"

Well, that did it. Yama's guards released their dogs and advanced on Nandin. I saw that surly little animal scatter the dogs and give the first death-guard a stupendous blow that broke his head in. There was a great commotion but I fell face down into a pile of old leaves and could see nothing more.

"Torment a poor defenseless animal will you?" I heard bones breaking and dogs yelping and running feet and chains coming apart. Then Nandin gently picked up the end of my noose and flew with me to the high Himalya.

There he came to Earth and changed into his true form, into a sleek white humpy bull. He serenely carried me hanging still bound from his soft wet mouth. We entered a flimsy cottage. Nandin's breath smelled of sweet grass in the sun. Nandin stopped and I saw Shiva sitting tall and fair, his two eyes like honey looking in my soul, his third eye closed on his brow, his hair unkempt and wild, wearing an old worn deerskin and rags, and looking at me and looking, with Parvati the mountain's daughter on his lap.

Then Nandin the bull and Shiva both faced the door. In a moment a quiet green man in a red robe entered and stood turning his head to see this way and that and looked at us with his dark unmoving eyes.

Yama joined his hands with fingers touching and said to the great Lord Shiva, "In my scribe's dusty record book this Guha is a killer charged with crimes. He has sinned; his life has been shortened; his time is up; his days are over. Why did you take his soul away from me, and leave us with an empty place in Hell?"

The wind began to blow through Yama's long black hair. Shiva said, "Death Lord, Guha was the one person faithful in saluting me when I came to his forest. Before he died he once fasted and kept sleepless watch for my sake in a tree all night, and offered me food he needed himself, and showered me with water, and gave me ornaments of leaves. And he took such rage against men pretending to love me that he threat-

ened their lives and drove them out. Therefore, Oh Yama, I overreach you, his soul is mine and not yours to take."

❖ ❖ ❖

"Yama smiled and left us without a word," continued Guha. "Nandin took my soul back to my body and I returned to life. So when even the Court of Death cannot tell right from wrong, it is surely very hard for us to judge things."

Lakshmana answered, "But certainly our father did wrong."

"Who told you that? This banishment will kill your father; it is simply time for him to die."

"It is the fault of those promises."

"No," said Guha, "those wishes are but the blind instruments of Fate. King Dasaratha was not such a foolish man. Once before, in my presence Kaikeyi asked him for one of those wishes."

"What did he say? What did he do?"

94

"That was years ago, before you were born," said Guha. "The Ayodhya King came on a hunting trip, and Kaikeyi was with him, and he stopped to see me and ask permission to use my forest."

Listen, Prince—

I gave him the freedom of my wood, and that evening I sat with Dasaratha in his camp near by my house, and with us were Sumantra the charioteer and Queen Kaikeyi. The forest was noisy. The day-animals were speaking before they slept, the night-prowlers were talking and arising, and a full Moon beamed down on us. We were surrounded by screeching and singing and howls of warning.

Your father knew the animal tongues. Suddenly a stag barked loudly, another stag answered, the first one called again, and your father was overcome with laughter. Kaikeyi was very curious and asked, "Majesty, what are you laughing at?"

"It would not be funny in translation," laughed Dasaratha.

"You can tell *me*," Kaikeyi pleaded. "If you love me what secrets are between us?"

"There must be this one, for you cannot understand the animal languages."

She said, "Teach me."

But Sumantra replied, "The King cannot. If he reveals even half a word he will die. That is the agreement, the price of his friend Jatayu the Vulture King, who rules Dandaka Forest and who taught him this speech."

So Kaikeyi was still and said no more right then. Awhile later she again asked for that secret learning and was again refused. And after another while in passing she mentioned her two wishes but never pursued the subject, and I would have said all was forgotten when the King and Queen retired to sleep.

No one knows what she said to him in bed that night, but in the morning Dasaratha came from his tent looking deplorable, and walked by me in sad distress saying to himself, "All is lost, all is lost . . . ."

He said that over and over. He ordered his own funeral pyre to be built. He planned that day to tell Kaikeyi animal speech while sitting on the pyre. By the terms of his contract as Jatayu's student his heart would then burst, and we were to burn his body.

I didn't know what to do. I had not yet died myself and so had little wisdom. I refused to help make the pyre, but Sumantra did it anyway. Kaikeyi eagerly took her seat near that stack of wood and I saw Dasaratha come out of his tent in white funeral clothes and walk slowly toward her.

But he had to pass my house and my yard where I kept many wild hens and a red and green and gold bantam fighting rooster, and also several ewes with an old short-tempered ram. And as Dasaratha went by the ram said to my rooster, "How can this pitiful bungler be called King of the World?" And the rooster replied, "Why, if I even thought of spoiling my hens like he does that woman I'd be out of business here in the flash of an eye, teacher's curse or not!'

❖   ❖   ❖

"When your father heard that," said Guha, "he went back to his tent shaking his head, biting his tongue and smiling to himself. He got dressed right and told me what my animals had said. He refused Kaikeyi and she was glad of it. Do you think for any reason that he has changed now, other than his approaching death? Lakshmana, if we live long enough, it is Time that wears out our bodies. Old men grow tired at last, their hearts remember the past more than the present. Death comes nearer, then they feel they must rest; they are about to fall asleep after a hard day. Death stands behind a man's shoulder, he touches him and there is no more will to live, and the man welcomes him. Try what he will, Lakshmana, through no fault of his own your father's life fails at last."

Lakshmana said, "But then the King asks Rama to do what will kill him."

"I think so. He sees what he does but does not care."

"Why does Rama go along with this?"

Guha said, "I later learned bird and animal talk for myself, and listening to them I have heard that once the Ocean talked with his beloved rivers. They described for him the land and what grew there. Big strong trees he had seen, carried down to him on the flood waters. But he had never glimpsed a bending cane nor seen a blade of grass. No river had ever washed down such a yielding plant to him, not since the world began."

Guha's winejars were all empty, and Lakshmana's eyes were clear and bright as his own. The drinking contest was a draw. The sky started to get light. It was near sunrise, the glorious Sun was burning hot low behind the eastern hills, and day was breaking, and our blessed mother Night was departing.

Rama awoke. Sita slept with her arm across his chest and he gently moved it aside. He sat up and stretched. He looked around at the forest and up at the sky, with eyes like someone newborn, unafraid and accepting.

Rama smiled; he stroked Sita's hair and woke her. He walked over to Guha and said, "Hunter Chief, we will cross Ganga fast washing to the sea, my friend."

Sumantra came and said, "I'll leave the chariot and come with you, and I will carry you home after the fourteen years. All that time will be an instant with you or a hundred generations if we are separated."

Rama touched his right hand lightly on Sumantra's shoulder. "Turn back to Dasaratha, we will continue on walking."

"Shall I go back with an empty chariot having lost a life that was in my keeping, as though driving alone away from a battlefield, my warrior killed and fallen? What can I say when people ask me of you? Rama, as a stingy man cannot enter heaven with no good deeds beside him, so I cannot enter Fair Ayodhya alone!"

"Go," said Rama, "so that Kaikeyi will believe that I am in the forests and not mistrust our father. And Life willing . . . if you and I still live we will meet again someday."

Sumantra said, "You must never cast aside a faithful servant who lives by your way and serves you well."

Rama said, "Charioteer, do not be sad, for pain and pleasure must come in their turns to all men and mortal gods. Cheer my father. Guard him and keep him. He is very old, he must be protected from harm like a child. Tell him—*Lakshmana and Rama and Sita are well. They have no grief. After these fourteen short years you will soon see them return, and may that time quickly pass for you as if in sleep.*

❧

Then as hermits do, Rama and Lakshmana matted their hair up over their heads with the sticky paste made from banyan bark. Guha gave both of them a deerskin, and to Sita he gave a fine feather cloak all of green and gold. Guha's men brought out from hiding a raft of logs with seats of fresh-broken leafy roseapple boughs, and took the three across Ganga. In midstream Sita made a silent prayer to the beautiful River Queen. "Ganga, protect my Rama. Beautiful bride of the Sea, let him return safely to his own Ayodhya. Let it be so, and I will bow to you. I will sing songs in the holy shrines along your river beaches . . . ."

Then they were all alone in the forest, far away from the smiling fields and gardens of men. There they felt the sadness of no one being near to care what happened to them. They walked in single file. First went Lakshmana holding his bow and carrying their fire and few possessions. Two quivers were on his back and he kept watch for animals and pitfalls and trod down the thorns and sharp grass. Sita followed him and Rama came last, looking down, his bow not even strung, just a few arrows tied carelessly at his belt and in his mind the mantras that could make those arrows countless.

They went still to the south, walking all day along the river Ganga. From inexperience of the forest they could not go fast nor get very far that day. They wasted their strength in many ways. When evening caught them Lakshmana shot a wild sow and cooked her, and they could eat very little.

That night Rama said, "Lakshmana, you've got to go back in the morning or else Kaikeyi will poison our mothers. Even Kausalya's pet parrot would try his best to defend her and bite her enemies, but I'm of less use to her than a gaudy bird. I am sent away just when her pains of motherhood should be rewarded, and my mother of slender fortune must lie weeping in the dust."

"Forget it," said Lakshmana. "You're tired, go to sleep with Sita. Don't tell me about inevitable things that displease me."

"You are right, despair is a bad enemy," said Rama. "Alone or with me, Lakshmana, in our exile always guard Sita."

"I'll stay with you right through the gates of blazing Hell as long as you want me!"

Rama and Sita fell asleep, a lion couple on a desolate summit. Lakshmana stood guard at that lone place in the wide forest. His blue eyes looked into the black night. Truly, he stood guard naturally; he had no fear and no violence in his heart; he had no envy and once he had sworn by Dharma he obeyed Rama. He never doubted Rama was right, or that he was right to obey him.

The next morning was sunny. They followed an uneven trail and soon they could hear the meeting of the waters of Ganga and the Yamuna river rushing together. On the land between the rivers there was a clearing surrounded by deep green banyan trees with red fruit like heaps of emeralds mixed with rubies. Set in the clearing was a hermitage, the home of the saint Bharadwaja.

They entered and bowed to that old ascetic sitting on the grass, and Bharadwaja said, "I have heard. I see you after you have walked long. My place here is yours, stay close by me and I will care for you."

Bharadwaja, a great man, washed Rama's feet, and Rama said, "We cannot stay so close to Ayodhya, but tell us somewhere good to live."

Bharadwaja slaughtered a bull for their dinner. When they had eaten he said, "Go to the hill Chitrakuta ten ear-shots distant from here. Chitrakuta's peaks are clear and bright-colored. There deep rivers run, there live birds fair to view. From there many saints with hair white as skulls have gone to heaven, but now that hill is deserted by men."

In the morning Rama and Sita and Lakshmana crossed the Yamuna studded with islands. First going south a way, they then turned and went west along a little stream flowing toward them.

Two days later they reached Chitrakuta Hill, standing alone and towering above them, engarlanded by his own flowering woods thick with flowers of red and gold and blue and white and every color. He had crags and ridges, round stones and giant boulders. Through his stone ran veins of black and yellow and silver-colored ore. He was alive with singing birds. He was like the garden of the gods, like the Gandharva groves in the Himalya. Clear rivers and little streams flowed down from him like graceful braids; they ran over glittering sands and dashed their loud-laughing waves against blue rocks of lapis. The forest floor by Chitrakuta was wholly covered with flowers, the paths were overarched by joyful blossoms and by branches bending low with ripe fruit, and no man there to taste them.

It was all-colored spring in the forest. The bees hung their huge honeycombs on the high limbs. The forest trail where Rama walked seemed to be the eternal peaceful pathway of the saints. The fine trees up the steep-sloping hillsides above were a gathering of clouds, the wind played through them and they bowed and waved their leaves, catching gleams of the sun on them and smiling as clouds smile by their lightnings. The trees grew way up the hill; they crowned the heights.

The round chakravaka birds who cry plaintively in the night if separated bobbed on the water in the river ponds and swam in mated pairs. Ducks were afloat in the streams and herons stood among the waving lotus flowers near the banks. Blackbirds sang to the Sun. Timid deer grazed in meadows, and tigers and lions who had never seen men watched the newcomers through the leaves.

Sita, that beautiful young woman blameless and beloved, looked on the perfumed trees and shrubs never seen before.

Rama told her their names, and Lakshmana brought her flower-shedding boughs and bushy branches of tender green and rosy leaves. They found a homesite on a tableland of rills, above a gentle rise on Chitrakuta, overlooking the level plain below.

Near a cave, by a clear sweet mountain spring Lakshmana built on pillars a strong house framed with long bamboos and floored with grass, whose walls were of woven wood tightly lashed by cords to keep out wind, whose roof was leaves. It had one door and many rooms and fair windows, and seeing it Rama said, "Surely we shall live here. How did you learn to build so well and do all this for us?"

As soon as he finished the house Lakshmana killed a black deer and dressed it and threw it into a fire. When it was hot and well-done Rama took the meat and set it out along with grass and water for an offering to the hill spirits. Then a household god came to live in their home filling it with gladness and warding away wrong. Only then did Rama and Sita enter the house.

Having like Rama gone a long way, the glorious Sun was sloping down and ready to depart from the sky. The light-giving Lord of the Day carried away with him all Rama's red-dyed grief at leaving Fair Ayodhya. The loving embrace of blue evening made even the Sun renounce heaven and leave the sky.

It was twilight and the trees stood motionless. From all sides came the enveloping dark veils of our Lady Night, forgetful and restful. Rama and Sita beside him were asleep in their house, they had no farther to go. The sky slowly turned above with stars for her bright open eyes, and the splendid mild-beaming Moon rose to dispel the darkness and touch all hearts with his glad rays, and Lakshmana watched the midnight gradually pass away.

❧

When the Kosalas awoke at daybreak by the Tamasa River they found that Rama had eluded them. They saw that Sumantra's chariot was gone and made a great outcry—*Shame to*

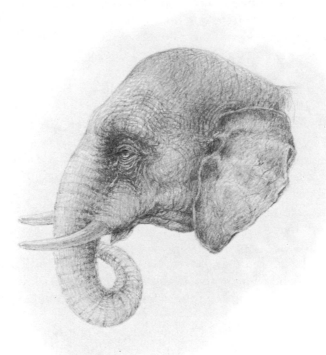

sleep! How could he? Our lives are over! Here is deadwood ready for our funeral pyres. Alas, all is Destiny!

Then they cheered and rejoiced. They had found Sumantra's false trail and they stubbornly followed it, tracking and looking, undaunted and obstinate, talking and waving and swinging their arms in the air, trying to listen for noises and telling each other to be quiet. They lost the fading wheelmarks within sight of Ayodhya. They entered the city. They were tired. They spoke quietly—*What else? How can we men defeat the supernatural?* They went home again.

The great grey elephants of Ayodhya wept as wild elephants weep when one of their Kings is captured in the forest. The Kosalas' faces were washed by warm tears, their hearts subdued. Everyone thought only of Rama, Rama they had lost. That night the lamps and lanterns burned dim, strange foreign stars clustered overhead and no one could sleep. In Fair Ayodhya the warriors ceaselessly burned and sighed.

✤

So passed the day after Rama was banished, and the night after that, and the next day. Then that evening Sumantra drove up to Ayodhya's walls at dusk, his face muffled by the end of his upper robe. He drove to the palace and walked still masked through the halls. He found King Dasaratha lying in Queen Kausalya's unlit bedroom, fanned by Kausalya and tended by Queen Sumitra, kneeling beside him.

Sumitra rose and looked at Sumantra. Her eyes were wet with tears and she said, "The King is blind."

"Lord!"

Sumitra said in a low voice, "Charioteer, listen. As your chariot sped away, grief struck down strong men. The King went to the city gate and watched unmoving in the direction you had taken, and Kausalya and I stood on either side to support him. Again he cried for you to wait, if but for an instant. He rose up on his toes to see the distant dust of your car, and when that dust was gone from sight and the south road was empty of you four, he fell and pressed his ear to the ground. When he could no longer hear the running horses we helped him to rise and led him slowly back. The people came out past us to follow you. We told Dasaratha, 'Do not follow far one who will come back to you,' but he heard nothing. He repented as though after burning his hand in a fire. He looked down at the straight wheel tracks as we followed them returning, and they beginning to be blown away by a doleful wind, and the sky darkening and all light failing. Stopping again and again, he said—*The last trace, the last trace of my son that I will ever see!*

"Sumantra, his tears soaked the ground; they bathed him as though he were already dead and being washed before the burning of his body, and our grieving people were his

103

mourners. We came to this room, he stumbled and fell onto that bed, and though he was not asleep he lay not moving for half the night with his eyes shut. And when he opened them at midnight he could not see. He blindly reached out to Queen Kausalya and when she took his hand he said, 'Mother of Rama, touch me for my sight follows your son and does not yet return. Oh Rama, they are very happy men who will see you return and embrace you. They are not men, but blessed gods.'

"So, old warrior, long have I stood here never leaving him, well pleased by my sweet son Lakshmana whom I love, in my mind praising his wisdom, bearing my hope shining within myself as the only flame of warmth left in all Ayodhya."

Sumantra advanced to the King. "I am Sumantra, covered with road-dust and hiding my face. I touch together my hands and salute you, Majesty. Will you not speak to Rama's envoy? Arise, Kaikeyi is not here!"

Dasaratha whispered, "What did he do? Where is he?"

Sumantra uncovered his face. He answered, "I left them in the solitude, walking alone in the forest. This morning he sent me back to you and crossed Ganga. He bows to your feet, for you are his father. He claims to be well. What I was first going to say about Kaikeyi on sudden impulse I have forgotten. I stood there speechless, and so Rama went away, and so Lakshmana left me behind, and so Sita disappeared into the trees.

"Hoping Rama might yet summon me I stayed awhile with Guha, but then turned back. Your favorite red horses were slow and spiritless. As I crossed back through Kosala, I saw that in all your kingdom the trees let fall their leaves and have no flowers, no scented fruit, no new buds. In your land the ponds are desolate, the streams are dry, the wells are bitter and silted. Groves wither, no creature moves or speaks, beasts of prey will not wander. The empty woods are stricken dumb; they have no nobility; they stand in gloom on all sides. Food has no flavor and no one wants to eat it anyway. Stones are burnt black. Grass is faded and dead. Crops and water-plants perish. Fish and gardens die. I drove a cheerless dreary road, my Lord. Where there had been gardens lean birds were drooping in the leafless trees,their bright plumes stained. No fires burn. Cattle give no milk. The air has no freshness. All sounds are faint and the world is indistinct. No one moves from where he is or or opens his eyes once closing them. There is no difference between a dear friend or an enemy or an uncaring man. People are not dead yet they do not live, all vitality is now lost and gone away . . . ."

The old King tried to rise. He trembled. "Charioteer, if I have ever done any good thing, drive me to Rama!"

"I cannot," said Sumantra. "I don't look back. I don't know where he is."

❧

They left Dasaratha alone with Queen Kausalya close by him. He slept uneasily for a short time but soon awakened. Kausalya still held his hand and said, "I am here."

Dasaratha said, "In my sleep I have remembered what I did long ago to cause all this misfortune. Gentle woman, as a man's deeds are good or evil so are the events which follow them, and which the man must face in their time. I have cut down sweet fruit trees for being slow-growing. In their place I've faithfully watered the rampant gay-colored trees bitter of fruit. Excited, mindlessly lured by pretty flowers on the branches, I came to expect a good yield. I looked forward to happiness but all the while I coveted delusion."

Kausalya said, "You lived a good life. You were a good man. Why do you blame yourself so? If you can't change what you've done wrong don't dwell on it."

"But the season has come," said Dasaratha. "Even when I was a young prince I leaned on a staff though I did not need it—and now I am old and have never stood alone. Asleep just now I have met Truth, I tremble."

◈   ◈   ◈

Listen, Kausalya—
When you were a maid unwed and I was young, my Love, I ever lived as I pleased, I never denied myself a thing, I knew

105

not any sorrow. I was a great marksman. I could shoot with bow and arrow aiming by sound alone and I was proud of my skill. Then once in the rainy season I rode out hunting. It was the evening twilight and the water had stopped falling for awhile. I rode along the Sarayu and the river twisted by in torrents red and black, dyed with ores and sands from the mountains and foaming in flood.

I stopped and waited by the river, planning to kill any game that came to drink. It grew dark. I could see but not very far. Then to one side I heard the sound of an elephant drinking and I sent an arrow flying at the sound. The arrow hit and I heard a cry—*Night, who has killed me?*

I felt cold fear. I had heard not an elephant but the sound of a filling waterjar. I ran to the voice and found my arrow piercing through a young man's heart. He knelt by the river. My bow fell from my hand and he fell over partly into the river. Blood poured from his breast and water poured from his waterjar lying overturned.

I held him in my arms and he looked at me. "Prince Dasaratha, what have I ever done to you? You have also killed my old blind parents who are lame and cannot move. They await my return with water. Never in their long lives have they injured another even for a good cause . . . take out your sharp arrow . . . ."

I said, "If the arrow is left alone it pains, but if it is withdrawn Death will come. I will go for a physician—"

But he sank in my grasp. His eyes fluttered upwards and with terrible difficulty he said, "No, I endure Death. I calm and clear my mind. Do not hesitate, it was but an accident . . . - boldly release my life . . . ."

So I gently bit off the arrowhead where it came out his back and withdrew the shaft. He drew in his limbs, sighed once and died watching me with no fear in his eyes, a peaceful man dying in victory. I straightened his deerskin robe and laid him along the river shore.

I thought long how to mend my sin and at last very frightened I filled the waterjar and carried it along a narrow way that bore his footprints, leading to his parents' home. I thought that it could not be right that he should die and they know nothing of it. As I approached the end of the path I heard an old couple talking about their son, feeding on the hopes I had destroyed. Then I saw them sitting like birds with broken wings, and no one to help them move about.

The old man turned his blind face to me. "Your mother feared you had gone swimming at night, my son. Answer us, do not be angry with old people who worry."

My footsteps faltered. In a voice of fear I spoke the hardest words I ever said. "I am Dasaratha, no son of yours but a warrior, a butcher. Without knowing, I have killed your son with an arrow, thinking him from sound to be an elephant drinking. Burn me with your wrath like fire, for he has died from my ignorance and from my sudden wound."

They were silent and I said, "Command me, Oh Ascetic."

He said, "We were unable to help our only son. We are like trees, who cannot rescue one another from the attacks of the winds. Had you not come to tell us this your head would have burst into a thousand pieces. Had you given him even a slight wound intentionally you would by now have fallen alive and screaming into Hell. Not to mention warriors, I can pull down Indra himself if he knowingly hurts a harmless forest man. Carry us to our boy."

I carried them. The old man and his wife fell over their son and their blind hands went tenderly touching his corpse. The old man said, "Ah, it is hard to get a son like you in this world, and you are dead!" He turned to me. "Where is he?"

I looked up. At first I could not see what path his soul had taken. I searched heaven with my eyes. I answered, "He is waiting by the door to the heaven of warriors slain in battle."

The old man said, "Prince, by your permission."

I said, "Yes." Indra opened the door and let him in.

"Go, my son," said the old man. "Born in our race you cannot come by evil." The parents poured the death-water for their son and the man drew me aside. "Kill us. Burn us three on one pyre."

. . . then he took him away . . .

"Yes, I will."

He said, "I do not curse you, nor does my wife. But I fear for you. Be careful in the future, be on your guard if you should have a son. The giver receives back the things he gives away. Will you not one day find your own death over your own lost son? Will you come by this same fate?"

I found some dry wood under a great tree where no rain had gone, and I killed them as they asked me to, and I burned them in fire that burned fiercely powered by their sacrifices, and the heat and flames of their generosity drove me backwards.

❖   ❖   ❖

"Queen," said Dasaratha, "that whole crime now comes home to me. If Rama could touch me I might live, but I have no other help. I cannot hear my own voice. My hand grows numb. I can hardly feel your hand, I barely speak. My death fast approaches. I have wronged my son, but he has done well toward me . . . Rama . . . . Where are you? . . . Rama . . . ."

Yama the Death Lord softly touched the locked doors of the Ayodhya palace and they flew open for him. Death holding his maces and bars in his hands entered unseen. Yama walked quietly beside him along the well-guarded halls, going gently to the King, casting sleep over Kausalya. Lord Yama reached into Dasaratha's breast and took out his mortal soul. Round the soul he put the diamond-wire silver noose of death and slipped tight the knot, then he took him away.

Two fires of grief past and present had dried away the life of the Ayodhya king. When that night was sometime passed he all unnoticed breathed no more, and departed this life. So did he die, the far-famed King Dasaratha, a warrior with no enemies alive.

bharata returns

*An orphan lion cub with his eyes still closed shut
from birth was given milk by a wild ewe who found him in
her meadow. He grew to call a ram "Father."He grazed
with a herd of sheep, knowing no other animals.*

*Then one day a jungle lion roared on a hill. Every lamb
and sheep fled, but the little lion looked up. He thought,
"How could I have run with sheep so long?"*

Lord Rama—at daybreak in the Ayodhya palace the royal
singers clapped their hands and sang the praises of Dasaratha
and his ancestors to awaken the old King, and all the birds in
the gardens sang outside. Serving maids threw sandal powder
into warm water for Dasaratha's bath. Menservants came to
the doorway of Kausalya's bedroom, and there they set out a
golden jar of Ganga water for the King to sip. They laid out
new-woven cloth and new bright metal mirrors and fresh-cast
ornaments and many new things of good fortune and excel-
lent virtue, so that the King would see them first thing on
awakening. So long as the Sun did not yet rise they awaited
Dasaratha.

Then golden sunbeams poured light in through the win-
dows and the King did not appear. The serving maids entered
Kausalya's room. The Queen slept beside Dasaratha, her hand
had slipped from his. They first spoke quiet words, and when
Dasaratha did not awake they touched him, and he was cold,
and they shook like water grass in the waves.

Kausalya awoke. Queen Sumitra came running. Kaikeyi
stood at Dasaratha's feet all forlorn and crying—*Oh Love!* The
sounds of lamenting for King Dasaratha filled every cavern on

110

Earth with sorrow, and carried through the sky to the end of every direction.

❧

The charioteer Sumantra put the King's body in an iron vat of oil. He sent out three swift horsemen to ride to the Kekaya land, to summon Bharata and Satrughna home to make the funeral.

The three horsemen rode fast. They overtook the winds. Their horses' hooves drove dents in the stones, they broke down the trees they passed near; where they crossed rivers they left them dry. They rode three black horses running abreast, running with head and neck and flying tail all in a line. They pounded through the forests haunted by bird-ghosts, they raced past brahmanas cupping their hands to drink water from Narayana's footprints at dawn. They went northwest and leapt the river whose waters turn to stone what they touch. They darted across Panchala and by Hastinapura the Elephant City, never stopping day or night. After four days a wall of dust appeared at Kekaya City, covering the mountain lakes and shrouding the sky. The sunset burned the dust red. Night came, and midnight. And the Ayodhya riders came from the dust and entered the city like thunder over a bridge in the dark.

Bharata had been asleep, but an evil dream had awakened him. In that dream he saw the ocean dry, saw the Moon fall to Earth, he saw the tusks of Dasaratha's elephants shatter, and the fires of Ayodhya go out, and saw smoke come from the hills of Kosala.

Bharata awoke in the night shaking and frightened. His grandfather Aswapati the Kekaya King was still awake. He tried to cheer Bharata with light happy music and comic plays, but the prince could not smile. Bharata's red skin was pale, his red hair was dark and damp with sweat. His throat was dry, his eyes were red as blood and he couldn't sit still.

Satrughna came to his brother and stood by him blacker than Night, and the gold bracelets on his dark arms flamed in

111

the torchlight. Bharata said to him, "I feel terrible. Suddenly for no reason I hate life."

Satrughna said, "Someone has died but I don't know who."

Then the Ayodhya riders entered, showing no sign of sorrow. King Aswapati and his son Yudhajit rose to meet them. The riders told Bharata, "Hurry to Ayodhya."

"Rest a moment," answered Bharata. "How is my father?"

The riders said, "We cannot linger."

"How is my mother?"

"We cannot rest."

"How is Rama?"

"Do not delay. Restless fate and fortune call you home."

Bharata said, "Grandfather, give us Kekaya horses for our chariot."

"I give." The aged King Aswapati embraced Bharata and Satrughna; he smelled their heads and pressed his hands down through their hair. "Go, my children, I permit you. Tell my daughter Kaikeyi that we are all well here, give her my love, and return to me when I remember you."

Bharata's uncle Yudhajit said, "We send no gifts. We are your friends in any threat or danger. Call us if you have the smallest need. Do not waste time on the polite ceremonies of leavetaking."

❦

Driving their chariot garnished with gold, by the fiery light of sunrise Bharata and Satrughna saw Ayodhya, and slowed their mountain horses. They looked down on her from the soft-rising hills to the north. They stopped. There was not a sound from the still city. The countryside was strangely quiet, as though Lord Shiva were walking abroad in the dawn, among the trees somewhere near.

Satrughna frowned. "The streets are empty. The doors are closed and shutters drawn across the windows. This is a sad view."

"Do you remember?" said Bharata. "In the early morning standing here we could always smell the scent of wines, and the wind would carry faint perfumes."

112

Satrughna said, "Our Great Father the Sun now rises and no one sings."

Bharata said, "Our homes are burnt out. Those are but their shells remaining."

The drove into Ayodhya. Their chariot wheels growled low and moaned as they passed through the Victory Gate, once guarded like the gateway into heaven. No guard stood there. No young couples drunk with Love's honey-wine came walking home from the parks at dawn.

They didn't see a living soul. Satrughna was brooding. He said, "If anyone still lives here, they ought to leave or they'll be dead by tonight."

They came up to the Ayodhya palace once flooded with light. Bharata said, "Dread of what awaits me hides in my heart and will not go!"

They entered the palace. The doors were half open. There was rust on the hinges and nothing was seen as it had been during the King's life. Satrughna went to find Rama. Bending his head, Bharata walked slowly to his mother Kaikeyi.

Kaikeyi rose from her window seat and Bharata knelt and held her feet, then he stood and asked her, "But where is my father? Why is your golden bed empty?"

Kaikeyi said, "My son, every marriage must end in sorrow unless both man and wife die together. He has gone to the next world under the law of Time. He lives no longer, he has died."

Bharata tore off his headband and let his long hair fall. He took ashes from an incense dish and rubbed them on his brow. He said, "I take Rama for my refuge, I take Rama for my protection. But how hard to bear! What did Dasaratha say when you last saw him?"

"He said—*Who will see Rama again?*"

Bharata stood grave as the ocean and still as the sky. Smoke rose from his body. His eyes burned like red gleams of Hell's light. "Where is Rama whose soft hands brush the dust from me when I fall?"

"Your father disinherited Rama so that you could take this kingdom without a rival, and he banished him and died from the grief of parting."

113

"Why? Whose wife did Rama take?"

"He took no other's woman. This was done to please you."

"Whom did Rama wrong, rich or poor?"

"No one. Why are you not delighted?"

"What did Rama steal?"

"Nothing, for no crime was he banished," said Kaikeyi. "I used my two wishes. The Kosalas are yours, Ayodhya is yours. You are the King!"

"How hateful!" Bharata ran from the room.

❧

He ran to Queen Kausalya's room. There were his friends. Kausalya and Sumitra were there; Vasishtha and Sumantra the charioteer and his brother Satrughna stood by them.

Bharata knelt before Kausalya. "Mother, we return from the Hills . . . I did not know! I'll never take it. I don't want to rule others, I don't want possessions. I know nothing . . . ."

"Enough, you are innocent." Kausalya laid her hand on his head. "You are the one injured. No one blames you." She held him.

Sumantra said, "I left Rama in the forest. This is a bad world."

Bharata said, "The whim of a whore."

"She's your own mother," said Vasishtha.

"Not any more," said Bharata. "What good is anything without Rama?"

Satrughna said, "Lakshmana did right to go beside him."

Bharata said, "True enough."

Satrughna said, "How will father look the gods of heaven in the eye?"

Bharata said, "Death will be small comfort to him."

"Be still a moment," said Vasishtha.

Bharata asked him, "Brahmana, why did she darken our fame? We all loved her and she always said she loved us. Why does she hate us now?"

Satrughna said, "And what has she gained anyway?"

"Crushing sorrow," answered Vasishtha.

114

Bharata said, "Surely desire easily outruns honor."

Sumitra said, "Everything will be all right, Bharata. My son Lakshmana is with Rama; my son Satrughna is with you, we are friends."

Bharata smiled at her. "Do you think so?" He looked away. "She trapped him and killed him like a deer lured into a snare by a sweet song."

Sumantra the charioteer said, "Rama—"

"What about Rama?" asked Bharata.

"He commands you to obey your father and not to take away his authority in his old age. He is covered by the blessings of Queen Kausalya. Vasishtha blessed him; he blessed them all."

Bharata said, "Did he promise?"

Vasishtha said, "Prince Bharata, listen to me. Rama said he would go away for fourteen years. He will never break his word. We need a King."

"What for?" asked Bharata.

Vasishtha said, "In a kingless land there is no rain. Families break apart in shame. Charity cannot be kept. Kindness goes. There is no law. Then who sleeps with an open door, or finds a safe road? Bandits will invade Kosala. Disputes will arise and not be solved. There will be no justice. Our ancient stories will never more be heard."

"What is there to do?" asked Bharata.

"Take my advice," said Vasishtha. "Rule us."

"No," said Bharata. "For my part I will go to the forest and bring Rama back."

Sumantra smiled. "I'll find him for you."

Bharata said, "The King did not consult with old friends like you."

Vasishtha said again, "Be our King until Rama returns."

"Watch it!" said Bharata. "Do not sell treasures with one hand and hold back happiness with your other. Or I will move out against you."

"There is a great ocean of grief to cross," said Vasishtha. "Regret and remorse are his whirlpools and tears are his tides.

115

Kaikeyi's wishes are his near shore, and fourteen years is his expanse, and the shrill words of the hunchback Manthara are his ravenous sharks."

Satrughna said, "*Whose words?*" He started for the door.

"Wait," said Bharata. "If Rama hears we have killed Manthara he will never look on us again."

Shrieks of crazy laughter rang through the palace, but Satrughna sat down and ignored them. Vasishtha said, "By the heavens, multitudes have censured Manthara and found no peace of mind from it! Burn the body of the King, Bharata. Do this much. Free the people; let their sorrow come out. One may fall and bear being kicked by another, but one cannot fall and bear ever so little sorrow. Sorrow deforms our thoughts and our reflections; it grows within and smothers our hearts. Sorrow has made Ayodhya unbeautiful to see; it has dishonored her. Who can live here? What is life without joy? Don't let sorrow beat down the Kosalas. Make the King's funeral and let us be done with it!"

"I don't want any part of it."

"You rightly despise the clutter of this world."

"But here I am," said Bharata. "I'll burn the dead King in Rama's name."

❧

Over the burning ground by the Sarayu black funeral smoke hung in the air. Bharata wept like a hurt boy and Vasishtha put his arm around him. Atop the pyre Dasaratha's face still showed as if he slept, a little pale. The rest of his body was buried under flowers and under solid perfumes that began to melt. The flames kindled from the firechamber of Ayodhya then reached up and hid the King's corpse.

That burning freed Dasaratha's spirit. It let him come out from Yama's shadowy land and get from the Moon his heavenly body, and in celestial robes take his rightful place in heaven.

Bharata said, "In my youth, Time's true nature was hidden from me, but now I see all his harmful ways. I'll never forgive,

116

I'll never forget what my mother has done. I want to go away and never hear her name. Vasishtha, how will she be born in future lives?"

"She will never understand, never know the True," said Vasishtha. "She will doubt life while facing the Sun. She will be a mad beggar eating dirt from a skull. She will be a miser living alone then robbed by thieves. She will be a poor man with a large family in a land ruled in fear by a bad King. She will be a great teacher who forgets all his learning and shameless turns to dice and women and puts his old servants out to starve in the streets."

"What else?"

"She will not do one good deed. She will betray friends and hand them over to the King's soldiers. She will give wealth to unworthy liars and dash the hopes of poor men who look up to her trustingly. She will refuse water to thirsty travelers by lying that she has none. She will poison wells. She will be an unwelcome philosopher who quarrels painfully over points of view and she will be born again as one who listens to such talk."

"What else?"

"In this very life she will not live to see Rama return."

"Is that all?" Bharata sighed.

Vasishtha said, "I have added nothing and left out nothing. All this will be her lot—unless you forgive her, Bharata."

Bharata said, "I forgive."

Vasishtha said, "Compassion is great enough where it can have no effect. Used to accomplish something it is supreme!"

"A son comes to life from the blood of his mother's heart," said Bharata, "therefore he is dear to her."

Listen, King Rama, our Master Valmiki knows. Once tears fell on Indra as he flew in the sky, and looking up he saw Surabhi the white wishing-cow of heaven gazing past him down at the Earth and crying. Indra flew to her and asked, "What is wrong? It must be a great injustice." She replied, "Lord of Gods, I mourn my sons fallen on evil days. See the two of them below, lean and sunburned and tired from

plowing." And Indra stood amazed and speechless, thinking how Surabhi's children number in millions and fill the worlds, how though she lived in heaven and was herself the very essence of good fortune she cried over two of them as though her heart would break . . . .

❦

The three widowed Queens of Ayodhya said watery prayers and bathed at the riverside. For eleven nights they slept on the bare ground. Then they gave away gifts in Dasaratha's name—food and drink and salt and homes, goats and cows, cloth and gold, silver and servants. After that, Bharata gathered his father's bones from the cold white ashes of the funeral pyre, raised them over his head and threw them into the Sarayu River.

That ended the mourning. At sunrise the next day the Kosalas awakened Bharata with loud shell trumpets and he went to them and said, "Never do that again, I am not the King."

Bharata told the charioteer Sumantra, "Only the son first-born may be King in our Solar race. I will take Rama's place in the forest."

Sumantra first asked the elephant-god Ganesha—*Remove the obstacles, widen the road, smooth our way.* Then he drove Bharata out of the city, passing under the groves of the Sarayu, under the flowers violet and gold.

Satrughna came next driving the three Queens in a chariot. After them came nine thousand war-mounted elephants, then six thousand chariots carrying light-handed bowmen, then many horsemen and footsoldiers running by the roadsides bearing shields like suns, then the wives and families of the soldiers came last leading mule-carts and pack-animals.

The wide road to Rama! The swift-rising Sun set alight the spear-points like a curving line of stars. The road gained loveliness as they proceeded. It was tree-lined. There were fair wells with resting places. There were fruit trees and orchards. The country people put flags by the roadside. They moved on, the people came all following Bharata, like the swelling high tide of the sea rolling on, like the entire Earth in human form.

They halted in grand tent-cities, and after three easy days they came to the first Sala trees of Guha's forest and stood on the far border of Kosala. The Sun hung aslant and low; it was the hour of evening.

Hidden within the Secret Forest, Guha looked out at them. From Sumantra's chariot flew the flag of the Kosalas, a green ebony tree shining on silver. Guha could see no end to all those people.

He sat down and cleared a flat space with the edge of his hand. He took nine bird bones from a leather bag and shook them in his hands three times saying, "Rama is my friend, who is Bharata?"

He threw his fortune. The bones said, "Don't hinder him."

While the Kosalas made their camp, Bharata and Satrughna came to the ocean-going Ganga and offered her clear cool

119

water to their father, so that in heaven Dasaratha's spirit was bright-shining with pleasure. Bharata bathed in Ganga and was no longer tired. He drank her holy water and gladdened his heart. Then he sat thinking how to make Rama come back, sitting under the same wide-spreading tree where Rama had been. That old tree threw out his heavy arms in joy to the sunset starry sky above, and Bharata said quietly, "From here, I bow to Rama in the forest."

There Guha met him bringing bread and butter and honey. Bharata asked, "Where is Rama? Do you know where he went?"

"All those people," said Guha.

"We want him back," said Bharata.

Satrughna said, "Dasaratha had died, now Rama is our king."

Little whistles and barks sounded from the dark forest around them. Guha grinned. "They've heard you. The bird people are singing of your fame, the deer praise you. They say you are an unclouded sky, beautiful in the daytime, beautiful at night. They call you a true man, a real friend, they wonder if there is anyone else like you on Earth, who would give back a kingdom . . . ."

Guha clapped his hands and torches gleamed into light and came carried by Guha's men, out from the trees. "I have hundreds of fisher-boats hidden along the river," said Guha. "Leave your chariots here, tomorrow I will take you and your animals all downstream to Bharadwaja." Guha took a torch. "See, under this great and ancient tree the hard rough grass still shows where it was pressed by Rama's limbs. Look, here are silk threads pulled from Sita's robe. Here slept Sumantra, here Lakshmana sat."

"It seems incredible to me," said Bharata. "Oh, had I not gone to Kekaya . . . ."

"No, no," said Guha. "Time does what he must, powered by the past. When Time does us wrong, we are lucky just to live on and get another chance at him, and what harm did you intend?"

120

"Then," said Bharata, "surely if Time will help me, Rama cannot long refuse to return."

The Sun had gambled away all his splendor, and Night spread over Earth. Then as a smoldering tree already burned by forest fire will show only by night that it still burns, so Bharata sighed in the dark.

the sandals

I see two birds on the same branch;
One eats the sweet fruit,
One looks on sadly.

The first bird wonders—
In what prison does he live?

The second marvels—
How can he rejoice?

With noise and shouting Guha's men ferried the Kosalas down the River Ganga, showing off with their boats in fancy formations, and the Kosalas who could not wait their turn floated among the boats hanging onto pitchers that were upside down in the water and full of air, and the elephants swam along like islands come to life. Guha himself took Bharata and Satrughna and the three Queens on board a serpent-prowed boat trimmed in gold and hung with bells, and steered them down to where Ganga's white waters met the deep dark Yamuna with a roar.

When all the Kosalas had been landed, the hunter-men and Guha swept back upstream in their boats and left them there. Bharata kept the Kosalas back and went alone on foot into Bharadwaja's hermitage, plainly dressed in a single robe and unarmed.

Bharadwaja met him with water to drink and water for foot-washing. They sat together and Bharadwaja asked, "How is the city of Fair Ayodhya?"

Bharata said, "Brahmana, are you well? I hope your fires burn as you want them to. You do not ask about my father."

Bharadwaja replied, "I know the King is dead."

"The King is alive," said Bharata. "The King is Rama. I want to get him and bring him hone."

Bharadwaja smiled. "Do I not know you, young prince? But why have you left your people behind you at the riverside?"

"They are thousands," answered Bharata. "I have soldiers and women and children. They would make holes in the ground here, and hurt your trees, and put mud in your water."

"Have them unpack and bring them here for dinner."

Bharata looked around, and saw only the woodlands around the little clearing, and Bharadwaja's small hut standing alone by a trickling stream. "I have been entertained by water and the sight of you. By your words have you well received us all."

"But you are too easily pleased," said Bharadwaja. "Tell them to come. I invite you all."

❦

Bharata walked back to the river and Bharadwaja went into his house and sat by his fire. There nodding his head he sipped water from his hand three times, and rubbed it on his lips and said—*I will entertain my guests.*

Down from heaven came the architect Viswakarman. He stood in the center of Bharadwaja's clearing and unfurled his great wings and swept them through the air. He turned; he moved his hands, and the trees moved back, the clearing grew. He built a dream, he made a garden where new wonders grew. Viswakarman knows all worlds. His arms shaped the air; he spoke names.

The south winds blew scented with sandalwood. The rivers of the world came there and ran with water and wines and milk and sugar syrup, ran through blue grass, among the coral trees brought from the wishing-forests of the Treasure-Lord. Heavenly Gandharvas played music and Apsarasas danced. Flowers fell from the air. Tree spirits were tumblers and dwarves, and the vines of the forest were beautiful women all dressed in flowers. Food appeared and buildings arose.

123

Viswakarman folded his arms and closed his wings and was gone, and the Kosalas entered what had been Bharadwaja's poor hermitage. Nagas in human forms met them and led aside their horses and elephants. The Kosala grooms forgot their animals and the animals forgot them sooner. Only Sumantra the charioteer would let no one else comb his red horses.

A Naga girl waited for each soldier, took his bow, untied his armor and fed him. The spirits of the air materialized and poured out drinks; the Gandharvas played dances; the Ayodhya warriors laughed and talked.

That was Bharadwaja's welcome. The Kosalas said—*Peace be to Bharata. Great happiness to the recluse Bharadwaja. We are within a vision of heaven. Why retreat, why advance, why move?*

❧

So entertained like gods the Kosalas passed the night in good cheer. They ate and drank all they could wish for. They fell asleep smiling in dreams.

Then, while they slept, the beings and spirits who had worked for their banquet went back to where they had come from. The stray fruits half-eaten, the heavenly flowers scattered and crushed underfoot, the goblets and bright dishes all vanished, and Bharadwaja's grove became again as it was before.

Bharata awoke early while the others were still sound asleep and went to the door of Bharadwaja's hut. Bharadwaja came out and asked, "Were you pleased?"

Bharata answered, "How wonderful it was! I salute you. I think . . . I begin to learn." Bharata looked around at the Kosalas, some of them just beginning to stir, the rest stretched out sleeping like the dead. "I bow to you. We will go on. Look after us with a friendly eye."

Bharadwaja said, "Set alone like a colorful jewel in the empty forest is Chitrakuta Hill beautiful to behold. Rama lives there, my child. A river flowing in waves bends around that hill, and part way up the high forest slopes above the river is

124

Rama's house . . . but introduce me to your mothers, let me meet them before you go, I would like that."

Bharata went to where his brother slept. "Get up, Satrughna, why do you sleep?"

Satrughna instantly arose and Bharata said, "Bring Queen Kausalya, and Sumitra and Kaikeyi."

Satrughna and Bharata and the three Queens stood before the hermit Bharadwaja. Bharata said, "This is Kausalya, she is Rama's mother."

Kausalya knelt and touched Bharadwaja's feet. He said to her, "Rama is very strong; he is the desired guest of the hills and woods, and the reasons for many things are lost in Time."

Bharata said, "This is Queen Sumitra."

"She is ever a kind friend," said Bharadwaja. He smiled and took Sumitra's hands in his. "Friendliness and love and protection, my Lady, I call that good, very good!"

Kaikeyi hesitated. Then looking down at the ground she walked once round Bharadwaja, and stopped, and at last looked up into his eyes.

Bharadwaja said, "No one must blame you, those are my words. Sending Rama to the forest will truly be for the great good of all the worlds, and what you have done will bring happiness to every man and joy to heaven. I bless you, Kaikeyi, you have done no wrong."

Kaikeyi smiled, and her son Bharata put his red arm around her shoulders and drew her close to him. Then Bharadwaja turned and bent his head to enter his small house again.

The Kosalas departed from Bharadwaja's retreat and left behind them Ganga the Queen of Rivers, and moved slowly toward Chitrakuta.

❦

The springtime trees of Chitra were perfect as a scene imagined from a storybook. They grew short and tall, thin and spreading, leafy and open. Their leaves were grass-green, blue-green, yellow-green, dark green, light green, crimson and brown and yellow, glossy and dull, smooth and sticky,

125

round and pointed like fingers, fluttering and still. The barks of the trees were rough and smooth and furry, grey and white and green and black, cool and warm. The flowers grew in bunches or grew apart; they were red, yellow, white, pink and honey-colored; they were green and blue and purple and orange and silver and gold and lavender; they were large and small. All among the trees were tapering vines and slender creepers, rushes and canes and reeds, ferns and shrubs and grasses and orchids and bamboo and moss.

There grew the climbers whose leaves close in the rain, and the trees that burst into blossom at a woman's touch, and the water lilies that open when deep thunder rolls through the blue rainclouds across heaven above. And to Lakshmana all these plants surrendered the supplies of a rich caravan. He got from them needles and thread and cloth, food and cords and soap, cups and jars and medicine.

> These trees in flower
> Have been engarlanded by the gods.
> This forest is a Garden,
> This Hill an ornament of Earth.

Rama loved the deep forest. One early morning he and Sita went for a walk above their house, by wild rose trees and shady lilac. Hill flowers carpeted the meadows. Sparrows who lived only on rainwater sang. From the soil the trees had drawn ores and minerals up through their roots, so that on their trunks and branches there were gleaming streaks of gold and quicksilver, and bands of blood-red ruby dust glinting from right within the bark.

Sita walked holding Rama's hard arm that was her pillow at night. With her walk Sita rebuked the wavy gait of swans. Wherever she went, Sita of slender waist was always at home in Rama's heart, sheltered by his love, as the path they followed was sheltered over by the trees.

They walked along a stream, past waterfalls and little islands. The water ran through the feet of herons and through the drinking pools of deer, and water tumbled over the rapids spilling like pearls and rolling away.

Rama and Sita swam in the river, then they climbed onto the breast of Chitrakuta. There Rama fell asleep, his head on Sita's lap while she sat back against a tree and stroked his hair.

While Rama slept, a black crow flew at Sita. She frightened him off with a stone. Rama awoke, looked up and saw her angry, trying to push back the robe that had slipped from her shoulder, her face glowing and her lips trembling. Rama smiled at her and sighed, and went back to sleep. But the crow returned. He attacked Sita, beat his wings against her breast and tore her flesh with his sharp claws.

Her blood fell on Rama and she cried out for him. Rama instantly awoke and saw the crow with red claws swiftly dart down inside the Earth. Rama put the Brahma Weapon on a grassblade and threw it after the crow. The blade burned with fire round its tip, and it pursued the crow wherever he flew. It chased him through all the heavens and under all the worlds and back to Earth. The gods shut heaven's doors against the crow and the saints looked away when he asked their protection. Even Hell was locked.

So the crow flew to Rama and said, "I find no other refuge against him." and bowed at Rama's feet.

"Surrender a part of your body for the weapon to hit," said Rama, "and I will protect your life."

The crow surrendered his right eye, and that eye broke from his face like shattered glass and he saved himself. The crow flew away and Rama comforted Sita.

Returning home they stopped to rest on a ledge by the mouth of a red-stone cave. Sita embraced Rama like a vine twined round a tree. Rama reached down and touched the red dust, and put a mark on Sita's brow with his fingertip.

Then they walked on downhill together. A monkey suddenly ran up a tree right beside Sita, and she jumped into Rama's arms in fright. He held her and her red brow-mark was printed on Rama's broad green chest. Sita was very happy and would not let Rama wipe it off.

When they came near their house they met Lakshmana bringing a black deer home from the hunt. Sita made wild wheat bread and Rama gathered honey. They ate under a

. . . but the crow returned.

golden vine by a clear silvery spring, and the woodpeckers tapped in the trees.

❦

The Kosalas caught sight of lovely Chitra Hill arising out of the Earth. They all had flowers in their hair like men from the south. They waited by a stream while Bharata went on alone up the hill.

Bharata found a trail that had been marked. He saw white smoke in the air ahead of him. Bark garments were hanging out to dry on the branches of a tree. By the path were stacks of firewood. Bharata walked out into a clearing on the mountainside and saw Rama standing by his house.

Rama stood very still, with matted hair and dressed in black deerskin. Bharata approached and knelt before Rama. He looked up and said, "Oh Arya . . . noble Rama . . . ."

Rama bent over and raised Bharata. "What is it? Why have you come here?"

"Our father who enjoyed all the world is dead."

When they heard that, Rama and Lakshmana and Sita took some cakes down to the river, threw some of them into the water and put the rest on the grass. Rama held water in his hands—*May this reach you, may it be so.*

Then they returned, and Rama sat with Bharata near their house. All the Kosalas quietly approached and watched them sitting together and wondered, "What will Bharata say to him?"

Bharata raised his hand and spoke. "Rama, peace to you: I decline the ownership and possession of the Kosala kingdom. We have no King. Return to Ayodhya with these people, I will replace you here."

Rama said, "I think a father may divide his inheritance as he pleases, and surely his sons will obey him. Bharata, a man's unbroken word is like a bowl of clear glass; once shattered, no one can put it back as it was by any art. I must do what I said I would do, stay here for fourteen years."

Bharata said, "Your absence already seems unbearably long. Father died soon after you left. Now I come seeking

129

you. A wife ought to love her husband more than even a thousand fine sons. Gentle Sita deserves to live in a palace. What unbeautiful thing has she ever done? The eldest son must be King. Father died desiring you to be happy, remembering you."

Rama said, "Keeping a given word, Bharata . . . that is more important than Kosala customs. I have no time for kingdom, Bharata. I have no time for any useless thing. It is not for me to do the work of others. Our father Dasaratha was a wall of Dharma like a mountain. Death is at last found to be a part of all life, and never can we escape it, and Death does not change a promise made. At the end of life, when this body is burned, a man takes Brahma's way if he has lived well; he takes a good way well-wrought by men of the past, and looking back at his family let him not see foolish sons set aside his last wishes."

Bharata said, "Come home. Men lose their sense as their Death approaches. Rama, why must men suffer ignorance? Ignorance will surely destroy a father's many kindnesses and a mother's pains. Why do we waste our food to set out offerings for the dead? Do the dead eat? Who do we feed? Small animals eat it all. Such blind rules are wrong, Rama. Engage your soul in happiness. Men are born for joy. Do not make ease your guide and do not follow discomfort. Do right deeds, forget to always say the right words. In land after land, one may find wives and meet friends. But I can now never get another brother."

Rama said, "The first betrayal may be easy or it may be hard, but after the first betrayal then the others soon follow. The heart, Bharata . . . keep note of your heart and don't stifle it. There lives the soul, clear, never stained, watching all we do or think to do, so let a man be still and find his heart. That is the only safe rescue. What use is a castle or a palace or a great stone fortress that is no defense against Time? Since we have come together, our separation some day is certain. While we are together as two men during this lifetime, let us keep the truth."

Bharata said, "It is true, that nights gone by do not return, and every day shortens our lives. But I think some things

130

endure. Surely love endures beyond our brief lives. All the Ayodhya Kings have loved their City. Our fathers have left Ayodhya shining pure white in her fame and glory. Now our City is miserable; she is an unhappy lake without a guardian serpent, unprotected, ruined, drifting and lost as an abandoned ship on the seas."

Rama said, "Death keeps a man company and after going with him a long way as his dear friend, Death returns with his soul. Man suffers scars and wounds, his hair turns grey, his strength departs and his memory flees; he seems not to know even his own children. Life is passing as a river ever flowing away, never still, never returning. Life is changeable as the flashing lightning, a pattern of as little meaning, and impermanent. Where can one live long? Life is bright and colored for a passing moment like the sunset. Then it is gone and who can prevent it going? Therefore, Bharata, once in this perilous body deplore your own condition. Mourn your own self and do not lament anything else."

Bharata said, "Oh Rama, kingdoms wash over you, but you are calm. You know the mysterious soul and the life where he swims. The Sun of our father's life first grew milder and then set, its journey done, and Night begins her course. Night is starless then, and then is water frozen to ice, and our City is like a fair woman forsaken. I came to see you, ask of me whatever will please you."

Rama said, "You say you love me, will you not wait?"

"Yes."

"That will make me very happy, Bharata."

❦

When the Kosalas knew that Rama would stay in the forest, they were proud and sad. They sat on the Earth and said— *Well said! Well spoken! We call that excellent, well done, well done!*

Bharata said, "Give me your sandals."

Rama took off his wooden-soled sandals that had colored flowers painted on them.

Bharata took them. "Rama, you are the true King. I will go back, I will rule Kosala in trust for you for fourteen years, and

your sandals will be on the throne. If I do not see you on the first day after those fourteen years I'll walk into a fire and die."

Bharata retraced his steps. In Kosala he put the sandals on the head of the King's own lucky elephant. Satrughna brought the royal throne out from Ayodhya and put it in the little village of Nandigrama nearby. Vasishtha brought all the signs of royalty to Nandigrama, and there Bharata led the elephant.

Bharata put Rama's shoes on the red and gold Ayodhya throne. Over them spread the gold-ribbed white silk umbrella and the white yak-tail fan of silver and emerald. Bharata and Satrughna put on barkcloth and sat at the foot of the throne.

Every day the ministers and noblemen of Kosala came out from Ayodhya all in bark like hermits. They would bow to Rama's shoes as to a King. The warriors were dressed like holy wanderers seeking for the Lord somewhere, begging their way. Rama's sandals lay quiet if justice was done before the throne, but if any case was wrongly judged the sandals swiftly beat together their loud wooden soles.

❦

In Ayodhya heralds furled the bright silk flags. For fourteen years there was silence in Fair Ayodhya and no sound of mirth or learning. Many days the Sun was clouded because of heaven's dark-hearted sorrow. Musicians unstrung their lutes and played no music, because there was no music in the forest where Rama was. The Kosalas took the wheels off their chariots and walked where they had to go, because Rama had no chariot and had to walk in the woods. The Ayodhya women alone still wore flowers and fine clothes and ornaments, because Sita went to the forest dressed in fashion. The gardeners kept their gardens of Ayodhya alive and watered the flowers in the hanging gardens on the hillside leading to the empty royal palace.

Ayodhya was like the pools by the seashore when the tide is withdrawn. Where once the waves had foamed and thundered on the stones, now in the little ponds were only tiny silent ripples born from a gentle wind from the sea. She was like a mare slain in war; now dead, yet an instant before alive and strong and in motion and attacking.

The mate of a young bull will not eat grass without him beside her. In summer a stream will dry away. Her water will turn warm, her animals will be lean and her fish will die. In winter her floods will drown small creatures. After many years a bamboo will flower once and then die.

We may be the playthings of Fate. We cannot breathe without taking life. As we talk here, we are ourselves the cause of the deaths of countless little lives. We have surely let old bodies go many times, as though changing from old clothes into new ones. We may have died more times in the past than all the times we have fallen asleep since being born twelve years ago.

Await the time. What use is impatience?

❧

Rama went barefoot for the rest of his exile. He thought Chitrakuta still too close to Ayodhya. One morning soon after Bharata had come and gone, Rama and Sita and Lakshmana set out towards the Vindhya Hills, south into the forests. Late in the day they came to a large lake fed by springs, with shores of soft white sands shaded by trees.

There were water-flowers, red and yellow and blue, and green water-leaves, and plump silver fish swimming, all spread out like an elephant blanket of many colors. There were cranes and fisherbirds and floating tortoises, and swans and frogs and pink geese. Rama and Sita and Lakshmana stopped and they could hear from within the water the sound of singing and of music. They heard laughter and drums, the ringing of ankle-bells and the pouring of wines, but the lake looked clear and they saw no one.

They entered a glade of green grass, and saw a house and an old couple sitting by it, and in the late sunlight the glow of Brahma power stood out as a halo around the old people. That was the home of Atri, one of the seven oldest saints in the three worlds, and his wife Anasuya. That is their earthly home; in heaven Atri lives in one of the seven lights of the Bear in the sky.

Atri welcomed Rama and Lakshmana, and Anasuya smiled and rose and took Sita aside. Rama asked, "What is that wonderful lake we passed?"

Atri replied, "That is Five-Apsarasa-Lake. Long ago the hermit Mandakarni stood there beside a little rain puddle and lived only on air. The longer he did that, the larger the water grew. He stood on the edge of a lake. Indra looked down from Heaven and saw that Mandakarni would soon drown the Earth. Indra sent five beautiful Apsarasas to stop him. Mandakarni saw the five dancing girls all lively as lightning and he changed his life. He married them all and made an invisible home within the lakewater. He had won enough merit to keep himself young forever. Mandakarni lives happily there and his five wives do everything to please him. When they drink and feast and dance we may hear their dancing-bells and sweet songs, and sometimes their fair-winged words, and even catch the scent of their five celestial perfumes."

Anasuya sat apart with Sita. Anasuya was very old; her hair was wispy white and her body shook with age like a leaf in the wind. She said, "Sita, with you Rama may have some pleasure in the forest."

134

Sita said, "He is my man."

"What shall I do for you?" asked Anasuya, whose name means Kindness. "Take a gift to please me." Anasuya opened a box and from it she gave Sita a never-fading garland of rare loveliness, and put it over Sita's head next to Guha's pink shell necklace. Then Anasuya gave Sita gold and silver ornaments that never tarnished and a jar of sandalwood cream that never emptied.

Sita took the ornaments and put aside some of her former ones she had worn from Ayodhya, and said, "These are very beautiful." Sita was surprised and smiling.

Anasuya said, "They will keep you beautiful forever. Oh Sita, look, the Sun has set. By the last rays of daylight the smoke rising from our fire is colored red. Open trees appear dense with leaves, nothing can be seen at a distance, and the hermitage deer lie by the altars. Night crested by stars and robed in moonlight has come, and day has gone from the sky and the Earth. Stay with us tonight, dear Sita."

❧

The next day Rama and Lakshmana, and Sita wearing those friendly presents, went on their way. They went west and a little south, walking the length of the Vindhya Hills after climbing their northern slopes. There Lakshmana found many places to build a home. They would live in one place for three months or eight months or a year, and then would move on to another place. They did this until thirteen years of Rama's exile had passed away, and it was late in the fourteenth and last springtime.

§

THIS ENDS THE
SECOND BOOK OF AYODHYA
HERE BEGINS THE FOREST BOOK

§

135

part two

sita's rescue

OM!
I bow to Lord Rama,
To Sita of beautiful fortune;
I salute Hanuman the monkey,
And the Goddess Saraswati:
JAYA!
Victory!

dandaka forest

It was almost the fourteenth summer when Rama and Sita and Lakshmana crossed over the Vindhya Hills and began to walk down the southern slopes. One evening after walking far they entered a large grove of trees, and many clear streams crossed the path with their branches of water. There was woodsmoke on the air, and Rama said, "We are coming to the home of Agastya, the brahmana who lowered the Vindhya Hills, destroyed two demons and settled here."

Sita asked, "How did he do that?"

Rama answered, "Agastya is a small man, but what is impossible for even the gods he can do easily."

Listen, Sita—

Long ago, the Vindhya Hills were jealous of the Himalya, and in envy Vindhya began to grow higher and higher. Vindhya told the Sun and Moon, "Circle around me now, for I am the new center of the world!"

Sun and Moon would not do that. They kept going around the golden hill Meru in the Himalya. But Vindhya rose until his peaks blocked the skies. Surya the Sun could not pass to the south. The stars and Moon were blocked and rainclouds and Wind could not go where they wanted.

Agastya came walking from the north. He got to the Vindhya foothills and saw how Vindhya had grown impassable. There were no trails and the hills were lost in cold clouds. Agastya asked Vindhya, "Best of mountains, I must go south for awhile. Let me go by and come back again."

Vindhya said, "Pass, brahmana." Vindhya bowed low to

Agastya, and these hills decreased to their present height, well below the sky-paths.

Agastya said, "Don't rise again till I cross you coming back." Then he settled here, south of the hilltops, and he has never yet gone back north, and Vindhya obeys him. Vindhya still waits for Agastya faithfully, with his head bent low.

Then men could cross these hills and travel here, but they were hunted by two demon brothers named Vatapi and Ilwala. Ilwala took the form of a brahmana, and speaking refined language he invited anyone he met to eat with him, and led his guest up to a little cottage by the edge of a wood.

Inside in the kitchen Vatapi took the form of a ram and Ilwala cooked his brother and served him outside, and when the guest had eaten the ram Ilwala would say—*Come out shouting!* Then Vatapi bellowing like a ram would tear his way out from the traveler's body and kill him, and Vatapi and Ilwala would drain and drink the corpse's blood.

In that way they destroyed nine thousand men. Then one evening Ilwala met Agastya and brought him home and served him dinner. Small as he was, Agastya ate up every shred of the roast mutton, and sat back smacking his lips and smiling.

Ilwala facing him took a deep breath and said—*Come out. Come out shouting!*

Nothing happened. Agastya washed his hands in a bowl of water and looked at Ilwala. "Beware of the Dharma-appetite," said Agastya. "I have digested your brother. I have sent him to Death as my delicious well-cooked dinner."

Ilwala's fingernails grew into blue poisoned claws. He leapt at Agastya. But with one fiery look from his eyes Agastya burned him dead as he jumped. He burned him with a glance that flashed real fire and real flames.

"We have met woods-dwellers before," said Rama, "but there is no one else like Agastya. North lives Lord Shiva, north are the Himalya hills, and Mount Meru the center of the world, and Kailasa Hill of silver, and all manner of weight, and Agastya alone by living here in the south keeps Earth from tipping over. He is very powerful, and the heaviest person alive."

Rama said, "Lakshmana, go ahead alone and greet Agastya and tell him we are here."

Lakshmana found Agastya clad in bark sheets tied with a belt of vines, sitting on cut holy grass that was blue as lapis stone, his feet crossed and tucked up over his knees as though he were warding away some evil. Lakshmana said, "Command Rama and Sita what to do next."

"I have been thinking of Rama in my mind," Agastya looked keenly at Lakshmana. "After a long time, by good fortune Rama has come to see me. Where is he? Let him enter my home, why have you not brought him?"

Rama and Sita walked past the flat stones where Naga Kings of the underworlds and gods of heaven would come to sit and talk with Agastya. Agastya rose and greeted them and said, "Sit and eat supper with me. The host who won't feed his friends will eat his own flesh in the next world, just like a false witness." He served Rama and Lakshmana and Sita a supper of edible flowers and bulbs that left them with no slightest thought of hunger.

When they had eaten, Agastya said, "Rama, let me see your bow."

Rama held out to him the bow he had brought from Ayodhya to use in the forest. Agastya glanced at it and set it aside. He said, "It is flawed, because the man who made it was at that time engaged in an affair with another man's wife and his mind was ill at ease."

Agastya's house was nearby. From within it Agastya brought out a long bow and a covered quiver, and gave Rama the bow. That bow was backed with diamonds and curving golden plates. Its belly was smooth and painted with colors like Indra's Bow of Rain. It was covered with gold on its tips and its bowstring was unbreakable.

Then Agastya opened the quiver and took out from it all that it held: two arrows made from long grass stalks, and vaned with vulture feathers, one bladed with brass, and other with silver. He gave the silver one to Lakshmana and the brass one to Rama.

Agastya said, "Rama of the war-chariots, take from me this sweet-sounding bow in exchange for your old one, and take this arrow. One day I found these things in the forest. I think they have fallen from heaven, perhaps during the confusion of Ravana's attack many years ago. This bow will better bear the weight of those weapons Viswamitra taught you. The blades of these arrows have never needed to be polished or sharpened, and so I think they may be infallible, shot by the right person . . . ."

The evening deepened into night and Lakshmana made a fire. Agastya said, "Rama, round my home on every side all the waters are clear. Live here with me. Harmless deer haunt this forest, bewitching people by their beauty. Aside from that, there is no menace here."

Rama, said, "Lakshmana would hunt those trusting deer for us to eat. That would pain you, we cannot stay."

❧

In the morning Agastya led Rama out onto a spur of the mountains, high on the hillside looking south. Below them the Vindhya Hills ended and the thirsty dry jungles of Dandaka Forest reached out to the south as far as they could see over the land.

"We are far from Lanka," said Agastya, "but the edge of Dandaka is the frontier of the Rakshasa kingdom on Earth. For the most part Dandaka is a huge wasteland. It knows no master but Ravana. Whoever goes down there must be himself his own protection. Oh Rama, Ravana the Demon King believes he owns the universe; what are men to him? Pleasures distract him and he scorns men as but his food, weak and worthless. Men live surrounded by chance and danger and they cannot tell right from wrong. Their lives are short and miserable. They are prey to hunger and thirst, disease and old age. Unending evils overwhelm them. Behold Man, ignorant of his own ways in the world—now merrily drinking and dancing, now blindly weeping all in tears.

"Fourteen thousand Rakshasa veterans garrison Dandaka, commanded by the demon general Khara. Away to the south they have an army station in a thistle grove, and watchtowers of stone around it. And in the jungle Gandharva sentinels sent by the gods watch in the trees. Serpents arch and bend up from underground holes, guards for the Water Lord Varuna. And whirling and sparkling in the night are the Yakshas, placed as sentries by the Treasure King Vaishravana. Every god fears that Ravana may yet move farther against him, and send demons to enforce his evil empire."

Rama said, "I did not know that there was anywhere on this Earth that Rama and Lakshmana could not freely go."

Agastya said, "Strike back at him."

Rama smiled. "I still have a year to wander." He turned and looked behind him at Agastya's hermitage. That grove of trees and little house could remove any weariness of body or heart. No Rakshasa could enter there.

Agastya said, "There are still a few pleasant spots here and there in Dandaka, but for the rest it is infested by blood-drinking demons. Be careful, especially at night. Don't let the Rakshasas surprise you and they will not win. If you meet them, prevent them as you go." Agastya embraced Rama. "That is the path. I use it sometimes, for a little way, to gather sticks. Rama, demons do not love men, therefore men must love each other."

Rama and Sita and Lakshmana, with their one new bow and two new arrows given by Agastya and with their arrows from Ayodhya, went downhill into Dandaka. The morning Sun, like a man newly rich, shone too proud over the forest. They left behind Vindhya of a thousand summits with his caves of lions and falling fountains, and his crystal rivers laughing aloud as they flowed down his sides.

The trees of Dandaka were like columns of wood and their

branches were twisted like the crooked hearts of evil men. Their leaves were brittle and dry. The air was wavy and hot; there was a hot wind, and huge hot boulders threw back the heat, and curled shreds of bark fallen to the forest floor rustled as the Sun got hotter.

All Dandaka was creaking in the heat, warning away men. The ground was uneven, trackless and deserted, overgrown with hard red burr-bushes and brush that cried out underfoot. Every pond that Rama and Lakshmana and Sita saw was encircled with wavy lines and blackened grasses that showed how the water had receded. The wind blew in gusts and they heard screams from the lines of dead whistling canes bent down in the wind. Dandaka stretched before them, fearsome and wild and wide.

Past stumps and trunks Lakshmana led them on into that hair-raising wilderness, and Dandaka grew deeper and denser and filled with noisy chiming crickets, and vultures sat on bare branches. Then at noon they saw the eighty-four thousand little Valakhilya saints of the wood. They were people smaller than a thumbnail, floating in the air, drinking in sunbeams, looking like motes of dust in the Sun.

They spoke to Rama and said, "Oh child, we are meek and unassuming. Here it is dreadful and lonely. It is a sadness to live here. Rakshasas prowl for flesh by night. They overshadow the darkness as though they would crush the mountains down. We must endure demons and submit to them. We have seen mountains of bones from the victims they have slaughtered, white bones, Rama, white bones . . . ."

Rama said, "Let me just walk on, through this forest. Give me your permission to see who will stop me."

"We see your strength," said the Valakhilyas. "Free this ancient forest, deliver us from the Night-Wanderers."

Rama answered the little saints. "I have strayed from the Dharma of warriors if this has happened while I was near you."

The Valas said, "We hide from Rakshasas of Lanka walk-

143

ing abroad through Dandaka, in form like hideous charred corpses from some cremation ground. They'll rush at you, Rama. They will hit you from behind with unfair weapons."

Lakshmana said, "If they attack us by day or by night we will hunt them down and kill them all."

The Valas said, "Oh Lakshmana and Rama like the Moon, they cannot bear you. More than anyone they will resent you; go on your way and be on your guard." The Valakhilyas clustered in the air. "Oh Rama, we are peaceful. We don't know . . . we think . . . we think war is better than fear, if you will fight it for us . . . ."

Rama and Sita and Lakshmana left the Valakhilyas and went along south for awhile, and Sita said, "We are not forest people. Do not carry war with you; in Ayodhya once again become a warrior. Don't let desire make you do wrong, do not kill demons without cause for war. I have heard that Lord Indra, when he envies the merit won by an ascetic, will take on the guise of a warrior, and go into the forest, and leave his fine sword with the hermit for safekeeping, and go away. So the ascetic will keep by him a sword sharpened only to kill men. Then he will begin to carry it with him when going from home. Then he will one day draw it. He will kill."

Rama said, "I won't start any war."

"How can you tell?" asked Sita. "Discard Agastya's arrows. After all these years we do not need them to hunt our food, and they are meant only for killing demons. Do not carry war with you, or by small degrees your mind will alter."

Rama said, "Princess, war is within us, it's nothing outside. No warrior neglects his weapons. He never gives them up. It is a shame to me that those saints must seek my protection that should be theirs without asking. Sita, while he may a warrior like other men enjoys peace, but misfortune and peril make him flame up in anger and resist."

"How can you tell what is right?" asked Sita. "You are only doing what you like."

Rama said, "Dharma leads to happiness, but happiness cannot lead to Dharma. There is some reason for all this. The

144

Valakhilyas have great power, yet they have done nothing against Ravana. The Demon King must surely have some strong defense that can't be broken by their merit, or they could all by themselves easily destroy all Khara's soldiers and suffer no loss doing it."

"Who are those tiny people?" asked Sita.

"No one remembers when they were born," said Rama. "They float through the air all together, like a cloud formed from streaks of light, and once by just a little of their power they created the King of Birds Garuda."

Sita asked, "How was Garuda born?"

Rama said, "Garuda is the mount of Narayana, and he lives with Narayana in a great heaven far above the realm of Indra and the lesser gods. He carries Lord Narayana on his back and never tires."

Listen—

Kashyapa is like Atri. He is another of the seven sages of old who live in the constellation of the Bear. The first Indra and six of the gods were his children. Their mother Aditi then retreated into the infinite heavens, she is the goddess of the unbounded Universe that goes on and on, free forever.

Kashyapa took two other wives and planned a sacrifice so they would bear him sons. Indra helped him prepare and offered to bring firewood, and the Valakhilya saints said they would do the same.

So Indra was flying in the air carrying great loads of wood. He looked down and saw all the thousands of Valakhilyas walking on the ground and staggering under the weight of one dry leaf, dragging it around the water pooled in a cow's hoofprint. Lord Indra laughed at them and flew by. The little Valas saw his shadow and looked up and said to one another—*He won't help. He wouldn't help us!*

The Valas pulled their leaf aside and crumbled it and lit it afire right where they were, and sang—*Let him come. Let a better Indra come!*

145

Indra could hear them chanting. He fled to Kashyapa and said, "The Valakhilyas will replace me with another King of Heaven. I take your protection."

"No fear," said Kashyapa. Kashyapa found the Valas humming songs over their smoking leaf. He told them, "Success."

They glittered with pleasure—*As you say, as you say.*

Kashyapa said, "Do not make another Indra, but make someone else instead."

Very well Sir. The leaf was all burned. From its ashes the Valakhilyas took two seeds. *For your wives. Sons for you then.*

Kashyapa went home. He told Indra, "Do not mock humble people." He gave a seed to his wife Vinata and a seed to his wife Kadru, and they swallowed them. Then Kashyapa left home and went away to be alone by himself in the hills.

A year later Vinata gave birth to two eggs and Kadru gave birth to a thousand eggs. They put each egg into its own jar of warm butter. They put the jars outside in the sunshine and rain, in the day and night. Time went by. After five hundred years all of Kadru's thousand eggs hatched into baby Nagas, but Vinata's two sons were still in their shells.

Vinata could not bear to wait any longer. She opened one of

her jars and took out the egg inside and cracked its shell. Inside she found her son Aruna, alive but not fully formed. He had no legs and his whole body was tranclucent. Aruna told his mother not to disturb her other son for another five hundred years. Then he flew away up into the sky. He became the charioteer of Surya the Sun. The light of dawn shines right through Aruna's skin and bones, and so the dawn is red, as he first drives the Sun's chariot each morning on its way.

Vinata left her second child alone to hatch. But Kadru thought that she was better than Vinata because she had so many more sons, and they were already born. So Kadru made a bet and cheated to win it. Long ago the Ocean was churned, and changed from milk into saltwater. Many things were created from that churning, and one was the King of Horses named Uchchaih-sravas, an all-white stallion. He belonged to Indra but during those years he could come to graze on the Earth, and Kadru and Vinata often saw him standing on a hill.

Kadru bet Vinata that the horse was not all-white, and each one agreed to become the slave of the other if she lost the bet. Kadru then made her thousand babies change into black hairs and hide in that horse's tail, and Vinata lost her freedom.

Garuda was born from that second egg. He struggled out of his shell and began soaking up the sunshine. He grew into a giant within a few moments of his birth. Garuda was a huge eagle, with golden feathers on his body and brilliant red ones on his wings. He had the head and wings and talons of an eagle, but he also had the arms and hands of a man, and his torso was a man's though covered with gold feathers.

Garuda looked around with his round yellow eyes. He saw that his mother Vinata did all the drudgery and housework and wore ragged sleeves and got only leftover snake food to eat, while Kadru lolled around in ease and idleness.

Garuda asked his mother why she was poor, and when he heard about the bet he went to Kadru and offered to ransom Vinata at any price.

The thousand Nagas were long since grown up. They all took counsel together, then Kadru said, "There is in Indra's

147

Heaven a cup of amrita, the nectar of immortality, churned from the milk sea long long ago. Bring it to us and we free your mother."

The wondrous fair-feathered Garuda opened his wings. They spread over the sky like a wind. Garuda flew to the hills for advice from his father Kashyapa.

Kashyapa was happy to see his son. He said, "My boy, eat a little something before you try to fly to heaven and steal amrita from Indra. But never eat a man. Remember that."

"Yes, Father."

Kashyapa continued, "There's a big lake behind this hill. There live two big animals always fighting one another—a tortoise whose shell is ten leagues around, and an elephant who stands six leagues tall. They are two men reborn. They are two brothers drawing out in lowly animal forms their senseless quarrel over an inheritance that began when they were men."

"What did they inherit?" asked Garuda.

"Money I think. Go eat them, son."

"Father, what's money?"

"Money . . . ." Kashyapa smiled at his son. "Money is . . . it's . . . it's really nothing."

"Yes, Father. Father, what's a league?"

"A day's travel with one yoking of animals. Remember now, never eat a man. Man is Master of all animals. If you swallow one he'll turn into fire or poison or a razor. Go now with my blessing, and seek your fortune."

Garuda blinked his eyes. "Goodbye." He flew up, then dove down at that lake. The animals were fighting as usual. The elephant was trying to pull the turtle onshore and the turtle was trying to drag the elephant underwater and drown him. They had been trying to do that same thing for ages, annoying all the hills with their yells and wails.

Garuda caught one beast in each claw and flew up high with them, looking for somewhere to alight to eat them. By the western seashore he saw a very old banyan tree, one of whose

148

limbs went way out over the water. That limb was so stout it would take ten thousand ox hides tied end to end to go round it, and it went out over the ocean for one hundred leagues.

The old tree looked up and called out to Garuda, "Sit on my great magnificent branch."

Garuda landed there, but his weight broke the branch. It cracked off right near the trunk and started to fall into the sea. As it fell Garuda saw the Valakhilya saints hanging from it upside down all clustered together. He didn't know what to do, but he thought they might be men and he ought to save them, so he caught the falling limb in his beak and flew up again still holding the two squirming animals as well.

Kashyapa had kept his eye on his son's first adventure. Now he approached Garuda in the air and yelled in his ear, "Fly easy, don't vibrate." He dropped down and talked to the Valas. "Victory to light. Forgive my son, he didn't see you."

Oh yes Sir, we know him, we know Garuda. The Valakhilyas left their perch and flew off someplace. Kashyapa showed Garuda a barren hill where he could drop the branch. The great high forest trees bent and waved and swayed like a field of wheat from the downwind of Garuda's wings. He dropped the branch with a universal crash, and then he sat on the hill summit and ate his breakfast, and his strength was doubled.

Garuda flew up toward heaven, slowly flapping his wings. In heaven, Indra's yellow marble throne got too hot to sit on. His thunders sizzled and rattled, his arrows attacked each other, and a dry wind arose full of dust and grit.

Indra and Agni the Fire God went to heaven's gate and looked out. Indra asked, "What's that golden gleaming fire down there? Are you trying to burn us all?"

"That's no fire of mine," said Agni. "That is Garuda, King of the Birds, created by those little Valas you made fun of."

"Some unearthly *bird*?" smiled Indra. "Oh, that's hard to believe . . . go see what he wants, will you?"

Garuda was floating like a hawk, on the wings of the wind from beyond, wondering where to go. Agni put on a cape of fire and a hood of flames to keep himself cool as he approached Garuda. Below were the Sun and Moon and all the heavens were above.

Agni sang a song to Garuda—*You are the elements of form, you are the light of life; Garuda moving in the sky, we take your protection.* He said, "Garuda; you are making the ether boil and warping the precise circles of the Universe. Diminish your energy and speak to me."

"Before I do that," said Garuda, "I need some amrita."

"Wait, just a moment." Agni went back to Indra. "Give him a little Nectar of Life."

"Never," said Indra.

"He'll take it then," said Agni. "He's too hot for you."

"What! Let me see!" Indra looked down again. "He doesn't look so great. Summon all my fighters!"

The amrita was kept inside Indra's palace. Indra set rows of heavenly guards around the building. They stood fearless in their golden breastplates that shone like suns. The spears they held started to smoke and their axes shed sparks.

Garuda came flying up over heaven's horizon. His wings blew up too much dust from the ground of heaven for the guards to see anything, and the winds he made sucked the air out of their lungs and they fainted. Behind the guards Garuda found fires fed by hurricanes. Garuda changed his form and grew eighty-one hundred mouths. He fled back to Earth and drank up eighty-one hundred rivers, and came back to Heaven and quenched all the fires.

Then Garuda took a tiny form, with just one head as before. He went inside Indra's house, and broke through a fine-mesh net of steel links. Behind that was a block of adamant and a round passage bored through it leading to the amrita. A fan of sword blades whirled in the passage with no room to go around it, but Garuda went right through the fan too quick for it to cut him at all.

At the end of the passage was a room with the cup of amrita in it, and by the cup were two angry serpents to guard it. Those snakes had poisonous breath, the glance of their eyes

150

would turn you to stone, and their tongues were electric pieces of lightning slickering in and out.

But Garuda was going too fast to be seen. He brushed between them like a ghost and took the cup of amrita and was going back out the passage before the serpents knew he had even come in. Going out he hit the sword-fan dead center and smashed it. He flew outside, grew large again, and took away the only cup of amrita in all the worlds held in one claw.

Garuda hurried along back to the Earth, not drinking a drop of amrita himself. Narayana met him as he went, and speeding on fast as Time they talked together as though they stood still on solid ground.

Narayana the One Lord said, "I make you immortal and forever healthy without taking any of that drink. I'll put you above me, on my flag on my chariot."

Garuda answered, "Lord, I will carry you on my back when you want to ride me, wherever you wish to go."

"Excellent, I make you King of all the birds of all the worlds for all Time." Vishnu left him then.

Near Earth Indra was hiding. He threw a thunderbolt and hit Garuda's breast. With that strike, all knowledge came to Garuda. He knew everything that ever had been or was or will ever be, knew it all in an instant.

Sita, listen. Indra's thunders are made from the bones of the giant Dadhicha. Dadhicha was an ancient warrior, the strongest person who ever lived, tall as a mountain. All men were that size in the days when Dadhicha was born.

Dadhicha went apart once from the others, and sitting like a sage he fell into a trance in the hills, and there as though asleep he outlived his time. His body grew weathered and had the look of stone. He never moved and seemed himself to be another mountain.

Then after Dadhicha had been that way for countless years, the Asuras made war against Indra. They were winning. Indra went to the hills and kicked the ground on a hillside in anger. But Indra was not standing on a hill, he was standing on Dadhicha.

151

. . . before the serpents knew he had even come in.

The giant opened his eyes and looked out over the fields of Earth, and saw the men and animals there. Dadhicha asked Indra—*How have men grown so small? Where is my King?*

That was a voice from the beginning of the world. Indra knew nothing, he had never known such men, or such a King. He said, "I don't know."

Dadhicha asked, "Who are you?"

"I am Indra. I rule heaven. Nowhere in any world have I seen a man large as you, nor heard of any."

"My King has died to you," said Dadhicha. "I am Dadhicha. My people have gone over, they have left and I shall follow behind. Why have you come to me, Indra?"

"I thought you were a hill."

Dadhicha laughed. "The worse for you then!" Indra smiled back. "I have overslept," continued Dadhicha. "I should have died long ago. I miss my King. So farewell, but since you have come to me, even by mistake, do not go without some gift, or you will anger me. What do you need?"

"A miracle," said Indra. "I am at war."

"And losing," said Dadhicha. "When I die, take my bones, they will be ready at once, for I will call down the ages past to me. My servant Time will age me to your eyes and you may fashion my bones into bolts of thunder . . . ."

Dadhicha began to age, and Indra watched amazed from the air. The giant called out—*I'm coming, here I am! Oh, for the Blessed Land . . . .*

Then there was nothing left of Dadhicha but his bones. Indra summoned Viswakarman, and the heavenly architect made thunderbolts out of the bones, shaping one bone with another, for they were the hardest things he'd ever met. Indra won his war and brought his rain down.

Now from respect for days gone past, when that unbearable thunderbolt hit him Garuda dropped one feather. The golden feather turned over in the air, the size of a war-shield. Garuda looked to see who had hit him.

Indra put down his thunders and came from hiding. "Let us be friends," said the Lord of the Gods. "Surely you can do anything . . . but if you won't drink that amrita why not return it to me?"

Garuda told Indra why he needed the amrita and said, "My bargain is to bring the amrita but I didn't promise anyone a drink of it." He went on down to Earth and Indra followed him invisibly.

At home once more, Garuda said to Kadru, "Here it is." The thousand Nagas all came up and crowded around. "Now free my mother forever."

"She's free, she's free!" The Nagas brought a grass mat. Garuda put the Cup of Life down on it. He gave the Nagas a strange look.

"What's wrong, what's wrong?" they asked him.

"It's just . . . oh, it's nothing I suppose," answered Garuda.

"What, what?"

"Well," said Garuda, "I wouldn't drink this down like a bowl of soup without washing first. After all, this is a treasure."

"Right! Quite right!" Then the Nagas and Kadru went to wash before tasting immortality. Instantly Indra took back the cup, and when the snakes returned the grass mat was bare. Still, they licked the sharp-edged grass hoping that some amrita had spilled over, and ever since then Nagas have had slit tongues.

"And the touch of the cup holding amrita also gave its power to our sacred grass that was used for the mat," said Rama. "And this story is true."

Sita smiled. "But—" Suddenly before she could say any more a long hairy red arm reached out from the trees to one side, grabbed her round her waist, and withdrew holding her fast.

Rama and Lakshmana ran after her. The arm that held her was so long, that they couldn't see where it came from, and as they ran it just kept pulling Sita away before them. Rama and

154

Lakshmana followed on and on through a thick stand of dark spiny trees laced with dead vines.

Then they came out of the trees and saw a red Rakshasa standing holding Sita. He was very tall and held her at his waist. His body was covered with up-pointing bristly red hair. He had ears like javelins and hollow green eyes. His mouth went from ear to ear. He began to howl. In his other hand he held an iron spit that had impaled on it three dead lions, four deer and the bloody head of an elephant that stared at Rama and Lakshmana with dead eyes wide open.

"Scum!" said the Rakshasa. He stretched out his arm again and put Sita up in a tree. "I am Viradha! No weapon can kill me! You travel here with a common wife, you dirty men, I'll drink your blood! Then I marry the girl!" He advanced.

Lakshmana shot Viradha full of arrows. They were sticking out all over him. But Viradha yawned and all the arrows fell off him. He snorted and caught Rama in one arm and Lakshmana in the other and walked away with them. Soon they were out of sight of Sita.

Then Rama broke the arm holding him, and Lakshmana broke the other, and they beat Viradha down to the ground with blows. Viradha roared and yowled until Rama held him down and quiet by his foot on the demon's throat. Lakshmana dug a deep hole, and they threw Viradha in it and buried him under rocks and stones and killed him.

A Gandharva of heaven arose out of that burial mound, a handsome drummer dressed in silks and silver. He said, "Oh Rama, I am Tumburu the musician, Lord." Tumburu smiled. "The Treasure Lord Vaishravana cursed me. I was gone from my post with an Apsarasa, and so love put me into a demon's body, and violence freed me."

Music was in the air. A darkly beautiful dancing girl came out of somewhere in the sky, and floating above Tumburu, and let fall from her hands a long drum with a head at each end. She looked at Rama and gave him a happy smile. Tumburu took the drum, slung it round his neck by a strap and let

155

his fingers run on it. Chitraratha the Gandharva King became visible in the sky, sitting holding a lute with lots of strings, playing dreamy tunes, and Tumburu stopped drumming.

The Gandharva said, "I was doomed to a demon's life till you should kill me, Rama, and then bury me the way the forest Rakshasas bury their corpses . . . I have reached out my arms for every moving thing in Dandaka, hoping to find you. Remember, any violent death in this Dandaka forest leads to heaven . . . ."

Chitraratha changed his music, it was time for the drums and Tumburu tossed his head and flew up to join his King and his girl, and they went higher and higher until they were gone.

Rama and Lakshmana went back and helped Sita down out of her tree. Rama said, "He wanted to die, and so he told us our weapons were useless."

⚜

Rama and Sita and Lakshmana kept going south through Dandaka Forest and reached the Godavari River. Lakshmana built them another house, near the river in a place called Panchavati where five whispering trees banked the stream, not far from a hillside cave.

One morning soon after they arrived they were all sitting out in the open by the house. Rama was telling some story to Sita and Lakshmana, when out from the forest surrounding them came the Rakshasi Surpanakha. She was Ravana's sister.

She saw Rama and desired him. Surpanakha was misshapen and mean. Her yellowy skin was rutted like a bad road. She had a pot belly and ears like flat baskets, claws on her fingers and toes, squinty eyes and messy hair.

She was gnawing a raw bone but she threw it away and leered at Rama. She pointed at Sita and said, "My dear, why keep that skinny girl?"

Rama stood up and said, "I am Rama."

"And I am Surpanakha! I have chosen you for my husband."

Lakshmana said, "A great gain."

Surpanakha said, "I'll take you to the broad city of Lanka by magic, dear Rama. My brother's wealth will let us live like a King and Queen."

Rama smiled at her. "You see—I am already married. To a proud woman like yourself, a co-wife is misery. Don't think more about it."

Surpanakha looked at Lakshmana. Lakshmana quickly said, "Don't take second best."

"Why make shy excuses?" Surpanakha cracked her knuckles. "It's natural to marry."

"Bless you, maiden," said Lakshmana, "but leave us alone. May all creatures be happy. A good wife is hard to find, may you soon be wed."

Rama said, "My brother Lakshmana is also married."

Surpanakha cried, "I see the trouble!" She rushed at Sita, and held out before her her claws curved like elephant hooks. But Lakshmana caught her. He took the gold-handled knife. from his belt, and swiftly cut off Surpanakha's ears and threw her down. "Were you not a woman you'd be dead!"

Surpanakha ran away bleeding and fled to the Rakshasa garrison commanded by General Khara. She flung up her arms and fell at Khara's feet like a stone falling from the blue sky.

Khara caught his breath in boundless wrath. In a voice deep and low as thunderclouds he said, "Arise!" The Earth trembled as he spoke. Landslides fell down from the hills around the Rakshasa camp.

"I've been attacked!"

"Don't roll on the ground! Who did it?"

"Two men and a woman. As if I had no protection!"

"Sound the alarm!" A Rakshasa soldier smashed a big hanging brass plate with a metal mace and kept on smashing it for a hundred and eight times. Khara yelled at Surpanakha, "Where are they?"

She yelled back, "Panchavati!"

The alarm stopped and the Rakshasa garrison assembled, fourteen thousand strong. Khara stood before them and said,

157

"Like Death, let us kill the three humans at Panchavati and please this lady!"

In Panchavati, Rama's Ayodhya arrows started to smoke. His new bow hummed. Rama strung it and said, "Lakshmana, we have sharply angered them! For a moment hide with Sita in that cave, and cover the mouth with trees."

Rama stood alone, glancing up into the sky, in the direction Surpanakha had gone. His green hand drew back his bow. His lips shook with anger and his eyes were red with blood.

❧

The Rakshasas came, flying low just above the trees and led by Khara. When they saw just one man facing them they hesitated. Rama called out. "Stop! If you value your lives!"

Khara replied, "Surrender yourself then."

Rama said, "I live here quietly. Why seek to injure me?"

"You are destroyed!" answered the demons. Rama spoke a mantra and he took three steps backwards to get his aim. Khara looked around, saw no one else but Rama, and waved his arm. The Invincible Legion of Dandaka attacked.

❧

Rama killed them all, fourteen thousand Rakshasa warriors and General Khara. He used what he needed of the mantras and weapons Viswamitra had taught him. Rama's golden arrows swept the sky like yellow lightnings. There was no escape.

Surpanakha was watching at a safe distance. She dove into the Earth and flew by Rakshasa power through the solid stone, right under the southern ocean. She surfaced in Lanka just outside Ravana's palace and ran inside to her brother.

Ravana was on his throne holding court. Surpanakha came in wailing—*Rama! Rama! Rama!*

She ran up the stairs to the throne and grabbed Ravana's legs in a grip like an iron vise. Her ears were gone. The court of the Demon King fell silent from shock and Ravana rose and cried—*Who dares?*

158

Surpanakha said, "Khara is dead."

"What?" cried Ravana.

"And all his soldiers."

Ravana beckoned with his ten left hands and Rakshasa physicians hurried forward. They snapped their fingers and restored Surpanakha's ears and gave her something to drink, and let her see herself in an unbreakable mirror. Ravana had her sit down and came down from the throne to sit beside her and said, "Now tell me."

"I am the only one still alive," said Surpanakha. "Like Hell itself, Dandaka is bathed in blood. In half a moment Rama killed Khara and his legion with whistling screaming arrows of dazzling gold, and the harmless men that we have killed for food in the woods watched from heaven as your army died. The kindly saints and hermits now may mock you and walk safely through dreadful Dandaka."

Ravana cleared his ten throats. All his eyes were looking all around. They danced in his heads like fiery coals. "Who did it?"

"Rama!"

"Who is Rama?"

"A prince."

A *man?* Ravana looked closely at his sister. "How many millions were in his army?"

"He had no army."

"What gods helped him?"

"No gods. Rama fought alone, and I take your protection for bringing bad news."

"Bad news? Why . . . a man? He's drunk poison. He's poked his finger in a black snake's eye! He is pulling lions' teeth inside a burning house!"

"The Wanderers of the Wood are dead and broken on the Earth," said Surpanakha. "Rama looks like a hermit, but it is only to destroy you that he has come."

"Me?" Ravana looked tenderly into his sister's face. "If they did me wrong, I would kill that tyrant Death, I would burn Fire and smother the Wind. Have no fear."

159

Surpanakha said, "Brother, you're a disgrace. You're all muscle and brawn, you rule by brute force and ignorance! Here you are lost in pleasure, idle and greedy and useless. You're not going to do anything, are you?"

"Enough!" roared Ravana. "By all the demons, Surpanakha, the Earth is wide and who cares what mere men do on every bit of her? Dandaka is a worse wasteland than the back of the Moon. There's nothing worth having there anyway."

"You don't know Rama," said Surpanakha, "but you are merciful. You will let the best bowman in the world live on your land with his brother and his fair wife Sita."

"Sita?"

"Whomever she warmly embraces will outgain the gods in happiness. It was Rama's brother who cut off my ears, but when Khara tried to avenge me only Rama fought us. The three of them can't do much harm there. At this very moment Sita must be holding Rama lovingly, and healing his wound by her caress."

"Then he was wounded!" said Ravana.

"He hurt his heel as he backed away barefoot."

"Then he retreated!"

"He was aiming, to shoot down your army."

"Go on, tell me about her."

"She is more beautiful than any of your wives, but all she thinks of is Rama."

"Indeed?"

"Her skin is gold; her eyes are dark. Her fingernails are round and red, her breasts are full, and her waist is slender as an ant's."

Ravana said, "Sita."

The Demon King dismissed his court and retired alone to his rooms. Surpanakha left Lanka and went to the Asura underworlds beneath the sea, and there she married.

Early the next morning Ravana went alone to his stables, armed with a bow and arrows and a sharp sword. He got in a small gold chariot that was pulled by asses with the faces of fiends. The chariot rose into the air and Ravana flew north,

160

across the vast ocean and then across our continent to Go-
karna. There in a hermitage lived his uncle Maricha, whom
Rama had shot as a boy but had not killed. Ravana's twenty
hands rested on the chariot rail. From the center of the rail
hung ten ornamental golden arrows tied together with golden
string. They were Ravana's only sign of Empire and Conquest:
ten arrows for the ten directions; South and the other three,
and the four in between those four, and up and down, all was
Ravana's.

the Golden deer

Sita of great beauty,
You are a woman.
To a woman everything is becoming,
Every one is her own,
May I be yours.

Maricha the Rakshasa sat alone in a clearing, clad in black deerskin. Ravana's chariot came soaring down and landed, and the Demon King walked over to his uncle. Ravana sat beside Maricha and said, "How good to see you, my old friend."

"Why are you here?" asked Maricha.

Ravana said, "The Dandaka demons have all been killed by—"

"*Stop!*" Maricha looked around. "Ravana, if you wish me to live, do not speak that name in my hearing! Fear of him has made me a hermit."

"Then you know about it," said Ravana.

"I saw Khara's legion die by magic sight."

"Magic," said Ravana. "That's what I want to talk to you about."

"*Ow!*" Maricha rubbed his knee and looked painfully at Ravana.

"What's wrong?" asked Ravana.

"Go away! Don't bother me. This talk pains me."

"You're making that up, Uncle!"

"He did not at first strike to kill me," said Maricha. "And now forever will I see him, wherever I look, dressed like the trees in bark, watching me where he cannot be."

"I won't let him get away with it," said Ravana. "His dear loving Sita is in the very bloom of her passionate youth!"

Maricha looked at Ravana as though he saw him already dead. "Innocent Sita? I have abandoned war, Ravana." Maricha sighed. "Happily, here I see so few fools any more. What enemy disguised as your friend mentioned Sita's name to you?"

"Surpanakha. They attacked her unprovoked."

"No," said Maricha. "Her heart envies you your fortune. She will ruin you by your own hand. She has spoken the one word of your doom, and there may be some use for dust from the trodden roadside, but useless is a fallen King."

"I will steal Sita by deception and he will die of shame!"

Maricha's eyes did not blink and his dry mouth hung open. "Give this idea away. Let the Sun and Moon stand in fear of you but let Sita be! Your army went down like a grainfield under a hailstorm. You will be nothing against him!"

Ravana said, "That was an accident."

"The whole world may well be an accident," said Maricha. "Forget it, let it go. His name is danger to me and to you as well. As a clever man hits on a secret and solves it, so did he eliminate your army. He hit them and they do not exist! And his brother Lakshmana is just as strong; he is his own second self."

"No matter," said Ravana.

"You have everything to lose and absolutely nothing to gain."

"You've got that backwards," smiled Ravana.

Maricha said, "This is the severing of the summit of the Rakshasa race. It is for your death that the forest hermits have so long poured butter on their fires. For your death and not Khara's did they direct that man to Dandaka. Wherever your soldiers looked they saw him before them, and for all their wrath and rage he easily killed them all. He can bring down the stars with his arrows, or break apart the continents and let in the sea, or raise Earth once drowned and create all Creation anew."

163

Ravana said, "He meekly submitted to an exile in the woods when his father banished him."

"Many quiet men are strong," said Maricha. "Just pray to your favorite gods that he never notices you."

"He has been disgraced once," said Ravana, "and is now a delicate failure, a false hermit with a holy hairdo yet scheming and desiring and bearing arms and tied to a woman, a laughable weakling. May such a life befall all my enemies."

"Do not scorn men!" Maricha shuddered. "Ravana, rare and unpleasant is the truth to an idiot King, but this greed will draw you swiftly to your doom. Ravana, be peaceful and content yourself with the wives you have. They love you, go home to them. Think of our people. Do not destroy them by the whims and envies, the vanities and glories of their King. You see things wrong. You imagine that man as someone small and weak. You think of Sita as harmless and inviting, a delightful woman whom you may play with safely and come to no harm."

"Uncle, do not always measure things and count them."

"Ravana, listen. Once I flew where I wanted over the Earth. I was swift and roaring, cold and heartless and huge as a hill. I wore a golden crown and was strong as a thousand elephants. Viswamitra kept trying to make a sacrifice, and his hymns were faint and scratchy, and I would let no god answer him. I bullied everybody and no one could stop me. Then Viswamitra brought that man, but he was still a boy. He had no sign of manhood on his face and he wore his hair as a child, but he protected the sacrifice. He was the soul of all the worlds, but I passed him by and went for the altar . . . ."

"Maybe so, maybe not."

"You are still thirsty for poison. Try doing right and people will be your friends; many of us care for you. Or else you will delight all your victims by destroying yourself."

Ravana said, "Cheer up. Pull yourself together. I've done all right so far, haven't I?"

Maricha said, "If it is not your Time, again and again snares

164

of all kinds may be set for you in vain, but when your death's moment comes you will not see the trap that catches you until too late. You won't listen to me, but I am your friend. However strong and great you once were, you are a straw figure now, falling into poverty."

Ravana smiled. "I don't listen to criticisms any more, just tell me the good parts. Come, delay defeats any deed. Change yourself into a golden deer and help me." He embraced Maricha and went on, "Let us plan this kidnapping with more delight. Let us be generous to each other; let us help each other through this life, happy and carefree as Kings." Ravana waved one of his hands over the ground and a jug appeared with two coconut halfshells. "Now, a taste of wine?"

"Well, I don't know."

"You lure him away, out of earshot, then escape." They drank. "Separate Rama and Sita, that's all I ask. I'll do the rest. I can handle Lakshmana. When he discovers what has happened, Rama will die of heartbreak."

"Rama. Rama!" Maricha rolled his tongue around his lips. "I can say it!" Ravana refilled their winecups.

The Demon King took a sip of wine with each head, one after another, and wiped his moustaches. "Kings must be adored!" he said loudly.

"Soft welcome words!" cried Maricha. "Just say how much you like the idea . . . whenever possible. Look for faults and you'll find them!"

"Precisely! I will give you half my kingdom. Half my World Empire."

"No." Maricha put down his cup. "It is Death that's paid me a visit today. Keep your kingdom if you've got one."

Ravana yelled at him. "Then I'll kill you!"

"You?"

"Yes, don't you fear Death?"

"What for? Why should I?"

"But—"

"But still, Ravana, it is better to be killed by the better

165

person. I won't escape him but I will lead him away and let him kill me." Maricha stood up. "I will go if you will promise not to brag to me along the way."

"Of course, anything you say." Ravana started to get up.

"Just one moment," said Maricha. He sadly tidied up his few old possessions and quickly performed his own funeral.

Then they were on Ravana's chariot, going through the sky to Panchavati. Maricha drew in the fresh air in deep breaths and stretched his arms and legs.

"There's always just a chance," said Maricha.

Ravana said, "That man isn't worth a finger-flick."

Ravana landed the chariot some distance from Rama's house. Ravana crept up close to the house, leading Maricha by the hand. Ravana said, "There they are."

Maricha became a deer. His face was of living blue sapphire like a moving mask made of a blue mirror. His antlers were ivory tipped with moonstone points and his hooves were glassy black flint. His lighted eyes were violet amethyst. His golden hair grew this way and that, and there were silver spots on his sides, and when he danced like a deer the golden hair ran the light in rays over his body. His underbelly was pale pink and his tongue bright red. He held his tail straight up and arched his neck a little and ran off.

The other deer scented a Rakshasa and fled from Maricha as he approached Rama's house. The tigers drew back and did not dare to roar. Maricha ate grass in a green meadow by the Godavari river, then ran past Rama's house, then stopped and turned, and lay down nibbling leaves.

Rama and Sita and Lakshmana were all at home, and Sita saw the deer. She called, "Rama, come quickly. Can you catch him?"

Rama said, "How beautiful."

Lakshmana came up and said, "There is no such deer on Earth. That is an illusion."

166

Rama strung his bow and took one arrow. "Wait here with Sita. I'll try to get him alive, or else I'll shoot him."

Lakshmana said, "See how his shape seems to shift and change around the edges."

"I'll be careful," said Rama. "If that is a Rakshasa illusion I will destroy it."

Maricha got up. He started to walk right for Rama. Then he noticed a man there. He backed and jumped and walked away into the trees just out of bowshot. He stopped and turned and gazed at Rama with his ears out.

Then Maricha went away running and jumping, taking long leaps with his forefeet drawn up to his chest and his back legs straight out. Rama went after him. Maricha didn't seem to see

Rama pursuing him and so Rama didn't shoot him for a long time, hoping to follow the deer home and capture him alive later. But though Maricha now and then seemed to tire, or sometimes lose his way, he tempted Rama farther and farther from home, and Rama began to lose sight of him.

The golden deer reappeared and Rama saw him through the stark trees of Dandaka, and decided to kill him. Rama shot a gold arrow and hit the lovely deer through his heart. Maricha leapt up high as a palm tree, then fell on his back, and at the point of death resumed his true form.

A black demon lay there dying. Rama ran up holding his diamond and rainbow bow. With his last breath Maricha shouted in Rama's voice—*Help me!* He threw back his head and died.

Maricha's cry was much louder than any man could shout. Rama knew they would hear it at Panchavati, and could not hear him from where he stood. Every hair on Rama's body was on end. He made sure Maricha was dead and ran for home as fast as he could.

～

Sita heard Rama's voice cry help and said, "Lakshmana, he is hurt!"

"That is not truly his voice," said Lakshmana.

"How much has Bharata paid you to betray us?"

"He is not in danger," said Lakshmana. "He told me to wait and stay with you. That deer was a demon, don't you understand?"

Sita wept. "Would you let him die? Oh, you don't care, you don't care!" She looked wildly around then started to go after Rama herself. Lakshmana held her back. She pleaded, "Let me go . . . Rama . . . ."

Lakshmana held her and looked her right in the eye. He sighed and frowned. She was breathing fast, she said, "Then is it me you want? Take me but save Rama!"

Lakshmana covered his ears. Real anger was on his face. He saw red. Red Sita, red trees, red sky. "First you have sent

Rama away to fetch you an illusion," he said. "And now you order me to obey a false voice. Do not move!"

Lakshmana looked out into the forest. He said, "Wrong words are nothing new for a woman." He drew a circle around Sita on the ground, with the tip of his bow.

"Do not step out of this circle and do not cross this line," said Lakshmana. "Let these trees witness that I have done right!"

Sita was paying no attention. Lakshmana thrust out his lower lip in anger. He took his quiver and entered the edge of the forest, bent low a bit, went under a branch and was out of sight.

The Rakshasa King Ravana watched him go. Then Ravana came boldly across the clearing toward Rama's house covered with the disguise of an old holy man, like a treacherous deep well covered and hidden by tall grass. Sita saw him coming and dried her eyes.

Ravana looked like a man. He wore soft red silk. There was one lock of white hair left long on his shaven head. He held a parasol and wore sandals, and he carried resting over his left shoulder a long triple bamboo staff with a waterjar slung on it. Ravana came and stood silently by Sita's house, as holy men do when begging their daily food. There was no sign of Lakshmana or Rama. All around them there was only the forest land of green and brown.

Sita's stepped over Lakshmana's line and said, "Worshipful brahmana, be our guest. Sit, take some water, wash and I will bring food."

Ravana hummed—*I walk the sweet Earth, Lord; I see you have made beautiful creatures, Lord; how fine and true, Oh Lord of Love.*

He spoke very fair. "How do you come to live here alone, my girl, in perilous Dandaka land?" He stood looking at her. "By the Book, fair are your jewels."

"I am Sita. These jewels were presents. Don't fear demons, for my husband Rama will be back soon."

"Ah," said Ravana, "his name can't be Rama, he must be Kama! You are Rati the wife of Love, wantonly hiding in the forest." He smiled like a father. "Oh, you timid girl, of slender waist and tapering thighs! You've had a lovers' quarrel with Kama. You belong in a palace. I can see you like jewels and luxury!"

"Brahmana, sit down and what can I give you? I am Sita, a mortal woman and my husband is the Ayodhya King. These jewels were gifts from Anasuya and this necklace came from Guha. Tell me your name and family."

"Beautiful," said Ravana. "I am the Rakshasa King Ravana. I rule the universe. Come to me, Sita. I will take you to Lanka with her engines and weapons, and I will put you over all my other Queens."

Sita laughed. "Garuda mating with a goose? A firefly courting the Sun?"

"Seek me! Cross the ocean with me!"

"A gnat trying to suck up a bowl of butter! Can you swim?"

"Don't play around with *me*!"

"I won't, don't worry," said Sita.

"You will have five thousand serving maids."

"Never." Sita looked again at the quiet forest and could see no one.

Woman, I am Ravana feared by the Gods! Ravana clapped his hands and his disguise fell away. He was tall as a tree. He had ten dark faces and twenty dark arms, and twenty red eyes red-rimmed like fire. He had yellow up-pointing fangs. He licked his lips with sharp tongues. He wore golden armor, long heavy gold earrings swaying, gold bracelets, gold armbands, ten golden crowns set with golden pearls, gold belt-chains crashing and gold rings all over his fingers. Fragrant white flower-garlands went over his shoulders and around his ten necks.

Ravana had a long ivory bow hanging down along one shoulder, its back rich with pearls, and by his hip he had a supple sword, of blue steel in a blue case. And on his back he had a long quiver formed of human skins stretched over a frame of men's bones, and the outside of that quiver was painted with demon faces drawn in blood, and those spectral

170

faces moved of themselves; they were grim or laughing at will, changing as though alive, following with their eyes. The quiver held fifty tall blue-black arrows of solid iron, vaned with thin iron blades.

Ravana shook his heads and rattled his crowns and looked down at Sita. Seeing that evil one revealed, the leaves did not flutter. The trees of Dandaka did not move. No breath of wind dared stir about in the woods. The fast-streaming Godavari river slackened her speed from fright. The glorious Sun, who every day looks down upon our world, this time dimmed his light from the sadness of what he saw.

"I will have you!" said Ravana. "Princess Sita, you are half divine, why mingle more with men? Rule every world with me. Sita, I stand in space and I pick up Earth in my hand. I close the Moon within my fingers and put the Sun in my pocket, and arrest the aimless planets. You will forget Rama with me!"

Ravana bent down, a black mountain come to life. Sita knelt near his feet hiding her face, clinging to a tree. Sita wore a clear yellow robe and Anasuya's ornaments and Guha's necklace. Her skin was golden, she was like sunlight in among the trees, and Ravana reached for her. In one left hand he held her long dark hair. He caught her legs in two of his right arms and lifted her, and his demon chariot came to meet him through the air.

Oh Rama,
After the theft of Sita who can escape Death from you?
That damned Demon might walk and breathe
But be dead.
He might win immortality, drink dry the Cup of Life in heaven, win
every god's blessing
And be dead.

❧

Sita cried—*Rama! Rama!* many times and struggled to get free but it was useless. Ravana was on the chariot, holding

"I am too old and tired to talk anymore"

Sita like a fireball in his bare arms, and the chariot began to move south.

In her mind Sita called the river Godavari, called the trees of Dandaka and saluted their tree-gods, took her refuge with the deer—*Tell Rama. Tell him.*

Then Sita saw a great huge vulture asleep high in a treetop and cried aloud to him—*Tell Rama!*

The vulture awoke. He raised his neck and looked hard after Ravana's passing chariot with round green eyes. His breast was yellow and back and wings were grey. Swiftly he spread his wings and went gliding in the air.

Instantly he overtook the demon car and stayed above it balancing on his still, open wings, with their tip feathers spread like fingers. He softly spoke to Ravana, "Brother Ten-Necks, I am Jatayu the Vulture King. I rule the birds of Dandaka. While he lived I was Dasaratha's old friend, we were born on the same day. Fear to do evil in my sight, Ravana, for I know the right ways of life."

"Go back to sleep!" said Ravana.

"I am King of the Air," said Jatayu. "Do not harm Sita. Free her or die, for not in safety will you carry her from my land, as if she had no husband. Demon King, I am sixty thousand years old, in my age peacefully ruling here and I forbid you." Ravana kept on going.

Jatayu said, "I am too old and tired to talk any more!" He hooked a talon through Ravana's chariot rail, a claw as long and curved as an elephant's tusk, and sharp, and hard as an iron gate-bar. Jatayu easily tore the rail away and on the wind of his wings he gently lifted Sita out of Ravana's hands and set her down unharmed beneath a tree.

Ravana cried out in shock and rage. He shouted, "I care nothing for you!" He turned the chariot to attack and flew at the Vulture King, holding his ivory bow and aiming an arrow.

Jatayu snapped that bow with one bite. He clawed the armor from Ravana's back, and with his beak tore out the hair from the Demon King's heads. With his wings he struck Ravana down and sent him falling. In blind fury Jatayu ripped the asses that drew the chariot to shreds, he shattered the car with one wing stroke and the golden chariot wheels spun through the sky like two suns, the iron axle smashed down on end into the forest, and everywhere fell bits of gold and crushed wood, and a rain of torn flesh.

The old war king Jatayu screeched in triumph. Ravana lay on the Earth faint and bewildered, streaming blood and only armed with the sword still at his waist. But Jatayu was exhausted. His vision faded and blurred and he could not see. From above he looked for the Demon King. Ravana saw his blindness and rose to attack.

Jatayu struck him by sound. Jatayu hooked his talons again into Ravana's back, and hung on, and with his mouth wrenched off Ravana's ten left arms one by one and let them fall. All Ravana's faces trembled in pain. His bones shook in agony, but those ten arms grew right back, and Jatayu could not see them but thought they were destroyed for good.

Ravana drew his sword with one left hand, and he cut off Jatayu's wings with it. The Vulture King fell dying, and Sita ran to him where he lay and held his head and wept over him.

Ravana roughly tore her away with bloody hands. He flew south with her, very fast, as though driven through the sky before an evil wind. Ravana was dark and Sita was golden. As Ravana went past he seemed a dark violet cloud holding lightning, smoke hiding a fire, a dark hill catching a sunbeam.

The loss of Sita outraged the worlds. Ravana flew over the Earth. He passed over hills and the hills saw him: they recited charms aloud with the sounds of their falling waters: they uplifted their waving arms of green trees: in anger they yawned, opening their valleys to the sky. Lakes looked up and whirled their waters: white open lilies were their fearful eyes, and watery foam and mists their robes thrown off in grief. The waterfalls wept.

Ravana's shadow raced over the ground, and where it passed lions and tigers ran after it, and clawed at the shadow to kill it. Ravana held Sita round her waist by one arm, and he ran flying, and fled for home. That was all he thought of then,

174

to win home to Lanka. Ravana carried Sita south across a dark river and looking down she saw two monkeys standing on a hill by a lake watching them, shading their eyes, one gold monkey and one white one.

Sita reached down her hands and broke the anklets off from her legs and let them fall down on that plain-looking hill. She took off her earrings and dropped them. Sita let all the ornaments of Anasuya fall, and she tied Guha's necklace in her yellow scarf edged with gold and dropped it also. Ravana did not notice. He sped away, and Sita's hair streamed out on the wind, and they left behind the two monkeys.

The two monkeys watched with their yellow-brown eyes never blinking, while Sita's gold and silver bells and bracelets fell ringing down and crying. The yellow scarf flashed down like lightning; the silver ornaments were the Moon and white stars dropping.

hanuman!

A real deer made of precious stones and gold
Never yet lived in this world.
Such a thing cannot be;
But Rama followed a golden deer
And lost Sita.

She is his Sita,
That girl born again and again
Like a flame from the furrow,
In the King's fields.

Ravana looked at Sita and he thought—*Mine*. He brought her to the back of his palace in the city of Lanka. Ravana smiled at her. His faces were all smiles and he said, "You will not see Rama again. Here you are safe, you have no more husband, and so there can be nothing wrong in our love."

"To Hell with you," said Sita. "You took me like a thief. And barely made it past an old vulture—."

"Quiet!" Ravana screamed at her. Then at once he composed himself. "My dear . . . capture is a good way to get a wife . . . I want your love. I will wait for you to love me."

"Do what you will with me," said Sita, "I will feel nothing."

"When you get to know me, perhaps . . . we shall see, my dear. Come inside with me now, change your clothes and eat and rest."

"I won't enter your kennel."

"Damn you! Hey, Rakshasis!" Female Rakshasas ran up. "Take her and imprison her in the grove of tall Asoka trees back behind my room and guard her day and night."

A demoness took each of Sita's arms and led her away to the

Asoka grove. Ravana told the rest of the Rakshasis, "Use hard words and soft, threats and gifts and temptations. Break her to my will and give her at any time whatever she may ask for."

Then the Demon King called after Sita, "When winter begins and the Sun turns north, if you haven't come into my bed I'll eat you minced for breakfast!" He went in the building.

In his high heaven Lord Brahma summoned Indra and said, "Sita must not die nor end her life in Lanka."

Indra asked, "Why me?"

Brahma looked at him. Indra said, "I'll see to it, Sir."

Lord Indra waited until night. Then taking the Goddess Sleep for his companion he approached Lanka carrying a bowl of heavenly wheat and butter.

Sleep spread out her arms over Lanka. *For the good of the gods. For the downfall of the Night Demons.*

The Rakshasis guarding Sita fell asleep. Indra entered the scarlet Asoka grove and touched Sita lightly so she awoke. She was not afraid.

"I am Indra, the Lord of Heaven, good fortune to you. My Lady, the demons sleep. I bring you food. Eat this and never will you hunger nor thirst for a year."

"How do I know who you are?" asked Sita.

"I am Indra, and you know me."

Sita took a little wheat and dropped it to Earth. "Whether Rama lives or has died let this nourish him." Then she ate.

Indra said, "Don't fear Ravana. He cannot force you, for he is under a strong curse, and he'll die if he does."

"Who cursed him?" asked Sita.

"While Evil lies borne down by Sleep I will tell you what happened," said Indra. "Anyone who desires an unwilling woman burns himself, and he who loves a willing one will find delight."

Listen, Sita—

Viswamitra the hermit, who led Rama to your father's land, used to be only a King. He spent a long time winning merit by austerities in the Hills. He was gaining on me, and I sent the divinely beautiful Apsarasa Rambha down to Earth to tempt him. She approached him on Kailasa Hill but Viswamitra turned her to stone for ten thousand years.

Viswamitra never stayed long in one place and soon he left Kailasa. The Yakshas of the Treasure Lord Vaishravana found Rambha. They thought she was a statue and took her into their palace gardens.

Years passed, and the spell wore off one day. It was spring. Rambha became flesh and blood again. She blinked her eyes, and sighed, and turned around. She saw Vaishravana's son Nalakubara walking in the gardens and fell in love with him then and there. They met, and after that Rambha came back to Heaven. She told me how tired she was. But at night she would go down the path leading from Heaven to Kailasa, to visit Nalakubara.

When Ravana's son Indrajit had defeated me in Heaven, and when Ravana had taken all creation into his supposed Empire, the King of the Rakshasas became dissatisfied with having only one wife. So he made Mandodari his chief Queen, but he started to ride all over on Pushpaka chariot, capturing women. Ravana took whom he pleased, caring only for beauty and for nothing else. He had hundreds of wives kept guarded on the huge chariot—Naga girls, hermits' daughters, mermaids of the seas, bird-maidens of the northern lakes, daughters of gods, woodland spirits, the wives of Kings and common men.

Ravana killed any one who tried to stop him. Hot women's tears streamed from Pushpaka, and their complaints were very sad. Ravana looked them over. He decided he had to have at least one Apasarasa, and he steered Pushpaka to the Himalya Hills and landed near the silver mountain Kailasa.

That night the clear rising Moon shone brilliant on the hill, and from the Treasure Castle of Vaishravana came song and music. A cool night breeze brought the scent of flowers, and stirred the trees, and made them let fall a silent shower of petals soft over the ground.

Ravana waited near the summit, hidden in the black shadow of a tree that grew beside the narrow way that leads up to heaven, and down to the Hills of Earth. He heard someone descending, and heard ankle bells and waist-chains ringing and swinging in step.

Rambha came picking her way downhill. Her body swayed; she was barefoot and trying not to step on stones, and flowers from the five wishing-trees of heaven were in her hair. Rambha the Apsarasa had all of a woman's artful graces and all of her natural beauties.

Rambha's summer robe was light as air, her eyebrows were arched like bows, her thighs and hands were soft to touch. Ravana stepped out in front of her and slightly bent near to her, and he said, "Where do you go? Whose time for ecstasy and bliss has come? What favored lover will drink the nectar of your mouth? Whose hard chest will touch your soft breasts?"

Rambha brushed back a lock of hair off her forehead. "You're Ravana, aren't you?"

"Rest here on this fine grass," said Ravana.

"You rule even over heaven," said Rambha. "And so if you are my King, I am a young girl to be protected and you are my father and my guardian." She stood looking down.

"Love me," said Ravana, "love me now!"

"But I am married, in my heart," said Rambha.

"Apsarasas don't marry!" Ravana threw her down and raped her. Then he went away and left her there, and Rambha went on to her meeting with Nalakubara.

Rambha wept when she saw Nalakubara and cried, "You are my husband, forgive me that a woman's strength is less than a man's."

Nalakubara called servants; he sent her with them and all alone he stood on a bare rock and he cursed Ravana. First he looked as far as he could see in every way, but the Demon King was gone. Then he let fall from his eye a tear, onto the stone where he stood, and that boulder shattered, cracks ran through it.

179

Nalakubara the son of the Treasure King looked south. He got a branch of a pine tree and held it, and it burst into fire and burned, dropping tears of fire itself, and Nalakubara said— *Ravana, when you next attack a woman who won't have you, your ten heads will burst!*

Oh Sita, had I been watching Kailasa that night! Those cursing words went right into Ravana's ears in Lanka where he had gone with his chariot full of captives. They heard the curse too. Up till then those captive women had lamented, but now that they knew they were safe, that only made them love Ravana. They felt sorry for him.

Rambha and you are the only women who have refused themselves to Ravana since that time. Such is Ravana's charm and appeal that some of these queens helped Ravana to steal them, and one lady killed her brothers who would have stopped her, and drank their blood, and turned to Ravana with a red mouth. I think women are more cruel than demons. Very often they are, when they may be so.

Yet, Princess, since Nalakubara's curse many times a madness has possessed the Demon King, and proof of this is his taking you although his wives love him. He has again hurt someone weaker than he. The tears that Rambha wept that night will burn him down.

❖ ❖ ❖

"For there is nothing worse than the tears of the innocent," said Indra. "Sita, you haven't on your body any sign of widowhood. Rama will rescue you; you won't dwell here long. Those monkeys will tell him that they saw you."

"And Jatayu?"

"By the Gods," said Indra, "Jatayu has had a place in heaven for a thousand lifetimes, but he won't use it; he won't be born anything but a bird, and he loves Earth. Over and over, again and again he gives his life for what's right, never once wondering should he do it or not, nor reflecting will it do any good, nor would it be better to live to fight another time! Ah Sita, I think Jatayu is very wise."

180

Sita smiled at Indra. The food he had brought her had taken away her rising hunger and sorrow. The Lord of the Gods touched his hands, knelt before Sita, and returned to heaven, taking the Goddess Sleep with him.

❦

In Dandaka Forest, Rama running for home met Lakshmana running towards him and shouted—*Go back!*

They ran home together. They found their house empty and looked everywhere for Sita. Rama asked the river Godavari, "Where is Sita?" But although Sita had told the river to speak to Rama, Godavari did not dare answer, remembering still the terrible form of Ravana.

Rama spoke to the trees, "Show me my Sita slender as a bough." He saw a glimpse of yellow and ran toward it. But it was a cluster of yellow flowers and not Sita's dress. Rama looked all around. He called, "I see you there! Come on out, I can see you!"

Lakshmana carefully examined all around their home. He went where Sita would go to bathe, or to draw water, or to pick flowers. He found the forest gods were gone. Wildflowers were faded, and the Earth herself looked worn and very old. He found a huge footprint. The highest branches of many trees were broken. Some deer came, and looked at Lakshmana, then jumped and ran south looking up at the sky, and back at the house, and at the Earth, and they were making little sounds.

Lakshmana went to Rama and said, "She was taken in an aerial car to some place on Earth south from here."

Lakshmana gathered their possessions, took the weapons and left the rest, and led Rama south by the hand. Lakshmana kept down his eyes, and soon he knelt. "Rama, a strange white flower lies here fallen, holding a drop of blood, still threaded with silk from a garland."

Slowly they continued on. First Lakshmana found broken bits of ivory inset with pearls. Then he discovered a sharp torn piece of gold armor; then a belt; then a sharp bladeless iron

181

arrow, feathered with iron, eight paces long and stout as a mace; a long quiver packed full of such arrows, the whole thing crushed and all the arrows broken inside; then a huge vulture wing-feather crushing to death beneath it two asses who wore the faces of demons; an axle standing on end; yokes and tresses hanging in the trees; the wreckage of a war-chariot overturned from the sky and fallen in many pieces; the ground bloodsoaked and raked with hooves and claws and marks not human.

Then Lakshmana found ten great bleeding dark arms torn off at the shoulders. Rama looked at all this and said, "Here the Rakshasas fought each other over Sita, and they tore her apart and this is her blood all over. They pulled her head off . . . ."

Lakshmana said, "These are all left arms. The hands wear costly gold rings. They are marked on their palms by the royal birth-wheels of an Emperor."

"What does that mean?" asked Rama.

"The Rakshasa King himself was here—look there!"

They saw Jatayu. The Vulture King lay on his back, barely alive. Lakshmana and Rama ran to him, and slowly Jatayu said, "Lord Rama, it was my age . . . my old age alone kept me from killing Ravana to save your wife!"

Rama said, "The plain truth is that there is no end to my bad fortune. You have given away your life for me, and despite that my life herself has been taken from me, and they killed her . . . ."

"She is alive. Sita lives!" Jatayu coughed. "But not without cost did Ravana go past me, strong though he was, well-armored and on a sky-chariot—." Blood ran from Jatayu's beak and he died.

Rama said, "See how in every race of creatures live the brave!" Rama and Lakshmana performed Jatayu's funeral. They burned his body, and Lakshmana put out food for the birds of Dandaka, strips of meat from the killed asses. To Rama, the fire that burned Jatayu was cool.

❧

Rama and Lakshmana went south, and all the happiness and life had been worn out of the land they walked on. That was the ground beneath the flight-paths used by the Rakshasas going between Lanka and the garrison that had been north in Dandaka. The Rakshasas had ruined it by flying overhead.

Empty houses sheltered jackals, and their yards were littered with broken things. There were no deer, only dogs gone wild. They found no more signs of Sita or Ravana until at last they came to the southern limit of Dandaka Forest, crossed a dark-flowing river and saw a lake, and a hill nearby covered with green.

That was Lake Pampa. In that place had lived a hermit named Matanga. Once when he was too tired to search for water, Matanga had brought rising from the Earth the waters of every ocean. His touch took away the salt and he made a freshwater lake and lived on its shore with an old woman named Savari.

In the year that Rama was first exiled, Matanga had died. But his virtue lingered and the waters of Lake Pampa kept the country green and fair, and Savari still stayed in their hermitage. Rama and Lakshmana walked by the lakeside and saw her house in a clearing, in a wood of coral trees.

Savari was very old, all dressed in white with long grey hair, and she had become very thin and short with age. She was sitting beside a newly made funeral pyre.

Savari rose to welcome guests, and Rama and Lakshmana sat down by her, and Rama said, "I am Rama. Are you well? Do you use little food and little anger?"

"I am Savari." She smiled. "Favored now is my birth and favored my long service to Matanga since you have come, my Lord Rama."

Rama asked, "Where are we?"

Savari said, "Ayodhya Prince, I stayed behind to receive you when my Master died; we knew you would come to Matanga's wood. He told me. Those little fires burning there by the edge of the trees were kindled by Matanga and he would tend them, but since he died they have burned on all by themselves, and those lowly blue flowers growing by them are

183

from drops of sweat that fell from my Master as he bent to put on wood. Those clothes of bark hanging there have not dried in thirteen years. Everything waits. That hill is Rishyamuka. It is guarded by little snakes, and over it Ravana carried Sita away through the sky.

"You saw them!"

"Rama, in misfortune seek for friendship."

"Where?" asked Rama.

Savari replied, "On Rishyamuka live the two monkeys Sugriva and Hanuman. We are not far from the hidden cave city of Kishkindhya, the capital of the monkey people, and the monkey King Vali has driven out Sugriva from there and banished him. Only Hanuman remained Sugriva's friend. Vali tried to kill them but they came here. Vali is Sugriva's brother, yet he has separated him from his loving wife."

"Done what?" said Rama.

"Hanuman doesn't know his strength. He and Sugriva fled in fear. Here they are safe, because Matanga cursed Vali once. Neither Vali nor any of his people can enter this wood that goes over the hill."

"Hanuman." Rama looked at the hill. "Who is this monkey Hanuman?"

"That white monkey?" Savari laughed. "Oh, no one can equal him. He is Sugriva's one loyal friend. He is brave and kind. He is the child of the Wind. What do you want to hear about him?"

"A friend," said Rama. "Tell me everything."

"Then," said Savari, "I will tell you the best story I know."

❧

Listen, Rama—

Mount Meru is at the center of the surface of Earth, no man knows where. On Meru the Sun will appear to travel around you. Bright sunlight has turned that mountain's soil into gold. The whole mountain is solid gold, but because the sunlight changed the ground so gradually none of the plants were harmed, and from the gold still grow grasses and trees. Birds and animals live there as on a common hill, and there is water.

184

Lord Brahma comes down to our world of Earth when it pleases him. Once he rested on Mount Meru. He shed a tear from his eye, and where it touched the golden ground, right then and there the first monkey was born.

Brahma named him Riksharaja and stayed on Meru to keep him company. Riksharaja played on the hill. He wandered around and explored by day and ate all the fruit he wanted. Every evening Riksharaja returned to the Grandfather of the Worlds and put some flowers at Brahma's feet.

Early one morning Riksharaja saw his own reflection when he bent over to drink from a lake. He thought it was the face of an enemy trying to take his water. Riksharaja attacked. He jumped in the lake, went completely underwater, and found no one there. When that monkey came back out onto the shore again, he had been changed into a female.

She was a monkey girl so beautiful, that as she stood on the hillside of Meru both Indra and Surya the Sun fell in love with her. That same morning, first Indra and then Surya came down and made love to her.

The gods' children are quickly born. That monkey girl had two gold-colored babies, and that afternoon she washed them in the lake. They splashed water all over her and by the time they were clean Riksharaja found that he was again a male.

Riksharaja took his sons to Brahma. They named Indra's son Vali and called his younger brother Sugriva. Brahma gave Vali the city of Kishkindhya. Brahma made more monkeys and populated the woods, and gave them the friendship of the bear people. Vali became the monkey King, and Indra gave his son a victory-garland of little lotus flowers cut from gold.

Riksharaja stayed with Brahma as his friend. They lived in Brahma's heaven and Riksharaja could see whatever happened to his sons. Vali seemed to get everything, and so Riksharaja asked Vayu the Wind to father a son, a monkey who would always be Sugriva's true friend.

Vayu the restless Wind went to Kishkindhya and looked around. The best-looking monkey girl he saw was Anjana. If Anjana took human form she could have the love of any man. She was walking atop a green mountain near here, when Vayu

Hanuman saw the glorious sun rise . . .

came to her. He gently stole away her clothes and embraced her in his long arms.

That same day, Hanuman was born. He was a little monkey with white fur and a red face and brownish-yellow eyes. Anjana was married to another monkey. She left Hanuman all alone by the mouth of a small cave on that hill and went home.

Little baby Hanuman was hungry. Night came, and went by, and dawn approached. No one came to feed him. He lay on his back by his cave looking at his toes, and the sky grew lighter and lighter. In the east there was first a pale grey light, then there was silver, then gold and rose.

Hanuman saw the glorious Sun rise into the air like a big ripe mango fruit. Newborn though he was, he knew what fruit was. He licked his sharp bright little teeth, crouched down and jumped with a leap and a bound up into the sky and went flying straight at the Sun.

His father the Wind came blowing over Hanuman from out of the north, cool and fresh from the snows. He saved Hanuman from being burned up. Hanuman drew near to Surya and the Sun beamed at him. Hanuman smiled back at the Sun. The fire of daylight was burning all around the Sun's chariot, and the flames sucked up the air and pulled Hanuman into the crackling white fire.

There Hanuman tumbled and spun unhurt inside the Sun's fire. It was time for a solar eclipse. The immortal disembodied head of the Asura Rahu advanced to swallow the Sun alive. He came close and opened wide his black mouth.

Hanuman bobbed and swirled in the updraft of the Sun. He was trying to get out of the fire and fighting against the currents of air and flames. Then he came sailing out and accidently put his foot right in Rahu's eye.

Rahu went to Indra. "Another Rahu is eating the Sun!"

Indra said, "Look, are you sure?"

"He hit me in the eye!"

"More trouble!" said Indra. He got on his great white elephant Airavata, who was wearing fancy hangings and was painted with leaves and flowers all over his skin.

Rahu led the way. This time Hanuman got a good look at him. Rahu was just a round head. He looked like a bigger mango than the Sun did, and Hanuman jumped him and bit his ear.

Indra cried—*Stop that!* Hanuman turned. He saw Airavata. The biggest fruit of all!

Hanuman attacked Airavata and Indra. He came at them waving his arms and swinging his legs, all out of control. Airavata stepped aside and Indra pushed Hanuman away with the flat side of his thunderbolt.

Hanuman fell back to Earth. He broke his jaw falling on a stone by the mouth of his own cave. Vayu the lord of the Winds saw this and was angry. He went to his son Hanuman and took him inside the little cave, and held him.

The Wind hid himself. The bodies of living creatures became hard as wood and their joints stiffened into knots. Like a banner lowered and put on the ground, the ever-moving air moved no more and lay still. Vayu looked out in anger at all the worlds and stayed with his child, and that was the vanishing of the Winds.

Lord Brahma came to Hanuman's cave and with a touch healed his jaw. Brahma said, "Wind, you are breath. Having no heavy body you pass through all beings." Still Vayu silently held his son. Brahma said, "I made you for life and for life's happiness."

Vayu said, "Who can go where the Wind waits?"

Brahma said, "Hanuman on the lap of the Wind, shining white, you will live as long as you wish to live; you cannot be killed."

Vayu stirred. Then Surya the Sun entered the cave, dressed in gold and jewel-crested clothes, wearing earrings and armbands shining in colors. He smiled at Hanuman. He blinked his eyes and there were blinks of black in the cave, and his lighted jewels went out and came back alight. Then Hanuman slept, as deeply as Night sleeps, and Surya the Sun set three mangos down beside him.

That pleased the Wind. He came out and the worlds could

breathe. Hanuman awoke the next day, ate his breakfast, and met his father the Wind outside his cave.

Vayu carried Hanuman to Lord Shiva. Shiva taught Hanuman to change form at pleasure. Nandin the bull taught him languages. Hanuman learned poetry as well, and as he increased his skill at poems Hanuman discovered that he had been wearing golden earrings all his life without knowing it. No one else can see those little gold rings except some person as yet unknown to Hanuman, who will meet him and be his friend and master, so said the bull Nandin.

Hanuman grew up and lived with Sugriva in Kishkindhya. Vali was the King. At first Vali was well-liked, but he soon became petty and mean, and the bears withdrew their friendship.

Vali would go out of Kishkindhya looking for fights. He would stand on top of hills and throw their peaks into the air and catch them. By the entrance of Kishkindhya cave there was a pile of the white bones of those who had accepted Vali's challenges.

Dundhuvi was a giant buffalo, and he was the only other animal as ill-mannered as Vali. Dundhuvi lived in the underworlds, and whatever anyone said to him he took offence at it. Dundhuvi was born angry and impatient and all set to do anyone wrong, and as he got older he got worse, and he left his home to seek new enemies.

Dundhuvi arose from the underworlds through the ocean, swam ashore, and stood on the seashore swearing and cursing and pawing the sand. He looked at the waves. They just kept on coming, they didn't seem to care if he was there or not.

Dundhuvi hooked his horns in the surf and bellowed— *Fight me!*

Waves swept the shore. The long watery arms of the Ocean hissed and pulled and swirled around Dundhuvi's feet—*Go back. Go back. Go back or drown.*

Dundhuvi retreated two steps. "Afraid to show yourself!"

189

he yelled. A great wave arose, foaming and rumbling, coming closer. Dundhuvi walked quickly away on stiff legs with his head in the air.

Then he saw from the distance the snowy Himalya, a low-seeming row of hills white as Shiva's smile, a lotus white. Dundhuvi climbed up into the Hills and battered them with his horns. He broke the rocks and yelled—*Coward! You coward!*

The Mountain King Himavan appeared above Dundhuvi, and he turned his rocky face to look down at the buffalo. Himavan stood on bare metals that struck out from the mountain. He was clothed in a white robe of snow and falling water, with a belt of ice locked fast. He resembled an old man with grey eyes and long white hair, but he was very tall.

With slow gestures Himavan touched together his deeply lined hands. He said, "Do not bring war over the world's edge." The Himalya summits towered away into heaven. An avalanche cracked and fell. "Would you harm my men of Peace . . . ?"

A storm came blowing and the black pines moaned, the dark deodars cried and ice broke like glass from their boughs. It began to sleet.

Himavan spoke. "The strong are not angered . . . we know, and you do not know . . . ." Cloud closed out the world. The Hills and Himavan disappeared. They were standing, hard to move, lost in the blasting white wind.

The frozen snow and ice tore down at Dundhuvi, biting and whirling along on the screaming wind that cut over the blades of the sharp ridges above. Dundhuvi ran.

He ran until he got to Kishkindhya. There he stuck his head inside the cave city and roared like a drum. Vali came out on a balcony of his palace. He had his arm around his Queen Tara, and he gave her his wineglass and said, "Don't stay while you can still go, you dumb ox!"

Dundhuvi said, "I'll return when you are sober. Don't worry, enjoy yourself!" He roared again just to hear the echo.

Vali said, "But I am only drunk at the sip of a fight!" He put on his golden garland and jumped down. Dundhuvi backed off outside the cave, and Vali came out and faced him like a fire placed on the Earth.

They fought for a long time, but in the end Vali caught Dundhuvi's horns and broke his neck. He let the body fall. Then he swung the dead buffalo around by the tail, and let him go.

Dundhuvi's corpse fell right there on Rishyamuka hill, and as it flew overhead through the air blood poured from its mouth and touched our altar here. Matanga cursed Vali to die if he ever came here. He gave the monkeys who lived here one day to leave, and then he put the curse of death on any of Vali's people who would enter Matanga's Wood. Matanga thought of this forest as his son, and the monkeys would tear the trees.

Dundhuvi's son was the Asura Mayavi. Mayavi came to Kishkindhya for revenge. At midnight he challenged Vali.

Sugriva and Vali both came out. They chased Mayavi and saw him enter a cave hidden by grass. Vali ordered Sugriva to wait outside and entered alone. "I don't need any help to win!"

Sugriva waited there for a year, then blood came out of the cave. Sugriva heard the cries of Asuras. He went just inside and called Vali, over and over. There was never any answer, and Sugriva could hear the Asuras of the underworld coming up and their noise got nearer.

To keep them from attacking Kishkindhya Sugriva left the cave and sealed it with a stone. Sugriva became King of the monkeys and bears. But Vali was not killed. He spent a year down in that cave searching for Mayavi, and then Mayavi and many other Asuras attacked Vali. Vali killed them. He came up the cave passage to Earth and found it closed, and kicked apart the stone Sugriva had put there, and like a ghost he returned.

Sugriva willingly surrendered the crown-diadem of Kishkindhya. But Vali wrongly exiled Sugriva for treason. Vali holds Sugriva's wife Ruma a prisoner. Only Hanuman has

stayed with Sugriva. They remembered Matanga's curse and came to live on this hill, after many wanderings.

❖ ❖ ❖

"Whoever hears this story of the monkey Hanuman," said Savari, "gains his every desire. Rama, the King of the Monkeys and Bears cannot be a thief. He can't take the wives of others. The true Monkey King is on this nearby Rishyamuka Hill, and the quest for Sita is in his hands. Oh Rama, Vali is strong, but Sugriva has sunlight in his soul, though Vali has darkened his happiness."

Lakshmana said, "We will go to Hanuman and Sugriva at once, with your permission."

"Be Sugriva's friend," said Savari, "for he knows all the worlds in fine detail. He can find her wherever she is. Now I wish to die . . . ."

Rama said, "We will leave you now." They left Savari and walked on along the lakeside.

I greet my Death.
Yama, come my Friend
And take me home.

Savari lit her pyre. She bowed her head and walked into the burning flames. Her old body fell from her in ashes.

Rama and Lakshmana looked back. They saw the golden flames rise and saw a chariot coming, armored in silver and drawn by ten grey horses running on air.

That was Indra's chariot flying gold and silvery flags. Indra came to Savari's fire. Under a white umbrella hung with flowers Indra leaned over the chariot rail not far above the ground, and spoke to Savari.

All around the marvelous chariot were the Gandharvas of heaven, wearing crimson cloth and holding drawn swords. Across their chests were blazing chains, and they were all twenty-five years old, the eternal age of heaven.

Savari became a young woman in a golden robe standing in the fire. She rose up and Indra took her on the chariot, and like a streak of light they went away up through the many skies of the world.

Matali the heavenly charioteer drove through the stars, turned through those fields of far lights. He passed above Indra's heaven, and went by the sky-homes of the saints. Above it all, they stopped at Brahma's realm. Lord Brahma saw Savari and said—*Welcome home.*

Rama and Lakshmana bathed then, in the waters of the seven seas in Lake Pampa. Rama said, "How shall I live without my Sita?" They climbed onto Rishyamuka Hill covered with trees. Sugriva and Hanuman stayed hidden near the summit and watched them coming closer.

THE BOOK OF THE FOREST ENDS.
THREE PARTS ARE PAST, AND FOUR REMAIN.
HERE THE BOOK OF KISHKINDHYA BEGINS.

193

On Rishyamuka Hill when a man falls asleep, if he has bad in him he is beaten by Asuras in a dream, and wakes up sore and bruised all over. But if a totally good person sleeps there he dreams of gold and wakes up really rich.

Rama and Lakshmana were climbing when a poor woodcutter appeared from the woods. He bowed and smiled at them. He put down his bundle of sticks and sat on it.

"What whim has led the Sun and Moon to visit me here?" The woodcutter wiped his hands. He smiled and nodded his head. "Are you truly gods walking on foot through the world? Oh, you two, you look at me like lions, my boys!"

Rama smiled. He looked around the hill, as though he had stepped fresh from the world's beginning to look around and see what had been done. He looked at the woodcutter. "Oh Hanuman of golden earrings."

"Rama, I remember you now." Hanuman shook himself. There he was, white with glossy fur, a long tail curved gracefully, long thin arms, feet like hands, a red face and white teeth and light eyes almost all yellow. "Why do you want Hanuman?"

"Ravana took Sita."

"We looked long after her," said Hanuman. He grew bigger. "Get on my shoulders," he said, and took them on uphill to meet Sugriva.

Sugriva had gold fur, and his throat looked like a piece of shiny gold. Rama embraced Sugriva. There was a small fire and Rama and Sugriva walked around it for a pledge of friendship, and each of them promised to take the other's joy and sorrow as his own.

Then Sugriva and Rama and Hanuman and Lakshmana sat down, and Sugriva the Monkey King said, "See what fell on our hill." He brought out Sita's scarf, untied it, and all Sita's ornaments were there. "A young goddess whose eyes curved back round to her ears was carried away by Ravana."

Rama asked, "Are these hers, Lakshmana?"

194

"Yes."

Sugriva said, "I know every place beneath the Sun's many rays."

Hanuman said, "Wherever he took her we can find her. Yet we have to hide on this hill, and Sugriva must suffer for the separation from his wife."

Rama said, "Let this meeting be the turning point of your fortune."

Lakshmana said, "Truly, a friend is protection against injury and a help for sorrow."

Hanuman smiled. "We'll keep these till we may give them back to Sita."

At that moment elsewhere in the world Sita felt her left eye wink by itself, and the same thing happened to Vali in Kishkindhya, and Ravana's ten left eyes also winked. That is a good sign for females and a bad one for males. Hanuman served roast fish from the lake and water in lotus-leaf cups shaped like boats.

After they had eaten, Sugriva said, "All Vali's other enemies are dead and their wives are widows. I don't know what we can do. Look, over there is the immense corpse of the buffalo Dundhuvi, and Vali threw him here all the way from our city."

Rama got up, and went over to the corpse and pushed it with one toe. The tough dry skin and all those bones went far over the horizon.

"Ah, now it's light as grass, but Dundhuvi was heavy when he was killed," said Sugriva.

Rama opened his quiver. He took out a war arrow. The arrow was gold plated, thicker than a finger, half as long as a staff, marked with Rama's name and vaned with the feathers of the fastest birds and steel tipped.

Rama strung his bow and said, "It is wrong for people in love to be separated!" He shot and his arrow went through seven old ironwood trees stout as turrets.

The next day Rama and Lakshmana and Hanuman and Sugriva went to the mouth of Kishkindhya cave and hid in the forest. Sugriva said, "I've run in fear from Vali for a long time!" He tightened his belt and stepped out in the open, and called for Vali to come out of Kishkindhya and fight.

Inside, in the monkey palace in the cave city, Queen Tara said, "Listen, that is Sugriva. Something is wrong. Take warning, there is danger."

Vali replied, "From him?"

"Our people have seen Rama and his brother nearby."

"My brother's a coward, why would anyone help him?" Sugriva called again.

"Don't go out," said Tara. "Be kind to your brother, and return him his wife, she is so sad here."

Vali said, "He is the one starting the fight." He sent for a sentry. "Who is with Sugriva?"

The guard said he had seen no one. Vali said to Tara, "Rama would not hide to harm me; he would never break the fair rules of war."

Tara laughed. "Rules?"

Vali gave her a pat. "My dear, the only reason to consult a woman is to find out what not to do!"

"No woman advises any man she does not love, even among monkeys. Be his friend."

"Oh, I won't hurt him," said Vali, "I'll chase him off, that's all. And it is actually wrong for wives to command their husbands."

Lovely Tara tied Indra's golden garland over Vali's shoulders. Vali ran out of Kishkindhya like the golden Sun popping up over a hill. He saw Sugriva and grabbed him, and the two monkeys were wrestling all over the clearing in front of Kishkindhya.

They were moving so fast they both looked the same. At first Rama could not aim. Then one of them was winning, and he wore gold flowers and Rama shot at him from the trees.

The bowstring twanged. There was the arrowy sound of air being torn like cloth, and the sound of a blow. The arrow hit Vali and went right through his heart.

Vali lay fallen on his back and only his golden garland kept him alive. Rama and Lakshmana stepped out of concealment and Queen Tara ran out from Kishkindhya with her son Angada. Weeping softly, she told Angada, "That is Death there in the form of an archer leaning on his bow, and from a distance he has killed your father the King."

Sugriva and Rama and Hanuman and Lakshmana stood near Vali. They were pale and stared aimlessly at the ground. Sugriva was crying and his tears were mixed with blood from a cut under one eye. The Kishkindhya monkeys gathered whispering, sad whispers like the night wind heard by a lonely man.

Tara fell like a star and embraced Vali. "My Lord, send away these people and turn to me."

Vali looked at them all. He smiled at Tara, and he said to Angada—*My son, for anger I die. Help Rama.*

Vali the shelter of hundreds was dead. Time, you have no friend and no kinsman and no family. The long-leaping monkeys trembled.

❦

Hanuman picked up the golden war arrow that had pierced through Vali's heart, and turned the shaft in his hands and watched its mark—*Rama . . . Rama . . . Rama . . . .*

Tara touched the corpse. "Why won't you reach out to me? If you are angry, at least speak to your son . . . Oh . . . !" She looked at Rama. "Will you eat your kill, noble man?"

Hanuman spoke to Tara. "Vali has left us on a long journey. The affairs of life are now our task. We live on, but in heaven Vali will win the hearts of the dancing women in their bright robes and their coronets and red flowers. Look on what was his body for the last time, Queen."

"Give me that arrow," said Tara. "Vali was my mate. I loved him, he was a good King."

"Here, take it."

"Hanuman, I am myself but a part of Vali."

"Oh Queen," said Hanuman, "a mate is this world's best gift to anyone."

"They say that Death has met us all."

"Many times, I have heard."

"When a weakling has been abused and has at last a chance to get even, he is allowed to leave the True."

"My Lady, your King kept my King separated from his mate."

Tara said, "Surely that is wrong, to part two people in love."

Hanuman said, "As wrong as war, my Queen. That was not right."

Queen Tara answered, "Oh Hanuman, tell Rama I forgive him, I forgive his murder—" Tara drove the arrow through her own heart and died.

The Monkey Prince Angada looked at his mother and father and looked at Rama. Angada said, "I'll help you. Grief

198

does the dead no good, and the wives and sons of our warriors never lament, not by day nor in the night."

That evening the monkeys brought out their royal hearse, like a war-chariot without wheels. Monkeys carried it on their shoulders, and other monkeys dressed the dead King in jeweled clothes.

They took Vali away on the bier covered with flowers, only his face showing. The monkeys went away from Kishkindhya, up toward the banks of a hill stream. Some walked before the hearse breaking apart jewel ornaments in their hands, and letting the pieces fall to Earth, and others cast down broken pieces of shiny silver. Then behind the corpse came singers—*Glory! Glory to the Moon. Glory to Water. We burn Vali. Vali slain by one arrow!*

When they had gone Hanuman said to Rama, "Come into the unconquerable cave city of Kishkindhya. Tomorrow we will make Sugriva our King."

"No," said Rama. "The rain is coming."

Sugriva said, "Rama, it is after midsummer, but still we have a few days . . . ."

Rama said, "King, go into your city. Lakshmana and I will live in the woods somewhere by here. You've been a long time away from home."

There was a faraway thunder. Sugriva said, "People can't travel in the rainy season, that's true enough, Rama. When the rain ends, I promise you, we will find Sita and obey you."

"I'll take you to a good place to stay," said Hanuman. "Follow me, my Lords."

Hanuman went bending low through the trees, up the slopes of Prasravana Hill, the hill of Springs, and led them to an airy wide cave, well lit, with water near, and he touched his hands. "I could have saved Sita by now more than once," said Hanuman.

Rama started to speak, but the wailing of grief from Vali's funeral came to their ears just then. Rama said, "Leave us alone, Hanuman."

199

the search

The Truth upholds the fragrant Earth and makes the living water wet. Truth makes fire burn and the air move, makes the sun shine and all life grow.

A hidden truth supports everything. Find it and win.

As Hanuman turned back down the hill the rains began. First, Lord Indra opened Heaven's gate and threw a thunder-stone tearing and crashing through the dark clouds in the still and heavy air. Then another thunder came, sloping on a shallow path, rolling and rolling nearer. Hanuman ran for home, thunders fell crashing closer and striking down, and round black clouds grew like pavilions in the sky and covered over all the world.

The ever-moving wind half-blew past the hills; then he swept impatiently down on Earth, snapping the flags of the cities, pressing through the forests and over the hills, driving the dust along the hot fields, throwing himself headlong against the world. Peacocks unfurled their tails like colored fans dancing on the mountain in the trees. The sky rumbled, and over Prasravana Hill a golden lash cut into the sky and the lightning fell and the rains were born. The Earth shook and the mad wind sang. The sky broke open, the rain down-poured, and all the world's water fell in an endless torrent.

The cold heavy rain fell on and on in big drops from Indra's dark blue clouds. Lightnings blazed and thunders exploded; the violent wind whirled and rattled the bamboos; and the racing air sent the rain streaming up and around and sideways in every way. The rays and lights of the Sun and Moon were gone. The dust was slain, and Earth with all her trees was soaking wet, in the night and in the storm. All light faded, the long dark night began, and the wind broke down the bamboos so their pearls fell out and rolled in the water.

Soon after the rain begins, the sound of the water changes. Very soon the brittle dryness of a year has gone, and all is wet through, and day after day the lasting rain falls into mud and beats down on wet stones and breaks the leaves. The hill seems made of water. Then all things reveal that they are but made of water.

The swift hill-rivers rushed brimful and laughing down the hill, dark brown in flood, roaring and foaming with white-crested waves. Water ran down the stony trails and the land below disappeared underwater. The world was an overflowing lake and the hills were islands. The heavy dark clouds had to rest on the high mountain peaks and seemed to take root there, and rows of white herons flying in the wet wind were a white garland for heaven.

In the dripping forests the brahmanas sang the holy Veda, and around them the rivers ran like sacred threads over the shoulders of mountains, ceaselessly murmuring with water. Elephant kings, those enemies of trees, walked themselves like mountains wrapped in dark clouds, and turned back in anger at the lightning storms and the cloudbanks of thunder, tossing their white tusks, waving their ears and trumpeting, thinking that some other elephant hung with a golden chain had challenged them in a deep voice.

Then the rains relented and the wind withdrew; you could catch the fresh breeze like cold water in the hollow of your hands. The wild plane trees flowered dark red, and Autumn came and smiled at the world. In the evenings the sunbeams came pale and yellow through the clouds. Hills and trees were fast asleep shrouded in white mist. The woods steamed. The pouring red rivers that had washed down the metals of the mountain became clear, and there were birds again upon their waters. By Rama's home, the lovely rivers fell downhill, and the weeping boughs of trees trailed in the water and tried to hold them back, but though the rivers were pleased, though they turned back a little, still glittering and sparkling bright, adorned in silver, they excitedly approached their lord the Sea.

The sky would open and show the stars for a moment in the nights. By day new shoots unfurled and the buds opened on the trees, and from water-soaked meadows grew green moss and green grass and green fern. Full waterfalls cascaded and plunged with noise. Lions again walked through the morning dew and purred softly in their new coats of fur, and in the pines the birds sang to shake the water from their paled wings, and flew out from their homes and back again.

Then the Sun! All the watery drops shone like rainbow jewels fallen on the grass and leaves from an Apsarasa's necklace broken in love. At noon the Sun felt good, he was steadily fleeing far to the south, leaving the far Himalyas covered with snow. Fire was comfortable in the cold west wind, and the night hours grew freezing and long. Roseapples ripened and then fell, waterflowers opened and blackberries blossomed. Then the lotuses died from the frost and left only their dry stalks above the water that was so cold thirsty elephants like cowards withdrew their trunks when first touching it.

The mild yellow Sun took the cold Moon's good fortune, and the Moon was veiled as a glass breathed upon, and dim. On Prasravana Hill Rama watched the white moonrise and thought—*Earth is in tears.*

Then for many days heaven was clear over all the world, and the river banks emerged from under water. In the north snow came at night on fast dark winds. On the warm plains the golden grain slightly bent its heads. The peacocks furled their tails and gave up love and games. Many-colored snakes came from their pits, and wide-winged swans returned to the lands around Kishkindhya. Elephants rolled in the dust, birds rose in flights from the grainfields, silver fish swam in the slow rivers, and it was almost Winter.

From within Kishkindhya cave Rama and Lakshmana could hear the monkeys singing and dancing to drums, and still they waited for Sugriva to come to them. Monkeys kill no game, and all round their city the small and harmless deer were unafraid. Rama felt Sita's loss the more when he saw them so secure in their woody homes. New flowers began to reappear. Rama saw a new open lotus and said, "These petals are shaped like Sita's eyes . . . . When Ravana eats her, she will cry out to me in fear, and her round breast once colored with red sandal-paste will be bathed in bright scarlet blood."

"Better to act than wonder and dream," said Lakshmana. "I'll have a word with Sugriva."

Lakshmana took his bow and set out for Kishkindhya, thinking over what he would say and knocking trees aside with his leg, thinking how Sugriva would answer and breaking rocks to bits with his feet. He entered the cave and saw Kishkindhya city's bright towers rising; he jumped over the monkey barricades, leapt their moat and approached the wall. The monkey guards looked down and Lakshmana stared back at them and sighed, and at that sigh the sentries ran away.

Angada the monkey prince opened the main gate. Lakshmana said, "My child, announce me—*Lakshmana waits for your promise at the gate.*"

Angada ran for Hanuman, and Hanuman ran to the king. He found Sugriva sprawled out asleep in his drinking room and grabbed his feet and shook him. Sugriva awoke with a start and blinked his bleary red eyes. "What are you doing?"

Hanuman said, "Get up, you fool!"

Sugriva sat up. "Who has been telling you tales about my imaginary shortcomings?"

"You've been drinking for over three months," said Hanuman, "and now Lakshmana is at the gate."

"Oh gods of heaven give us a little peace and quiet around here, can't you?"

"Are you still drunk?" asked Hanuman. "Get up, go to him, kneel, fold your paws together like a family man, and bow down that he may abuse you and spare your life. A promise-

203

breaker is so vile no beast will eat his body when he dies, and an angry friend is worse than an enemy."

Sugriva said, "Cold water, Hanuman, not talk . . . ."

At the gateway Lakshmana grew tired of waiting and entered the caverns of Kishkindhya city, walking down the sloping outer halls where beside the path fresh water flowed down stone channels to the city within. He went through rooms and past flowery gardens, and saw many monkeys in their robes and garlands, and they greeted him silently with touching hands, raised to their brows. He came to a wide road watered with perfume and lined with sandalwood trees. At the road's end he crossed over a clear river on a footbridge, and went through a golden-arched gate in the crystal walls of Sugriva's palace.

The tall white and silver roof spires rose up into the cave above, and one long tower pierced through the top and disappeared. Lakshmana walked through a grove of blue-flowering trees, stepping his way over low flowers colored like gold melting in the cool shade. He entered a doorway and crossed seven rooms where women on gold and silver couches were stringing flowers. Then he came into the heart of the monkey women's quarters—a dancing hall of marble and jewels, with soft seats round the walls and tables for banquets—and stood guiltily in a corner.

Lakshmana thought—*I don't belong here, where shall I go?* From within some unseen secret inner apartment came happy women's voices and music and the jingling of bells and jewel belts. Lakshmana couldn't remember how he had come in. There were fine-cut window screens everywhere in the walls and too many doors. Then Lakshmana pulled his bow, let go the string, and the bowstring rang out like the snap of a whip. Lakshmana looked for some escape.

Nearby, Hanuman heard the bow-cry and he jumped. *He's really here!*

"Relax," said King Sugriva. "He can't get out. A job for the Queen."

Sugriva called Queen Ruma. "Dear, good men like Lakshmana out there will not usually hit a woman. Go to him, read his heart and console him."

The good-looking Queen Ruma went before Lakshmana with many downcast looks, her feet unsteady, her eyes red with wine, her golden belts flowing about her hips. She said in a husky voice, "Oh Lakshmana, why are you angry with your loving friends?"

Lakshmana said, "It's your husband, my Lady."

"After long fear and shame," smiled Ruma, "he is lost again in the early springtime countryside of happiness, and led astray by summery love. Carefree, even a man in love forgets who he is, what of a monkey? Forgive us our pleasure, be not angry against us. And he is still true to you, come."

She led Lakshmana to Sugriva. The golden monkey King now sat on a rich carpet, and rose to join his hands together, wearing a gaudy garland round the ruff of gold fur that was his neck. "Welcome, Lakshmana, welcome."

"Best of monkeys," said Lakshmana, "Vali's path is not so narrow that no one else can follow him, also killed by Rama's arrows. Remember past kindnesses and beware; there's nothing that can't be accomplished by a little work."

Sugriva smiled. "But we care! Climb the watchtower with me."

They went up a long winding stairway of silver, out through the cave roof and onto a balcony high above a hilltop. Lakshmana looked out at the valleys he had just left. Everywhere, hordes of monkeys and apes and big shaggy bears covered the land.

Sugriva said, "Thirteen days ago, I laid my commands on my people, and I asked for help from the bears. We are all aware of illusion; we are versed in arts and the law; we are strong and we come from all over the world. Oh Lakshmana, when we fight we hurl entire hills and rock faces, we stamp down the forests like grass underfoot and splash the water from the sea. If we trip, the Earth cracks, if we want rain we capture the clouds and just wring them out, if we give a small celebration the noise knocks the birds stunned right out of the sky, and we number in millions . . . .

❦

Hanuman went to tell Rama the animals had come. Sugriva and Lakshmana went back downstairs from the tower, and in the throne room of Kishkindhya they met Jambavan the King of the Bears, an old dark bear with a crown and earrings of gold, with smoky grey eyes, huge paws and long arms, who stood on two feet or on four, just as he wished.

"Who came?" asked Sugriva.

"I will tell you," growled Jambavan. "Outside your cave are the white tree-dwelling monkeys who change their forms at will; the tall blue coconut monkeys strong as elephants; the yellow honey-wine monkeys with sharp teeth; the charcoal monkeys, born to the daughters of Gandharvas, who worship the Sun; the grey apes from the woods skirting the Edge of the World, who are handsome from eating only berries; the black ones with snaky tails, from the caves and hidden passes of Ganga, who never praise themselves; the red ones with lion-manes; and all the great bears of Earth have come here dark as gloom, brown and black and terrible to meet."

"Leave your families here with ours in Kishkindhya," said Sugriva, "and go out to find Earth's daughter who has been stolen. Because for her Rama laments, and the dark-eyed forest people weep to hear him."

Sugriva told Lakshmana, "Fleeing from Vali I have come to know every place in the world." He sat on his throne and sent for the General of the East. An old grey monkey entered, moving slowly, his eyes bright and round, dressed in hides tied fast with a bowstring, a red cloth tied round his forehead, white bow scars all over his arms. He looked sharply at Lakshmana and then at Sugriva, and said nothing.

"Search the Eastern quarter of the world for Sita," said Sugriva. "Go through the silver mines and the mulberry groves where silkworms feed; search the mountains and the

206

rich cities embraced by the Eastern Sea; search the hillside houses of the barbarians whose ears fold across their chins like scarves, those curious men of red hair and yellow bodies and hard round faces black as iron, who eat men, who have but one foot and yet outrun the deer. Search those islands where bristly hunters live on raw fish and mermen swim undersea, where the hillmen run on four legs and strange fishermen never leave their boats all their lives. Search the Gold and Silver Islands whose sharp hills pierce heaven, where live the swans and the gods. Go through the wilderness and the deep woods of stony rills, the mountain crags, the hermitages and sweet gardens and bowers, the farms and villages and sandy deserts, the bare ocean islands cut off by dark waves and storms howling at sea. By the Eastern Sea of salt beware of the huge hungry demons hanging head-down like misshapen rocks on the cliffs over the surf, who die every day when struck by the sunrise, but fall into the sea and revive, and return to hang again on the cliffs. Go beyond, to the limit of the world's land, to the shore of the primeval milk sea, whose breast ripples with white milk waves like strands of pearls, where silver lotuses shine with filaments of gold. Stop by the tall golden palm tree that Indra planted on the last shore to mark the end of the East. There through a crevice cleft in the Earth you can look down and see far below you the serpent Sesha white like the Moon, who upholds Earth on his coils, who has a thousand heads with wide lotus eyes, who is clad in blue. Farther east, far out to sea is the submarine fire burning, coming out from the mouth of a horse, changing the milk to salt seawater again, from under water boiling up steam to make the rains, waiting for when the world ends the next time to consume for food all this wondrous universe of life that moves and of creatures immobile. You may hear from afar the cries of feeble ocean-beasts in fear of those flames, and across that lonely sea you will dimly see the beginnings of the impassable Mountains of A World and No World, the boundary hills surrounding the Universe, their far sides in perpetual darkness, so high that all other mountain peaks

207

would lie at their feet, and our noble summits would but form their base. On their flanks trees and high abodes rise up beyond our vision, nor can we ever approach them. Over the milk sea, across the barrier Hills of A World and of No World, no creature can go. They encircle the universe. Past them in every direction is eternal night—boundless, treacherous, without Sun and Moon and light. And again, that darkness itself and all the cosmos is held within the white shell of an egg.

"In the East dawn first appears bright with brilliant glory reflected from the sunrise gates of gold, and people living there awhile also become golden colored. Search everywhere I have said to look, and wherever I have not named. Stay away no longer than one month from today."

The Monkey General of the East bowed to his king, turned on his heel and walked stiffly outside the cave city. One quarter of the monkey soldiers set out following him. Their weapons blazed, their supply wagons rumbled along, the dust from their march trapped the sunbeams in the sky and hid the day. There was a bewildering noise, the floor trembled in Sugriva's throne room, and they were gone.

Then the red-haired monkey General of the West entered before Sugriva, muttering to himself. He came to a halt, smashed his brass sandals against the stone floor, swept off his iron helmet that trailed long green plumes and parrot feathers, swirled his red cape, fell to his knees with a crash of bronze armor and cried—*Victory to the King! Jaya! Jaya!*

Sugriva said, "Explore the West for Sita. Search her out by force and by skill; discover what has happened to her; learn if she is waiting somewhere on the way West."

"*Majesty!*"

"Listen to me," said Sugriva. "In the West the Sun's light ends and there the kind Lady Night has her home. Follow west the cool forest streams that flow from the high cold lakes; search the wide western kingdoms and empires, the hot plateaus and tablelands, the natural arbors of entangled creepers and vines so hard to penetrate. Where the Sindhu river falls

208

into the Western Sea is the Hill of the Moon, with a hundred crests and ten thousand ridges lost in the sky, where live those giant wild birds who carry up to their nests whales from the sea and elephants from the land, and keep them there for little pets. Their nests are so large that the elephants happily roam and wander within them eating their fill in the shade of huge trees, and round the edges where the rain collects the whales swim and dive. Search this place. And near here as well, do the hermit Gandharvas store food for the rains and keep orchards. Take no fruit from them, let none of these creatures see you. Past that place is Diamond Thunder Mountain, a steep hill of blue adamant. Cascades run all through channels deep within it, and along those dark swift waters boars and lions roar, forever excited by the din and echo of their own voices. Westward of that hill begin the golden flower trees that lead up sixty thousand low hills of gold which surround Sunset Hill. The Sun dispels the darkness of the world up to this point. You can go this far. Do not go beyond, where the Sun and Moon are put out, and nothing can ever be seen. Look wherever you might expect to find Sita, and wherever you would think that she could never be. Return here to me within a month."

"*Jaya Sugriva Raja Maharaja Jaya!*" The General of the West battered his way to his feet, touched his hands together in a salute and left the room.

The white-furred Bear General of the North quietly removed his satin shoes at the door and gracefully entered unbidden, and knelt to the monkey king. "May you be pleased to command me, Lord."

"Survey for me the northern quarter of the world," said Sugriva. "Carefully search the Bharata and Kuru kingdoms. Go on into the bordering deodar forests of the bird tribes in the foothills, and cross the hair-raising lifeless desert beyond, and enter the enchanted lands of the Northern Kurus. Keep your wits about you. As wild animals who are free to come and go, search Kailasa Hill pale and silver as the moon, and go through the palace of the Treasure Lord Vaishravana, who is

209

bowed down to by all creatures who can bend. North of that, cross the Stone river where Apsarasas swim and play. Don't let the water touch you, but lean across by using the tall bamboo stalks lining the banks. Look among the magic Wishing Trees, and the trees that bear drinks and pearls for fruit, and the ground vines bearing couches and blankets like melons on stems. Examine the passes and the sloping sides of the icy Himalya, and listen there closely for the sound of music and the voice of sweet song and happy laughter; because what may seem to the eye to be but a bare mountainside at first, will often be an illusion, that hides the playgrounds of the Naga serpents beneath a spell of invisibility. Discover these hideaways and search them. Those Himalyan Naga people are blessed and fortunate, they are never sad nor want any beautiful thing, and every day they gain marvelous abilities and skills. And among the Hills is Mount Meru the center of the world, invisible to doubting people, round which revolve the Sun and Moon; indeed, in half an instant the Sun swiftly passes over Meru at noon. Farther north are treeless hills that hold the homes of horse-faced men and women. It should be dark beyond there, for Winter fast approaches, yet in many vales and caves live luminous saints, and the Northern Kuru land is visible by their bright light. On and on to the Far North stretches that land, eternally silent, shining with all the loveliness and reality of any ground warmed by the Sun, though there are few ways for moving creatures and the wide sky is empty of stars or clouds or light from heaven. Go on if you can, and you will reach the North Sea whose waters are black. Look at it from a distance but do not touch the surf and do not lose sight of Mount Meru behind you. Those North Sea shores are made of grey stone and black slate and shrouded in fog. There the cold wet wind blows onshore forever and the sea-spray freezes to salted ice in the air. Waves break like glass on the shore, darkness blots the air, fire will not burn, each day and night become a year and time is lost in eternity. Turn back quickly from this fearful northern border of the world, and let not more than a full month pass before you return."

210

The Bear General of the North touched his sword-hilt and said—*Yes*. He rose and left the room, and so out from Kishkindhya had gone three-fourths of the animal warriors, gone to search in three of the four directions, when Sugriva said, "Summon Hanuman, bring me Hanuman."

❧

Hanuman came in with Rama, padded over barefoot to the middle of the floor and sat down. The golden monkey prince Angada brought some rugs and also sat, and Sugriva left his throne to join them, and there also sat Rama and Lakshmana and the towering old Bear King Jambavan.

"Now the thing is," said Sugriva, "we saw Ravana fly South. Lanka is South. I make Prince Angada leader. Oh Rama, Hanuman the Son of the Wind will surely find Sita; if you will, stay here with me until they return, and let Lakshmana stay, and let Jambavan go, and let them return in a month." Sugriva stood up. He withdrew a scroll from his robes and gave it to Hanuman and said, "You know what to do and how to do it . . . here is a little message for the Demon King if you should chance to meet . . . don't lose it before you memorize it . . . ." Sugriva smiled and returned to his inner rooms and fell asleep.

Hanuman joined his hands. "Rama, we'll come back soon. Lanka is hard to reach and far away, but I know every province and city and puddle and footprint and demon stronghold in the world. When Vali would chase me and Sugriva we would fly so high that we saw below us all the world like a picture, clear as your face in a mirror. We saw Earth herself turning in space with a strange whirring noise like a firebrand swept quickly through the air. She was like a wheel, and her cities were like small golden coins and her rivers were crossing like threads. Her forests and meadows were tiny patches; the Vindhya and Himalya Hills all covered with rocks looked like elephants in a pond as they rose from the flat Earth."

Jambavan the bear smiled. "Sugriva trusts this Hanuman, and Hanuman relies with even more confidence on himself, and I will also accompany him."

211

He withdrew a scroll from his robes . . .

Rama gave Hanuman a wide gold ring. "This is mine and she will know it, for her father Janaka gave it to me after our wedding, and on it is written my name three times—*Rama, Rama, Rama!*"

❧

So with only one thought in their minds, the monkeys and bears fanned out from Kishkindhya into the four quarters of the world. They gave orders and ignored them, passed impassable torrents and climbed unclimbable crags, sifted the sands of the deserts and combed the meadows. They drove the yellow tigers yowling from the glens and the butterflies flapping from the gardens and the village cats running from the fields so that they all fled together. The monkeys and bears rushed along and shouted in high voices and low—*Step Aside! Move over! Let me by, it won't take me long!*

The animals of Kishkindhya ran up along the narrow ways that lead from certain holy temples to the hidden side-doors of heaven. They looked into sealed royal vaults and pawed through secret treasure-rooms forgotten from the past. Disguised as men, they bumped into people and picked their pockets; posing as bandits they shook out the tents of travelers as if they were cleaning rugs, and rattled the caravan wagons like dice to see what would fall out from them.

The monkeys and bears asked the birds a thousand searching questions. They peeked inside closed flowers, talked to the wild beasts and spoke to the tame buffalo. They listened to leopards in the quiet jungle and to men in the city bazaars. They followed streams to their sources in the hills to be sure they were not the water from Sita's tears. And at night they slept on the ground under fruit trees, making their beds beneath their breakfast.

Hanuman and Jambavan and Angada and a quarter of the animal warriors went South. After half a month they were not far from the Malaya Hills where sandalwood forests grow, when they entered a dead forest. Once in that wood, a hermit's son had died when he was but ten years old. His life had

213

run out then, and for that his father cursed all the land to lose its life. There was no food to be found, not even a bee lived there.

Angada led them on through valleys choked with thorns, through twined thickets and dense underbrush and clumps of thistles. They crossed chasms and ravines, and the Monkey Prince made them every one stay in the sight of another, until at last, tired and exhausted, the monkeys and bears collapsed under the dead trees to rest, lying on the dry grass curved over the hills, far to the south.

Then round a hillside flew two swans. His voice faint from thirst, Angada said to Hanuman, "Let's look around there." The birds flew by dripping water from their wings. Around the hill they saw the rocky mouth of a cave. A long narrow lightning scar seared the stones just outside it, and by the entrance grew water-loving trees, and they could feel a cool wet breeze when they looked inside.

But they could see nothing. It was dark as a black night pouring rain. First Hanuman went on in; Angada grabbed his tail, someone else held Angada's tail, and so forming a chain all the animals followed. The floor led down, then the slope steepened and the stones underfoot were wet. Hanuman slipped and started to slide. Angada stumbled and couldn't hold him back; then all the animals began to fall after Hanuman, still holding onto each other, unable to stop, falling faster and faster. The floor became the wall of a tunnel leading down. There were no handholds and nothing to stand on.

They fell for a hundred leagues. Finally they saw a light below, coming up to meet them, and then they dropped down into the bright lighted underworld. They fell all in a heap somehow unhurt, beside a wide splashing river running with cool white wine, with goblets growing from silvery rushes alongside, flowing in a channel lined with delicious little oysters.

It was a large cavern lit up by magic mirrors and chunks of gleaming gold set in the walls and ceiling high above. They all had a drink. Then Hanuman looked around and saw a white

214

palace with gold balconies and windows screened by nets of pearls. There were pools and ponds of water and wines set out in a park, and playing fountains, and petals on the paths. And in that park the living fish were real gold and the turtles were chased silver.

The monkeys and bears started to celebrate their rescue. But by accident Jambavan the bear broke off a branch from a lovely red rosebush. Blood ran out from the break; the roses lost their color and were drained white. Then Hanuman made everyone be still, and with Jambavan cautiously approached the enchanted palace.

A beautiful young girl dressed in a soft black antelope robe was sitting in the shade of a bell tree, on a bench of purple lapis, by the jewel stairs that led into the house behind her. One by one, all the monkeys and bears came and sat down quietly around her.

And though they did not know it, that marked the end of the month's time. From wherever they had gone, all the rest of the animals came again to Kishkindhya, from East and North and West. The General of the East covered his face; the General of the West sighed; the General of the North returned covered with ashes. Sugriva said, "Oh Rama, now it is only Hanuman the Son of the Wind who will succeed in finding Sita . . . but the time is past and where is he?"

❧

In the cave where they had fallen, Hanuman asked that girl, "Who are you and whose home is this?"

She said, "I am Swayamprabha, a mortal woman, though here things are not always what they seem. This is Maya's Cave of Trees. The Asura Maya of masterful art and illusion built all this."

"How did you get here?" asked Hanuman.

"Little monkey, I am a dancer. I dance, and I dance so well that Apsarasas from heaven come to watch me, and in this way I became self-luminous and a dear friend of Hema the Apsarasa." Swayamprabha smiled. "I'll give you mangoes and

215

bananas and honey, and will you not tell me why you were going through the desolate forest on Earth above us?"

"I am Hanuman. We are looking for Sita."

"Oh," said Swayamprabha, "I am pleased, I am well-pleased with meeting the quick-footed monkeys and the furry bears!"

While the animals ate, Hanuman asked, "Where is Maya?"

"He could be here right now," smiled that winsome girl. "Maya the Asura is a true artist, a magician of marvelous power. Whatever Maya creates is perfect and complete, while it lasts, before it changes. All is illusion, Hanuman . . . he would often say—*believe it and make it true* . . . ." Swayamprabha's dark eyes filled with tears, ". . . before he died . . . ."

Hanuman was all ears. "What happened?"

"Indra killed him," she said, "by the mouth of this very cave. Hema the Apsarasa inherited this place, and I take care of it for her. She was Maya's consort, and that angered Indra."

Hanuman said, "Hema's daughter is Queen of Lanka."

"Yes, it was soon after her marriage to Ravana; it was in a storm on Earth above . . . you can still see the path the lightning made blasted into the stones!"

"Still—" said Hanuman.

"You're right," said Swayamprabha. "Indras come and go. Maya is a true genius, the Master of Time. He could escape that down-lighting thunderbolt."

Hanuman grinned. "And Indra saw it hit?"

"Absolutely! He saw Maya blasted to bits by thunder, right below his very eyes!"

"All one thousand of them!" said Hanuman.

"Indra had kept Hema closely guarded after her daughter was born, and Maya got the child somehow, and only the two of them, father and daughter, stayed all alone in empty rooms."

"But now Indra is off guard, I think, and in some beautiful home—"

Swayamprabha laughed. "The Asura Maya is a consummate actor; they never found his body. Who knows? He might return, he might be very angry to find thousands of monkeys and bears in his cave . . . ."

Hanuman saluted Swayamprabha. "How may we go?"

She answered, "So you will go to Lanka? But once anyone enters this captivating cave of illusions, especially by mistake, he can never return alive to Earth by his own power. But I will help you, call the others." She put on her dancing bells.

The monkeys and bears assembled. Swayamprabha said, "Fair fortune to you. Stand still, close your eyes and cover them. You must not look until I tell you."

The monkeys and bears covered their eyes with their soft paws and hid their faces in their hands. They heard Swayamprabha's dancing bells chime, and it seemed they could smell the ocean.

You can look. They looked around and found themselves facing South, standing by the shore of the Southern Sea, with the coastal Malaya Hills close at their backs. They smelled the sandalwood trees, and from within those hillside forests the southern Nagas watched, coiled in their serpent forms, hidden in the branches behind the pointed leaves.

❦

The blue sea, far and wide, vast as the blue sky! A light breeze lifted spray from the wave-caps, and the waves fell lightly ashore, and slipped back sighing into the deep. A delightful river crossed the beach, lined by trees that hid her waters and islands, and veiled her, like some young girl going to meet her secret lover.

Prince Angada shaded his eyes and stared toward the Sun. Then he slumped to the ground and cried—*Hanuman!*

"What?" Hanuman ran up fast.

"Look where the Sun is! We've lost our other half a month! How long were we inside there?"

Hanuman stared at his shadow. "The month is up alright . . . I thought we had more time. Through ignorance we entered Maya's treeful cave underground and lost all the time . . . ."

217

Angada got up and stamped his feet. "We were tricked by illusion! Rama's work isn't done, the King's orders aren't obeyed—oh, happy are the dead!" He turned to the others and shouted, "I won't straggle home a failure, I'll starve myself to death right here!"

The monkeys and bears swung their arms and yelled, "We will die with you!" Except for Hanuman and Jambavan the bear, they all sat facing the south, all over the seashore. They fell silent and entered meditation and resolved to die.

Hanuman and Jambavan turned away. They walked on down the beach and left the others there behind them. It was a beautiful day, in the early afternoon. It was quiet. The waves were low and long between. The river ran over round rocks and spoke in whispers, and the gentle wind blew in off the sea.

The old bear Jambavan shuffled slowly along, and the sunlight made his dark fur seem to glow, tipped with reddish lights. He stretched out in the spotted shade beneath an ancient honey tree, and Hanuman lay back against Jambavan's soft flank, and yawned, and began to daydream.

Jambavan snorted and blew some sand away from his nose, and said in a rumbly voice, "Monkey, how was Sita lost? Tell me Rama's story."

Hanuman closed his eyes and put his hands in his lap. "This tale is full of peril and safety," he began. "It will armor noble souls with courage, and bring heart failure to cowards. It will perplex the wise and baffle the foolish, and make them both follow their hearts. It gives reasons for acting in every way; its chapters haunt the mind; its verses make heroes hunger for glory. Its lines shed warm love, its words bring smiles of rage and tears of joy. Oh King of the Bears, this story is not for worried ears and weak nerves, for it holds dread and rash chivalry, sweet honor and elegant danger, and graceful bravery and bountiful generosity beyond knowing."

hanuman's jump

Look!
The Son of the Wind leaps into the air,
And flies through the clouds with a roar,
While the enemy waves on the green salt sea
Splash and foam below!

Oh, gold and silver found wild
Are better than coins tamely won;
Treasures found on a hunt are as good
As the pleasures of fancy in heaven.

The little wind carried every word down past the other animals and up into the Malaya foothills. Hanuman said, "Listen well, Oh Jambavan. Once in Fair Ayodhya there was an old King who had no children . . . ."

Hanuman told of Rama's birth and marriage, of his exile and his father's death, of how he killed the demons of Dandaka Forest, and of how Ravana made a golden deer, and of the theft of Sita. The monkeys and bears around Angada began to fuss and squirm. They strained to hear the story, and began to wring their hands and sigh and exclaim things under their breaths.

Then suddenly a flying shadow fell over the beach. Down from the blue Malaya hills swooped a huge vulture. But his flight feathers were burned. He couldn't slow his fall; he waved his wings at the air and landed heavily on the shore. His wings threw up a cloud of sand that buried Angada and all the suicidal monkeys and bears up to their ears in grit.

Hanuman and Jambavan were out of the draft, and Hanuman went right on with his story. The vulture picked himself

219

up. He turned his head and looked at the monkeys and bears he'd buried, first with one big round orange eye, then with the other.

"It's true," said the vulture. "People are really rewarded for past good deeds, for here are fat little animals all set out in rows for me by the kindly gods. They've lived all their lives just for my dinner!"

Then down the wind came Hanuman's words, and the vulture heard him say, "Great was the deed of Jatayu. Old though he was, for Sita's sake he nearly killed Ravana before the Demon King tore his soul from this life."

The hulking vulture turned and peered under the honey tree and said—*Who speaks of my little brother Jatayu, King of the Air?*

Hanuman replied, "I am Hanuman. This is Jambavan the Lord of Bears. The animals of Kishkindhya are searching for Sita. Ravana took her from her husband Rama, and he killed your brother when Jatayu tried to stop him in Dandaka Forest."

"My name is Sampati," said the vulture. "If I could still fly I'd go to Lanka and kill Ravana for that!" Towering over the beach he rubbed one leg against the other, like scraping a thousand scythes over pieces of slate.

Prince Angada jumped up out of the sand. Courteously he introduced himself, and said, "Please let us die in peace. All is vain. We can't find Sita, and now whatever I have not seen and heard and done must wait for my next lowly life."

"But monkey prince," said Sampati, "I thought you knew; she is in Lanka, if she lives at all."

"How do you know?"

"My eyesight is as clear as the good Dharma law," said Sampati. "The vulture race can see movement from afar, for a hundred leagues. We have magic golden eyes."

"Are you sure?" asked Angada.

"Prince, I am Sampati, swift as the wind. Eight thousand years ago Jatayu and I went flying together. We went over wood and forest, streams and kingdoms, and higher, and over clouded lakes where snow-geese swam, and over hills of grey stone, and always higher, until we went so high, we saw the Sun shining near and large as the Earth! Then the heat struck us down, and I fell, shadowing Jatayu with my open wings. I fell in a glare of light that made all the worlds seem burning, with no shadow, and no way to know where I was. Then all at once I lost the wind. My brother and I fell apart from each other. I found myself here on these southern hills and slowly my memory returned.

"My wings were useless, and after all these years I have only today recovered enough to rise from my back. And this year, this summer as I lay helpless I saw Ravana fly overhead with Sita. I kept him in sight all the way to Lanka, and he has not left the island with her since then. She is somewhere behind the city walls, over the sea.

"None of my people knew where I was, until one of my sons found me yesterday night. He was very sad that he could offer me no food, and said he would bring me some later today. He said, 'Father, I caught nothing today. It's the first time I have failed on a hunt since once before the rains, when I prepared to attack a dark demon with ten necks as he flew in the air over a mountain pass, going south, not far from here. He carried a fair woman and peacefully begged me—*I admit my defeat and take your protection.* I could not attack someone who had surrendered to me and I let him go on. And then I heard the sky-voices saying—*That was the doomed Rakshasa King Ravana. By good fortune Sita still lives, and passed you safely by.* But I will bring you food tomorrow.' So it was her, Prince Angada, and there are two of us who saw her carried away. Age has not weakened my mind and eye, though my life now hangs loosely upon me, for I have not eaten since I fell from heaven."

The animals who were still buried in the beach looked worried. Angada told them, "Stop thinking. Bring us some vulture food."

"Say no more!" they cried, and ran to the mountain woods.

Hanuman said, "Sampati, Rama himself burned Jatayu's body, and now your brother lives in heaven. We may live for

221

thousands of years and never hear of a braver deed than his. Had Jatayu been even one day younger he would have won. All noble creatures love Rama, and in his kind service will live their lives for him, and do gentle good to each other, and bad to Rama's foes."

The food arrived, and as Sampati ate, young new feathers began to grow from his wings like golden down. Then Sampati said, "Ignore your time limit, for truly Ravana took Sita at a time when what is lost is soon regained, at a moment most unfortunate to a thief."

Angada asked, "How far is Lanka?"

"Just about a hundred leagues, no more," answered Sampati.

Angada looked out at the sea. One place his still water reflected the image of all this world and all the sky; elsewhere, blown by the wind, he rose in playful waves as high as hills. Angada felt waves of doubt run through the monkeys and bears.

"Who will leap the ocean and bring back news of Sita?" asked Angada.

The monkeys and bears answered, "I can jump ten leagues . . . I can go thirty . . . seventy . . . I can jump a hundred but I can't get back."

Angada said, "I'll try myself."

"You can't," said Jambavan, "you're our commander. You're the root of our search, it's we who must resort to you and serve you."

"Then there's not a hope."

"No hope!" said the old bear. "Oh, there was a time—" He turned to Hanuman who stood beside him. "Listen, little monkey, are you going to stand there looking at us like an idiot?"

Hanuman said, "What?"

"You're young and strong, what have you done to help us?" said Jambavan. "I didn't hear you say anything just now about how far you can jump."

222

Hanuman said, "I'll do it."

Oh King Rama, Wind is Fire's best friend. Wind shatters the hills and moves across the eye of heaven. He cannot be seen, but only the heavy things he moves are visible. Hanuman is the son of the fast-racing generous Wind. He equals his father in flight. To enhance the sorrow of the Rakshasas he wants to leap into Lanka. There was dismay and faint sorrow, and it was time to be strong. Then like a storm Hanuman drove away low spirits, like a light he brought courage.

§

THIS IS THE END OF THE
BOOK OF KISHKINDHYA.
HERE FOLLOWS THE SUNDARA KANDA,
THE BOOK BEAUTIFUL.

§

❖ ❖ ❖

In his mind Hanuman had already crossed the sea and entered the demon city. He climbed one of the Malaya hills to get firm ground under his feet. He began to fill up with power. He grew very large and heavy, and his tread pressed down the hill and crushed the caves of serpents. Out from underworld came the richly dressed Nagas, bruised and hissing, their hoods spread wide. In their anger they rolled on the ground with tongues flaming; they spat fire and bit the rocks in passion. Their venom cracked the hill, and gleams of red metal and stone showed from within the Earth.

Hanuman climbed higher. With smiles of amazement, the heavenly Gandharvas and their Apsarasas rose half-dressed from the hill into the sky and looked down to watch. Hanuman climbed up through their hillside parks, where Gandharva swords and bright-colored robes were hung on the

Hanuman stood on the hilltop . . .

trees, and golden winecups and silver dishes were on the ground in fair shady gardens hiding lovers' beds of lotus petals.

Hanuman neared the summit. His feet squeezed water from the hill. Rivers tumbled down, rockslides rolled, bright fresh-broken veins of gold sparkled, tigers ran off and birds flew away. The tree spirits fled, and in their dens the wildcats yelled in a frightful chorus, like the cry of the mountain himself through the voice of all his animals.

Hanuman stood on the hilltop. He held his breath and sucked in his stomach. He frisked his tail and raised it a little at the end. He bent his knees and swung back his arms, and on one finger gleamed Rama's gold ring. Then without pausing to think he drew in his neck, laid back his ears and jumped.

It was grand! It was the greatest leap ever taken. The speed of Hanuman's jump pulled blossoms and flowers into the air after him and they fell like little stars on the waving treetops. The animals on the beach had never seen such a thing; they cheered Hanuman, then the air burned from his passage, and red clouds flamed over the sky and Hanuman was far out of sight of land.

That white monkey was like a comet, pushing the sky from his way and bumping clouds aside. The wind roared under his arms and was pushed down from his breast as he passed, and made the ocean pitch and roll. Sea spray rose and steamed up the Sun. Beneath Hanuman as he went, the green salt water parted, and he could see the whales and fishes like people surprised at home. The air around Hanuman became electric, and sheets of light gathered and crackled—blue, and pale melon green, and flickering orange and red.

Halfway across to Lanka, the golden mountain Mainaka lived on the ocean floor, and from under sea he saw Hanuman coming and thought he would be tired. Mainaka spread his glistening golden wings, rose from his watery bed and surfaced on the sea. Water poured from his shining sides and looming up against the blue sky he spoke to Hanuman.

"Rest awhile," said Mainaka. "Let me repay my ancient debt to your father the Wind."

225

Hanuman stopped and leaned on the air. "Who are you?"

"I am Mainaka, the son of Himavan the Mountain King, the brother of Ganga the beautiful river Goddess. I have long hidden deep in the ocean from fear of Indra. In return for the sea's faithful protection, I have stayed as an outer gate against the Asuras from under Earth, who dare not approach me. Come down onto me, land and rest."

Hanuman asked, "What did my father do for you?"

Mainaka said, "In the olden days, long ago, all the large mountains of Earth had wings like I do. We flew where we wanted, but when we landed we were sometimes a little careless. We bowled over the little hills and flattened kingdoms flat as a floor. We got a bad name with the forest men, and they complained to Indra. Then with furious thunderbolts the Lord of Heaven cut off our wings, till out of all the hills only I could still fly. When Indra chased me the Wind carried me away, and here I took refuge of the sea. The wings of the broken mountains have now become clouds. So blessed be you, gentle Hanuman, rest and continue refreshed."

"Forgive me, but I must not break my flight," said Hanuman. He only touched that golden hill with his fingertip and sped away to the South.

When he had gone, Indra came from heaven and told Mainaka, "Keep your wings if you will, for you welcomed Hanuman and you have cared to keep him from danger," and Mainaka went back below the waves.

In the strong sea-currents that lay twenty leagues off Lanka lived the old Rakshasi Sinhika. She saw Hanuman flying and said, "This is the strangest bird I've seen in eight hundred years!" She swam to the surface and seized his shadow, and in the air Hanuman felt himself being dragged down and held back.

Sinhika stood on the water holding Hanuman's shadow in her claws and looking at him with tiny red eyes. She opened her ugly mouth and bared her yellow scaly teeth, and started to pull at his shadow.

"Watch out!" said Hanuman. "Beware, I am on Rama's service, and his kingdom is all the world . . . ."

She pulled him closer. "You can never escape me!"

"Oh yes, I will if I want to!"

She saw how large Hanuman was and opened her mouth wide as a cave with a long tongue. But Hanuman became quickly small as a thumb and flew down her throat like a tiny hurricane. He crushed her heart with his sharp fingernails, turned, and darted up out from her ear. Sinhika threw her arms about and collapsed on the sea. Her blood burst and spread through the water, and the fish came quickly to eat her.

Then Hanuman regained his jumping size and flew on in the sky, where birds fly and rainbows gleam, where heroes ride in bright chariots drawn by miraculous lions, where the smoke of fires rises and the rains and winds live. He went on through the pure sky embellished by planets and stars and luminous saints and by the holy Sun and Moon, the support and glorious canopy of this live world, the sky made and well made by Lord Brahma long ago.

❦

The green hills of Lanka Island rose from the horizon. Hanuman saw the shoreline of warm white sand and scattered stones and water pools, and behind that many tall swaying palms, and plane trees, and forests of aloes. He saw rivers meet the sea, and saw where pearls and cowrie shells and fine corals had been spread to dry. He flew inland, over stacks of gold and silver from the demon mines that lay blazing in the sunlight, and then he saw the City.

Beautiful Lanka was built on a level place just below the highest summit of the three-peaked hill Trikuta, as though built on clouds. She had four gates facing in the four directions and her strong golden walls were the color of sunshine. Preceded by a little breeze, Hanuman landed under an overhanging cliff on the hill not far below the city, amid fruit trees in full flower and bearing fruit as well, in a soft scene like heaven. Blue rivers laughing with flowers fell running down channels and stairs of ruby, and trees of every color growing uphill reached out to catch the faint pink clouds. The warm sea-wind smelled like pepper and cloves and fragrant spices.

Hanuman ate some dates and thought, "Not a hair out of place, I'm ready to do it again! I call that little ocean a puddle . . . not like other people . . . I'm better than any bird . . . ."

Carefully Hanuman crept out from hiding, just enough to see the main highway to Lanka's north wall. Around the walls ran a deep moat fed by a mountain river, shark-filled, running in a bed of iron and wearing pale floating lotuses and lilies. The tall red-golden gateway panels were painted with green plants and twining vines, with fish and trees and flowers, flights of birds and clouds and stars. Elephants stood under the stone gate arch, and Rakshasa bowmen looked out from the crowning roofs and turrets. Seen from below, Lanka was a lofty city moving in the sky and built on air, embraced by clouds and held by sunbeams.

"We'll have to kill them all," thought Hanuman. "We can't be friends, they are too proud to approach. They would never betray Ravana. They can't be bought off, they are too bold and strong."

Beautiful Lanka was decked out like a maiden. Waters and woods were her clothes, bristling spears and darts on the wall were the ends of her long hair; the many-colored waving banners and the cloth-of-gold war-flags nearby them were her jewels and earrings; the high stone missile towers were her breasts cleaving the sky. She was Beautiful Lanka of the Waves, well-defended, built in time long past by Viswakarman the architect of heaven. She seemed a city woven from beauty, made by the mind from a wonderful dream half-remembered.

The late afternoon shadows lengthened, and Hanuman thought, "I will first meet Sita somewhere in there, and she will tell me what to do."

Then as the twilight of evening came and Night fell black over the dark world, Hanuman diminished his size, and took the form of a small long-haired silver tabby cat. He tied Rama's ring round his neck and it was lost in fur. He hid in a ditch and said, "If they see me, a cat roams free at night, and may explore wherever he is curious to go. Three times I take

228

refuge in Rama, who is the safe shelter of all who flee for help from any thing."

In the dark Hanuman sprang over the moat and walked away from the road, down along the base of the wall to where there was no gate, prancing like a cat on four feet, going a little sideways, his legs stiff and his tail like a plume straight up in the air. Suddenly a dark-skinned woman appeared from nowhere before him, her face crooked in an unlovely smile, flames for her hair and a bleeding tigerskin for her dress, standing there in a halo of glowing lights and moving colors that looked like the burning clouds at the destruction of all the three worlds.

She looked down at Hanuman and said in a despicable voice, "Now be careful, be on your guard! Advance half a hair's point farther and I will kill you!"

"Who are you?" asked Hanuman.

"I am Lanka herself, surrounded by protections, ruled by the hand of Ravana. You cannot enter me, little cat!"

Hanuman said, "Gentle goddess, I am curious to see your

hidden charms and attractions. I am a mere monkey, just let me take a quiet look around—"

"Never till the end of Time!" She hissed and kicked Hanuman hard, but he didn't move at all. He sat, and fastened his left forefingers into a fist. Then he jumped up and hit her right between the eyes. Lanka fell on her back. Hanuman helped her to rise, and she put her foot in his way, and drew it back, and stood aside.

"When a monkey knocks you down, know that a fear and a curse have come to the Rakshasas . . . so have I heard," said the goddess. "You have vanquished the realm of Lanka with one blow; enter if you will."

Hanuman leapt over the high wall, where there was no door, by night, and landing within he first touched the ground with his left foot, putting that foot on his enemies' heads.

❧

Hanuman went to the shadow of a tree, and knelt and joined together his hands. "I trust in Rama," he said. "World-famous Lanka is inconceivable and lovely, a fortress city whose moat is the sea. She shines in her glory. No one can subdue her by force. She is guarded by Rakshasas standing with their weapons uplifted in their upraised hands, yet I have entered. I remember the ancient saints, and call to mind the warriors of the past. I trust in Rama, I trust in Rama . . . he is very strong—and alas, that for their one king's wrong this noble race of demons must perish!"

Then to help Hanuman, the small clouds withdrew from the sky. The bright round Moon was revealed, the friend of the sea, reaching his long silver rays over all, making the shadows blacker, afloat like a white swan in the clear starry sky, in the bottomless lake of heaven. The Moon was full, it was the last full Moon before winter. Watching Hanuman that night over Lanka was our Lady Lakshmi of good fortune, who sometimes wanders on Earth's high hills or walks at evening by the seas, standing in the sky beside the Moon.

Hanuman waited, and Heaven turned above him. The

Moon gleamed like a mirror, like the face of a king gaining a kingdom. Midnight came, when among humans couples end their quarrels with love and sleep together; and among Rakshasas, in the forests the hideous Night-Wanderers, astonishing and terrible, go out to eat flesh and drink the blood of carnage. In Lanka began the night-life of every enjoyment; and at midnight Hanuman began his search for Sita.

The brick streets of Lanka were lined by tall adjoining houses set behind trees and built of white stones marked with a thunderbolt and hook by Viswakarman the architect. Behind the main streets were gardens and alleys, and there prowled Hanuman, looking in the lattice windows and running over the roofs. He heard the sounds of every indulgence—lutes and horns and two-headed drums and late-at-night laughter; chattering parrots and demons clapping time; running feet, and here and there droning sing-song chants from the holy Veda.

He saw many a fair demoness, and some of the Rakshasas also appeared much like men of good height and form. But other demons were black, or a ghastly pink, or pale and nearly transparent. Some were unbelievably handsome, others were maimed and deformed, repulsive and frightful even in their splendid clothes. On the streets carrying torches Hanuman saw the night patrols of Rakshasa warriors from every demon nation, clad in rich and regal heraldry, or in feathers and quills, or wearing rotting raw skins, or walking naked with shaven heads. They were armed with studded bludgeons or knives or blow-pipes or handfuls of holy grass enchanted into spears and javelins. These were the warriors who had conquered heaven and received the surrender of the seven netherworlds.

Hanuman saw many things, shamelessly looking in windows and doors. He saw the royal spies with matted hair like holy beggars. Their plain-looking hermit's staves and rods were secretly loaded with heavy metal cores, and they concealed blades and razors in their hair, and wore mantras tied on their arms with strings, and death-spells were hidden in their traveling fire jars that they would carry innocently slung over their arms.

Hanuman saw demons who looked wise and powerful even when drunk and asleep with wine, with women, or with their arms round their beloved bags of gold. He saw army officers with coppery lines of sandalpaste on their bodies, talking and waving their strong arms, stretching tough bows and looking disdainfully at maps and beating their chests and sending out orders—*Hurry up! Wait!* He saw violent, swift demons who never slept, lying in the dark rolling their dismal staring eyes and wearing earrings of charred bone, all alone in the dead of night. He saw courtesans entertaining the rich; by joyous smiles and long slow side-glances of their eyes they trapped all hearts in loveliness and glamor and made all life a pleasure. He saw young new-married wives with their husbands, held by bashfulness and bliss both at once; and girls sad for separation from lovers dear to their souls, weeping heartbroken. And over all the wind chimes and little temple bells, the hum of mantras being chanted grew louder as the night went on, the very sound of the power of Lanka, filling the air.

Hanuman worked his way to the center of the city. There a lesser wall ran in a great circle, made of sixteen colors of rose gold, enclosing the palaces of King Ravana. Hanuman jumped over it and landed in a garden. Bright-flaring lamps burned on golden posts and standards of silver, and the gravel on the garden paths was made from jewels. All around him were garden temples where black incense burned, secluded libraries and detached pavilions and arbors and retreats. And rising above them all, in the center of the great park was a spired palace with royal golden domes, a building clad in costly gems and starred with diamonds, a mansion only different from the best one in heaven in that it touched the Earth of Lanka.

Hanuman slipped past hooded watchmen who sighed impatiently into the night, expecting an attack, looking forward to stopping some invasion. He went unnoticed past fanatical birds set out in crimson amaranth trees and trained to scream an alarm if they were disturbed. Hanuman searched one side of the castle grounds, and then the front of the garden, and then he entered a great courtyard on the third side of Ravana's palace, running the whole way from front to back.

That courtyard was as large as half a city, and there filling it entirely was the huge aerial chariot Pushpaka that Ravana had stolen from his brother Vaishravana the Treasure Lord. That colossal chariot was transcendently beautiful, a car made everywhere of flowers, made by Viswakarman in Heaven, the chariot of Spring, driven by the mind, and lightly resting in Lanka two fingers off the ground. Pushpaka the Car of Flowers is a field of treasures; he is a joyful way to travel, a vehicle of swift vision and soaring fancy; he rides as smooth as the transport of a man by a dear wish come true.

Hanuman got on that car and searched it. By the light of the full Moon he could see a forest of flagpoles like rows of tall trees against the night sky, and from them flew a skyful of flags and silken streamers and pennons bright and colored. Pushpaka had hills and green lawns, sweet-smelling rosebeds and ivory benches covered with brocade. There were figures carved out of gold of wolves and horses placed by houses made of vines. There were ornate and curious iron railings and far-looking balconies, little silver doors set with rubies that led somewhere under the green grass, wind-nets of tiny silver bells, crystal windows and secret passages, a gallery showing pictures of elephants bathing, silk tents and a theater, fishponds and moss gardens, overgrown paths and glades of ferns, and a swimming pool with a splashing fountain whose water fell over a stone image of Lakshmi standing on a big open blue lotus of turquoise, holding in her hand a little red lotus bud cut from coral.

Viswakarman the Architect of Heaven always considered Pushpaka chariot his masterpiece. When Pushpaka flies at night with his running fires and lights on, it seems that all the sky moves with its starbeams and planets; bells ringing and flags flying, by day he is a marker for the Sun's path, and one may look up and see how all his chariot hull is built of rainbows tied together.

Pushpaka can fly behind a thousand horses or without them. The materials used to build him have come from all the Universe, from these worlds and from other worlds. In some places the rays of his yellow topaz garden walls will keep day-lilies open at night; and elsewhere even by day the night-lotus is ever open, held in the rays of dark emeralds that stop the daylight and cast beneath them a deep shade and an illusion of Night, like being somehow within a lightless heavy raincloud.

Pushpaka chariot is Earth's ornament embodied to view, and a gathering of all wonderful things. He goes through the air in infinite motions. On him, you go where you will. You can look out the windows, or ride out in the open air under the Sun, standing on carpets, among jewels all around you that wink when the great chariot turns in the sky and the sunlight moves overhead.

Hanuman searched all through that vast and beautiful chariot as he would have explored an old climbing tree with many holes and branches. There was no one aboard. Nothing moved. Hanuman stood at the forward rail sniffing the air. At first he could still smell the carved sandalwood of Pushpaka and all his flowers, but then the wind turned just a bit, and brought from somewhere the scents of foods fit for a King and of well-mixed iced drinks, and the smell of the costly perfumes palace women use at night after bathing.

Hanuman left Pushpaka and followed his nose to the side of the royal palace set in the very center of Lanka and surrounded by its own gardens, and he caught a glimpse of many lights as he approached. Hanuman thought—*Find the pleasures of the senses, and there find the Demon King.*

❧

Hanuman went into the palace. He went bounding and sniffing past a thousand enduring pillars and columns, through stately chambers and long rambling halls lit by hanging war-shields and the gleam of magic bows stacked close together. The corridor walls were made of deep blue tiles and bands of bricks glazed crimson, and set high above were large windows covered by networks of gold and crystal, or of soft ivories and silver, or curtained over with silks. There were rooms of precious stones and serving dishes and full metal winejars, and of these many rooms none had been built by conquest, all were made for the asking.

The scent of food and wine and women grew stronger. Hanuman went on over alabaster floors and up a stairway of cool lapis and burnished gold, until he reached the end of a silver-paved hall and opened a tall jade door with a cut amethyst handle big as a coconut. Behind that the doorway was closed by a hanging woolen curtain colored in stripes, a drawn veil shaped like the Earth—four-cornered, and flat, and as wide as the world with all her lands and people and homes.

That was the entrance to Ravana's bedroom. Hanuman ducked under the left corner of the draw-curtain and stood just inside with his back to the wall, looking out at a huge floor lit by flaming lamps of gold and covered with sleeping women so tumbled together that Hanuman could not tell where one lady left off and the next began.

There was hardly space to step anywhere. Those were the countless wives of the Demon King asleep in disarray, lying all over each other, women beautiful and bright as flashes of lightning now locked fast in Sleep's embrace. Hanuman thought, "When even the form of a heavenly star is less than enough, virtue's divine reward for a good life must be to receive such fair shapes and lovely limbs as these!"

Once arriving in that room of women, it would be harder for any man to remember who he was or where he stood or why, than to fly across the sea in the first place. And though Hanuman was not a man, still when he looked at each one he thought no other woman could be fairer, and when he saw the next sleeper she was in turn the best and most beautiful as he looked at her. Truly, among those magnificent women the

235

rays of the one's beauty showed off the charms of another; they slept deeply after an evening of drinking and dancing and playing music. Their fragrant hair was loosened and their bracelets scattered; their beauty marks of sandal paste were smudged and their colored robes unclasped and their waist-chains ran loosely straying to the side; their hazy garlands were disbanded and their pearls had gone and their earrings were lost.

Hanuman feared to do wrong and never broke a good law unless he had to. "It is surely wrong," he thought, "to gaze even by accident at another's wife lying unclothed or defenseless or asleep. But I take refuge in Rama, I take shelter with him. The mind commands the eye and sends out sight in good or evil fashion. By Rama's help, my mind will not change by this looking. I am saving Rama's life by seeking for Sita, and surely a woman may be found among other women."

Even the bedroom lamps looked openly out at all those women while they had the chance, as Ravana slept. Hanuman picked his way among the love-skilled Queens of Lanka who were draped over the floor and looked at their faces. They smiled or frowned or sighed in their sleep; their pillows were others' arms and legs and laps; they pulled each other's robes and wrapped themselves in them. With their eyes lashed shut in sleep they were desirable as closed flowers; when they touched each other they smiled and drew closer, believing they pressed Ravana with their breasts. Even asleep the dancers moved enticingly; the girl musicians slept embracing drums and hugging lutes like their long-absent lovers.

The golden lamps on the walls watched over them unblinking, and in their light the gold and jewels of those Queens made a river of lights and colors and shimmering waves of gold and silver. Their pearl necklaces were white water-birds asleep between their breasts, rising and falling; their strings of turquoise were families of blue teal and their hips were the waves and the riverbanks; their faces of golden or white or deep blue skin were the lotuses; when they stirred sleepily, the small bells sewn on their silken clothes were the ripples moving with little sounds; and the bruises and scratches of love on their tender breasts were signs of where the lion and tiger had come to drink.

Then across the room, in a corner Hanuman saw a crystal bed raised above a short flight of jeweled steps, under a white umbrella of seven tiers fringed with colors. Flame-red Asoka flowers hung from the four ivory bedposts, and at the head and foot mechanical men, silently driven by falling water in some hidden way, gently fanned the air with yak-tail chowries.

Hanuman drew near and looked up onto the bed. The pale yellow silk sheets were trimmed in diamonds and the many soft pillows were covered with fleecy ram skins. And on that bed lay the Demon King Ravana fast asleep—heroic and dark, wearing white, with twenty arms like gate pillars marked with cool blood-red sandal paste, with ten devilishly handsome heads, with his faces aglow from long heavy gold earrings, sleeping like a deep-breathing hill. Ravana slept unsuspecting, all worn out from love and wine. He was the dear desire of every Rakshasa daughter, and the happiness of every Lanka warrior.

Hanuman shrank back in awe. The back of Ravana's bedroom opened onto an outdoor drinking terrace. Hanuman quietly went out there, and climbed onto a long table heaped with savory leftover roasts and perfumed rice and good cooking made to thrill the seven thousand nerves of taste. Delicately, still in the form of a cat, Hanuman padded between the plates, and there he sat entranced, looking over at Ravana from a little distance. Hanuman was a monkey of the woods, he did not desire fair women and he ate no cooked food . . . but he could not take his eyes off Ravana lying asleep there in the majestic lamplight.

Ravana lay like a collection of wrongs, a mass of harm and injury and brutality and darkness of heart. On the Demon King's broad breast were the old curving white scars from the tusks of Indra's elephant Airavata; on his strong dark arms were the burns of thunderbolts and lightnings and scars from

237

the bowstring; around nine of his necks ran thin lines to show where he had once cut off nine heads and burned them as an offering to the gods.

At last Hanuman looked away for an instant, then back at Ravana. *As long as he stays there*—he thought. He looked over the foods on his table and poured himself a drink. Then Hanuman ate some melons and peaches, and lapped up some cream, and began to purr and wash himself, just like a cat. He licked his paw till it was wet, and washed down through the whiskers by his mouth, and up over his ear. He wasn't thinking about anything special and his cat's eyes roamed idly here and there.

All at once he stopped washing and squeezed his arms like a monkey. He saw Mandodari the Queen of Lanka sleeping apart on her own bed, very beautiful, the mistress of all the palace. He thought, "Rich with youth and so beautiful, she is Sita! It's her!" He kissed his tail, jumped off the dining table and ran in gleeful circles. He sat and slapped his hands on his knees and smiled and hummed a joyful tune, acting just like a monkey. He ran over and up and sat perched atop one of Ravana's bedposts.

"Oh no!" Hanuman had another thought. He sighed and stopped still. "That's not her. What a shameful apish idea— *Where would Sita have any place in this bedroom?* That's the Queen of Lanka, the daughter of illusion . . . though Ravana may well wish that she were Sita. First taking a false form, the Demon King was barely able to steal her at all. Sita will drink no Lanka wine nor ever love another husband . . . when do elephants mate with hogs, and who finishes a good meal with a glass of vinegar?"

❖

Hanuman jumped from Ravana's bedpost to the bedroom terrace, and from there he leapt into the yard behind the palace. Only behind Ravana's mansion had he not yet looked.

With a little snap, Hanuman discarded his cat disguise. He

was again a white monkey, and Rama's ring was on his finger once more. A low stone wall enclosed a grove of Asoka trees behind the palace, and Hanuman sat on that wall slumped over, staring blankly ahead at nothing, scuffing his heels against the stones. The little leaves of all the trees around began to stir in the faint wind of the end of night.

Hanuman was tired out. It seemed he had opened and closed half the doors and windows on Earth; he had looked in rooms and burrows and holes, and even under water along the bottoms of Lanka's lakes and ponds, and he could not find Sita.

Hanuman held his breath a long moment, and then sighed. He talked to himself and addressed the empty gardens. "She is surely dead, for the vulture Sampati blinked his tired eyes, and missed seeing her fall from Ravana's grasp somewhere into the sea. Or Ravana delighting in evil has killed her. He flew so fast she could not breathe, or he crushed her—Sita is dead, she lives no more, and sadly she cried out for her Lord Rama with her last breath!"

Tears dripped from Hanuman's yellowy eyes and ran down his red face. His words grew all choking wet. He wrung his hands and shook his head and switched his tail. "Ah, how unhappy! What heartbreak, what a failure! I can't return with nothing to answer Rama, never again will I laugh and play with my friends of the forests . . . or run through the trees . . . I have lost all my skill in searching, my fine garland of fame has expired—*Oh I can't stand it, I'll die*—"

Every word of all this empty talk went down the air to the long ears of Vayu the Wind Lord, the rain's lover who clears the air. Vayu stood behind the winds of the worlds and sighed, and stirred, and started to whisper at his son Hanuman. That miserable monkey lay draped on his stomach across the low wall, sobbing and rubbing his eyes, and in from the ocean, over the shore a little wind swirled up the flanks of Trikuta Hill and into Lanka.

Hanuman still complained. He held his paws over his face

239

and gave a last gasp. "It's suicide, and my body may then at least bring meager happiness to some poor bug . . . ." He went limp.

Then from afar came the Winds, nearer and nearer. The million flat leaves of the mountainside trees trembled, they rustled and tried to speak and waved like dancers' hands. That was the first time since Ravana had come to Lanka that the Wind had dared to blow hard, but now he came in wild and free again over the walls of Lanka with all of his great might; he came flat out like an ocean gale with nothing to stop him, daring Ravana. He threw down the rows of flags and sang through the catapult wires; he banged the palace shutters and broke off branches like cannon-shots.

Hanuman heard the running wild Wind speaking—*How long? How long?* He opened his eyes and peeked out through his furry fingers. A whirlwind was headed straight on at him, pressing down his hair. Leaves and flowers sailed past him, twigs were snapping, trees were waving, and from Ravana's garden paths loose jewels whipped from the walks and flew singing past his ears. Vayu the Wind took a deep breath and blew his son right over the wall—*Away with you, Oh Child how long, how long will you seek to annoy me? Follow the winds, follow the winds . . . .*

Hanuman tumbled and rolled under an Asoka tree. He picked himself up and brushed the dust from his fur. The wind died down. Hanuman was in Ravana's Asoka Grove. It looked like a wood, but was too neatly kept; it resembled a garden, but it had grown too wild. The beautiful asoka trees had round crests and clusters of long red flowers, and with many other trees and plants they were in a long inward park behind Ravana's sleeping rooms.

Dawn swiftly approached. After a hush, the awakening birds and deer began to talk, but their voices were strangely unhappy. Hanuman wondered, "What grief can there he here?" He looked around. "Where is Sita? She is somewhere faint and forlorn as the misty Moon, hard to see as a streak of gold covered by dust, hard to find as a bright yellow reed

240

broken grey in the frosty wind and lost when winter comes, fading away as the red scar from a new arrow wound, from the fresh cut of some sharp heavenly weapon."

In the center of the grove Hanuman saw a tall overgrown Sinsapa tree of golden leaves and small white flowers standing by a pond, with torches flickering round it but no one there. And as Night departed and the Sun rose from the sea, he climbed that tree and hid in the leaves, lying along a stout limb and thinking, "Sita always loved to walk the woodlands and bathe in ponds like this among wild creatures; soon she may come here at sunrise."

hERE I am

All Heaven's stars may fall
And Earth may break apart,
Fire may burn cold,
And waters run uphill—

But Sita never turns from Rama.

Oh Rama, the pond below Hanuman clearly reflected the world in the calm at sunrise, and the sunlight traveled swiftly into Lanka, down from the top of Trikuta Hill, and gleamed on the golden city walls. In the still morning Hanuman heard Rakshasa priests within their temples singing to welcome light to the sky. Then in Ravana's bedroom the drums started to go off and the lutes tuned up, and the bards of Lanka sang praiseful songs to awaken their King.

Then some Rakshasis, female demons acting like guards, came from among the asokas and put out the torches burning round Hanuman's tree. They were a gruesome ugly group of hideous horrors; they bore the faces of rabbits or dogs or owls, swine or tigers or fish; they had the legs of cows or elephants or horses; and the ears of buffalo or goats' beards or fangs like snakes. They were a small host of furies and gluttons and scolds and fiends. Some carried sticks, some had three squinty eyes, some were bald and some had ratty stiff hair like a mangy camel. They wore misfitting clothes. They had hanging bellies and blotchy flapping lips, voices like rasps working away on sheet metal, and flat crooked noses set askew or upside down on puffy faces. They were leering or grim,

242

dwarfish or tall, and most still drunk from the night before. Hanuman saw his fill of low brows and broken nails and bloated faces. And it seemed not one of them had ever bathed in all her life, unless she had been caught outside in the rain or fallen into a river, and the bloody gore of past dinners and murders stretching back for years on end covered them like a cloak of garbage. They made Hanuman's eyes sore.

The first thing when he woke up every morning, Ravana the Demon King thought of Sita held captive. He got out of bed smiling and straightened his robe. He slicked down his hair and his ten moustaches and went out a back door and through a gate in the wall around the Asoka Grove, blinking his glaring red-shot eyes in the sun. After Ravana, came about a hundred of his wives, sleepy and stumbling. And Queen Mandodari walked beside Ravana giving him sips of wine from a bowl, one head at a time.

Hanuman saw that Ravana was heading his way, and as the Rakshasis below him formed perspiring ranks and foul rows, Hanuman shook himself and diminished his size till he was no bigger than a hand, and fled up the Sinsapa tree to a higher branch. There like a hidden bird he watched from far within the dark shadows of the leaves.

Then he saw her. Hanuman saw a fair woman of the human race arise from sleeping in the dirt under another nearby tree. She came over and sat with her back against the Sinsapa tree, her legs drawn up and her worn dusty yellow robe covering all her body, her glossy black hair tied in a long braid that fell down her back to her hip.

Hanuman thought, "It is Sita, much changed since I saw her carried away." But he wasn't sure. She seemed bewildered, lost and fallen. Hanuman kept staring at her and looking, puzzling as one will do when trying with learning long unused to read another tongue. Here was a woman imprisoned as a Naga girl held on her way by staying charms and spells. She was a river dried away, a torn leaf from a doubtful book, a muddied lake; she was dead love and disappointed hopes.

"Forget him!" *yelled Ravana.*

Beneath him Hanuman saw an inspiration thwarted by distractions, a reputation lost, a just and royal law disobeyed and a prayer unfinished.

But it was truly her, it was Sita of fortunate looks, thin from grief and fasting, lean and trembling. That was the robe she had worn, and there below him Hanuman could still find her fair brows and white throat, her round breast and red lips, her lustrous black eyes with curling lashes, large and wide. It was Sita born from a furrow in the Earth. Even in captivity her every limb was lovely; she was still beautiful to all eyes, as is crisp Autumn's sky after the rain's end.

Hanuman thought, "Oh Ravana, we'll get you for this! Here is Rama's joyful Queen fast plunged into grief! My master Rama is truly strong, for he yet breathes without her and has not entirely consumed himself with sad thirst and longings."

Ravana came to the Sinsapa tree and without speaking knelt and bowed his heads at Sita's feet. He rose and smiled, "My dear, how can you fear me? I am helpless in the bonds of Love. Don't be shy . . . how does it become you to lie on the bare ground when you can be Mistress of my kingdom? Desire me, be kind; reward my love, for youth is uncertain and passing, and beauty will not last forever."

Sita put a grassblade between herself and Ravana. "For your own death you touched me," she said. "Ravana, even in a picture have you never seen black Kalee dance, and the horrid skulls of her necklace laugh, and the darkness of Death come down like Night?"

"But every god serves me these days!" said Ravana. "There are three hundred and twenty million warriors here; if I need the help of one, a hundred come forward. Rule over my other wives and my city as you rule in my heart. Why hold yourself back? If you command it, I will do good to all the world. Favor me, dear Sita."

Sita said, "You see everything reversed, because you are so near to your own death. If you are really strong, follow Dharma and take me back, no one will harm you."

"*Forget him!*" yelled Ravana.

"Why, you are but his prey," said Sita. "Can you not feel the noose of Death?"

"Oh timid girl of slender waist, enjoy yourself. Look at this wealth around you; open your eyes, it will all be yours."

"You are a magician selling sunlight as if you owned it," said Sita. "Are you mad to tempt me with wealth, when all the treasures of Earth belong to my one Lord? I am his alone. After the Lord of Men has held me I can never seek another. For you, I am a red-hot iron image awaiting your embrace!"

"The *nicer* I am," said Ravana, "the worse you treat me!"

Sita answered, "Then know me for the daughter of a *real* King and a true man's wife!"

RRRrraarrR! Ravana gave her a terrible look, he roared and shook his heads and hands. His twenty red eyes went spinning and rolling in different-turning circles and opposite ways. He ground his grim teeth. His robes swirled like the stormy sea. He seemed to be having a fit and up in his tree Hanuman nearly jumped out of his skin.

But Queen Mandodari took Ravana's arm and said, "My Love, pass her by and come with me. She's not better than I. She still loves Rama, for one insect will only love another of its kind. Sita's thin destiny will not let her enjoy your grand company . . . ."

Then Mandodari full of love turned Ravana around and led him back to their bedroom, speaking softly—*Whatever you will, my dear Lord, whatever you say.* And as they left, behind Ravana's back his other wives, daughters of gods and of great kings, consoled Sita with their eyes. Then they left Sita alone with her guards and followed the Demon King.

Hanuman tightly held his tree and thought, "Does that fool go through this every day?" He looked at Sita and bared his teeth. "For this Lady were the demons of Dandaka Forest slain, for her was King Vali killed from ambush, for her I flew the ocean—it would be entirely right had Rama for her sake overturned the Universe. Like the waters of a river flowing by, Time cannot be called back, and so Earth's daughter of golden skin finds herself a poor prisoner here; yet she and Rama are never parted from each other's thoughts or they would die."

The Rakshasis told Sita, "Our unconquerable King stands in a regal halo of white glory, and for your good luck he has fallen in love with you. He pays you court politely and acts so charming. Why cling to Rama who lives with animals?"

Sita replied rudely in the voice of a lioness who talks to a little dog. "Don't be too bold with me. I would never even spit upon your unwashed king. Fall in love? No, but he will truly fall! Asking and answering, Rama will find the way and come to get me."

"Look," they said, "we're satisfied. You've acted well. But there's no need to go on any longer." Their eyes could see no more there than a prisoner unarmed, alone and powerless.

Sita looked at them. "Shut your mouths, don't menace me!"

"What?" they cried. "We're just too kind and soft-hearted and easy going!" Some of them had knives, now they drew them and shook them at Sita gleefully. "We've put up with you so far just to help you! Our words to you are always well-meant, it's for your own good, face reality!"

Sita laughed.

They screamed, "Be happy! Or else!" One demoness drew closer and cried, "Or else we'll eat you up. Liver for me!"

Bones to crunch and snap, blood and froth to lap! The Rakshasis started pushing and shoving each other, all yelling at once. "Ravana will be happy again, why quarrel, divide her into equal servings. Get the axe and kettle! Lots of sauce! Let's dance! Torn ribbons of soft flesh for the crows!"

Hanuman crouched into the shadow of the tree trunk. He clicked his tongue against his sharp teeth and hissed in his breath; he curled his tail and darted his fiery eyes about; he flexed his fingernails and got ready to jump down fighting from the yellow Sinsapa leaves.

But just then the old Rakshasi Trijata hastened forward and stepped beside Sita. At first glance she looked like any nice old woman wearing her hair in three white braids, but her

247

eyes were upside down, set in her face with their outer corners touching her nose. She was the only one who treated Sita well.

"Shut up!" Trijata faced the others. They stopped shrieking and shouting at once. "Be still," she said, "for last night in a dream I saw terror and the overthrow and conquest of Lanka." She raised her two hands before her breast, her palms outwards, saying without words—*Peace to you.*

Trijata turned to Sita. "Princess, I will tell you all my dream, so you may save us from death—

"You stood wearing white atop a snow-white hill beaten by white sea-waves round its base. On that hill I saw Lakshmana sitting on a pile of white bones, drinking milk and eating rice. Then Rama came to you riding a white elephant with four ivory tusks bound in white silver. He wore white flowers and white clothes on his green limbs, and he sat on the elephant's back on an ivory throne.

"Then like light meeting the Sun you were beside him. You embraced Rama and were on the elephant with him. You raised your arms and held fast in your hands were the Sun and Moon.

"Then I saw Ravana dressed in red clothes and red flowers riding a hog, drinking oil, the hair shaved off all his heads, fleeing Lanka. As he rode to the South our city sank into the ocean behind him. Ravana was demented; he shouted insane words and laughed and wept like a maniac. He rode into a dry lake-bed, and there a dark woman wearing a red shroud and a necklace of skulls twined her dusty arms through his necks. She pulled him to the Earth and dragged him away, always South, to the Land of Death.

"Sita, I saw our Good Fortune running North like a frightened girl weeping, bleeding from many cuts, and a tiger fell in running beside her to protect her, and guide her to safety. They ran to Fair Ayodhya . . . ."

Trijata shook her head and looked at the other guards. She said, "Like a field of grain, evil ripens slowly in time. When a fruit is ripe, then may it fear the fall. Console Sita and ask her

248

forgiveness. There is no unlucky mark on her body. She'll never be a widow. This captivity is not her true fate, it just seems like it, and I have seen her rescue while I slept. Even at this moment, danger comes at us here from Rama's sending, so ask her pardon."

Sita smiled at them and said, "When this becomes true, I will save you all."

The Rakshasis disbanded and went to guardposts away by the Asoka gates and along the walls, and Sita sat alone under Hanuman's tree. Hanuman thought, "Demons can take any form; how can I speak to her so she will trust me? If I talk in Sanskrit like a brahmana she'll think I'm the Rakshasa King . . . ."

So in a quiet voice no one else could hear, Hanuman said in the animal language, "Rama—Rama—"

Sita raised her head and listened.

Hanuman went on softly speaking. "—Rama killed that false golden deer. He spoke to the dying Vulture King Jatayu. Rama is Sugriva's friend, and all the animals of Kishkindhya have searched for you. I found you, I alone leapt over the sea. I am Hanuman, the Son of the Wind . . . here I am above you."

❦

Sita looked up into the Sinsapa tree and saw a white monkey like a tiny bunch of little lightnings, his red face smiling down at her, his light yellow-brown eyes shining with fires and lights. She rose and held a low branch and said, "Who are you? Now I have let my mind slip into illusion."

Hanuman came down to that branch. "Mother, it's me, Hanuman. I serve Rama. But who are you? Are you a bright star-spirit hiding from her Lord in jealous anger, or are you Sita?"

"I am Sita." Silently she began to cry and tears poured from her eyes. "What star-spirit sheds tears on hearing the name of a mortal King? Oh Hanuman, every sight speaks to me of him, and I fear you are also only a phantom in my mind."

249

"Ah no, I am not!" Hanuman came closer. "Listen, too much crying's bad for your eyes! Everything's going to be all right . . . very soon, Sita . . . ."

Sita looked down at her feet on the Earth, and every detail was clear and distinct. It was no dream; and when she looked back, by her own heart Sita read Hanuman's inmost thoughts and feelings.

Hanuman said, "You're welcome! I've already put my foot on Ravana's ugly heads!"

"Oh my *pretty* monkey!" She squeezed him and ruffled his fur. "You've come like medicine to a dying man, at the last painful moment. Where did you find Rama? How have monkeys and men met as brothers?"

"Remember when you dropped your ornaments from the sky onto a hill by a lake?"

"Oh yes!"

"That was me and my King Sugriva. We were in hiding. We saw you and gathered up your things. Then Rama and Lakshmana came to our hill of Rishyamukha, wandering in a beautiful forest, and we showed them your jewelery. Sugriva and Rama became friends, and Rama restored Sugriva to his wife and made him King of Kishkindhya, and for his part Sugriva will rescue you, the monkeys and bears will come to Lanka . . . ."

So they talked confidingly together, Sita standing with her head near the golden sinsapa leaves and her sweet voice soft and low, and Hanuman stretched on a branch that began to bend a little from his weight, as he started to grow bigger again from the happiness of his success.

"This is his ring," said Hanuman. "Take it." Sita read the name on the wide gold band—*Rama, Rama, Rama*—and Rama seemed to be there touching her.

"If one can keep on living somehow," said Sita, "real true happiness comes to each of us once in a hundred years! I remember all the good times I'd forgotten!"

"Everyone was looking for you," said Hanuman. "We only waited out the rains. Take heart. I am famous all over the three

250

worlds. I'm hard for enemies to look at and impossible to stop."

Sita's face was beautiful. She looked at Hanuman and smiled a luminous slow smile bright as the day-star. Her dress slipped from her left shoulder a little, and Hanuman could see part of her arm revealed, he saw her slim muscles under the golden skin strong as steel within silk. Hanuman grinned at her. Then he fell into a short animal trance and said half to himself—*A huge black woman strikes her belly with her many hands, driven to anger until she shall devour the Rakshasas, impatient to reach out and draw them into her terrible mouth . . . .*

Sita pulled up her robe and caught her breath. "What are you saying?"

Hanuman blinked. "You mean about the rains?"

Sita smiled a sad sweet smile. "Hanuman, has Rama lost his love for me through long separation?"

"He hardly eats or sleeps. To him the cold nights are like flame and the gentle moonbeams burn him. Get on my back and I'll take you home."

She laughed, "Here again I see your monkey nature!"

Hanuman said, "My first womanly insult." He jumped from the tree and became big as a white hill eighty spans high. He was crouched ready to leap, with a coppery face, nails and teeth like thunders, yellow lantern eyes like dazzling brass plates. Then before anyone else saw him he was small again. He ran back to Sita and up into the tree.

"I believe you!" smiled Sita.

Hanuman beamed. "I could take back all Lanka with her stupid King and her walls, and no one could catch me."

"No, let Rama recover me if he will—but now that beautiful man is freed from a wife like me."

"Princess, if Rama sees a flower you once liked he falls into a fever. If he hears your name, it will sometimes comfort him, or else will worsen his pain. Now he is distracted, but once he knows for sure that you are here, I swear by all the delicious fruits of the forest, he will come with a large army to save you."

251

Sita was both sad and happy, like rain in the sunshine. She said, "Blessed are the gods who can steal a look at Rama where he hides, and blessed are the holy men who never love or hate. People cannot thwart Time; behold all of us so sad."

Hanuman replied, "When Rama's hot anger breaks over the world the seas may well boil away. Dear Sita, before Love's eyes Time does not lay on year by year the little heart-blinding spells of age. Before true Love, the maces of Death are frail stage-weapons, fragile and useless for combat. Death gives way to Love and has never dared to war with him."

Sita sighed, and her breath burnt a few sinsapa leaves that hung down near her face. "Soon you must leave me and return, my Hanuman. People will fancy what they see and forget those who have gone. Shamefully I loved a jeweled deer and sent my man away. Here there is no cliff to jump over. I haven't any knife or poison, and only my own braid to hang myself. How is one better than a slave to this life that will not end when it is over and done? Often I weep longing to die . . . ."

"Destroy your sorrow," said Hanuman. "You're the most beautiful woman I've ever seen."

"Oh Hanuman."

"But you are, you are supremely fair. Oh Sita, Rama is like a fire-temple, burning from his own fires within. Love's shadows and his darkness are really lights. Tell me what to do for you."

"Does Rama remember the crow that clawed me when we lived on Chitra Hill? Take him this message—*For me you sent the dread Brahmastra weapon to kill a little crow, so why do I appear to have no protector now? Am I helpless? Have you enough love left for me to set weapons against the demons? On that day far from care, on Chitrakuta Hill my red brow-mark was printed on your green chest and near your heart.*"

"I'll tell him, I promise," said Hanuman.

Sita said, "Stay nearby awhile, rest here with me today. I have no one. When you leave I will miss you, and who knows if you will ever return? It is very hard to enter Lanka, and I fear

252

no one but you can cross the sea. Complete good fortune, and a friend to share it with, is very rare and unlasting. My monkey, spend this night with me and go tomorrow."

Hanuman smiled a sunny smile. "Why would King Sugriva send any of his best monkeys out on an errand like this? I am a common animal, the poor child of the homeless Wind. Nothing can stop the monkeys and bears, nothing can stop Rama and Lakshmana. We can go anywhere as fast as we want to. We fight on the ground or up in the air; our weapons are uprooted trees and blocks of stone broken out of the mountains. Let me go back and bring them here to you, here and now, this very day."

Sita looked at that remarkable and amazing monkey again and again. Her sadness had come and gone, as clouds will draw across the clear night sky, and cover the moonlight, and go again. "Faithful Hanuman, at the year's end Ravana will kill me. Speak so Rama will save me, let him do it, and farewell."

"Farewell, it won't be long."

❧

Hanuman ran unseen to the wall of that Asoka Grove farthest from Ravana's palace. He got all set to jump back across the ocean when an instant monkey thought crossed his mind.

He looked back at Sita. Her face was fair as the Moon. His eyes brightened and he thought, "Will I leave her once more in danger with no sign of good cheer?"

He popped over the low wall and out of Sita's sight. He got bigger again. He said to himself, "I won't hurt Sita's grove and I won't touch the good chariot Pushpaka . . . but all the rest . . . right or wrong!"

A great idea! Hanuman was off like a bolt from a bowstring. He plowed through Ravana's lawns and flowerbeds and pushed over his pavilions. He threw benches and bricks through the palace windows and splattered the sentries with wet muddy lotuses. Horses shied and elephants stampeded, and the deer stared roundeyed and frozen in panic. Dust and

253

leaves fell all in a wind over Lanka; and standing amid the wreckage of Ravana's gardens, Sita's Rakshasi guards saw an infernal monkey crackling with energy, growing bigger and bigger.

That was a wondrously harmful sight, a true regret to their eye. They ran to Sita and asked, "Lotus-eyes, who is that?"

"What do I know of your terrible Rakshasa magic?" answered Sita.

Ravana heard the racket in his courtroom. The palace bodyguard of eighty thousand fighters did not wait for any orders. They served together always, and knew and loved each other; in full armor they flew out the tall windows and saw Hanuman sitting on top of the big main gate in the circular outer wall around Ravana's home.

Hanuman cried out—*Victory to Sugriva the King!*

What King?—shouted the regiment.

Hanuman grabbed an iron gate-bar and stood in the air. *My King!* He beat them all to death with it and the ground shook.

On his throne Ravana could hear that Hanuman was winning. His ten heads turned here and there and his eyes roved over his court. Then commanded by a royal glance, the good-looking young warrior Jambumali arose, the son of the demon General Prahasta. He bowed and left the court, and once outside the door he broke into a run.

During those moments, after he had hammered to death the royal bodyguard, Hanuman pounced from his gate onto the goldplated Rakshasa city temple across the street. In back of that building priests were talking senselessly or rolling in the dirt or just smiling like religious idiots. Inside there was an image of the goddess Lanka made of sapphire. Hanuman stuffed her down a drain and slapped his armpits so loudly that big pieces of the golden ceiling fell blackened by ages of incense smoke.

Hanuman fled outside, broke off a marble column, and flew to the top of the temple roof. *Let me bless my beloved demons one by one, are you ready?* He spun the pillar around so fast that it caught fire, and coals and flares and sparks whirled up in the

254

air, and the priests ran for their lives, the temple burst into flame and exploded.

Jambumali heard it blow up. A piece of flying stone just missed his head, with a sound like a hummingbird flying by his ear. The noise awakened everyone in the world who was still asleep that morning.

Jambumali got on his light two-wheeled chariot. It was brightly colored and drawn by three white mountain ponies, as curved and fanciful as the toy car of a princess, but made of adamant and armored in death-spells. He drove to where the temple had been. Two pillars still stood there; on one of them a loose plank was balanced, and on that plank Jambumali saw a monkey picking cinders from his coat. And though his anger grew like a fire fed with butter, Jambumali looked calmly at Hanuman with the gaze of a young lion; and Hanuman looked back, thinking, "How young he is!"

Jambumali got down from his pretty car and walked nearer to the ruined temple. He held a red bow curved in two curves with the straight grip between, decorated with solid gold flowers. He had a soft quiver slung over his shoulder, covered outside with embroidered silk showing colored birds and dancing girls, heads of ripe grain and flowers; inside his arrows scraped and swore, and their tips danced with light.

Then very quickly Jambumali shot an arrow straight up in the sky and cast his mantras, whispering—*Come down falling!* Hanuman's plank tilted and started to slip.

It was a perfect quiet morning. Hanuman's board stuck there on that column at an impossible angle and did not fall. Hanuman yawned and stretched out and closed his eyes. Jambumali stared.

A tremendous piece of stone fell tumbling down out of nowhere just missing Jambumali. Another boulder fell, they were falling all over. Jambumali cursed. Those were grains of dust! Something else was falling, a huge long tree-trunk. The arrow returning! A giant long shadow growing, too fast, a whistling and a wind—

Jambumali was crushed and killed, there was no more sign

255

of his body or bow. Hanuman himself knew some small magic also. He saw Ravana watching from the palace, and he howled like a metal drum so that the windows rattled. *Rama!*

❧

Ravana instantly turned and walked down a narrow stair and through a tunnel under the city wall. He came out a secret door into a grove of the hillside woods that was hidden from view by magic. There under a downgrowing banyan tree sat his son Indrajit. Indrajit had once taken the god Indra prisoner in war, now he sat pale and thin beside a hermit's waterbowl, with a butterjar for feeding a little fire, wearing deerskin with a grass belt, in a field filled with the slaughtering posts and altars of many sacrifices.

Ravana went to approach Indrajit but the preceptor Sukra stopped him. Sukra had come from the Asuras undersea to teach Indrajit. He said, "Majesty, do not speak to him just now or make him break the vow of silence. He has been fasting to center himself in the spirit . . . ."

Ravana said, "What identity does he seek? Is it well done to worship my enemies the gods?—I do not understand my son!"

"King, don't speak of what you can't understand," said Sukra. "Do not say 'I won't believe,' for this is real. This is the final hour and moment of the five-day rites called the Gift of Gold. Every power that Indrajit has just won by meditation and endurance and devotion, he now offers back to Lord Shiva."

"Why do that?"

"A small gift for your good fortune," answered Sukra, "for against you will come Ramachandra, Rama like the Moon, and you will—"

"Silence, brahmana. I need him now! Let him study war, not mysteries, and return to my side here in this world of passing sights and nets of pleasures and of pain."

Then Indrajit arose. "Father, the gift to Shiva is done and I am ready. Or else, why would I part from Shiva the Lord?"

Ravana said, "My son, bring me that animal. Beguile him by

256

unreality and take him by force. Use things that begin one way and end in another."

Smiling, Indrajit said in a gentle voice, "This life is an echo in the air and a wave on the sea. That is Hanuman. I'll take him if you want him; war or peace, it's all the same to me."

Then Indrajit's fairseeming form changed. Gone was the friendly lean ascetic. There was Indrajit the raven-haired warrior, dressed in blue and yellow silk, his skin dark red like spilled blood, a yellow flower in his long hair, his eyes sharp green with cat's pupils, a golden chain wound nine times round his waist, a white spot of sandalwood on his brow, a great round blue steel shield in one hand, a bow backed with gold serpents in the other, a full quiver slung over his back and a sword at his belt in a silver sheath.

"Long life to you, my Father." Indrajit went to the burnt temple in Lanka. Hanuman was waiting for Ravana's next champion to come against him, lying there on his unbalanced board.

Indrajit knew Hanuman could not be killed. So on an arrow he put a mantra that can be sent but once at anyone, and never sent again. He shot the spell of Shiva's noose, and Hanuman fell to the ground tied invisibly hand and foot and unable to move.

But before Indrajit could reach him or speak, other Rakshasas ran from hiding and in the blink of an eye they had tightly locked Hanuman in chains. Indrajit bit his lip and sighed. For the binding force of Shiva's noose will never hold nor return, when there is any other bond laid over it.

"Boundless ignorance again takes command," thought Indrajit. Cursing and kicking Hanuman, the demons dragged him off to the palace. Indrajit saw that by no sign did Hanuman show that he was free. "Those fools—*I bow to Shiva who places us all in true danger now*. Oh, let lust and anger keep their distance, let all this unreal world be far from me!" And Indrajit went back to his grove of meditation without speaking a single word aloud.

257

the new moon

The footrest on your high throne
Is worn smooth from the crest jewels
Of lesser kings,
Bowing their crowned heads in surrender.

But good fortune is a wanton harlot,
Going where she will—
Oh Majesty, is she still yours?

The Rakshasas pulled Hanuman into Ravana's court. There on his red and gold throne, in a better hall than any room in heaven, the Demon King sat like threats of darkness. Ravana had earned all his wealth and power by his own strength. He was fortunate and splendid and rich. Ravana had the patience and strength to protect all Creation from harm, but he did just the opposite and took the worlds for his possessions.

Ravana's throne was covered with doeskin and was set in the center of a long indoor altar, made of a golden frame filled with Earth, a low-banked hill running on each side away from Ravana to the corners of the room. At each end Rakshasa priests tended fires and hummed songs, and when they made their offerings they could choose from among the spoils of the Universe and the treasures of the three worlds.

The entire Majesty and Glory of the Rakshasa King! The demons carried Hanuman close. Ravana was very tall. He wore ten crowns of flaming red flowers and gleaming gold. A gold breast-chain hung from one ten-armed dark shoulder to the other, forged of flat heavy links from which were hanging

258

golden devil-faces with amethyst eyes and open ruby lips and long shiny ivory teeth.

Ravana looked at Hanuman with twenty eyes, and from the smooth emerald floor Hanuman in chains looked steadily back. And the Rakshasa King remembered what the bull Nandin, wearing the face of a monkey, had told him on Shiva's Hill of Reeds long before—*Animals with faces like mine will destroy you.*

✿

Ravana's younger brother Vibhishana came from the ranks of courtiers and bent over Hanuman. His face was black and his eyes dark blue. He said, "This is Lanka, long built here, long prospering. You have killed our people and broken our holy temple. But good fortune to you. Do not fear, but tell us the truth. Who are you and where did you come from? Why are you disguised as a monkey?"

Hanuman replied, "I *am* a monkey! I've a message for Ravana."

The Demon King leaned forward on his throne. "Insensate animal! What message?"

"Majesty," said Hanuman, "I am Hanuman, I am Rama's slave. I came to find Sita. Hear the words—*In the cave city of Kishkindhya your brother Sugriva, king of the monkeys and bears, asks after your welfare. Listen to his desire: in Dandaka Forest Sita was harmed, and I have promised Rama to find her; therefore do not confine another's wife but return her.*"

"How did you get here?" asked Ravana.

"I jumped."

"Don't make me laugh!"

Hanuman grinned. "Don't worry, I won't!"

Ravana opened wide his eyes in anger. "Unlucky beast, you've lost your weak wits from seeing the beauties of my city."

"Lord of Lanka, I am the son of the Wind, fast or slow, irresistible in my course. I'm an animal; what you call beauty

Ravana looked at Hanuman with twenty eyes

won't turn my head. I crossed the ocean, as a person without attachment to worldly desires easily crosses the ocean of existence. Withdraw your heart from Sita, or that will be a costly theft, for it's by her energy that I jumped over the sea."

"Impossible. Vibhishana, cut off his head!"

"No," said Ravana's brother. "You can brand or shave a messenger but not kill him."

Ravana said, "What good are you as a demon? I've killed them before!"

Vibhishana said, "But I wasn't here before."

"All your life you've been timid and weak as a woman."

"Just the same," smiled Vibhishana, "here I am standing up and telling you no."

Then the Rakshasa General Prahasta rose from the audience and said, "Have a heart, Ravana! Give us a chance. In the army we've eaten your food and spent your money, and all we have to show for it is peace! You must release Hanuman. It is sweet to make a real war and win! Set free this monkey who killed my son, because if he does not return no one else can ever find Sita, and we will never fight against Rama."

Hanuman lying in chains said to Ravana, "Are you bored with your great-seeming wealth and do you wish to end your life? Whatever happens to me, how can you believe that Rama will abandon his beautiful wife and let Sita be taken from him and not recover her? Actually, your conquests are uncertain and your treasures unnecessary. Past merit still protects you, but somehow I think you strangely desire death."

"No, you tiresome little monkey, I do not desire death!" Ravana swirled to his feet. "You have now seen us both. Tell me truly, how Rama compares to me."

"Truly," said Hanuman, "you are the bright Full Moon, the light of the night world; and my Rama is the New Moon, a thin shred of light, no more."

"Excellent," said Ravana. He summoned a band of grim demons. "Monkeys take pride in their tails. Set his tail aflame, carry him around through Lanka and then throw him out."

261

They slung Hanuman on a couple of carrying poles and took him outside. They started to wrap his tail in oily rags. They wrapped and wrapped, and it seemed the whole length of Hanuman's tail wouldn't be covered by all the cloth in Lanka. So the demons just bundled up the end of his white tail. They set the rags afire, lifted the poles to their shoulders and carried him around the streets yelling—*Look what happens if!*

In the Asoka Grove Trijata told Sita what was happening. Sita gave her a cool smile and went to a little shed where the guards kept a tiny flame always burning in a clay cup filled with butter, to light their nighttime torches.

Sita looked into the little flame and said—*If I've kept faith, be cool to Hanuman.*

The fire flamed and bent to the right—*Yes, I am good to him.*

So Fire let the Wind be cool right next to his son's tail and Hanuman felt no heat, though flames played in the air and burnt the oil in the rags. The demons carried him bouncing along, and Hanuman thought, "I've seen their incredible King, why stay in chains?" He broke loose, lashed out with his fiery tail, and sprang into the sky like a lightning streak.

Hanuman flew, setting fire to rows of mansions and houses with his burning tail. Flames devoured Lanka like a cremation yard; smoke blocked her roads and vultures settled on her golden walls. Burnt were sweet sandalwood and diamonds, corals and fine silks, golden vessels and piles of weapons, furniture and ornaments, ropes and elephant cords, beds and perfumes and hides and armor, all burnt.

The carved windows blazed and bricks melted into glass. Down fell roofs and towers and burning beams. The water-born pink and blue pearls shattered in the walls; the golden moons and silver crescents melted away. Along whole streets the houses collapsed outwards and fell over aglow with fires. Gates and grills snapped and smoked, and living flames blossomed alive in the air. The demons cried alarms and jumped into their lakes and ponds, fire brigades tore past, and thin

262

rivers of hot iron and molten bronze ran down the streets like quicksilver.

Hanuman flew to the very top of Trikuta Hill and looked at what he'd done. He had to shade his eyes from the heat; it seemed Lanka was flaring brightest, before she would die. Even the restless waves of the sea were red from the burning.

Indrajit had been brooding in his grove outside the walls. He said, "I will destroy the six senses. Eye, I will pierce you; mind, I will cut you . . . ." And his senses answered, "You will pierce only yourself, you will cut only yourself . . . ."

Then Indrajit forever wearing different forms heard the wails of woe and saw the fire. The Prince of Lanka swiftly bathed in a stream and put water in a bowl. He threw aloes thorns on his altar and lit them, and sat down on scattered grassblades. He spoke to Fire, "The grass isn't even woven into a mat. The time is long ago and we have no skills. You are not the fire of Lord Shiva's third eye spreading wide your tongues. You are not Shiva's wish."

Indrajit dipped three fingers into his waterbowl. Agni the Fire God rushed out of Lanka and a cone of sparks and fire came over Indrajit's altar.

"Heat and thirst!" cried Agni.

Indrajit said, "Ashes!"

"Smoke and anger!"

Ashes! Indrajit sprinkled water on his aloes fire, and Agni the Fire Lord backed off a little.

Indrajit said, "I hold you."

"Fear me," answered Agni.

"No, my Lord. Never are you patient, but always you burn. Never are you filled by burning, hard are you to stop once grown. Oh evil companion, I am a storyteller myself, I am an actor too. Now I send you away and I watch the doors for your flames' return."

Then a finger's depth of water appeared and covered all of Lanka, clinging to walls and ceilings and floors, and the fires had to go out. Hanuman sitting above the city quenched his tail in a mountain spring and thought, "Never again! What have I done? I've burned Sita!"

Hanuman held his head in his hands. "A fool will try anything. It's never too late for him to ruin a successful affair. Any kind of evil can be easily done in thoughtless anger." Back he jumped into Lanka, through the clouds of smoke and steam. He landed on a hot street, ran to the back of Ravana's palace, and headed for the Asoka Grove.

Nothing was harmed there. Sita was safe by the sinsapa tree. How could Fire have burned Sita? It is she who can burn Fire if she will.

That amiable woman smiled and said, "Oh Son of the Wind, have you returned for your honors and decorations? We praise your wit and wisdom, your brave courage and fine knowledge of politics."

Hanuman knelt before her and touched his palms together. "My mother, I salute you in the dust. A fool's excuses are worse than his crimes. Blessed are people with good sense."

"By good fortune I see you unhurt," said Sita. "My Child, if you are tired after all this, rest by me."

"Let me leave while I still can," said Hanuman, "give me your permission. Jumping the sea is easy. It's all this running from guards and watchmen that tires me. I will come back with Rama. Ravana has truly already been slain by your anger, and yet awaits only Rama's strength as the means of his death."

Sita said, "Monkey, in one reckless moment one can kill the innocent and boast wrong words, forget friends or lose all the harvest of pleasure, profit and dharma. You did none of this. They set your tail afire and you burned them back! So throw off your care as a snake abandons his old worn skin and leaves it behind him. Hanuman, when you stop to think you are strong, you are intelligent and good, you know time and place."

"I feel better already."

"Listen, Lanka will be soon rebuilt. If you so heedlessly destroy these demons you will cloud Rama's fame. Take this

264

to Rama, get him to act." Sita untied the corner of her robe and took out the pearl mounted on a gold leaf that her father Janaka had tied into her hair on her wedding day.

"How did you keep that all this time?" asked Hanuman.

"Head pearls are common," smiled Sita. "Say this—*I seem to have no husband. Rama best of men, seeing this gift was like seeing you. Now I part from it and keep your ring. I will live on here for a month and not longer. Do you still think of me at all? I send this pearl so you may know—you are loved by me, you are loved by me.*" Sita smiled her warm white smile that had never an equal then in all the worlds, nor ever shall.

❦

Hanuman hid Sita's jewel in his belt. He walked round her in three right-turning circles, bristled up his fur and flew off to the north.

Hanuman left Lanka behind him. He flew booming along through the air like the wind through a canyon, and the monkeys and bears waiting on the seashore heard him coming. They ran up a grassy hillside and made a circle holding hands, and Hanuman landed in the middle.

"I talked to her; she's alive!" Animals encircled Hanuman; they brought him fruit and water and fresh boughs to sit on; they came up smiling to touch him; they sang and cheered.

With gold bracelets on his arms and wrists, Prince Angada embraced Hanuman. "No one is like you. Can we go get her?"

"Don't do that," said Jambavan the Bear. "We were only to find her."

"Just leave her there?" asked Angada.

Hanuman said, "You usually do the right thing, Prince."

Then all at once came Angada's order—*Return*—and the miraculous monkeys and bears leapt from that hillside and flew home to Kishkindhya, supporting Hanuman's flight by their admiring looks and glances. Near Kishkindhya they saw King Sugriva's Honey Park. There the Monkey King kept his finest forest honey wines under guard.

The animals smelled ripe warm fruit and nectar in the sun.

265

They looked at Angada for permission, but before Angada could answer Hanuman shouted, "Let's go! Follow me!" and landed in that Wine Forest.

The yellow monkeys and the sable bears said, "All the world honors Hanuman. We'll follow him even into wrong; what to speak of perfectly correct things like this?"

The animals descended from the air. Down from the trees they pulled the rare and ancient honeycombs, fermented and dusty and venerable, and broke them open. In a moment they were all fearlessly drunk, staggering and lurching along, all talking at once. The monkeys were swinging in the trees and waving their tails, and the bears were nodding and dancing.

That Honey Park was guarded by the elderly peace-loving monkey Dadhimukha, who lived in a small cottage in a secluded corner. He heard people breaking his trees and splashing in his streams. White-faced, he went swinging down through the trees to see what was going on, and came to a mob of bears all bristly with glee, who were singing and imitating birds and thumping their feet on the ground.

Dadhimukha dropped from the trees and told the bears, "Stop it!"

They laughed. "We'll drink to that!"

"Get out!"

"We just got here!"

Dadhimukha sucked his teeth dry. *Oh yes?* He furiously pulled up a tree and swept the bears away. More bears came. Dadhimukha struck them down with his fists before they could speak. He threw them here and there, pulled handfuls of fur from their coats and showered them with insults and blame. But they just laughed and kept on eating great gobs of wild honey. Some of them said, "Catch me first!" and ran; others sat there and said, "Leave us alone, help!"

"Why ask?" yelled Dadhimukha. He slapped the bears, and they didn't seem to feel it. Belligerent drunken bears began side-arguments among themselves. Still more bears came. Some of them started to weep over life, and others with stern authority rebuked them for crying and then wept themselves.

Others laughed and bumped into trees, and old Dadhimukha was swallowed up in bears and chaos.

Hanuman whizzed out of the bushes. He had orange-petaled flowers and red berries, vines and blue-green leaves and buds stuck all over his white fur. He looked like Spring running lightly over the world. Hanuman waved back the bears and smiled at Dadhimukha. "Father, let's not fight over nothing—"

Dadhimukha snorted. "Repent, world-famous Hanuman!" He kicked Hanuman and sent him rolling like a ball into an orchard. Hanuman banged into a tree and juicy fruits fell down all over him. "Respect your betters," called Dadhimukha.

Prince Angada came running up, but that swift old monkey bent down, caught the prince's knees and threw him over. "Stop right there, all of you!"

But it was pretty hopeless. Nothing could stop the pushing and shoving, so Dadhimukha flew to King Sugriva. Sugriva was sitting outside Kishkindhya cave, with Rama and Lakshmana on their hill, awaiting some word of Hanuman. Dadhimukha's clothes were all torn; he bowed before the Monkey King and said, "*Lord of the Forest!*"

"Speak."

"Hanuman's army has fallen on your favorite ancestral forest from above. I tried to gently reason with them—"

Sugriva coughed. "They're drinking my honey-wine?"

"It's all gone."

"I forgive them." Sugriva's tail stuck straight up with joy. He turned to Rama. "He's found her! This is a wonderful return." He told Dadhimukha, "Why make such a fuss over the small faults of my children? Arise, calm yourself and send them all here to us."

Dadhimukha found Prince Angada dozing and starting to float on the air in the Honey Park. "The King awaits. He's with Rama on the hill; go to him."

A rumbly sound spread through the wine park and the bears were stirring. A wind came up. Animals ran from

267

Kishkindhya Cave to get a sight of the southern search-party returning; they climbed the rock-rooted trees and amid blossoms and leaves they waved the tag ends of their robes and cheered.

There was Hanuman, flying to Rama's hill. Whatever the obstacle, Hanuman like strong love leaps over it and goes on. The high forest hill danced in the wind, his treetops swayed. Wind tossed the flowering branches together in collision as though he were stringing them touching on a garland-thread.

Hanuman landed before Rama and touched his hands to his head. *"She lives!"*

> *Yellow trees like lions' manes and golden crowns;*
> *Mangos white as fame like dancers on the hills:*
> *Love has weakened you, here comes the swaying wind.*
> *You've run out of fighting Dharma;*
> *You've slighted your warriors:*
> *What will you reply when people ask of Sita?*

❦

Hanuman and Rama and Lakshmana and Angada and Sugriva sat on a wide flat stone, in a smooth meadow high on Prasravana Hill. The other animals gathered round to listen, and with a glad heart Hanuman said, "My Lord, Sita is held prisoner in Lanka, on an island beyond the end of the sea. She is within the city walls of Lanka, behind locked yards and garden gates, in an Asoka Grove behind the lordly palace of the Demon King, guarded by Rakshasis.

"Ravana has threatened her death if she will not submit to him. But her heart carries her love to you; her thoughts are the well-bred chariot horses, driven by her spirit—*Here we will go, and this will be true.* She's true to you, but she is all alone, like a tuneful lute without a player.

"She is gifted with beauty. I saw Ravana's bedroom, and Sita's loveliness makes all those sleeping consorts seem vile and monstrous, of lurid hue and form. Her dark eyes are as wide as lotus petals, her skin is golden, her breasts are close-touching and firm, and her posture bent slightly forward by their weight.

"Her waist is thin as a swordblade, her brows just meet and then go back to touch her ears, her hips are round and smooth . . . and her soft smile . . . though she is there without any ornament at all, what is mostly missing for her is the ornament of a husband, her ornament of you."

Hanuman looked to the South and thought of Sita. "I gave her your ring and she sent you this." He gave Rama the wedding pearl.

"Emptiness," said Rama. "Echoes and emptiness . . . that's all I have."

"Don't let your loss make you lose heart," said Hanuman. "You can't give up after all we've done for you; you must bring her back to life and music!" He told Rama all he had seen and done in Lanka. "Sita herself will live but one month more imprisoned. She says—*I love you*—and tells you of the time you sent the Brahma weapon against a crow, and of when her brow-mark was imprinted upon your chest. She kept that pearl by her with great care, and I took it for you in my hands."

"I begin to remember our love and happiness," said Rama. "Tell me what else she said."

"She said, 'Hanuman, blessed are you, for you will soon see Rama the best of warriors. Speak to him so he will act. Demons cannot withstand Rama. Let his life return, let his heart regard me again. Speak so he will act. Inspire him to kill Ravana; he can do it.' " Hanuman fell silent.

"What else?" asked Rama.

Hanuman twitched his tail. He stretched his fingers and toes and his white fur rose on end. Then he said to Rama in silent mental speech, "Oh Lord, if men from ignorance still praise you—sad for them, it is a lie. If your spirit's broken it was weak to start with. Sita was fooled when she wed you, and Shiva's long bow would have broken anyway just sitting in its box. Where are your wits that you're not suspicious of despair? Sita's never thought of a second husband. She has no

269

one else but you, and in fear you left her. Like a coward, like a common ordinary stage-actor you traded her over to another. You told her to go to him though you'd long loved her. Why do you serve Ravana as best you may, and give him Sita for his pleasure? You forsake her. She is encircled by evil. You've let Ravana throw you away for his own good. Rama, do not be a meek little man, fawning and unclean, unholy and afraid . . . ."

Only Rama heard those silent words and his face darkened. "What did you say?"

"I said never fear to love well," said Hanuman. "If you can't bear it who will?"

Rama wept. He embraced Hanuman and then held his shoulders at arm's length. "It's alright."

Hanuman said, "Now make me a promise, Rama, an unfailing promise."

"What?"

"Kill Ravana!"

❧

THIS CLOSES THE
BOOK OF BEAUTY.
HERE THE WAR BOOK BEGINS.

❧

◆   ◆   ◆

"Let your arrows pierce him through," said Hanuman. "Ravana is mighty strong, but he is poor, for it has been very long since he stood out in the open grass under a green tree he did not own."

Sugriva the Monkey King said, "Rama, open-hearted people like you suffer more in sympathy than the selfish do. Your heart is undefended. Grief undoes good fortune. Good things are ready to happen, do not prevent them." He swept his hand round in a circle. "Look, here we all are! Make a plan, do something great!"

Lakshmana said, "Who approaches close-guarded Lanka of the Waves and returns from the demons? Who even approaches? We cannot cross the sea . . . ." He looked at Jambavan. "What do you think?"

"Get out of my way!" answered the old Bear King. He looked at Rama with a deadly gaze. "Attack! Don't think and listen. Act! Call out our animal rage, Rama, release our violence. We are senseless wild animals—blood all over, their blood, our blood—who knows, who cares? We fight, that's all, and if we're at bay we fight worse than ever, we fight till we die! We feel no pain then, and when have you ever seen us surrender?"

"That's right," said Sugriva. "We never reason and think if things are hopeless or not. Rama-chandra you are the King. You are the Moon; does the Moon go out because dogs bark and howl at him? Where can Ravana hide from you? Be brave, do what you think best."

"I will stand straight," said Rama. "I will never bow down before sorrow again. Warriors who won't get angry can't win."

Jambavan the bear smiled and growled low. "Anger is madness, that's what you need in war. I've dealt death—I smell fear, I close in . . . I've felt the blood spill and tasted it, all my life . . . ."

King Sugriva said, "Release us from your hold and let us go. Order us. We will gladly enter fires for you."

Rama replied, "We will cross the ocean, and once beyond that, Lord of Rivers and Streams, we will lay siege to Lanka."

Rama said, "Let Hanuman tell us again about the defenses of Lanka, for he has seen her armies and walls."

Hanuman answered, "Beautiful Lanka's wall is like sunshine. There are four heavy wide gates facing in the four directions. Lanka is on the steep brow of a hill, but outside the walls there is enough level ground to fight. All the Rakshasa soldiers are loyal. There is a moat, and at three gates draw-

271

bridges, but where the main road enters at the North the gate-bridge is immovable, lined with a railing and benches of gold. Set on the walls are many hostile machines and engines to repel attack. There are catapults that will not reveal their aim from their positions, loaded with secret weapons bound in cords and hooped in iron that when fired break apart into spikes and maces and kill by the hundreds. There are cannon that spew out red hot nails and knives, and swords strung together on barbed chains, and burning arrows which pursue their target though he twist and turn to flee. There are patrols in the forests and many ways are mined with traps and pitfalls. Lanka is a celestial fortress, a joyful city of heavenly beauty taken by demons. She is artificial but looks natural; her sentries never sheathe their swords; she is the jewel mirror of arts and inventions and the home of happiness and comfort.

"Against us are Ravana, and his son Indrajit who is invisible in battle, and his brother the sleeping giant Kumbhakarna. General Prahasta desires war against you; his armies are calm and mindful and alert. But for all that, consider Ravana already dead. Rakshasas can overflow the world, the Sun can go backwards across heaven, but no army can frighten old Jambavan and his bear tribes, or resist Angada and our people, or stop Lakshmana, if you will yourself lead us to save Sita."

Rama said, "Tomorrow Sita's birthstar is ascendant; the planet of Death will be in conjunction with the Moon; we will leave for the South at midday, at the fortunate moment when the Sun is highest."

The next day the animal armies said farewell again and left their families behind in Kishkindhya. They began to march. The brown and yellow monkeys went first, covering Earth like a far-reaching field of grain. Angada carried Lakshmana on his shoulders and Hanuman carried Rama. Behind them came Jambavan with his dark bears and white ones, whose faces now bore war-marks of vermillion. More and more apes and monkeys followed them. King Sugriva went from side to side and front to back, urging them on, and the welcome wind

272

blew from the north as cool as the Moon to touch, and the days were clear and bright.

Advance parties made a roadway, they drained swamps and brought water to dry camps; leveled hills and filled hollows; broke boulders into gravel and cut away brush; and did all their work under lucky signs, at good hours on prosperous days. In three days they first began to smell the sea, and then sandalwood, and then they started to arrive at the Malaya Hills. Monkeys and apes and bears crowded onto the mountains by straight roads and side paths. They went down to the seashore between the cliffs overlooking the waves, raising fine clouds of colored dusts from the slopes of bright metal ores, waving their arms as they talked and knocking over trees with their gestures.

Rama saw the deep-sounding brimful Ocean. At dusk he took his bow and went down to the surf with Sugriva. The crested racing waves fell over the rocky coast, and broke on the round white stones and beaches of sand. The wind blew onshore and carried the salt foam of the sea onto the land, and the daylight failed. The sea became like the sky and the sky like the sea, there was no difference between them. The stars of heaven appeared above, and from far within the sea sparks of light showed gleaming out from the Naga castles under water, guarding the sea-doors to their underworlds. Dim grey clouds moved under one corner of the sky, and grey waves ran over one side of the seawaters, stirred by the winds. Night came, and the Moon rose reflected on the Ocean's silver breast. Waves caught the moonlight and laughed; they rose and fell and came forward endlessly, one after another forever.

Rama told Sugriva, "Camp nearby and keep a watch for strangers, and leave me here alone."

Then in a while the animal talk died down and the watches of Night began. Rama heard the silvery waves—*Who? Who? Who shall cross us?* He thought, "I am richly gifted with misfortune. When will I ever again slightly tilt up Sita's face and when will we embrace? What can I do? I am a lovesick

stranger, a poor man all alone, wronged and begging help."
His hands trembled—then he caught himself, he remembered
what he'd said—*Dismay and sad thoughts I'll never feel. I reject you;
I banish you!*

Then not speaking, Rama touched a wave of the Ocean with
his hand and lay down with his right arm for a pillow, not
eating, not sleeping, not moving. *Ocean, speak to me.*

The Night went by, the light of dawn appeared and the stars
were going. The wind diminished, and there was no answer.
Rama stood and strung his long bow; he put an arrow on the
bowstring and held it drawn back to his ear and said to Ocean,
"Fools mistake patience for weakness. Honor's for those who
boast and victory serves great heroes who bribe the strong and
attack those too weak to fight! You would disregard anyone,
were he unarmed and quiet!" The arrow flew hissing and
tearing into the waters. Smoking seashells and underwater
stones flew up in the air.

"Damn you!" Rama brought down the winds. Loud waves
of hesitation rose straight up; the water whirled. Samudra the
wide-souled Ocean rose from his dark bed below and sat on
the waves looking at Rama.

Samudra was mild and peaceful to see. His dark skin was
wet like a cool lapis stone. The Water King wore bright gold
bracelets and bands, and a green robe. Seawater poured from
his long white hair and beard, foaming in torrents down his
smooth chest, carrying a flood of rolling pearls down over his
shoulders.

Sea-mists and clouds were behind Samudra, and the beau-
tiful rivers of the world swam near him in the shapes of fair
women. The Sea Lord touched his hands and bowed his head
a little toward Rama. "I am the sea. This is another world . . . ."

"Don't try to net me with illusion," said Rama. "One glass
of wine has a lot more pleasure than all your tasteless waves."

"Oh Rama," said the Ocean, "the worlds are made of water;
it is my eternal nature to be fathomless and uncrossable."

"You are very large and know not my power. Let us by,
or dry towers of dust will blow through your bed and
choke you."

274

"Oh man, I drink down all the worlds and sigh."

The sea became silent. The waves died and the air was still and waiting. There almost seemed to be no air to breathe. The tides stopped.

But only for a moment. Samudra smiled. "Blessed be you, Rama, blessed be! I am immeasurably old, my soul is wide as my waters. What is wrong, Rama? Never was I your enemy but only your friend. Why use fear on a friend? The Goddess Earth and myself, Wind and Light—forever do we four keep our nature and never do we change. Why would you pass me by?"

"For Love."

"Indeed," said the Ocean Lord, "my heart is as large as the sky who is over me. I will help you. The monkey Nala who is with you is a son of Viswakarman, and he was born with the imperfection that whatever he throws onto water will float and not sink." The Ocean King smiled. "I will support on my surface any foundation Nala lays down. Oh Rama, as long as you wish, for you I will be bound by a bridge . . . ." Samudra of the Seas vanished back into his own depths.

Rama found Nala the monkey, and Nala said, "Did he say that? I used to just float stones for fun! Why then I'll throw out a bridge . . . .

"Get everybody to help me." Nala set to work. He looked to the South. He looked back at the Malaya Hills. Then he sat in the sand drawing lines for a long time, glancing up and out at Ocean, looking back down at the sand, absorbed in his work and seeing no one else as all the animals gathered around him.

Nala gave his orders. First the animals made stakes and lines and measuring rods; then they made the other tools; then they collected the materials from the hills. Then they began to build a bridge that would be a hundred leagues long and ten wide on a foundation of stones and boulders. Over the rocks they laid down a roadbed of poles, then Nala paved the road with grass and wood.

When they heard of that bridge-building the little people of the squirrel tribes came to help Rama. They wet their fur in the surf and rolled in the sand. They quickly ran out onto

275

They quickly ran out onto Rama's bridge . . .

Rama's bridge and shook themselves, and the sand fell into all the tiny spaces left in the paving and made it firm.

But they were forever underfoot. Hanuman scooped them out of his way while he carried big stones along. The squirrels ran to Rama and said, "Master, brutal Hanuman kicks us and hits us and shames us."

Rama ran three of his fingers down their backs to cheer them, and from that time until now every squirrel in the south has on his back the marks from the fingers of Rama. The squirrels went back to work and Hanuman told everyone else, "Watch your step; don't harm the little tree people!"

the BUILDING OF the BRIDGE

*Do not let the ways of the world
Dismay your heart,
Being a warrior.*

Lord Rama, on the day after Nala began that bridge, in Lanka
Ravana called his council of noblemen and said, "Bring your
minds with you for once."

When they had assembled Ravana said, "We have repaired
the damage he did, but yet Hanuman all by himself invaded
my unreachable city and will return with Rama. What must I
do? What must you do? The superior person will gladly take
good advice before acting."

Those empty-headed Rakshasa elders replied, "Yes, we
agree!" They said, "Majesty, you rightly rule the Universe.
Everything's been just fine so far. We will free the world from
monkeys."

Then Vibhishana stood and spoke. "Rama will pardon us if
we return Sita. She has not been harmed."

"I'll have no more of that!" Ravana was as angry as a liar
whose word is questioned.

Vibhishana said, "All the gods' animals are running loose!
They are building a bridge and plan to cross the sea and
surround Lanka. You want war, but what do you know of their
strength? What protection do you take against them?"

"Are you trying to anger me?" snarled Ravana.

"Well," said Vibhishana, "to tell the truth I don't have to;
it's an angry mind that won't understand all this."

"They will never go back over that bridge!" said the Demon King. "I find nothing to fear from simple animals. Have you no shame to suggest surrender?"

"King, no one else dares tell you the truth; you have no real friends left but me. You could hide in the veil of the winds, and use the Sun for a shield, and the sky for a wall, and still lose to Rama. He will kill you; there's no escape."

Ravana said, "What do I care? I do what I please!" He motioned with his hands—*Sit down, you have finished.*

"No," said Vibhishana. Four strong armored Rakshasas loyal to him came forward and stood to guard Vibhishana, cradling maces in their arms, facing the four directions. Vibhishana looked around the royal court of Lanka. He saw General Prahasta and his captains of the demon war-bands. Still as always, priests tended the palace altar to each side of Ravana's high throne, setting out their jars of curds or fire or butter or rice, gossiping uselessly in the corners.

Vibhishana said, "I blame you for a coward long loving evil. You're a sneak-thief—"

"Silence!"

"What will you hold against me? How can you stop me? For these hard words I deserve your praise. Are you incapable of reason? Do you want to live on congratulations and embraces and elegant flattery? For the second time I warn you to give back Sita, and send gifts with her."

"Do you think I'll stop and change my ways though the whole world says I'm wrong?" asked Ravana. "Kings have nobility, cows have milk, and kinsmen have envy in their hearts! My brother, blind with selfishness, would betray me! You would unfold the way of defeat. It truly must not please you that I am Emperor of Creation, and for myself I would rather live among open enemies than with you in my family."

"Open your eyes and mend your ways," said Vibhishana. "Wake up and do right! I don't speak just to talk; I have for my heart's purpose the rescue of the Rakshasa race, but I'll not go on repeating myself forever. You are a slave and wrath your

279

Master. We have surely been through this all before in other lives. Consider right and wrong. For the third and last time, give her back."

"Get out!" said Ravana.

Vibhishana answered, "Good fortune to you, now I go far away."

Vibhishana left the palace with his four knights. They put on their helmets and flew across the sea, north to Rama's bridgehead. Already the beginnings of the bridge struck out like a line parting the sea, aimed curving at Lanka, pointing like an accusation before all the world.

> *I'm not an actor or a singer,*
> *Not a fair woman nor a clown;*
> *Then what have I to do*
> *With the palaces of Kings?*

☙

Sugriva saw Vibhishana and his bodyguard and told Rama, "We'll end their short lives today." But Rama said, "Wait."

Vibhishana stood in the sky and looked here and there with his dark-blue crystal eyes. He saw Hanuman and beckoned to him. Hanuman came close and Vibhishana said, "Rama! I take Rama's protection, I take the true King's shelter!"

"Why are you here?" asked Hanuman.

"Ravana rejects my words. Except for that I could save him. It would be the easiest thing in the world to give Sita back. But now, white monkey, I must try myself to save even a part of our race on Earth."

"Come on down, I'll be your friend as you were mine." Hanuman led Vibhishana by the hand to Rama, and as they went the monkeys and bears drew back from them. But Vibhishana smiled at the animals, showing his handsome fangs, and swept off his helmet when they reached Rama.

Vibhishana said, "The protection of Rama! I am yours, may you be my safe refuge for all time."

Rama said, "No fear to you from fearful things."

280

Hanuman said, "Rama, in Lanka this Prince Vibhishana saved my life from his elder brother Ravana."

Vibhishana said, "I will help you when I can, but I cannot fight against our people."

Sugriva the Monkey King was there. He said, "He came to spy and kill us in our sleep."

"I want to do right, that's all," said Vibhishana.

Hanuman said, "His true nature will show."

"I don't believe him," said Sugriva.

Hanuman replied, "King, you're trying to make me mad again! Withdrawing from Lanka proves his wisdom. Stop forbidding things and saying *No* like a King. Be more cheerful; like an animal . . . must every Rakshasa choose evil just to please you?"

"He's Ravana's brother isn't he?"

"Sugriva," said Hanuman, "this is only because *you* have not met Ravana. You were home drunk in bed. Therefore in ignorance you can talk a long time about this when there's really nothing to say. I take this Vibhishana for my own friend, and if you don't like it . . . ."

Rama said very evenly, "I will fight Ravana but not the innocent. Vibhishana's face and gestures and words are open. He has done no wrong. He is not clever or busy. One must blame the blameworthy and favor the good wherever they appear. Lowly people who know everything may follow their suspicions, but when someone seeks my refuge he cannot be slain, he will be saved though it will cost my life."

Vibhishana said, 'I'll be a powerful friend, Rama, I'll pay you back some day . . . .'

> *Never murder one who is not fighting,*
> *Nor a warrior who hides or flees bewildered,*
> *Nor any one wounded.*
> *Though he has just now stopped war,*
> *Though his cunning hands touch over a proud heart,*
> *His betrayal blocks your Dharma like a frontier barrier,*
> *A wall of stones.*

The monkey King said, "Without Dharma there is no strength nor power. This is no wonder for you, Rama. *Jaya, victory to you.* I also welcome Vibhishana as an equal friend."

On the first day Nala built his bridge out for fourteen leagues over the sea. The second day he built twenty leagues more, on the third day he added twenty-one leagues, on the fourth day twenty-two, and the fifth day he built twenty-three leagues more onto all he had done already and bridge touched Lanka Island. Then Rama and Lakshmana discarded their deerskins and unmatted their hair.

It was a slightly curving bridge finished in grey stone and supported by arches that rested steady on the sea. That fifth evening Vibhishana and his four knights guarded the southern end but no other Rakshasas appeared. Early the next morning the animals began to cross the wooden pavement from the north, running so swiftly that the first of them began to arrive on Lanka that same afternoon. Sugriva was standing on the north shore ready to go across when a hawk flew in from the ocean and sat on the branch of a nearby tree.

That hawk was Suka, the most trusted minister of the Demon King. Suka said, "Lord of the Monkeys, I am sent here to speak with you. Listen to Ravana's words—*Dear brother, I have only friendship for you. Best of Monkeys, why build a bridge like a rail of anger over the sea? Do me no harm; return to Kishkindhya and rule the forests forever.*"

Sugriva saw Angada stalking that hawk from behind and answered, "Why tell Ravana about our little bridge and disturb him? Just don't pay us any attention and we'll go away . . . after all . . . ."

Prince Angada grabbed Suka out of the tree and squeezed him tight in his paws. Suka gave him an angry look. "Take care, you are at chance, you are in danger! Kill me at your own peril—for if you do, the fruit of the countless evil deeds I've done from the night of my birth till now—all will be yours!"

"What'll I do?" asked Angada.

282

"Drop him quick!" said Sugriva. Suka flew back up in the tree. Sugriva told him, "Say to Ravana—*You have killed one old vulture. You do not see me this day; you do not know I am stronger than you. Rama rules Earth forever.*"

Suka flew home. That day Hanuman and Angada carried Rama and Lakshmana over the bridge. By evening Jambavan and Sugriva and most of the animal armies had all crossed over, and on the Lanka beachhead they sang of fame and victory in their camps along the cool wooded streams, and the aloeswood crackled in their fires.

The next morning the animals climbed Trikuta Hill and began to assemble outside Beautiful Lanka, on the western side of her walls. By the time they had almost all arrived it was past midday and those golden walls were sunlit. Then from the battlements the Rakshasas blew blaring shells and glaring horns and beat their drums. The animals then for the first time knew that many of them would die there, and fell silent a moment. Then they yelled back twice as loud; they roared a lion's roar of victory.

Ravana in his palace spoke to Suka. "Nobody could believe in a bridge across the sea! And all those animals unbelievable! . . . but send someone out to count them."

"I'll send two," replied Suka. He called the faithful spies Sardula and Sarana. "Go outside the walls, count the enemy; find out their plans and dreams, and return."

They said, "Victory to Ravana!" Outside Lanka they took monkey shapes and mingled with Sugriva's army, until Vibhishana happened to glance at them. Vibhishana's crystal blue eyes were sharp-sighted, and he kept them illumined with black kohl dust round his lashes. He could see clear in shadowy light; he could see a still black ant in the black shadow of a black rock on a moonless night. He could have found a lost hair in the darkest corner of a lightless basement vault.

Vibhishana saw Sardula and Sarana for the demons they were. He snapped his right fingers three times and broke their disguises, caught one under each arm and dragged them to Rama.

Sarana was so afraid that he shrank away to nothing; he

vanished completely and was never seen again by anyone anywhere. Sardula stood alone before Rama, despairing of life and barely able to breathe.

But Rama only said, "If you have discovered all you came to find out, go safely home. If you have missed anything see it now, Vibhishana will escort you."

"No thank you," said Sardula.

Rama said, "Now your King Ravana may use against me that great force he used to steal my wife!"

"And farewell," said Sardula.

Sardula found Ravana on a high balcony overlooking the ramparts of Lanka's wall, facing west. The Demon King said, "Why are you pale, did they catch you?"

"Alas, I am covered with shame," said Sardula. "I can't count them. Some are still at the bridge, some are still climbing the hill. Sir, Vibhishana sees through us."

"And you call yourself a spy!"

"No longer. I resign, with your permission."

"Are you afraid?"

"Well no, but my stomach hurts!"

"Yes, you may go, you are no warrior," said Ravana.

Sardula looked at the King. "I will point out and name their best fighters for you, before I go to live with my wife and family in the Naga lands under the world."

"Never mind," said Ravana, "be still. This goes beyond the making of a report and the declaration of this and that. Peace be to you, Sardula; this is real. What you can see from here and what I see are different things, and I am master of what must next be done."

Then Ravana was alone. He saw the broadshouldered monkeys and scowling bears climbing uphill, carrying huge rocks and uprooted trees. He looked out at his moat and thick walls. He saw his loaded slings and firebombs. And he saw the animals all looking up at him with their ancient eyes; the ancient eyes of the animals, the first friends of man in ages past . . . .

In his bedroom, standing by the back door to the Asoka

284

Wood, Ravana summoned his two magicians, Lightning-Tongue and Thunder-Tooth, and said, "By spells of deception and illusion make for me by magic the severed head of Rama, and his bow with an arrow set on its string."

Thunder-Tooth said "Yes." Out from beneath his robes he drew a bow with diamond and gold on its back and many colors on its belly, strung and holding a golden arrow which was marked—*Rama*.

Lightning-Tongue took his wand from his belt and turned aside. He bent down, straightened up, and held out in his hand a gory green head, bruised and dusty and stained with dried blood. Ravana rewarded them with pearls. He took the bow and told Lightning-Tongue, "Await my call."

Ravana went over to Sita in the Asoka Grove and said, "This is your Lord's honored bow still strung." He snapped it in two.

"Dear Sita," said the Demon King, "Rama arrived on this island last night with his armies. At midnight General Prahasta fell upon them as they slept. He beheaded Rama with a curving broadsword; he turned aside a little and fatally stabbed King Sugriva; he crushed Hanuman to death beneath an elephant; with a bloodwashed axe he cut off Jambavan's legs and broke his neck. Prahasta's warriors used a net of flying chariots to pull the traitor Vibhishana from the sky; they left Angada rolling in the dirt and torn by agony and arrows. Now animal corpses cover our shores and litter the wooded hills by the sea and float drowned on the red tide. They lie hewn and mangled in caves where they ran to hide and then to die; their bones are broken, their sinews severed, their tendons torn and their blood spilled out. Dumb and speechless, stricken and badly wounded, Lakshmana alone ran away and fled to safety. And if any others still live they are dying now."

Ravana told one of the Rakshasi guards, "Call out from the palace that cruel Lightning-Tongue who brought me Rama's head!"

Ravana said to Sita, "Here, I'll show you." Lightning-

Tongue approached holding that head of illusion by the hair. He looked at Sita and slithered his long forked tongue over his thin lips. He threw Rama's head down right at her feet, bowed to Ravana and swiftly departed. "Prahasta killed that mere man and sent these relics to me. See for yourself the final sad death of Rama and marry me!"

Rama's head stared up at Sita with dead green eyes. She saw the familiar brow, the long dark-green hair tied back with a war-cloth, the kind mouth, the broken emerald war-earrings. She wept piteously and said, "You foolish man, I was really your death and never your wife."

Sita sat and held the head in her lap, and her shining tears fell down upon it—*You died to save me, what could be worse?* Sita began to let go of her life. She quietly opened her hand, and let life slip and fall away through her fingers.

"Hey Ravana!" The back door to the palace banged open, and in full armor General Prahasta came swiftly striding through the Asoka trees towards the Demon King. His bronze armor clanged, his sword slammed and rattled against his iron-clad legs, he waved and smashed his metal arms against his sides—and from without the palace wall, from the city Sita heard the deep white-faced drums of Lanka pounding, and the beating of the brazen gongs, joining in one after another from every direction.

"Victory! Victory! Excellent success!" shouted Prahasta. "Aha, it's *War!*" He cracked the fingers of his steel gloves and smiled. Elephants were trumpeting in the city. Lines of lance-points tied with colored sashes went by just visible beyond the palace walls. The gates of Lanka swung shut on diamond pivots and closed with a jarring noise, then the brass bolts falling, and the latch-guards of steel. Chariots clattered through the streets, the arsenals and armories opened their doors, and by heavy chains the three drawbridges of Lanka were raised into the outer walls.

"Forgive my interruption," yelled Prahasta. "Did you see them? The sea is a hundred leagues across and rough with huge breaking waves, yet Rama has crossed it like a village cow-trail. Rama has come!"

The ground of Lanka shook. Ravana smiled at Sita the best he could. "You must excuse me, Princess, there seems to be something . . . ." Ravana and the long-handed General Prahasta turned and left the Asoka park, and when Ravana had gone Rama's head and bow melted and disappeared. On the big city walls the fire-machines were ignited. Shooting over the sky appeared the gleaming reflections of many colors thrown from squadrons of polished Rakshasa shields and golden chariots, a dire luster like the raging wildfires of summer.

Sita was still bent over weeping, so blinded by tears she could not see that the false bow and head were gone. The old Rakshasi Trijata came beside her and said, "Daughter of Earth you are no widow. What you hear is our call to arms. Now the warriors will gathered to discover why they are called—Rama is right now in a field outside Lanka. He is alive!"

Sita could not understand. "Kill me, let me fall by my husband."

Trijata reached down and lifted Sita's head, so quickly that her teeth snapped together. Trijata was angry; her bare toes made the grass curl and smoke. *Disbelieve it! Disbelieve it! Disbelieve it!*

When Trijata said those words three times her speech broke through and reached Sita's heart, like welcome rain falling on the hard dry fields of Earth. "Listen—" said Trijata. "—are you listening?"

"Yes . . . ."

"My every word is true—Rama knows himself and cannot be surprised asleep, nor can Prahasta so easily kill those animals as Ravana pretends. Look, that head and bow are gone. They were wrong and untrue, they were an illusion spread about you, a momentary glamor and a passing spell."

"What?" Sita was bewildered.

"Rama advances on our city with a great army of woodland

animals. They may well deny it! Ravana has gone to a war council. I take refuge with the Sun who makes our days and gives our joys and grief; I swear by the Sun who goes round the world like a dancing horse round a circle—*this is Truth!*"

Trijata continued, "Out in the streets everyone is armed. Weapons are a sign of fear made visible, and we are afraid. Hear the horses neigh while their hair stands on end, hear the archers calling. Our bloodthirsty soldiers flourish their weapons and shake them at the sky, to bully the heavens and terrify the serene planets and stars and frighten the clouds. But this time they don't fight gods! The creaking high saddles are tied upon the elephants' backs, the horsemen mount, the jangling chariots are harnessed. Like water that pours into the sea, the Rakshasa warriors rush here from all sides, mailed demons of wondrous forms, all doomed to die . . . ."

A Rakshasa patrol swept by overhead armed with swords and triple spears, their cowls and capes crackling and snapping like whips in the air behind them, their shadows tearing through the Asoka leaves. Trijata smiled and said again, "Lakshmi embraces you. Your sorrow will be demolished. Dark-eyed Sita, I can take any message to Rama."

> Rama and Lakshmana are your help,
> Not long will you dwell in this
> Dreadful demon city.
>
> I'll wait for my beloved,
> He is not far away.
> My Rama is not far from me,
> I'll wait out the time.

"Find out instead what Ravana plans to do with me," said Sita.

Trijata became a wasp and flew to the windows of Ravana's courtroom. She returned, took back her real form and said, "He won't free you, Rama must first kill him."

In Ravana's war-meeting was the old Rakshasa Malyavan, who with his two brothers had asked the heavenly architect Viswakarman to build Beautiful Lanka long ages before. He sat there, and he thought he had some warning to give Ravana.

As Malyavan had grown older and older he had come to look more and more like a man. He had lost his fangs and teeth, and he trimmed the claws on his slender fingers till they looked like nails. His short hair was white; he was very thin and dark; he dressed simply in a white cloth, with no ornament and no colored borders. Malyavan had eaten but one bowl of rice a day for many years; he had seen his brothers killed; he slept very little. He sat against walls and trees outside and smiled with his eyes open and his head leaning back in the sun. He told ancient stories to children and awake at night he watched the streets of Lanka.

And as the world grew dark in the evenings, Malyavan had many times lately seen a withered man with his head shaven going along the streets, wearing a brown worn shroud, covered with dust and ashes, coughing a dry cough, peering into the doorways of the demon mansions with his hollow eyes and grinning like a skull. Beautiful Lanka had been built for the asking, once she had been young and now Time walked her streets. How had those dirty monkeys and bears come so far to hurt her?

Malyavan slowly got to his feet in Ravana's courtroom. He stood and saw all the assembled officers and warriors sitting silent, staring straight ahead and awaiting orders. Then for a moment a memory of war's blind anger changed Malyavan's face, and as though he were young still, he looked at them all with a proud and evil look that faded right away again. Ravana watched him as he looked around.

Malyavan tried to remember what he ought to say. In one of the open windows behind Ravana's throne was a wasp that was really Trijata. Beside the wasp stood a blue-and-green bird eavesdropping who was really a Rakshasa, one of Vibhishana's four warriors, staring Malyavan right in the eye with his head tilted to one side. There was something important to say but Malyavan had forgotten what. It seemed to him, all this had happened once before. He smiled a wrinkly smile at the king and raised his open hands before him—*Blessings upon you, I will go.* Malyavan shuffled away and left the room without speaking.

When the war-meeting had ended that afternoon, Vibhishana's courtier returned to him and said, "Ravana believes himself already victorious. When we attacked heaven we had altogether fewer warriors than now attend each gate of Lanka. The least of Ravana's soldiers is as strong as ten elephants, and every warrior now paces behind the wall of Beautiful Lanka saying—*I will go first.*"

Vibhishana went to Rama and said, "Even if he knows the difference, Ravana will still rather do wrong than good. He will fight. There stand the Rakshasas, golden in their armor on the walls, like a second wall on top of the first one."

Rama said, "When we fight let no animal change shape, and with your four knights be with us in Rakshasa forms."

Then Rama told Prince Angada, "Go as my messenger and ask Ravana once more."

Angada flew into Lanka. He saw Ravana walking the walls and like a fiery golden ball with the sunlight in his golden fur, Angada dropped from the sky beside Ravana and was surrounded by dark demons pushing forward like heavy clouds.

"Who are you?" asked Ravana.

"I am Vali's son," said Angada, "and these are Rama's words—*Too long, Ravana! Give back Sita, or bid farewell to your friends and come out to me, I am waiting to kill you.*"

"Ah," said Ravana, "I will not blow out like a light from windy words. When I win this battle I will at last finally impress Sita and she will love me back." Ravana smiled ten wide smiles and his twenty eyes laughed. "Angada, you are a good messenger, you added nothing and you left nothing out. Won't you stay to dinner?"

"Ravana all your wealth is wasted, what's the use of being rich if you won't spend your gold to do good for other people?"

"Someone said that already," replied the Demon King. "Come, make yourself at home, I will protect you here."

Angada said, "Majesty, I hope you don't think I believe that for one moment, do you? You think it's so superior to be evil! You think it makes you *better!*"

"You are yet only a rash child, a meal time visitor, a pleasing presence; but keep it up and one of these days . . . ."

Angada tossed his head. "Shall we all put out our eyes? Is the Sun dark, because some men are blind?"

Ravana frowned. "You are speaking like a fool! We could all die at any time—" He bent down and thrust his ten faces suddenly snarling close before Angada. His lips were drawn back and his moustaches quivered; his wide-rimmed red eyes were aflame and veins were throbbing on his brows crowned by diadems. A deep low growl came from his ten throats.

Angada was faint with fear. His heart froze. The blood drained from his face and he couldn't breathe. Ravana said, "Now you are caught in the meshes of war; there's no way out of this for you! Fools have sharp eyesight and they stay forever on the good Dharma-Wheel, but the wise do not see so well." He reached out for Angada. *Who the dark Demon King seizes in his grip, who he holds in anger dies crushed and cursed, he never lives!*

Then Ravana just touched Angada. He brushed him away like a little piece of cloud, and off Angada floated . . . .

Ravana called after him, "Tell Rama—*Grief to you! Men are vile, may this war increase your pain and bring joy to the demons!*"

Angada recovered his strength and backed away into the air. He returned to Rama. And in Lanka, Ravana rang all the brass and iron bells, the great bells of Lanka rung with swinging logs. From the ringing mouths of bells came . . . daring . . . defiance . . . .

The crimson Sun set behind Sunset Hill at the western edge of the Earth, beyond the sea horizon. The sky grew pale lavender while still holding light, like the color of old silver. Then it was dark and the stars came out.

Angada said, "Ravana will not listen; he cannot clear his mind."

Rama answered, "Then where will he escape while I live?"

the siege of lanka

This perilous Life is a drop of water,
A hanging raindrop on a lotus leaf;
Soon it falls back in the pond below
And is lost.

Indrajit,
In war or peace
You are falling away.

Early the next morning Ravana was leaning on the wall over
the northern gate looking out, leaning on his twenty arms
spread side by side by side along the ramparts, under the
shadow of a royal white umbrella. He patiently watched Rama
and his army while two demons fanned him with white
chowry fans made from yak-tails and trimmed with peacock
feathers. He wore white robes like fame and glory, adorned
with rubies red as blood; and for a long time he quietly
watched the animals.

Ravana saw the golden-haired Sugriva fathered by the Sun;
the black-and-brown bear Jambavan; Angada with his long
fine yellow hair, pacing with his arms folded, yawning in
anger and slapping his tail on the ground; the white monkey
Hanuman, come back again to Lanka, strong and gracious;
and beside him Rama of tangled hair and dark green skin,
holding a bow whose arrows can slice the Earth or pierce the
sky—Rama King of the World whose anger is Death, sur-
rounded by animals all willing to die for him.

Sugriva told Rama to stay behind the army with Hanuman.
Lakshmana walked back and forth in front of the animals, his

skin like pure gold, his lips swollen with wrath, not easy to pacify. *Aaah* . . . the Rakshasas on the Lanka walls sighed like the long-traveling wind storming in from off the sea. They flaunted their glorious war-banners on shiny golden flagstaffs. And back from the monkeys and bears came another deeper sigh, deep and loud as weights of water pouring through a broken sea-wall. *Aaaaa* . . . .

Then at the same instant Lakshmana pointed at Lanka with his bow and Ravana raised a mace over his head. In Lanka the Royal Artillery Commander waved his sword. Batteries of Rakshasa artillery roared fringed with fire; the monkeys and bears closed ranks; the big north gate of Lanka opened; and the youngest third of the Demon Army came out to attack, led by Prahasta on a war-chariot.

But the demons could not win in daylight. Bears broke their cars and killed them with their own axles and flagpoles; long-armed apes caught them and pressed them to death; monkeys flattened them with uptorn trees and cliffs and chopped them up with captured axes like firewood. At noon Prahasta ordered a retreat, and the Rakshasas poured back into Lanka, and the huge northern gate snapped shut like a trap. They waited for darkness.

❧

Then Night fell, increasing the strength of the demons. At dusk the War Chief Prahasta and King Ravana were on the wall again, and the darkness grew. Pale silk flags and standards crowned Beautiful Lanka with all their colors fast-fading and moving in the twilight wind. Up on the wall the air from the city below carried the scents of incense and the murmur of Rakshasa prayers to welcome Night. Demon soldiers were everywhere kneeling before fires built in the streets, stringing their bows, tying on their armor, and then putting on over that many garlands of flowers blessed with mantras of safety. And on the battlefield outside the animals built many fires to light the ground.

Ravana said, "Let the young warriors rest. Arm the veterans."

"That's what we're doing."

From a stone flask Ravana poured out a glass of soma juice somehow stolen from heaven and gave it to Prahasta. General Prahasta drank it down and ate up the glass along with a dried string of red-hot peppers. He crunched the glass and chewed on the pepper seeds and smacked his lips. Ravana backed away from him a little.

Prahasta said, "I'll go out with them. I'll drive away the animals and isolate Rama. I'll entertain my friends with his flesh!" Little flames began to come from Prahasta's mouth, licking over his lips.

He touched his hands together and bowed his head and saluted Ravana. Ravana said, "Be careful." Prahasta came down from the wall and tied back his flowing hair and got on his chariot.

General Prahasta's chariot had two wheels covered by sheets of gold, that turned like rolling suns and rumbled like the clouds. Steel scythes were mounted on the axle hubs, and a long iron spike pointed forward from the harness pole that was all painted with crescent moons. Sixty four mottled green serpents drew that car, harnessed by unsolvable knots; the chariot bristled with racks of swords and harpoons; it was armored with bullhide warshields and metal plates.

Things were loaded all over Prahasta's chariot. He had slaughter-sledges, butcher knives and meat-hooks, chains and claws and clamps; he carried bombs and rockets and poisons and appalling jealousies; delusions and bad dreams, diseases and ambitions, many crises and confusions. Wrong-way road signs and false maps of mirages were tied on with broken promises. Small iron wheels spun in the air, their rims striking sparks against flint-stones and whirling in flames in the Night. There were lights and shadows and lying smiles, prisms and colored lenses and crooked brass mirrors and baleful green cats'-eyes. There were puzzles with essential parts missing and loaded dice and heartbreak and many first loves lost.

It was quite a sight to see! From a high flagstaff in the center of the car flew Prahasta's flag showing a serpent of emeralds and a clawing lion of topaz stones sewn onto blood-red silk.

From that central flagpole a defensive net covered the chariot like a tent, made of glowing diamonds closely tied on blue steel threads, woven tightly with spun strands of adamant, guarding Prahasta as he fought and leaving small hidden ways for him to shoot his arrows.

It was fantastic. Still, Prahasta was a great archer; he had never turned back from a fight on Earth. Prahasta flexed his twisty bow and rolled his eyes. He leaned forward and told his charioteer—*Take me to War!* The chariot leapt forward protected by hatchetmen in winged demon helmets. Again the north gate opened, and General Prahasta led out from Lanka the elite veterans, and Grand Army of the Rakshasas. The teeming soldiers followed, riding and shouting, bells tied on their arms and legs, mounted on chariots drawn by running scorpions and toads, riding on the backs of porpoises and camels and giant goldfish, on lizards and pigs and huge blue rats.

The Rakshasas laughed in anger and blew ten thousand out-of-tune shells. They came onto the battlefield and charged at the monkeys and bears. The animals fled back between their fires and the demons cried—*Easy! Easily done!*

But it was a trick. In one motion, all of them together, the animals threw great stones out from behind their own lines, over their own warriors, over Prahasta, and aimed them to fall in front of the following Rakshasas. They made a roadblock, a strong stone wall that cut off Prahasta, and when demons tried to fly over it the animals beat them back with trees, and closed in behind the General's chariot.

Arrows long as chariot axles flew from Prahasta's bow. None missed. He struck five or seven animals with one single arrow, or hit one monkey with seventeen arrows, or pierced a bear with twenty-seven or with ninety. The monkeys and apes and bears gave way and drew back from Prahasta, all but Nala the bridge-builder.

Nala alone faced Prahasta's chariot. He dodged a thousand flights of arrows and rockets that flew at him. Then he just stood still and let Prahasta shoot. A big brass club bounced off

Nala's head, but it only killed a mosquito who was about to bite him. Nala stood among the falling missiles and arrows with his eyes closed like a proud bull standing in a rainstorm.

Then Nala opened his eyes, narrow in rage. He watched every move Prahasta made. The heavy Rakshasa chariot turned and bore down on him. There was noise like peals of thunder; the ground shook; Nala could see every armor plate, every diamond, every stone in the war-flag, every mirror flashing lights. He almost felt the serpents' breath.

Then quicker than the twinkling of an eye Nala threw his weight onto one foot and Trikuta Hill lurched off-center and Prahasta's chariot overturned. The serpents who had drawn the car slipped their harness and dove into the Earth. The chariot splintered to bits, Prahasta's bow broke, his protective net fell down, and suddenly the Demon General was standing free from the wreckage, holding a mace under his arm, spitting fire from his mouth and rubbing his hands together in a bath of flame.

Prahasta swung his mace in both hands and struck Nala twice; swinging out he hit his shoulder and on the back-swing gave a glancing blow on Nala's hip. Nala pulled one of the golden wheels off the broken chariot. When Prahasta raised his arms to strike again with a downwards blow, Nala threw the wheel in under his guard. He struck Prahasta over the heart. He knocked the mace from his hands and drove the life out from his body.

When they saw Prahasta killed that midnight, the Rakshasas bent back like tall trees in a windstorm; they tore loose their hair in shame, and returned leaderless to Lanka, looking down and not speaking. On the war-field west of Lanka Prahasta's chariot was smashed; it lay bent and smoking like a dead bolt of thunder fallen from heaven. The charioteer was dead. Prahasta lay on his back, terrible to see. His remorseless eyes were open and from his mouth little flames still darted out between his teeth that were burned black by his fury.

Nala stood wounded over Prahasta, one arm hanging broken and blood on his leg. Rama approached him carrying a

297

torch. As Rama came near, Nala knelt and bowed to him. Once kneeling he was too exhausted to rise, but looking up at Rama's face his eyes still glittered and glowed like the eyes of a cobra just struck a blow with a rod, spreading wide his hood.

❦

The monkeys and bears carried their dead up the hillside of Trikuta and laid them in a forest. All the demon arrows, stone-sharpened and hardened in fires, were removed from the dead and wounded, and broken and burned.

The demons also left many dead behind them killed by the claws and teeth of animals, but to conceal his losses Ravana from within Lanka spirited those corpses away into the sea. Prahasta's body was gone without a trace.

In the city Ravana called his minister Suka and said, "One must make his own good fortune wherever he goes. Six months have passed—awaken my brother Kumbhakarna!"

The giant Kumbhakarna slept for six months after every day he was awake. He lay stretched out on his back inside a huge one-room mansion, the largest building in Lanka. Suka told the demons in the kitchen to start Kumbhakarna's breakfast, and with many servants holding torches and lanterns he went to the long giant house. Cooks arrived driving carts full of steaming rice and vats of wine and crisp roast buffalo, and Suka opened the great doors to let the scent of food inside.

Kumbhakarna didn't stir. Suka entered. He fought the windy push and pull of Kumbhakarna's breathing and drew near his ear. Kumbhakarna's hair and beard were six months wild; his hairs were like young forest trees, and when he was awake and felt like hunting, that giant would tie a boulder to each hair and go stand among his prey and shake himself, and crush his victims under stones.

Suka reached in his robe, pulled out two big brass cymbals and smashed them together by Kumbhakarna's ear. Kumbhakarna yawned, and his monstrous throat looked like a red mine-shaft leading down to Hell. A team of eighteen trained elephants ran in through the door, up Kumbhakarna's side and across his chest; there they made a line and sprayed his face with cold water.

Suka kept battering and banging his cymbals, and Kumbhakarna awoke. Trainers called the elephants back just in time. Kumbhakarna sat up, opened his eyes, reached outside for a vat of wine, and drank it down and sighed, "Ah, it is full Night!"

The food-wagons drove in, and Suka stood quietly at a safe distance until Kumbhakarna had eaten. Then he approached and said, "Prince, General Prahasta has been killed in war. Lanka is surrounded by Rama and his armies."

"Rama? Rama?" asked Kumbhakarna. "What god is Rama? . . . never mind, I'll help you."

Suka replied, "Here in Lanka you alone sleep happily, knowing nothing of our fate. Rama is a man, and his warriors are monkeys and bears from across the sea. Our soldiers have been twice driven from the field, and Ravana wants you at the palace."

"No fear," said Kumbhakarna, "be calm. Behold the magnified evils of being awake and subject to reason. My only law is dreams . . . ." He bent his head, went out the tall doorway and washed his face in a lake.

As Kumbhakarna fully awoke, he became so dark and menacing that he seemed to soak up all the light from Suka's torches and from the stars of heaven, and by a sudden fancied dimness in his courtroom Ravana knew his brother was coming. Rakshasas lined the streets to the royal palace and called up to Kumbhakarna—*Don't step on these fragile temples. Houses are there, here stand soldiers.*

After a few steps Kumbhakarna was near the palace. He sat outside near Pushpaka chariot, where he would have room to talk with Ravana. The Demon King came outdoors and saw his little brother blotting out the sky, and ran to meet him with ten happy smiles.

Ravana said, "Scatter my enemies like a strong wind!"

Kumbhakarna asked, "What have you done wrong while I slept peacefully?"

"I'm at war with Rama because I took his wife Sita," answered Ravana. "His animals have killed our warriors who were never before defeated."

"Give her back," said Kumbhakarna.

"But I am in love with her," said Ravana.

"A tremendous mistake. Stop yourself."

"But cast the blame where it belongs, it's not my fault she's so good-looking and easy to see! No one in any world is like Sita, but she won't get into my bed."

"Best of Kings," said Kumbhakarna, "here you are speaking of the waking world of impermanence, of suffering and unreality. Those are the animals of Lord Narayana, and this is the death of the Rakshasas."

"I won't believe it," said Ravana. "What I don't like I don't hear!"

"Oh, let alone the animals, Rama can himself defeat you all alone. Do some good before you die. They are eager to kill you; why won't you make peace with them?"

"Not for fear of all the worlds!"

"Majesty," said Kumbhakarna, "after you've done this thoughtless deed full of flaws and holes, then you call on me. You've begun at the end and ignored the beginning."

"What do you know about it anyway?" asked Ravana.

"I know forgetfulness, and sleep . . . as a child falling asleep . . . what I knew then years ago, as I fell asleep, I still know. Forget. Sleep and forget her . . . ."

Ravana rubbed his eyes. "Yes, I am tired and spent—" But then he shook his heads, took a deep breath of the night air and sighed. "But I have lost myself in longing."

"Your entire education was a waste," said Kumbhakarna. "For nothing did you read the holy Veda and throw your heads into the fire when we lived in the high Himalya Hills."

"Well, it's done, isn't it! Why must you tell me about the aftermath of evil? If I'm wrong I need you to save me all the

300

more. Ah, if you could only see her, like an idol of gold, the very handwork of Maya himself . . . ."

"There's no greater wrong than stealing another's wife," said Kumbhakarna. "Lord of Night, what else but a harvest of misfortune could follow? You have many ladies in your own house; be happy with them. Enjoy in peace your honors and kingdoms. Keep for a long time your wealth; preserve your life. Return her to Rama and get more sleep. A King is the root of his people's happiness, and if he is wrong their lives are in danger and their nation will die. Your ministers cannot take this to heart, they do not serve you well. They plot to kill you. They do not fear your anger. Majesty, those two men Rama and Lakshmana are the flame and the wind meeting—will no one tell you this except me? I will kill Vibhishana for not caring to prevent you doing this."

"Vibhishana did try to stop me," said Ravana, "and when he failed he went over to Rama. He's out there on the field right now."

"Now he was right to do that, and surely it was wrong of you to force him to go. Give back Sita. You have no gift of protection against men and animals . . . ."

"She is my beloved . . . ."

"And I am your friend," said Kumbhakarna. "Listen, I have an idea. Take Rama's form by magic, go to Sita, and she will willingly love you."

"No, I can't," said Ravana. "The transformation would have to be complete; I'd have to take on all Rama's virtues as well to fool her, and then I could do no wrong, I couldn't lie to her and say I was someone I wasn't. Help me to cure my sorrow. In my mind I am sure of your victory!"

Kumbhakarna smiled. "Then they must first kill me to get at you! Dear brother, have a good time, do as you please. Be merciful while you may and think no more of Rama."

Ravana was very happy; he beckoned for his warriors and told Kumbhakarna, "Consider well your own strength and theirs, do not go out alone."

But Kumbhakarna said, "I want no helpers. Everyone here

who has been awake and kept silent about your careless love is your fawning enemy. The simple truth is that Rama and the animals have outwitted you all; they've built a bridge while you sat around saying it couldn't be done! Let these others help you feather your conceits, but I alone will kill Rama tonight and drink his blood!"

Ravana felt reborn. Kumbhakarna smiled at him again and went back the way he came to put on his war-clothes. But though he seemed in good humor Kumbhakarna thought to himself, "Dharma is the root of all good fortune, and you have uprooted Dharma; the happiness of others is light for the spirit but you have darkened the worlds."

Then Kumbhakarna put sympathy aside; he put his heart into the stone age. He donned his armor of bronze and his helmet of gold. The chains of his belts were heavier than the chains that raised the drawbridges of Lanka; his bracelets were like the metal tires on chariot-wheels; his garlands of flowers were as long as a day's journey.

When Kumbhakarna had dressed he drank down two thousand vats of war-wine, and from his long house he took out his black iron spear decorated with animals inlaid in gold. When Kumbhakarna touched it, deadly blue fires burned round the spear-point like the fires at the birth of Time, blazing for a moment large as a funeral pyre. Kumbhakarna walked to Lanka's wall and over the western gate the Rakshasas raised his flag, a black banner hung with crimson flowers, showing the Death-Wheel of oblivion, a giant wheel sewn on it in golden thread.

❧

On the battlefield that Night Rama could see the bearded Kumbhakarna, dark and startling, visible behind the high walls like walking Death. He asked Vibhishana, "Who is that?"

"My brother Kumbhakarna has awakened," answered Vibhishana. "He'll make one mouthful out of our whole army. He is the very crown of our cruelty and the banner of our

302

strength. Did he not sleep so long he would by now have eaten up all Life on Earth. If he can reach them, he will scrape up your animals and swallow them like little grains of rice . . . . But tell the monkeys and bears that this is an uplifted war-engine, a huge machine; for if they know he is a living being they will die of fright at the thought, whether he touches them or not, and we will swiftly lose this war."

"I'll send them to the back." Rama summoned Sugriva and told him, "Withdraw from the field."

"No," said the Monkey King. "They say that the gateway arch to Kumbhakarna's house rises so high that every noon-day the Sun must pass under it on his way around the Earth. They say that giant is so heavy that he draws in the flood tides when he walks near the sea. But people talk too much! Why should we move aside? Why give way, leaving you be-hind us?"

Kumbhakarna stepped over the wall, swinging his mon-strous arms in anger. Like a pillar of light, his spear-shaft caught the torch-beams of Lanka on its golden ornaments. Kumbhakarna saw the monkeys and bears and thought, "Animals like these were always the innocent ornaments of our gardens. Rama is the cause of this war; I will kill Rama and end it!" He turned in Rama's direction and cried out his horrible, unnatural war-cry, a shuddering sound, so low and deep it could be felt through the ground, and yet shrill and piercing, and getting louder—

And that cry alone broke the formations of the animals. They fell unconscious, or lay trembling and unable to move, or ran to hide in quiet places, not looking back, and a curtain of dust rose from their feet running in panic.

Kumbhakarna took a long step towards Rama, and beneath his foot Earth lurched and swayed like a swing. The animals' war-fires spilled and rolled burning over the land. Prince Angada tried to stop the fleeing monkeys and bears. "Think of the King, think of your good name and fame! Your wives will scorn you—"

Still they ran past him—*Life is dear!*

Hanuman jumped hard and high at Kumbhakarna.

"Sound an alert! Return!"

But each animal thought, "He is after me!" In an instant the army had fled. But Hanuman came from somewhere and stood quietly beside Angada, and they saw Sugriva not far away, and Jambavan the sullen Bear King had stood his ground. But between Rama and Kumbhakarna there was only Lakshmana.

Then from where he stood Hanuman jumped hard and high at Kumbhakarna and bit a piece out of his ear. Kumbhakarna whirled, very fast, and struck Hanuman down with his great spear. But that blow broke the iron shaft, and as Hanuman fell stunned Kumbhakarna threw aside the piece he still held and advanced on Rama unarmed.

No one remained except Lakshmana, but his arrows could not penetrate the stiff coily hair that covered Kumbhakarna's body wherever his armor did not. Kumbhakarna looked way down at Lakshmana and said, "You also are dead, when Rama dies!" Then he stepped over him and quickly advanced on Rama.

Rama took three steps backwards and aimed an arrow with bent knots like thunderbolts. He released it; it flew and struck Kumbhakarna in the chest, right through his armor. Kumbhakarna paused and stood still, and blood poured from his wound.

That wound alone was fatal, but his hatred for Rama kept Kumbhakarna alive and his murderous heart did not fail. He cried out—*I am not Vali the monkey shot in the back; I am Kumbhakarna poised over you!*

Rama shot a straight-flying arrow with a broad razor head and cut off Kumbhakarna's right arm, which fell crushing trees and rocks. Still Kumbhakarna kept coming, he yelled—*I tear Earth apart and pull down stars; I fall on you like Doom!*

Rama cut off his left arm. It fell into the sea and bruised the whales, and Kumbhakarna shouted—*No one can slay me; no one can stop me!*

Again Rama twice drew back his bow, and with two thirsty arrows cut off Kumbhakarna's legs. The giant fell only a

305

few bows'-lengths from Rama. Still he managed to move, something carried him on, and his mouth opened and closed —*Let all Creation see the might of Kumbhakarna awake, and tremble!*

Then with one final arrow Rama beheaded Kumbhakarna. The giant head rolled downhill into the sea and sank to the bottom. It was near the hour of dawn and Rama stood alone against the sky. For a few moments he kept shooting his gold-covered arrows up through the air and into Lanka, and the snap of his bowstring struck terror into the Demons' hearts. With golden arrows Rama was scattering the Night. The sky lightened behind Lanka. The stars faded, caught in the skies of heaven and defeated by the eastern Sun rising all in flames. Soon Rama stood in sunlight and unstrung his bow.

❧

When he heard that Kumbhakarna's life was lost, the hot fumes of anger filled Ravana's heart. He stood on the wall and saw his brother's body and limbs blocking the fields outside Lanka. Smoke swirled out of his ten mouths and hung in the air round his heads like a dismal shroud.

The old Rakshasa Malyavan came and stood beside him at sunrise, and Ravana said—*Truly how has Rama done this?*

Malyavan answered, "He did it with glorious arrows lighting up all the directions of Earth, arrows washed first with gold and then with blood."

"Grandfather, as you look at me I am defeated although I seem alive. All is truly forever chance and change."

Malyavan said, "Like a mirror gleaming through from within a black velvet bag, we may sometimes glimpse Reality shining here and there when it takes us unawares."

Ravana said, "Once when I was here at home, the cautious Wind blew cool from touching the waters; the waves of the surf stepped lightly; the careful warm sunlight was never burning hot; the Moon paled from dread when I went outside into my gardens. At my command trees blossomed and clouds poured rain and the sea-tide stopped." Ravana sighed. "But now, when talking the name Rama comes out in my speech. I

306

see his face when I close my eyes. Monkeys have bridged the sea, and stones float for them unfairly, against the natural laws, and what never yet happened in the world has happened here! . . . This sad peril is all my fault. I have banished Vibhishana who was my conscience, and my young brother who loved me is dead. Where does Kumbhakarna go all alone?"

"He is in the bright heaven of warriors killed in war," said Malyavan. But he could not console the King, and he walked slowly away and left Ravana alone.

Ravana hung down his heads and wept for a long time. Then he said, "What have I to do with Empire? What shall I care now for Sita? I must avenge you, Kumbhakarna. *If I cannot kill Rama, then Death is my good fortune and this life is useless to me!*"

Then a voice behind Ravana said, "Oh King, banish sorrow!"

Ravana turned and looked into Indrajit's quiet eyes. "My son!"

Indrajit said, "I shall make my sacrifices to the Fire. Sire, be happy; drink your wines and sleep. Enjoy all pleasure, for your enemies are already dead and Sita is about to become yours!"

the invisible warrior

Do not complain about how heaven turns above,
For heaven will endure long enough without you.

I am all this,
All this Life;
I am all this.

That same fell Indrajit, able to assume shapes at will, stood there on Lanka's walls in the form of a golden young man. His hair was gold and his eyes were flecked with all the colors of gold. His skin was gold. He wore a golden war-robe and a golden belt and thin gold-leather shoes. He hid behind himself every enchantment and he was beautiful to see.

Ravana said, "I am in a deep and narrow pit, with steep walls, with no place to grasp them anywhere . . . and no way out . . . ."

"Father, I'm whoever I want to be." Indrajit knelt to Ravana on one knee, he touched together his hands and said—*I am Fire in the dry grass.*

"Now there's a thought!" Ravana was happy as a man high on a clear hill on a springtime morning, with his love beside him.

"Majesty!" Indrajit rose and pointed to Rama far away. "He does not know me, so he comes against us. Why does he stir the sweetly sleeping fire? What shall I do for you on my invisible chariot unswerving as the Truth?"

"Just kill Rama and Lakshmana, that's all."

"Yes!" said Indrajit. "Though my fire is an illusion, it will

308

burn; the water will drown, it is no more false than Death itself."

✧

Indrajit went outside Lanka to his hidden grove and built a smokeless fire on his altar. He raised a vessel of clear butter to his head. The fire burned in seven tongues of flame all playing about in the heat-waving air—one tongue black and one deep red and one starting to smoke; one swift tongue, one sparkling, one threatening, and one having all brilliant forms within it.

Indrajit took a sip from the bowl of butter. He poured it in the fire and quickly stepped back. The flame streamed up in golden splendor when he fed it. *Lord Brahma, I have won from you one hundred and eight kinds of illusion; I have won a quiver of arrows that never run out, and an invincible bow, and charms bringing darkness and ignorance, and the power of invisible flight, and an aerial chariot ever victorious. Give me my many prizes.*

Up out from the red flames rose Indrajit's dazzling fire-born chariot drawn by four tigers, a fire-hued war car decorated with the golden faces of demons or of deer. It flew a red flag showing a lion of green with sapphire eyes, a banner hung with gold bell-bracelets all around. It bore a bow and a quiver of arrows of crooked ways, vaned with vulture feathers.

There were all Brahma's boons given Indrajit for freeing Indra. The cruel Indrajit smiled. *You shame me, Lord. Oh Brahma, your life endures while I exhale one breath!* Then Indrajit got onto his tiger chariot and dressed himself all in bows and arrows and swords and lashes and hammers, and tied back his hair, and whatever he touched turned all to gold. He wrapped himself in illusion and spread enchantment around himself with a wave of his arm, and vanished.

On the battlefield Vibhishana frowned. He shaded his blue eyes and looked up into the blue morning sky, where a few small white clouds had gathered. He told Rama, "Indrajit approaches us invisibly. I cannot see him unless I know just

309

where to look; even Brahma cannot see him. For combat, he has called his chariot forth from the fire, and while he stays on that car he cannot lose a fight to anyone. To Indrajit now the thunder of heaven is but a whisper and Death's dread noose a bit of string. Your army are deer sent against a lion; there is nothing he cannot do."

Clouds spread over the sky. From within them Rama and the animals could hear the creaking of Indrajit's chariot-wheels and see the flashing of his gold weapons. They heard the flag-bells ringing and the four tigers growling—then there was a sharp noise from the sky like iron cracking and a flaming axe came from the clouds. It was falling fast aimed right for Rama. King Sugriva bravely jumped up to shield him, and that axe struck through his bold heart and killed him.

Indrajit stood firing down from the back of the beyond. Down came a rain of death. Thirty-three crescent arrows killed Prince Angada, and his blood made his gold fur red. An iron hook dashed in the chest of Nala the bridge-builder; he fell coughing and choking, and died strangled and frightened. Ten diamond-tipped arrows pierced the bear King Jambavan and he fell; a barbed bronze spear tore through Vibhishana's shoulder as he stood beside Rama and pinned him to the ground. The frightful cries of the dying filled the air.

Hanuman flew up into the clouds. He couldn't see Indrajit, but he saw a magic sword running at him like lightning, all by itself. Hanuman grabbed it, but that weapon became a fair young woman. She cried in fear, "Let me go! It's wrong to hold an unwilling woman!" So hearing that one word—*Wrong*—Hanuman released her. She became a sword again and cut him down from the sky.

Indrajit's assault covered the field with dead, and Rama stood among the rolling heads and broken bodies of his animal friends. He tried to aim by watching where Indrajit's arrows appeared to come from, but those arrows didn't fly straight, and their sources always shifted and changed. Rama shot his golden arrows out over the whole sky, and some few

310

of them fell back from the clouds with their points covered with blood.

Then only Rama and Lakshmana remained standing, the two best men of all this world. Indrajit shot his arrows at them until there was not one fingertip's space left unpierced on their bodies. Their gold armor was no use. Those many wounds killed Rama first. He fell dead. Lakshmana couldn't believe what he saw and wept. He tried to blink the tears from his eyes, but more arrows came through his heart and killed him before he could see again.

And at mid-morning, Indrajit unbearable in war returned to his grove of trees outside Lanka. He became visible and got out of his chariot. The car and the tigers disappeared in a ball of flame. Indrajit said graciously to his servants, "Go through the underground passage into Beautiful Lanka. Tell my father—*Have no doubt, have no care. Rama is dead, I killed him.*"

When they left, Indrajit sat under his banyan tree, whose leaves were green, whose flowers were red as all the blood he'd spilled. Indrajit laughed. Then he said—*Om!* He leaned back and closed his eyes, and speaking no more he began to breathe slowly in and out, slowly and deeply, centering his mind only on his breathing. He made himself one with the breath of Life. The clouds left the sky, and Indrajit shut himself away from the world—*I breathe. I breathe.*

❧

All that day the battlefield was like some slaughter yard in the sun. But when the ancient goddess Night came and increased the power of all Night-Wanderers, Vibhishana the Rakshasa stirred where he lay. He looked up at the stars, the open eyes of Night. He grasped the metal spear-shaft in both hands and twisted apart the tough bronze where it entered his shoulder, and pulled himself up leaving the spearhead in the ground. He sat bleeding and trembling in pain, but he joined his hands to honor the weapons Indrajit had used and spoke a secret mantra that healed his wound.

311

Vibhishana used his keen night vision and looked around for some friend alive. From the back of Rama's army all the way up to Lanka's walls were dead monkeys and apes and bears, many of their bodies cut into pieces. He remembered that Hanuman can never be killed and saw something white move a little in the gloom. Carefully Vibhishana got to his feet and went to see what it was. He found Hanuman sitting up, alive and covered with sword-cuts.

Vibhishana and Hanuman together searched among the dead, and there they found Jambavan near death and but faintly breathing, badly injured and burning with hot fever. Vibhishana bent over him and gave him water. "Riksharaja, King of Bears, are you alive? Have these sharp arrows yet spared your life?"

With great effort Jambavan replied, "Demon Prince, I cannot see. Tell me, does Hanuman the Son of the Wind still live?"

Vibhishana snapped his fangs. "You do not ask about Rama. You do not show such love for anyone else as you show for that white monkey Hanuman."

"Hear why I ask," said Jambavan. "While Hanuman lives, this army also lives; but if he is dead we are truly destroyed."

Hanuman held Jambavan's feet. "Here I am once more!"

"Life! Then we have narrowly escaped with life!" Jambavan's voice was weak but he smiled. He asked, "Indrajit?"

Vibhishana answered, "Now it is Night; this morning Indrajit killed Rama and Lakshmana and everyone else, except us three. He left and has not returned; he must be hidden in his grove of trees, in meditation. I have just revived, and I found Hanuman alive."

"Then this is not the time for grief and not the place," said Jambavan.

Hanuman asked, "Old bear, what do you mean?"

"Only from you have we any hope for our lives," said Jambavan. "My child, there is no one else. Instantly go back over the sea and north into the far high Himalya. At night

312

from the air you will easily see the glowing Medicine Hill of Life, crowned with annuals and herbs, bright and luminous, long ago transplanted from the Moon. Those fragrant plants are potent to heal any hurt and restore life to the dead . . . bring them back . . . hurry—"

Hanuman bent his back, opened his mouth and jumped straight for the snowy lap of the Himalya Hills. He flew like a blazing comet, fast and generous, speedy and bright! He went over the dark sea and over the land. Soon he saw the River Ganga falling from heaven into Lord Shiva's hair; he saw Shiva, always visible to animal eyes, tall and fair and smiling, with a new moon in his hair, the new moon like Rama . . . .

Ahead on the horizon Hanuman saw high on a hill the flickering lights of many luminous plants shining with their own light like cold white flames of fire, shining in the clear night like silent lightning. On that Mountain of Life there is no difference between day and night. When the Sun departs, lights glitter and stream out from those medical herbs on the high summits and ridges; their new leaves sparkle and gleam, their stems glow like liquid silver, like moonlight on the waves as they bend in the wind, and the whole hill shines like a gem.

Hanuman looked down on the Himalyan rivers and mountain passes and caves, the icy cliffs and dark forests and the hidden retreats of holy saints. But the glowing plants felt him approach. They drew themselves down under the ground, their lights were hidden and they were lost in the dark night.

There was no time to dig them out. Hanuman said—*You foolish grasses with no compassion!*—and in three shakes of his shoulders he uprooted that whole entire mountain where they grew and held it over his head in his hands.

Hanuman flew back to Lanka, so fast that the Hill of Life grew very hot and all the herbs began to steam and bake. When he arrived outside Lanka, Hanuman could see nowhere to set the mountain down. As he stood on the air wondering what to do next, the scent of those herbs spread over the battlefield, and that fragrance alone was enough to restore the

313

. . . the scent of those herbs spread over the battlefield . . .

dead animals to life and heal all their wounds. But the dead Rakshasas were under the sea in other worlds, beyond the reach of any medicine of Earth.

Jambavan ran over and looked up. He saw Hanuman holding a huge hill bearing all its trees and stones and elephants and colored veins of ore and pockets of snow and falling rivers. Hanuman shouted, "Where do you want it?"

"—Oh Lord!" Jambavan laughed till he cried.

"What? Where?"

"Oh blessings, best of monkeys," said Jambavan. "We are saved! Turn away, put it back again where it belongs!"

The monkeys and bears formed into a guard around the battlefield. They held trees and stones; they looked calmly out in every direction. All night, when even a straw blew past them they struck it down lest it be Indrajit, or some Rakshasa magic.

Sugriva the Monkey King washed Rama's eyes with palmfuls of cold water and said, "We were all dead." He told him what Hanuman had done.

Hanuman returned again and landed with a thump beside Rama. "My Lord, you live!"

Rama embraced Hanuman and said, "Listen. So far by good fortune I see you all alive again, but were I to lose any of you, then without you my life would be empty and worthless. Never seeking in the world again could I find other friends so true. Why did I bring you here? Go home, King Sugriva. Take your people and no more of dying. Retrace your steps to Kishkindhya."

King Sugriva said, "After all we've gone through," and looked at Hanuman.

Hanuman answered, "Dear Rama, we are indeed your old good friends from long ago, and your companions of ancient days come here to help you. We are your forefathers. We are your ancestors the animals, and you are our child Man. As for our friendship, why we've known you a long long time, Rama, and the number of those days is lost in Silence . . . ."

❦

That same evening just after nightfall the old Rakshasi Trijata hurried to Sita in the Asoka Grove and said, "Alas, all is destiny; in war victory and defeat are all uncertain!"

Sita asked, "What is it?"

"I don't know," said Trijata, "I'm not sure. Indrajit is supposed to have killed Rama and all his army. They say he has now destroyed the root of this war. But Ravana has been asleep all afternoon and no one has seen Indrajit since this morning."

"How dared they—"

"But wait," said Trijata. "Indrajit deals in illusion; don't be enthralled by his spells of doom. Daughter of Earth, I went over the wall and I saw Rama and Lakshmana and all their animals lying out there riddled with arrows; a strange sight, I cannot believe it's true."

Sita didn't cry. Her soft black eyes grew hard and there was a terrible anger in her face. Trijata said, "Lakshmi of the Lotus! Oh wait, my Lady—though covered with arrows, the light of Life still lingers in their skin; their muscles are not slack, nor their weapons dull. The dead do not look so. I speak to you from affection, I have never lied to you. Set aside your anger until you are sure. Throw it down . . . Sita, for the moment forbear . . . do not destroy us . . . ."

Sita sighed and was still. Then the other Rakshasis came and told her, "Come with us; get onto Pushpaka chariot. We've something to show you on the battlefield, you'll see!"

Trijata whispered, "It would be merciful to obey." Once on board the giant chariot the Rakshasis said, "Handsome Rama lying slain, and Lakshmana dead beside him!"

Then by thought they made Pushpaka start to rise into the air. But when that chariot was only a few hands' breadth above the ground Trijata cried, "I knew it! This is fine!" She smiled at Sita and stopped the flying car so he would rise no higher.

The other Rakshasis turned and screamed, "Welcome news! It's plain as day, they're dead!"

"No they're not," said Trijata. "This proves it's a lie. The flower chariot Pushpaka will carry no widow!"

"What? What?" they yelled.

"Stop it," said Trijata. "Be silent before I lose my temper. Why *me*, why must *I* suffer such fools all the time?"

Sita looked up at the northern sky and asked, "Trijata, what is that huge object glowing with heat and racing at us?"

"Hanuman and the Hill of Life," answered Trijata. "Dear Sita, how can Hanuman do all these impossible deeds so easily?"

Sita smiled. They could smell the fragrant medicines. "It must be by the power of his wholehearted love for Rama."

Trijata brought the chariot down and said, "Sita, your sorrows are long and I wanted to comfort you. But instead, you have brought me happiness, and though I'm born in the demon race you have won your way into my heart."

❦

Ravana slept all night, and when he awoke on the third morning of war his sentries from the walls told him how Rama was alive again. The Demon King went at sunrise to Indrajit's invisible grove and sat down by his son and softly said, "Help me once more."

Indrajit bowed his head a moment, then he said, "Majesty, for everyone there is the choice of two ways, right or wrong. Look at Rama. Regard his army. See his bridge! All this time millions of monkeys and bears have camped just outside your Lanka—and you could still not believe you were in any real danger—but even if Time and Death themselves overlook you when your life is full you can find no safety from Rama if you keep his wife. There is always a choice, Father—the Way of Life, or the path of Death."

"Kill him for me!"

"But I did that once," said Indrajit. "Think for a moment, remember the past. When you were young you grew strong by following Dharma and by sacrifice, and so you ruled the worlds. Yet once on the throne of power you slighted Dharma, you had no courtesy towards life. You drove out kindness, and denied freedom to the Universe, and made Creation

317

suffer. The worlds are large, but your selfishness overmatched them. Now your wrongs devour us. In the far forests your intended victims drain our strength, and the smokes of their offerings spread over Earth's ten directions, and innocent holy men have promised we shall die."

"What of it?" said Ravana. "You are the best of warriors. You defeated the gods."

"Then bring on the gods!" answered Indrajit. "However great you may be, do not live hostile to every other soul. The fear and anger of the helpless has taken on the form of an army of animals. Death has led you on. You took Death on your lap the day you stole Sita, and Death have you courted all this time."

"Why, you captured Indra!"

"Now Dharma is on Rama's side," said Indrajit. "His army and his weapons are but the material instruments of Time. Now Rama rules Earth with all her creatures. All is Dharma, Majesty; there is no second thing in existence; there is Dharma alone in the world."

Ravana said, "My son, act now!"

"Then I will sacrifice to Fire—"

"No! If you love me, why offer more smoke to my slaves the gods?"

Indrajit laughed. "The gods are no one's property!" He got to his feet and put on a sword. "I won't use the fire offering unless I fail again."

Ravana arose. "Fight for me on Earth, as you did in heaven!"

"Yes, we seemed to have conquered heaven," said Indrajit. "But all we see is illusion. All is illusion, Demon King; loops and nooses of deception hold us. The gods of heaven—all they do is to obey the Dharma-Law, and all I do is tell the Truth to them . . . and I may sometimes use it for a controlling spell because it is so rarely heard."

Ravana embraced his son and smelled the crown of his hair. They went together through the tunnel to Ravana's palace in the city. Indrajit left his father there. "They will leave us in peace, don't worry."

Indrajit went outside and got a flying Rakshasa army char-

318

iot. He made a magic figure of Sita, lifelike and seeming to
live, looking sad and thin and very beautiful. Then the chariot
flew moving low over the Lanka wall, and in sight of Rama's
army of monkeys he caught the false Sita roughly by her hair
and drew his sharp sword.

Hanuman and many monkeys were near Lanka. Hanuman
recognized Sita. The Sita on the chariot cried—*Oh Rama! Oh
Lakshmana!*—and burst into heartbroken tears.

Hanuman yelled, "What are you doing?"

Indrajit said, "I would do anything to give you pain." He
smiled and raised his sword. A scream cut the air and Indrajit
cut Sita apart. He struck her left shoulder while he held her
hair and cut down across her body, carving her in two along
the line of the sacred thread lying across her breast, and half
her body fell to the chariot floor.

The simple monkeys gasped in horror, and from their
throats came a hopeless cry. Indrajit wiped his sword's blood
on Sita's hair that he held; then he dropped the rest of her
down into his car, turned in the air and descended once more
into Lanka and out of sight.

The monkeys all ran. Hanuman tried to find Rama. He met
Jambavan the bear and Lakshmana together, and rubbing
tears from his eyes he said, "Indrajit killed Sita!"

Lakshmana was speechless. Jambavan said, "That ends the
war; Rama will die."

Out of nowhere, Vibhishana the Rakshasa suddenly ap-
peared beside them—*Hanuman, what is this?*

Hanuman told him and Vibhishana said, "That was an
illusion."

"Oh no, I saw it, it was real!" said Hanuman.

"It was false!" Vibhishana grimaced and his face shattered
and fell in pieces at his feet. His eyes broke like glass and were
gone. He looked at Hanuman with empty eye-sockets in a
horrible scar-covered skull. "Monkey, thus are you blind!"

Hanuman swallowed hard and stared at him. Vibhishana's
eyes and face reformed and he said, "Take my word, it never
happened. Do not grieve and please your enemies."

"What can we do?" asked Lakshmana.

Vibhishana replied, "We must hurry. Tie your armor and your hair; get your bow and arrows. Let Jambavan gather all his bears. It was foolish of Indrajit to touch Sita even in thought. He did not fight or remain before you because this time he did not have his tiger-chariot. Without it he has no divine protection in war, and cannot stay invisible if I reveal him. But now he hears us talking, he even knows what we think, and he will make the offering in his hidden grove unless . . . ."

Lakshmana asked, "What hidden grove?"

"It's not far from here, outside the walls," said Vibhishana. "I will make it visible." He knelt and bowed his head. *Queen of Dreamers, King of Dreams—*

> *Friends are impermanent,*
> *Wife and child are unreal;*
> *The world is untrue,*
> *And sorrow is a lie.*
> *Mother Night, we are shadows!*
> *Mother, show me my brother Indrajit!*

❧

It got dark over that mountainside as though under some huge umbrella. They saw Indrajit near the southern wall, in a grove of ancient down-growing trees, in gloom and dark shadow. A flame burned on an altar of Earth and Indrajit knelt feeding it with butter from a double ladle of black iron. His back was to Lakshmana and Vibhishana. Tied to a stake, a black goat lay just killed in a pool of blood. Indrajit's hair was loose and he wore a crimson robe. By the altar were piled many armloads of javelins, each strung with a hundred little bells.

Lakshmana and Vibhishana watched with their blue eyes. Bears surrounded the grove at a distance. Still Indrajit didn't look up. He made a mark with ashes on his brow and spoke something. Cracks opened in the ground and up from the underworld Naga serpents came and bathed those javelins in their venom.

Indrajit's fire danced. He filled his ladle and stepped back. He was about to make the final offering; already Lakshmana could see the tigers beginning to emerge in the dark, pawing the air from within the fire; he could vaguely see the chariot, with its every golden face forming . . . .

Vibhishana said, "Ready?"

"Always have been." Quick as a lightning flash Lakshmana shot one arrow. He broke the iron ladle out of Indrajit's hand. His bow screamed like an eagle, and the Nagas dove underground in fear of their enemies, looking back up into the sky as they fled. Then Indrajit turned in a swirl of crimson. Then he knew he could be seen.

When Indrajit took his eyes off his fire, Agni the Fire Lord rose from the sacred flame and opened his mouth, and the seven tongues of flame came from his lips. He looked around for Indrajit. He saw Lakshmana, he saw the butter-ladle broken and Indrajit distracted. Then in surprise Agni turned away with a smile, and his form faded from the altar, and Indrajit's fire turned into a flaming madness. Burnt and gone were the tigers and their war-car.

Raven locks and red anger! Indrajit faced Vibhishana and Lakshmana. He looked at Ravana's brother. "Traitor, you have revealed me!"

Lights blazed in Vibhishana's dark-blue crystal eyes. "Why spear my shoulder?" He lay back his ears and snarled. "War was ever all you knew and all your skill."

Indrajit laughed happily. "May your new masters forsake you when all your old friends have died!"

"Say what you like," said Vibhishana. "How dare you defend the theft of Earth's daughter?"

Indrajit tightened his belt and gathered his hair. He drew in his power; he stood there now in silver armor and wearing a sword, firelight glanced from his silver helmet; he held a silver bow, and a quiver of silver arrows and a silver dagger hung at his side. He said, "Lakshmana, if you missed seeing my power before, see it now. *I ask you for the gift of single combat.*"

Lakshmana said—*I give.*

Indrajit narrowed his eyes and dropped down. He fell onto

321

his left knee, held his great bow out flat before him and shot a thousand arrows at Lakshmana. Lakshmana cut them down as they flew and mocked Indrajit—*They're sharp and strong as lotus stems!* Lakshmana shot seven arrows and cut Indrajit's seven armor strings, and the silver mail fell down like a cluster of stars spilled out from heaven at night.

So fleet and swift were both warriors' hands that no one could see them notch an arrow or draw their bows, just as no one can see his soul behind his own senses; all you could see were the arrows flying. Arrows veiled the sky and made it even darker below; sparks and noise filled the air when they struck head-on. Indrajit seized a poison javelin and threw it; Lakshmana with arrows cut it down and left it in pieces no bigger than fingertips.

Indrajit again raised his bow, but this time Lakshmana broke it with an arrow. Indrajit threw an Asura hand-arrow; it separated into a spray of flint darts, and like a swarm of needles they wounded Lakshmana a hundred times. The many darts that missed drummed on the trees and tore smoking holes through the leaves, as painful to meet as loud angry words from a friend. Lakshmana shot back. He hit Indrajit three times in the face, and pierced his body with five arrows that went right through the marrow of his bones and came out red, and flew on underground into the Earth covered with blood.

Indrajit drew his sword and whirled it over his head. That blade groaned and flamed at the cutting edge, but Lakshmana shattered it like glass with his arrows. Then Lakshmana slowed his hand, and carefully withdrew Agastya's arrow from its pocket in his quiver, a long grass arrow with a silver blade. He put it on his bowstring and pulled it back to his ear and said—*Kill him!* He released the bowstring and beheaded Indrajit.

For an instant Indrajit seemed to stand alone in light. Then forward fell his lifeless head, and backward fell his body. The altar and fire and weapons and offerings were gone and the grove was no longer dark. In death Indrajit's corpse and his head took on their true forms. Nothing beautiful remained. Seeing his look had long since made Indrajit abandon the desire for unreal and temporary illusions that depart and perish, and deal for himself in true reality and freedom.

❧

Monkeys and bears fell into each other's arms, and Hanuman carried Lakshmana on his shoulders to Rama. Rama said, "That was a deed hard to do. We could never win this war while Indrajit lived; all Earth is grateful to you." He made Lakshmana lie down, and using herbs and moss Rama stopped his bleeding, and did not let his brother's life flow out.

It was a little past noon. The demons on the walls drew Indrajit's remains into the city by speaking mantras, by magic nets of words. They covered him and brought him along the streets and carried him to the King's palace, but no one dared tell Ravana. At last the minister Suka heard what had happened and quickly went to Ravana. He found him alone in his bedroom and said, "After delighting Lakshmana by the gift of many arrows, Indrajit is dead."

Ravana bowed his heads and wept burning tears that seared through the floor—*My son, my son . . . .*

Ravana sat for a long while in silence, then he said, "My loyal brother is dead and now you, my son! Now I begin to think much more of Yama, for he has brought you, Indrajit, under the law of Time!"

Suka said, "One lives while others remember him. Ravana, you might think people forget but they don't. They seem to worry over their petty cares, but they remember, they all remember the past and the dead, every Night . . . ."

Ravana didn't hear, but spoke as though he still could talk to Indrajit. "This realm is empty without you. Once you crushed the proud and empty gods for me. Now where have you gone, leaving your inheritance, leaving your father and your people? The old should die before the young—why am I left here all alone to make your funeral?"

Suka said, "Majesty, death is not life's end, and when the

323

course of Time must bring something to pass, not wealth nor desire nor strength can make the smallest change. Ravana my King, this is still the way of warriors—*He who dies for his King wins heaven.*"

Ravana said aloud to himself, "Yama, Death Lord, come, tell me how this could be?" But Yama heard only that one word—*Come*—and stood by unseen and made no answer.

Suddenly Ravana grabbed a sword and ran for the open door to the Asoka Grove. But Suka stepped into the doorway first, held the walls and braced himself, and Ravana ran right into him and knocked him down.

The Demon King stopped, and with great care helped Suka to rise, and looking closely at him said, "Suka my friend, forgive me, at least I must kill her."

Suka held Ravana's arms. "Majesty, do not draw the sword of an Empire to kill a woman, or else you let anger lead you into shame!"

"Ah, Suka—" Ravana sighed. "Has Death destroyed my reason?"

"Tonight is just past the eve of the New Moon," said Suka, "and Night will be of her darkest. Fight Rama then."

Ravana sheathed his sword. "Yes. I accept your speech, those are good words. Let us quickly burn my son's body. And after, I will go out to war."

Ravana and Time

Valmiki the Poet held all the moving world inside a
water drop in his hand.
The gods and saints from heaven looked down on Lanka,
And Valmiki looked down at the gods in the morning of Time.

Oh Sita,
I sing this song.
Rama will untie your braid;
He will free you.

Remember his love for you.
My poem will outlast Time;
I sing this song,
Oh Sita.

When he had finished Indrajit's funeral, in the late afternoon Ravana commanded Suka the minister, "Let my armies attack now and kill the animals. At dark I will meet again with the nobles of Lanka, then I'll kill Rama . . . ."

Demon warriors crowded into the streets; their chariots and elephants and horses filled the high roads that led to the western gate of Lanka. Captains rounded up their bands of soldiers and called off all their names, and the battle-flags upon their tall staffs cast long black shadows, and banished all the lovely light of day around them.

The old Rakshasa Malyavan was dozing in an alley when the noise and dark shadows awoke him. The armies of the demons were marching again and shaking the Earth in rhythmic beats, as though somewhere nearby a giant or a great god was beginning to dance, jarring the ground with his feet as he

took the first steps, starting the Dance of Destruction, timing
his steps, the timing strong and sure—

*Oh Shiva there before the waters were, never born, never de-
stroyed—*

And Malyavan remembered.

❧

The shadows of Garuda's wings, the cry of Narayana's huge
shell trumpet, the days of Malyavan's youth falling again over
Beautiful Lanka of the Waves. There in the sky above, the
dazzling red-and-gold Garuda, and on his back Lord Nara-
yana tall and dark-blue, wearing saffron robes, a soft round
jewel on his breast, his dark eyes smiling, murdering the brave
Rakshasas . . . .

Malyavan ignored all the war-noise, he'd heard it all before.
He went slowly by side-streets to a corner of Lanka's walls. He
cast a dissolving spell and went through the stones, and
walked through Rama's army unseen, and climbed by a nar-
row pathway up onto the highest summit of Trikuta Hill.

Standing in the air right above that very hilltop, long ago in his youth Malyavan with all his strength drove a black lance into Narayana's side and cried, "I swear I'll kill you!" And how easily the lance entered, it was not hard to wound Narayana, like wounding water. But the bird Garuda wheeled on the winds. He missed Malyavan, but his talons tore off the steel chain that the Rakshasa wore over his shoulders. Arrows flew like rushing comets, and Malyavan fell through the shrieks and screams, Mali was dead and Malyavan ran to the world Undersea.

Old Malyavan looked around. Trikuta Hill looked like the otherworldly landscape of Infinity . . . a place out of the past . . . .

> *Through the floor of the Sea,*
> *Through the silent doors of Eternity;*
> *Blessed be you,*
> *Blessed be.*

❧

Shiva and the silence! Fortunate to see, gracious and auspicious the great Lord Shiva stood by Malyavan, and there was not a sound on the hilltop. Shiva the great ascetic seemed a tall fair-skinned man, with four arms, wearing deerskin and a snake, holding a trident, his throat a beautiful blue, and for a moment Shiva looked carefully at Malyavan, and saw his heart, and his eyes never blinked.

Shiva's two eyes were like honey, and his face was wrinkled with smiles. On his brow his terrible third eye was closed, and the new moon hung in his hair, low in the evening sky.

They stood there all alone. Malyavan looked down, and at his feet he saw the rusted links of his ancient shoulder-chain, long-lost and eaten by Time.

I saved your father. I found him newborn and abandoned and faintly crying on a lonesome barren hill. Shiva stood still and held out his hand.

Malyavan remembered his beautiful mother, the smiling daughter of a heavenly Gandharva. A little wind blew by his ears. A hundred thousand tiny silver bells were ringing and ringing, and all this beautiful world dissolved . . . .

Come, I will take you home again.

❧

Late in the afternoon of the third day of war, the Grand Army of the Rakshasas gathered again by Lanka's west gate, an army of great honor and loyalty. Their fires flickered and threw off dark smoke and sparks, and their hair stood on end. Carrion birds wept on the housetops, facing south and biting their side-feathers; and by Ravana's palace gate jackals barked and howled with live flames on their breath. Clouds of ashes grated harshly in the sky and blew low down the city streets showering blood. In heaven there was a blue stain on the Sun, and the stars attacked him although it was still day.

Outside the golden walls there was a great explosion, and Indrajit's enchanted grove was destroyed and gone, leaving only a crater of smoke. Many omens appeared; the light was dim and wrong and the wind was dark; high things were low and the low were high.

The west gate opened and the movable bridge dropped like thunder. Then a pale headless corpse stood in the gateway, and with his wounded arms sadly tried to push back the Night-rangers of the Woods. On the hillsides by the city many trees fell, and birds flew over Lanka in left-turning circles. The Rakshasa warriors stumbled as though caught in snares; the whips fell from their charioteers' hands and their eyes watered.

The demon sentinels looked out from Beautiful Lanka's high golden walls, and out on the battlefield they saw the bears watching them, staring at them, sleek and dark, gathered round their King Jambavan like the sending of fate. The bears' eyes were wide with wrath, and their mood was murder. Behind them stood wild apes and monkeys from the highlands who had already grown their thick winter's coats hard for weapons to bite through, with many grey hairs that

328

made them look like long-murdered ghosts, or seem all silver in the sun.

But the bold Rakshasas were not afraid. They drew their glowing swords with a noise like a grindstone grinding iron, and came outside the walls—warriors like hills, like living flames, very strong and cruel. Then like the crest of a wave the front lines of the Rakshasa army rose up into the air and threw down spears and maces and fires on the animals. The demons advanced through the sky in their wondrous waving robes and the animals died by thousands, and backed away from them as summer clouds will fly before the winds. And all unnoticed in the havoc and ruin of war the many house-gods of Lanka followed Ravana's armies out of their city, now homeless, looking afraid and sad to leave, and not knowing where they would live now.

Only Jambavan the Bear King did not back off. All alone he snarled and snapped and pulled down the demons; in a terrible rage he ripped them apart, and left them there in small pieces that a crow could swallow whole. He tore open their throats; he bit and shook his head and broke them; he clawed out their hearts. His mouth was wet and red, his claws were red and his eyes were wild, and he reveled in blood and bleeding demon flesh.

Tall and handsome, wearing the war-crown of the bear kings, old Jambavan took on the whole army of demons. He hugged them to death; he struck them with great round-swinging blows that tore off their heads. Jambavan was unbelievably strong. Whichever weapons the Rakshasas tried to use against him Jambavan destroyed; none could hurt him; and he crushed their chariots with trees. With just a little animal courage he badly damaged them beyond repair. He was Death on that field.

The demons thought—*We're outnumbered!*—and there was no chance in that fight for their unreal illusions. When they joined hands to cast a spell the monkeys broke their arms with stones, and called out warnings in the ancient animal tongues.

329

But there on the city wall were the two magicians, Lightning-Tongue and Thunder-Tooth. They had their heads together, talking and looking at Jambavan, rolling their eyes and licking their ugly fangs. Their arms started to grow longer and longer, and razor blades appeared on their fingertips, and they stretched out their hands for the Bear King.

Hanuman and Sugriva streaked through the air. The two Rakshasa magicians drew back their arms, and they whispered to each other—*Just wish . . . I wish . . . .*

The monkeys were too quick. Hanuman cried—*No fear and follow me*—and struck Lightning-Tongue from the side, caught his throat in both hands, shifted his weight, threw him down and twisted his head right off. He threw the head into Lanka like a ball. It burst into a hundred and eight pieces and the brains went flying out in fiery sparks.

Sugriva made his fingers into a fist and hit Thunder-Tooth from above, so hard that he drove the magician's head down into his belly and jammed his thighs up into his body. But that didn't bother Thunder-Tooth a bit. He just stood there grinning with his mouth at his waist and his eyes on his breast, headless on stumpy legs. Then he winked one eye at King Sugriva and touched his tooth. A staircase that seemed to lead down to Hell rose out of the ground, and Thunder-Tooth ran down it away out of sight and the whole thing disappeared before Sugriva could follow.

"Never mind," said Hanuman, "let's help Jambavan."

They flew back to the Bear King but there was no need. Jambavan was humming war-songs, the Rakshasa attack had failed, and it was nearly evening. Rama called back the animals and stood in their midst as though within an impenetrable forest. The light was fading away from the sky and the animals carried their many dead up into the hillside forests. King Jambavan drank some honey-wine and said, "Ah, it was nothing . . . ."

The few remaining demons withdrew. The west bridge was pulled up and the gate slowly closed. Then as before, from within Lanka the Rakshasas removed their dead from the battlefield and cast their corpses underwater into the sea, and the tides were red.

So on that war-land outside the city there were left only a few painted iron shields and brass clubs, some supple curving swords like clear water, curious bows and arrows with glass points, many trees and stones, torn banners and broken wheels, and shiny gold bracelets winking like fireflies in the dusk fast approaching.

❧

The day went by and was past, and the sunset quickly faded from the west. The new moon set and in Lanka's streets the demons lit their fiery torches made of burning bones.

Ravana sat on his throne in the royal courtroom, in the center of that long indoor altar of Earth where the grass had long grown green from the lights of the glorious lamps, and from the brilliance of the weapons hung round on the walls, and where two holy fires still burned at each end for the blessing and good fortune of the Night Demons. Ravana leaned back comfortably; he closed his twenty eyes and smiled ten smiles.

Then leaving their chariots and animals in the palace court-yards the nobles and elders of Lanka entered the room. Each one courteously bowed touching Ravana's feet with his head and took his place by rank. The greatest sat on raised cushions near the throne, the next ranks sat behind them on grass mats, and all the rest sat on the emerald floor. The smell of fine sandalwood and incense was mingled with patchouli perfume and the flower scent of colorful war-garlands.

They sat gazing up at the faces of the Demon King. Ravana folded his hands, ten by ten, and said, "I am Ravana. What do they say of me, out in the world?"

A herald rose from the ranks dressed in silver and black and answered, *"You are Ravana, King of the Night-Wanderers. You are Lord of Lanka on the Waves, the Protector of Heaven and the Guardian of Truth, the Defender of Love and Enemy of Evil. In anger you are a dark stormcloud threatening all that is wrong and moving if you*

331

will against the wind. You have jailed lies and you imprison all deceit—Majesty, rule right forever!"

Ravana sighed. "Yet Earth fears me, I am her misfortune. I've never seen my armies lose a war, but now Rama has come, and our legions swiftly diminish like a water pond in summer. Rama defeats me by his mere presence, what to speak of his arrows? Tonight I am going out to fight him, and I ask you, leave Lanka now and hide somewhere to save your lives if you fear for my defeat."

No one moved, no one said anything for a long while. Ravana asked, "Will anyone wish to speak here in my council before I go?"

Then Suka the Minister of State arose from his corner seat holding a winecup. He said, "I drink to knowledge," and drank, and looked at the King.

"Come here," said Ravana.

Suka went before the throne and touched his hands together. He knelt and bowed his head. "Majesty!"

Ravana smiled. "Speak quickly, Suka."

Suka stood and said, "Soon or late, a King must hear his people, or he has no time to be a King."

"What do they say?"

"They say—*Why is Ravana blind? Why won't he hear?* They cry—*Where is my father? Where has my husband gone? Where is my son now?*"

"What else?"

"They ask, where are your wits? They ask why your fat and wrinkled sister had to see Rama in the greenwood, and why they must die for her belly's lust? They ask how can we fight Rama? It would be good to take the shelter of Rama."

"What do you think?" asked Ravana.

"Oh King," said Suka, "spare me from fame and the abuse that goes with it! How can you come to your senses when your senses are stolen by Love? What other person ever matched your sacrifices or received such boons as you got from Lord Brahma long ago, in those days long past? Now you've lost your way, and what is surprising in that?" Suka looked around him and shook his head. "It is wondrous and most marvelous, that now the people of such a King as you must face defeat. We can see no one in any world to dry away our tears."

"What would you do yourself?"

"I don't know," answered Suka. "Your brother Vibhishana did right to take Rama's protection; it was a good deed for him, well done at the right time."

"Then why did you not go with him?" softly asked the Demon King. "Why have you stayed by me?"

Suka said, "Once taking you for my King I think it wrong to leave you, Majesty."

"But you could live anywhere unknown; you could easily escape."

"Oh Ravana, this life is over in one instant, why spend it in shame?"

Ravana held out a long scarlet sash. "You always freely chose to serve me, therefore I commission you my messenger. Wear this and carry a letter from me to Rama."

Suka slipped the sash over his shoulder. Ravana gave him a heavy Rakshasa letter written on a flat stone and sealed within a stone envelope. "Deliver this in the morning. Go to where Rama's bridge touches our shore and wait the night there, and then at sunrise take it to him in my name. Fear no one."

Suka took the stone letter. "Ravana, the like of this citadel and city of Beautiful Lanka as she was during your long reign was never seen before, nor will she ever be seen anywhere again."

❧

Ravana dismissed his council and went walking through the halls of his palace swinging his arms, with garlands of flowers over his broad shoulders, and the jewels on his bracelet and armbands swung their all-colored lights over the shadowy walls.

Near the doorway to his bedroom he met Queen Mando-

333

dari. Ravana smiled at her, and held her gently in his twenty dark arms, and there was a dream in his eyes then. Ravana said, "It's nearly done, everything will be alright."

Mandodari the beautiful, the daughter of illusion dressed all in silks replied, "When I first saw you, you captured my heart. You have brought me delight, I love our life, I always approach you in joy."

"You must believe me," said Ravana. "Put your hope and faith in me once more, just one more time."

"Yes," said the Queen. "You are my Lord, and I will ever hold this thought, near to my heart, like a treasure . . . ."

Ravana embraced her. "Farewell my very love . . . ."

It was dark outside, and Ravana climbed alone onto the top of a watchtower that stood near the palace, and from there on its flat roof he could see the battlefield and his city below him, and above, all the stars in the black sky. Ravana laughed. How had Lord Brahma the Creator dared make so many stars!

Ravana saw the gods gathered in the sky to watch his war with Rama, and the Demon King looked back at them with his fiery red eyes, and spread wide his twenty arms.

At that moment all the bells of Lanka pealed, the great gongs and brass drums rang out in the night, and kept ringing, and the little drums raced and sounded like thunders, and Ravana lifted up his dancing foot and brought it down and jarred all the worlds and shook them.

Ravana began to dance. His heart beat fast and he breathed in deep the fresh clean air, and in the heavens the charioteers of the gods tried to calm their animals. Ravana felt he'd just broken an iron band tied round his chest for years. The night air was cool and all the world was young forever.

Stunning thunder and noise poured out of Lanka, and Ravana threw back his heads and waved his arms and spun around. He called down the Wind, the Wind in the trees, the long dry North Wind rising. From afar out at sea to the north there was a little whisper, and the gods saw the air stir, and

334

saw the bright luminous wheel of the rays of the Wind rolling towards them, violently arising and rushing aloud away past them to the ends of the worlds and beyond, far beyond.

Gales came in from the storm-wave ocean and tore up the side of Trikuta Hill. Ravana heard the wild Winds running in from the high Himalyas, booming through the black pines and the dark deodars far away, blowing forever across the ice and snow. Then the tiny wind-bells of Lanka sang, and the great gold walls rocked and trembled.

The North Wind swept flat over the land and blew out every fire in the Universe and every light. Hanuman bent over Rama to protect him and thought to speak to his father, but that was impossible; they could hardly breathe; the air was swifter than thoughts, and it was as if they were falling away with a speed beyond knowing, and all the Earth was falling with them.

Rama and the animals saw Ravana dance. Blue flames shimmered round his form high above Lanka, electric thunders crackled bright in his long loose hair, and fiery sparks streamed downwind from his arms as he turned and moved in waving circles. In the wind and in the Night his twenty dark arms opened and closed like the petals of a graceful flower rising and falling. And Ravana looked out at Rama and the animals as though to consume them, as though they were already dead, as though he danced among charred corpses in some horrible demon drinking-park set in a cremation ground.

Then Ravana clapped all his hands and stamped his feet three times and ended his dance. It was full Night. He drove the storms away. The Wind fell like the sounds of waves growing softer and softer; at first still crying, then wailing by and weeping away, and at last only rustling through the leaves, and then gone.

There was sudden silence from the city and the worlds were clean empty of sound. Ravana disappeared from view and then, as he came down the winding stairway inside that tower the Demon King met Time waiting for him there, Time wearing a body so shriveled and old that he looked dead even

335

. . . like the petals of a graceful flower . . .

when he moved. The way was too narrow to pass and Ravana had to stop.

"Oh welcome, Ravana." Time looked up and grinned happily. "Now at last your life is over, and you must pay me for the sins of a lifetime. You are about to die, and now for all Eternity Hell awaits you, and even your memory will be lost in endless years of silence. You will never again meet a friend or see any place that you love. Your glory and sweet memories will be lost like precious golden dust blown from your hand before your eyes, and the wonderful Earth will vanish from your sight for evermore. Go wear your best jewels, for who will wear them later? Look round at the beautiful world of life; see Lanka well, for now she is in my keeping. For your great wrongdoing I have fallen in beside you all unseen, moving where you move, waiting in your shadow for the moment— how have you eluded me so long?"

"Indeed," said Ravana, "I smile at your folly."

Time answered, "Oh do you think so, Ravana? Do you believe, Demon King, that I only control others, that Time will never rule you but only others . . . ." Then the face of Kala, the face of Time took on the cruel look of someone who has lied and pretended and waited his chance, and is at last in power over his enemy. "I'll have the last word; I'll humble you and kill your strength and spirit. The bright golden dawns of future lights won't be for you, I'll press loneliness into your heart and chill your bones, and there is no return . . . ."

Ravana laughed. "You little liar!"

"What? You stole Sita and you'll pay—"

Ravana threw out his arms like twenty bars across the narrow stair and looked down at Time. "Why I have all the time there is."

"What!"

"You are the thief and not I," said Ravana. "For a few moments' pleasure you take whole lives in payment. And whatever you give you steal back, by fraud, from hiding, when you're not watched. Death and misery are your good friends—but you are yourself unreal; you do not exist; you cannot steal from me."

337

"Do you know who I am?" cried Kala.

Ravana answered, "A marketplace of sorrow, a well of lies."

"Never!"

"You're a fraud and you know it. Why . . . you're not looking so well." Ravana smiled. "May you feel worse tomorrow!"

"Oh take care!" said Time sharply. "Watch out, injustice angers me . . . ."

"That's a laugh! I'll faint from fear just as soon as I find someplace to fall down, alright?" Ravana twirled his moustaches. "Listen—

When my dancing footfalls stopped,
I broke Time's small back
With my last step."

Kala said, "Ravana, you are mad. There's no help for it, you are doomed . . . do what you will while you still can . . . your old home is empty, your friends have died, and all the good times are long gone by . . . things can never be still, nothing can remain the same, all must change and die and come apart . . . it will be as though you had never been . . . . Time will pass Ravana, time will pass . . . now be aware . . . ."

"We know better than that," said the Demon King, "Love is eternal and we are beyond your reach."

"Just a moment! Don't be absurd, you don't believe all those old stories do you?"

"Oh, I believe them *just enough*—"

"There must be some mistake! No one is beyond my power."

"This time *you've* made a mistake—you have wrongly faced Ravana who has gambled his life for love . . . and always will, I guess."

"Never try to cheat your fate," said Time.

"When we sleep, where are you then?" asked Ravana.

"What?"

"And when we wake from a dream, you are pitifully slow to restore the scenery of the world around us."

338

"Nonsense!"

"All loss of love or life is a lie, old age is an illusion, and only bad things perish."

"Really, I fail to see what—"

"I'd forgotten you had that problem," smiled the Demon King. "But I must be on my way now, I can't be late, and my time is far too valuable to waste on anything but daydreams. Be careful, turn and go, back away from Ravana who will fight and die for love—for Good Love never dies . . . ."

"How'd you find that out?!"

"Oh Kala stand aside. Pretend to rule styles and fashions if you will, but don't talk of being over me. You're but a poor slave yourself. You mean nothing to me. I command you to go."

"No! I won't!"

"*Aha!*" Ravana swiftly bent down and looked close into the wasted eyes of Time with that terrible demon look he had. The muscles on his arms stood out in knots and his hands moved round Kala like a cage. "Do you dare menace *me?*" The Demon King drew back his lips and his coppery eyes glittered, he made ready to seize Time and crush him with his steely strength—and Valmiki the Poet safely watching all this caught his breath in shock at that threat!

Then Ravana touched Kala but lightly with one hand and stood straight again. Time started to sweat. He sneezed and looked around; his face was worn and battered and his voice cracked when he spoke. "Why, it's all dusty . . . everything here, it's all covered over with fine dust . . . ."

Ravana stood with all his hands on his hips as he watched Time fade and vanish with a puzzled look, ever still trying in vain to say something more. Ravana stood on the empty stair.

Valmiki the Poet laughed with pleasure. *Oh Ravana, delightful, beautiful—Well done, Demon King!*

❧

Ravana hurried to war. He put on his night-armor finely woven from dull black steel and ten dread dark helmets that

339

hid his faces. Over his two-wheeled war-car he raised the battle-banner of Lanka, a cloth of gold shining bright, and said, "I send out many warriors and few return. Now I must go myself, let Earth take warning . . . ." And he thought to himself, "Death, now whirl your maces and rods and strike with your clubs—I am at chance this day . . . ."

On that chariot Ravana loaded a hundred tough horntipped bows as hard to stretch as the mind; and a thousand quivers of his own arrows, long and thick, vanes and shaft all made from one piece of blue iron; and a long straight sword; and an irresistible eight-sided mace. The chariot was armored by shields and plates cut from dark brass, and drawn by four white horses. Tied loose on the central flagstaff were the ten golden arrows for the ten directions of his Empire.

With his many hands Ravana needed no charioteer. He leapt like a lion into his car and drove out from his palace into the city streets. His horses broke into a run and the Rakshasa people along the way yelled and cheered, lining the wide streets, changing their shapes and colors from their emotions, and the chariot wheels crashed and clattered over the yellow bricks.

Then the Demon King left Lanka through the fifth gate, by the Gate of Illusion. The monkeys and bears were watching all the four city walls to see which one would open, when Ravana and his horses and chariot winked into view coming down through the air and hit the ground just west of Lanka with a smash like a mountain falling flat upon the world.

Ravana stopped a little way forward of the wall and looked out across the plain, where at a distance he saw the moving golden ends of Rama's bow like waving torchlights in the darkness, and saw Rama facing him on foot and unafraid.

&

'Look, there he is." Rama pointed with his bow, and a lightning flash snapped across the sky though there were no clouds. "He's come before my eyes as though before a serpent who kills by looking."

The monkeys and bears all ran to Rama, and many of them were partly hard to see or all invisible from fright. With one hand Rama quickly strung his bow. He turned to Lakshmana and said, "Let my animal friends of the woods take cover, and you with them."

Hanuman was there and he said, "Don't worry about us, worry about fighting on foot against a deadly chariot."

Rama smiled. "Go back to the bridgehead. It's midnight, and from now on, the world is destined to grow light."

"He is a most glorious and magnificent king," said Lakshmana.

"His coming here is my good fortune," answered Rama, "for now before me is the root of all evil, and the only one left to die cut on the edge of battle."

Then they all left Rama standing there alone, his long green hair no longer matted like a hermit wears but tied back with a green silk war-band; but still he wore barkcloth over his golden armor, still he walked barefoot without the sandals he'd given Bharata—partly seeming a wanderer, partly a warrior, partly a King.

Still Ravana waited and did not move. Then suddenly a starlight came down from heaven toward Rama. As it approached and drew near to Earth Rama saw that it was a brilliant aerial chariot, a silver car with weapons hung in racks that shone like lanterns, drawn by ten silvery-gray horses flying abreast, coming closer and closer with many fan-blades spinning and the silver wheels all flashing; then in a cloud of dust, with a rumble of hooves and wheels, that chariot landed not far away and drove full speed over the battlefield to Rama, and stopped before him. There was a charioteer in the driver's box but the car held no warrior behind him.

"A friend wishes you well. I am Matali the heavenly charioteer." Matali stood beside Rama. "Lord of Men, this is Indra's celestial car. Best of Kings, these are his cloud-horses shod in silver shoes; they are my rain-steeds—the sky-climbers, the star-jumpers, the misty runners of the sky, and our paths are everywhere."

341

"Welcome to you," said Rama.

"Solar King, we'll take you to Victory!" Matali looked at Ravana. "Wherever I look, I seem to see Death, Death wearing many flowers waiting for him . . . ."

"I haven't forgotten," said Rama. "I still remember, we saw you when Savari told us the tale of Hanuman—and I had lost my Sita—"

"Oh this is a wide road for attack and no place for grief," said Matali. "Here I am in the dark in my cold bronze armor, and I've lost all my patience, and there's no escape for him. I'll thread the paths and follow the roads to win! It's hard to kill the Demon King! Get on!"

"The world will be without me, or without Ravana." Rama put his arms on board the car. "Now drive straight against him."

"*Om!*" The rain horses laid back their ears. Matali and Rama got in the chariot and Matali held the twenty long reins. He looked at his horses and glanced at the ground before them. Then his hands trembled slightly and were still, and the ten horses were walking. "*Go!*"

They went a little faster, at an easy gait. Then they quickened their step and they were half-running. *And I've been true*—whispered Matali—*I've been true, all this time, run!* And at last they went full running, silver shoes flashing, beautiful horses running abreast, beating down the ground—

Ravana's chariot leapt forward to intercept them. All at once the two cars were together, and the golden plates on the back of Rama's bow among the diamonds shone like fires out among the stars, all up close.

Ravana laughed in anger and lashed Matali with a whip. Matali struck back at him, but very fast Ravana backed and turned quickly and couldn't be reached.

Ravana shot eight bows at once. Thirty thousand dark arrows struck Rama. They tore away the bark he wore, and Rama's armor all of gold gleamed out in that night bright as the Sun.

The brilliant spires and towers of Lanka looked flaming and

afire in that blazing light. The glare and the gold came reflected back from Lanka's wall and confused Ravana's aim, and Matali drove off a way and stopped.

Fierce and furious was that fight. Oh Rama! Waves were on the water in Valmiki's hand; storms swirled.

He saw Sita. In the clash and sting of war she loved you.

Now hear the melody of our sweet song, swiftly plunged into strife.

Majesty, it is Night, and people change at Night!

Swarming at Rama came a million arrows with iron arrowheads of sharp animal faces—the keen faces of wolves and eagles and sharks, iron teeth that closed and bit when they struck flesh. They tore down all over; but Rama answered them with flights of his Ayodhya arrows again all gold-covered, bearing his name, feathered with white and blue heron plumes; and he dropped them severed from the sky.

Then light-handed, Rama cut off Ravana's heads with arrow-blades, and the lifeless heads rolled away with their long earrings and shadowy helmets, dusty and bleeding dark. All Fire-tempered, Rama's arrows with sharp heads and even knots flew howling like hurricanes.

But the heads grew back. Hundreds of heads rolled killed, but there was Ravana again, never turning back from war, bearing to Rama ill-will and weapons. There in his chariot stood once more the Demon King of many talents, many felonies, many evasions.

Rama squeezed his long green arms. First saying the Mantra, he called the Fire-weapon and shot an arrow straight up. Down upon Ravana fell arrows that burned. Their bright-burning points were windows of light; heaven through the dark was full of windows open to all the worlds above.

Ravana spoke the rain-mantra over an arrow and released it. Clouds came out of nowhere. Water drenched the world, the fire-arrows went out and blackness fell.

Rama used the wind-weapon. He shot an arrow into the

343

clouds and his unbreakable bowstring rang out over the whole island of Lanka. The air sighed and the seven winds of heaven swept down their paths moaning and whirling, and by the bridgehead rolling breakers trailed white on the grey sea and the tall palms bent their heads and gave up their old leaves from the past. *Free,* sang the seven winds, *Free the world, Free!* They screamed through the high rocks on the summits above Rama's battlefield; the rainclouds fled before them, the sky was clear, the stars sparkled.

Ravana fired an arrow into the ground and from Earth arose steep walls of high mountains. Great solid rows of black stone, barren and lifeless, blocked the sky with jagged ridges and peaks and stopped the Wind. Those were the bare black hills of Hell, baking hot, and they creaked with the strain of the cool night air until, with a noise like a salvo of cannon, deep cracks broke through them and red canyons of heat glowed from deep within.

Rama fired Brahmastra, Brahma's weapon, and shot it arching up to fall on the line of hills. The arrow grew long and stout as a spear. The Wind entered its feathered wings; there were the Sun in its metal blade, skies and rainbows in its shaft, and all the worlds in its weight. It reached its height and began to curve down. In a burst of brilliance it scattered apart into 180,000 rocketing thunders. Bolts of light stabbed at the hills from above, and wherever they hit they turned the brittle stone to diamond. The Hills of Hell shuddered and dove back out of sight below ground.

"Enough of this," said Rama, "there's work to do! Now I take off my fancy rings!"

Matali looked over his shoulder. "But you aren't wearing . . . ."

"Charge!"

"Alright! And here he comes—"

From a standing start, in the wink of an eye Matali's horses were racing. Rama stood free, not holding any support, not swaying or even a little off-balance. The two war-chariots drove right at each other. At the last instant Matali turned. The

344

cars tore past each on the other's left, throwing out clouds of dust and stones from their wheels. The horses seemed to touch, the axle hubs just missed, and Ravana wasn't fast enough. He had no time to shoot. Then they were by, traveling swiftly apart. But just as Rama passed he shot an arrow deep into Ravana's left shoulders and the Demon King had to hold onto his flagstaff with his right arms to keep from falling.

The chariots slowed and circled round facing again. Matali maneuvered for position and said, "Now I begin to see the end of Ravana's life."

And far north across the sea, the harmless woodsmen of Dandaka Forest walking in the silence of Night under the huge trees could see in the sky violet ribbons of light from the war of Lanka in the south, and they wondered—*Rama . . . Where is Rama-Chandra, the lovely Moon of Night?*

> *Only the sky will cover the sea;*
> *Only Rama can fight the Demon King.*

❦

Rama and Ravana dueled with arrows. One after another, Rama broke the bows out of Ravana's hands until ninety-nine were gone and only one remained. The Demon King shot arrows long and short, thick and thin, quick and slow, from close range or far away; but Rama's armor was hard and impenetrable, he was unharmed and many arrows melted away when he saw them come.

Ravana seized his mace of iron set with lapis stones and embellished with gold, hung with iron-mouthed bells and entwined with red blossoms, for years daily washed with blood and now smoking and straining to strike, an eight-sided mace which would return from flight into the thrower's hands.

Ravana drove to attack. He gripped the iron handle with four hands and swung as the chariots met. It was too soon and the blow fell on the charioteer and not Rama, but Matali knocked that mace hard aside with his bronze fist.

Then Ravana drew apart and stopped. He whirled his mace

345

in a circle rising and dipping his heads; and the mace moaned
—*Woe . . . Woe . . . Woe*—

The mace went faster and faster. Matali drove to deceive
Ravana's aim and Rama reached for Indra's weapons-racks.
He took a spear, held it in one hand, slapped it with the palm
of his other hand and threw it. That great dart went at Ravana
resonant and vibrating with sound, with a noise like the
thunder of a rockslide, a loud falling noise like a cliff falling,
the dark world falling, Ravana falling . . . .

And the Demon Lord let go his mace; it sped, and Rama
stood in its way. Ravana's chariot turned to run.

Rama's spear broke Ravana's flagpole; the cloth-of-gold
war-flag fell. Rama broke the ten arrows of the Rakshasa
Empire, and when he did, the running demon car lost its rattle
and clatter and its wheels turned on in mournful silence. The
flag of Lanka lay in the dust.

Matali couldn't outdrive Ravana's mace, but he dropped his
reins and stood up himself in its path; and it glanced off his
broad chest and knocked him violently from the car, and went
by Rama deflected just enough to miss him.

Rama wept and bit his lip. The mace turned to go back to
Ravana, but Rama threw himself from the chariot and seized
it. He knelt and broke it like a stick over his thigh—*Good
Fortune to you!*—once, into two pieces—*Peace to you!*—and
twice, into four. Deep red blood ran over his green skin.

The four pieces of the mace kept pulling back to Ravana,
and Rama cried—*Would you?*—and hurled them at the Demon
King. Ravana quickly turned aside; and as he had spurned
them, the four angry chunks of iron tore into Earth and van-
ished noisily underground.

Matali lay on his back unconscious. His heavenly armor
was torn, and his ten horses stood still, their faces near his,
looking down at him. A flood of sorrow filled Rama's heart to
see him hurt. Rama touched him and untied his breastplate,
and said, "Here indeed your loyalty has had unjust reward!"

Matali revived from Rama's touch. He looked up and saw
Rama bending over him, saw his horses raise their heads, and

following their look saw Ravana's chariot coming again, but moving strangely slow. By some chance he yet lived, and he felt the life flow back into his body.

Rama brought water from Indra's chariot, and some cloth that he began to rip apart for binding Matali's wide wounds. The silver car was stricken and dented. The horses pawed at the ground with their front feet. "Majesty," said Matali, "I'll be well, there's time enough for that later."

Rama said, "Good. It's fast nearing dawn, but drink just a little." Then after Matali drank, Rama sipped water three times. "Lie still, I don't need the car now." Rama took up his every-colored bow, and there stood Rama the great archer, Rama the good bowman, the friend of every man.

He was all fiery to see. Wild little flames came from his skin, his green eyes gleamed, then swift as thought Rama shot his arrows. He broke off one wheel of Ravana's chariot and it tipped over and left the Demon King also standing on the ground, holding his last bow and a sword, facing him; and the white horses ran away with the broken car.

Rama opened a long bamboo case at his belt and took out the brass-bladed grass arrow given to him by Agastya, and notched it on his bowstring. That arrow could rend walls and gateways of stone; it breathed and sighed. Rama pulled his bow. He took three aiming steps backwards and held his breath.

Ravana took on the brilliant form of Indra the King of Heaven. He was glorious and gracious, all illumined; he could scarcely be looked at, and a halo of radiance and energy danced around him. Rama was dazed by Ravana's false figure. He could not bear to shoot at such a divine form, at such fair beauty.

Matali the Charioteer was watching. He could be enchanted by no beauty but a fair woman's. He raised himself painfully on one arm and called out to Rama—*Strike, Strike, That's not my Master.*

That was then the destined time and true setting of Ravana's death. Rama thought—*I must believe it! Oh kill him!*—

347

Rama shot. The bowstring rang out, all over the Universe. That arrow first broke the sword and bow Ravana raised to ward it, then it hit Ravana's breast and struck through his heart, stealing his life, and never stopped, but came out from his back and entered the Earth.

Down from Ravana's hands fell his broken bow and sword, and the Demon King of Lanka fell dying in his own dark form.

At first Rama didn't move. Then he first unstrung his bow and put it aside. Then he lifted Matali into Indra's rain-chariot and the misty horses rose running through the sky and were gone.

At daybreak, at dawn Ravana died. He was a fire not burning, an ocean still with no tides. He could no longer speak. He could not know whatever might happen around him. He could not move; he grew cold; he had no thought; he did not breathe.

The Rakshasas who had watched the war turned away in fear from the walls and hid in Lanka. And darkly the Kings of the four quarters of the world glanced, but none saw what way Ravana went then.

❦

That last night, Suka the Rakshasa Minister stood by Lord Rama's bridge, wrapped in his night cloak and holding Ravana's stone letter under his arm. All night he watched the garish lights and signs of war up on Trikuta Hill, and Lakshmana with the animals stood watching him.

Then at sunrise the first long rays of light reached the three summits over Lanka. Suka dropped his cape behind him, and wearing the scarlet sash of a messenger he walked slow and easy toward the city, and the animals made way for him. Only Prince Angada opened his mouth to speak, but Sugriva the Monkey King put his hand on the young prince's arm and pulled him back and Hanuman stepped in front of him.

Suka stepped into the air and flew back up the slopes to Lanka, and she was golden in the morning when he stepped on the ground. The sunshine, coppery and yellow and red and white, touched her like melted metals from a mountain. It was still, and silent, and Suka thought, "I remember this silence,

348

the silence over all . . . ." Suka felt free. It was almost as though Ravana had sung again there on the battlefield the lilting songs that had won him his freedom from Shiva's prison, and Suka had also been released from somewhere.

Suka walked straight for Rama. Rama stood alone over the corpse of the Demon King. There was no one else about, nothing stirred. And where the wreckage of war was in his way, Suka by a look from his eyes blasted it silently aside and made his path clear.

He came to Rama and handed him the sealed letter. "For you from the Dead King."

And as he spoke of him, Suka looked down at Ravana. Suka's hooded eyes were half-closed, no expression crossed his face, yet for a moment Suka seemed to grow ominous and tragic; he seemed to darken even while standing there, in the sunlight.

Rama cracked open the stone envelope in his strong hands. He looked at the letter awhile, then turned to Suka. "Ah my friend," said Rama fondly. "Listen—"

❧

Lord Narayana, you are the witness, you make the Moon walk in brightness and the stars vanish in the daylight.

Dear Rama, Lord of the Worlds—Think and remember, how you promised Indra to kill me forever. Nothing is forever except yourself. Except dying at your hand, how else could I make you take me into your own Self?

I was only a Rakshasa, and you were very hard to approach. Yet seeking wisdom I learned many things. You do not know who you are again. I knew it all along, but even still you do not know. Nothing you do ever fails, one glance of yours and people sing again the good old songs.

I took no protection against men. You go everywhere, and know every thing that ever has or ever will be done. How was I careless? I was nowhere careless! Oh Narayana, Lo, I looked, I marveled—Men are mines, Men are precious mines. Oh Rama, did you think that dark was bad?

You see whatever happens and you support all creatures. I

349

"For you from the dead King"

saw that heaven was impermanent and Hell itself did not endure; I discovered that the time of every life is one day full; and I found how all creatures that are separate from you are ever and again reborn, over and over, always changing. I do not love things that come and go and slip away with Time, and Time himself I hate. I warned him when we first met that I took him for my enemy, I told him so.

Best of Men, there are many kinds of Love, and I never hurt her. I kept Lakshmi to lure you here. I offered you my life and you accepted it.

You are Narayana who moves on the waters. You flow through us all. You are Rama and Sita born out of Earth and Ravana the Demon King, you are Hanuman like the wind, you are Lakshmana like a mirror, you are Indrajit and Indra, you are the Poet and the Players and the Play. And born as a man you forget this, you lose the memory, and take on man's ignorance again, as you will, every time.

Therefore welcome back your Sita. The war is done, and so we close our letter.

❦

The two of them stood there by Ravana, still as statues in the new-risen sun. Then Suka took off his blood-red scarlet sash and folded it and laid it down on Ravana's breast.

Rama sighed and smiled. He broke the letter and threw it away. He said quietly, "Go, go, I do not care what all this means."

"I never dreamed of such a thing." Suka was smiling and smiling. "Oh, after all this long way around . . . ."

There was a soft whisper, and Suka became a rising wisp of smoke; he spread and dissolved in the air, in surrender. For many years he lived peacefully alone in the forests across the sea, and no one ever saw him sad.

This is an ancient tale.

❦

◈ ◈ ◈

We choose the god-like splendor
Of the best-loved Sun
To inspire us;
May the shining Sun
Brighten your Life!

We sing Valmiki's song.

Oh King Rama, grand and glorious, the all-seeing Sun of a thousand rays lives in the sky. He is the Lord of Day and the eye of the world. He gives Life. Every morning he wakes people from sleep, and goes his way alone through the heavens above and through the heavens in the heart. Salutations and greetings to the Lord of the Sky and Maker of Days.

Praise and victory to the good and friendly King of Light who moves our thoughts and our blood within us and opens our senses by his beams. He is mighty strong. He is golden bright and his seed is golden. We can see no evil; we see no men who get no sunshine. Therefore shower gold, spend and be generous to those you love. For your sake spend your bright yellow gold, give gifts while you can and do good, choose your deeds well. You are wealthy, you have unlimited gold to draw on.

I don't respect the floating borders of Earth,
I travel where I will,
I love everyone.
My friend the Moon has known this for long lifetimes,
I am the Sun,
All the same.
Ancient stories.
Ancient Sunpoems.

Every morning you are new. My Lord Sun I am asleep, my body is like a corpse, until you come and raise me to Life. You reveal all things to me; you show me what they truly are. I look

352

out on a happy world! I see you in your chariot behind your seven horses and you bring every kind of happiness. Dear Sun, behold me here below you, a Man, to myself the center of all these worlds.

You feed us all; every garden grows by your light. All our energy is yours. I bow to the Eastern Mountain where you rise, I bow to Sunset Hill in the west where you go down, setting low above the waters, in flame, all in gold.

You unfold the flowers of day. You are bright and beautiful. If there are clouds you are always behind them. You are the handsome ornament of all the heavens. Your heart is wide, it is immeasurably wide. How can I not speak of this? Why be silent about you? Take my song and give me light.

How can I be sad? Am I blind? The Sun shines on me. This very instant have I won brilliance for my wealth.

❧

Oh Rama, it is Truth, we think, that moves the Sun across the sky. Oh Lord, look up at him, so joyful and fine!

Whoever sings this song or hears it sung, he comes by no misfortune. When he is in peril of his life, or is ill, or is in a lonely place, or in any fear, this bright tune will bring him victory. No thief can touch him, he will never dare. This song is named *Heart of the Sun*. It is warm and safe and strong. It makes toubles go. It is supremely good. If you are afraid in the long dark night, remember it.

Ayodhya King, our preceptor the Poet Valmiki saw all of this war gliding already into the past, becoming a wonderful tale, a beautiful story.

May all creatures be happy. We sing Valmiki's song.

> *"Trust and be True:*
> *Serve Right as*
> *I serve You"*
> —*says the Sun.*

part three

the dharma wheel

OM!
I bow to the great Lord Narayana,
And to the blessed Lady Sita;
I salute you, faithful Hanuman;
And Saraswati, Goddess take my gift:
JAYA!
Victory to you!

heRe's love!

And so the War of Lanka was ended on the morning of the fourth day, just past the first night of the New Moon, near to the solstice of Winter when Spring dares begin again, and the Sun turns in his sky to come back to us. Rama took off his armor and the day grew warm. Surya the Sun was pouring out bright silver and fine gold. He threw his beams down cordially over that morning world—a fine reliable figure of light, a handsome person, a happy sight—indeed a part of the world well-made, very well done, all of it.

Hanuman and the Rakshasa Vibhishana and his four demon knights came swiftly to Rama's side. Vibhishana held a bundle and said, "Dear Lord, wear these clothes Lakshmana sends to you now."

"They're not Rakshasa robes?"

"He carried and kept them somehow throughout all your wanderings." Vibhishana smiled. "They're from Ayodhya. I don't know how he did it."

"Fair Ayodhya!" Rama dressed, and saw that Hanuman also held something. "Monkey, what have you got there?"

"All the ornaments she let fall upon our hill." Hanuman looked at the dead Ravana. "Master, is he really dead? What did Suka say? What else happened? When can we—"

"Oh enough, Hanuman!" Rama looked round at the world. "Long love is now remembered. Be still. I've recovered her, we are reunited and all the old lovely colors return and come again into my view. Go to her, tell Sita we have won!"

"I'm gone!"

Vibhishana said, "We ask permission to make Ravana's funeral inside the city."

356

"Why is it so quiet?" asked Rama.

"Every soul's already left Lanka but for a few who will soon go."

"I had not wished harm to your beautiful city; now she is desolate."

Vibhishana laughed. "How many times, Lord? You know how we love to disappear, but I will stay here when I may."

"Is there any water?" One of the four knights gave Rama a waterjar. "Kneel, Vibhishana." Rama poured water over the Demon Prince's head. "Arise, Lanka King."

Vibhishana stood. "Our folk will return, but don't fear us. We Rakshasas are the guardians, we are the protectors; so were we created by Brahma. We'll guard the temples and not harm good men, and I'll hide Lanka's golden beauty and keep our home from others' eyes. All will be well with us always."

"What's keeping that fool Hanuman?"

Vibhishana answered, "It's been but a moment!" His four Rakshasa knights carried away Ravana's corpse. The west gate of Lanka opened for them and they entered. "They'll burn him quick. You'll soon meet Sita. I'm here; I'm going to be your wish-protector."

Rama asked, "What will happen to Queen Mandodari? What will she do?"

"Ah," said Vibhishana. "The Daughter of Illusion! Our people all have other lives beneath the Sea—but Mandodari's father is the Asura Maya, the great Artist. And if he still lives he will come to her here; he will take her home. *Maya! Maya! All is illusion . . . All is illusion . . . .* Maya the ancient architect, Maya the builder of young dreams might take her back to his Cave of Trees, and who will meet her next no one knows."

Vibhishana and Rama stood silent awhile, then the Good Demon Lord of Lanka said, "Queen Mandodari would have restored Sita's clear yellow robe for this day. It will take her time to dress for you as well."

"I don't care what she's wearing!"

"There's the smoke, that's Ravana's pyre burning behind the walls. I wonder—I would marry Mandodari myself if I only found her somewhere, someday—but even Time can't ever find out too soon what Maya the Asura wants concealed. Who knows?"

❧

When she saw Ravana dead, the fair-skinned Queen Mandodari, dressed all in white, ran to him, and in the quiet city she held his hand in hers and bent over him silently weeping, shedding tears of sorrow, disconsolate with grief.

A Rakshasa priest approached her. "Faultless Queen, no one must mourn a warrior slain fighting, so say all the ancient preceptors at arms . . . ." He put his arm round her shoulder. "But I also am very sad this was his end."

Very swiftly some Rakshasas built a pyre of red and white sandalwood logs, and laid a soft deerskin on top, and they put Ravana's corpse on the deerskin. They washed the blood from his body and put a new gold thread over his left shoulders and across his chest. They laid a new bow and sword by him and put garlands of marigold flowers over him there, and covered him with a golden cloth bordered with blue deer. From brass ladles the priest poured butter and buttermilk over Ravana, and then he lit the pyre from Ravana's birthfire brought there in a burning jar.

All in a few moments the Rakshasas burned Ravana's body. The few remaining Rakshasas of Lanka walked by, throwing into his fire black aloes sticks and incense, handfuls of pearls and broken sea-coral, and the fire burned fast. Ravana's earthly body returned again into the five elements it had been made of.

Then Mandodari went alone to a mountain streamside in a park and bathed in her wet white robes, and set down by the waterside some seeds and sacred grass as offerings to the ancestors. She still had tears in her wide eyes. But so late in the year the water-lotus stalks should not have flowers. She shut her eyes and wiped her tears away, and looked again to see more clearly.

"Father!"

There stood the Asura Maya, the Architect and Astronomer of the Olden Gods, and he gently touched her. *Do not cry. Do not cry.*

But Mandodari only wept anew. "Come," said Maya, "I conjure you, speak to me."

"Oh," she said, "they may burn his body but never his heart that he gave me years ago. What is now left to Ravana of all his Empire? His body was happy and graceful in love; he was hard to look at in anger. I loved all his brows and his smooth skin with handsome scars—and now no more on Earth, or any world!"

"Are you sure?" Maya sat down beside his daughter and watched the water flow past. He said, "I liked it best when he whirled his twenty eyes, when he came crunching down the garden walks, when he drank and sang and wore all his flowers . . . ."

"They'll pay for this!" cried Mandodari.

"But—Why? What has happened?"

"What shall I do?" asked the Queen. "Which way is there to go? Where are all my people?"

Maya replied, "Why, what people did you own?"

"The people of this city! I am their Queen!"

"Who would believe it?" smiled Maya. "What city?"

"It's fading! Father, stop it, you can stop it . . . ."

"Come to our peaceful home; you are never alone and friendless."

Mandodari sighed. "Oh, let Lanka go, what good is she without my husband—" Tears filled her eyes. "A husband is most dear to a woman. With many sons and millions in gold, she cannot be happy without her husband. She is but a poor widow . . . ."

"I enchant you not to cry," said Maya. "Can you remember how to walk with me again, as when you were very young, as in those maiden days?"

I am the Asura Maya, a great Artist, the Master of Illusion. I will show you, my wonderful palace is still where it always was. I have food for all my family, and wine for you also.

359

"Father, tell me, why would my Lord forget our vows to always live together, and go apart along the unknown way, and leave me behind like a poor wayside beggar, and not comfort me?"

"Did he?" asked Maya.

"Oh Time destroys things so easily!"

"Does he?" Maya laughed and got to his feet. "Come on!" She stood by him. "Leave here everything that is Lanka's, and take away only your own deeds."

And besides that, only Love may go beyond, along with us.
See the world through my sight.
See—
All that magic!
All yours!

Then hand in hand they began to walk down a long hall of shady trees unfamiliar to the Queen, and Mandodari was like a little girl beside her father Maya. Her dress was blue and pink and silver; her shoes were gold and she smiled up at her father. Ahead of them there was an open door where sunshine entered.

Maya the Asura said, "Your mother has come back to us; our home is happy. Soon we will be like some story once heard as a child long ago, hard to remember, the bright shadow of what perhaps never was . . . ."

He led his beautiful daughter of illusion out through that garden door and far away.

Believe it and make it true. We are safe. Your love is here for you.

☙

Thus Death's long evening shadows grew and reached to touch Ravana lying fallen in the dust. Life is very uncertain, and even royal fortune fails at last, and turns away from the greatest kingdom. Ravana was lordly and his dark arms were strong; he bound the worlds in ropes of illusion; so did he die.

What can one count on, except that whatever one has, it will soon be gone? Better to do right.

360

Ravana boasted and made good his boasts. He broke apart the sacrifices in the forests. He had a beautiful wife, but lust veiled his eyes so that he could not see, and he went falsely to steal Sita. He courted Death, or else what was he doing?

Ravana is gone, so forgive him. His flesh and bones were consumed by Fire, and his ashes were scattered by the winds. And yet men say that pyre still burns and that flame never perished, and long afterwards it sometimes can be seen at night high on a hill on Lanka Island, shimmering through the spells that hide a golden city somewhere there.

&

Hanuman flew like a flash to the Asoka Grove behind Ravana's palace, his white robes streaming out, his white fur ruffled with joy. He found Sita alone under the golden Sinsapa tree. But now she was dressed as a princess. Her dress was new; she wore a woven crown of fresh and fragrant wildflowers and new leaves, and her braid had a ribbon. There by her tree were a bronze comb and mirror, and sandalpaste and dark dust for brow and eye.

Oh blameless Sita, you are the fairest woman in all Creation, and no goddess can compare to you. Your face is bright as the Moon, you are more giving and forgiving than your mother Earth, more beautiful than Lakshmi, if that may have been. And Rama, what is the use our singing of her charms when you and she have sung your two songs together?

"Well, this makes sense for a change!" Hanuman greeted the doe-eyed Sita, so bold and beautiful. "This is the first nice day there's been for a long time on Old Earth!"

"Oh, it's perfect!" Sita smiled, and her smiles were forever warm and loving; they would carry anyone away, intoxicate him more than any wine, and leave him floating on the waves, in the air high above himself. "Now I leave all sorrow behind me."

Hanuman hit his tail on the ground and tipped his head to one side and laughed. "Mother, we are all well. Thanks to you we have won. Ravana is killed and you must have no fear, for you will soon be in your own house with Rama."

"Good betide you, Hanuman! My white monkey child dearer to me than life, I am so proud of you! What have you got there?"

The tip of Hanuman's tail curved up. "Look!"

"That's my yellow scarf!"

Hanuman said, "Guess what else," and opened his package.

"How heartwarming!" said Sita. "My ornaments from Anasuya, and my pink shell necklace from Guha the Hunter King." She put them on, earrings and anklets and bracelets and necklace. "How do I look?"

Hanuman only smiled. Then he said, "Ask Rama."

Sita grew quieter. "How is he?"

"Come and find out!" Hanuman looked around with his clear red eyes. "Where is everybody?"

Sita smiled, and drove out even the name of care from Hanuman's monkey mind. "What have you to do with them now?"

"Right, it's all finished and done."

"Thank you for your graciousness and true generosity," said Sita. "I have no fit reward for you—but Hanuman, Son of the Wind, you will always know and remember the True. You will always be strong and faithful, noble and wise and daring!

Always excellent powers will grace you and crown you, and I give you my real love forever!"

"Oh," said Hanuman, "What else are treasures but your good words and love? They are rare and precious jewels. It's like finding a lost way, like lighting up a lamp in the dark, like picking up what's fallen down or showing what's been hidden."

"So promise me to pardon the race of demons now, and go tell Rama I'm ready, I await him. Where is he anyway?"

"Yes. The war's over. I promise," said Hanuman. "And I think he's waiting for *me*!" He leapt into the air and flew back to Rama's side.

%

Now we return to Rama, Lord of the World. Gradually the monkeys and bears came back to the field outside Lanka, friendly to each other but fearless in war, and Hanuman found Rama there among many friends, embracing the animal kings Sugriva and old Jambavan.

Hanuman said, "Go to her."

But Rama spoke to Vibhishana. "Lanka King, bring Sita here. Let her be seen."

Vibhishana obeyed. He went and told Sita, "I come from your own Lord Rama, with a glad heart."

One of Vibhishana's courtiers said, "My King and I myself . . . we bring our best and kindest wishes for you and all your friends, that is . . . for you and for the entire population of Earth . . . ."

Then Sita, whose waist could be clasped round by Rama's fingers, came out of Lanka. The monkeys and bears drew back to let her by, thinking—*Oh yes, this is from the old times back.*

Then as Sita walked to Rama, her gentle face aglow with love, King Vibhishana beside her, all the animals and Lakshmana also bowed to her. They were all kneeling in a circle around her, and they did not move.

Vibhishana the Rakshasa shaded his face with his dark hand and looked up at the sky with his blue crystal-clear eyes. There were two chariots in the air, gleaming bright, unwavering. Voices in the sky sang the praises of Rama firm in fight, and fragrant flower petals fell from heaven. The ravages of war all vanished and the last omens cleared away.

Agni the Fire God then appeared by Sita, and touched together his huge webbed hands shining with ornaments and rings. Agni said, "Rama's father Dasaratha is in that other chariot; he is very happy for you, my Lady." Then in his red robes, with his black curly hair and beard Agni took Sita's hand and led her to Rama.

The Fire Lord said, "Rama, from the portion of gentleness in you, people call you a part of the Moon. A king is the eye of his people, therefore Lord Narayana take back your Sita. Take her away with you; you have won her again."

Rama smiled. "Why call me by a great god's name?"

"But . . . . But my Lord—" Agni looked at him in amazement. "You mean you don't remember?"

"I am Rama, a mortal man."

Agni grinned, and shook sparks from his bare arms. His golden rings and hand-ornaments melted. "Have you any idea—?" Agni was all immersed in Fire there; he was a joyous furnace. "Oh Rama, I dwell within all life. I am the true witness never deceived. Again and again you have forgotten your secret. Sita has not the smallest fault, and she is innocent. Lakshmi of good fortune is your wife, and she loves you." Gold melted and fell from the Fire God in heavy smoking drops of metal, and his jewels shattered and crazed, his eyes were blazing.

Indra the Rain Lord came into view on the other side of Sita. He wore a thin cloak of fine-spun mist that was trimmed with dancing stars, and under that his old battle armor of worn leather hard as stone and unbreakable. He stood barefoot a finger's width above the ground. He was slender, and cast no shadow, and never blinked his deep black eyes. His straight hair was long and black; his skin was fair and white, and smooth as a girl's, except where his slim hands were covered with the old crossing lightning scars that were whiter still.

Indra King of Heaven said, "Narayana, Searcher of Hearts, what is this amusement, what is this play of yours? You have killed Ravana and freed people from fear."

Agni breathed out words from a furnace, like speech from an open burning hearth—*Remember her!*

Indra said, "The closing of your eyes is the Night of the World's End, and your awakening from sleep is Time's beginning. To favor men you are born as Rama, so let no one think men are weak and alone. It's heaven's own truth! It is you alone who gave to me the kingdom and rule of heaven."

Rama said, "That cannot be, how could I do that?"

"Oh forget it!" said Indra. "I mean—"

Agni said, "I am myself your anger; the universe is your whole body; the Moon is your delight." He pressed his hands together before his wide chest, so the fiery muscles stood out on his arms. "I can test the True. Only beside Truth, the lapping flames are dull and cool. Here is Sita. Here's Love."

Rama said in a happy voice, laughing as he spoke, "I've won the war, what more do I need to know! Give me her hand."

Agni placed Sita's hand in Rama's, then drew back his own arm quick as a serpent's tongue. Rama had burned him!

Sita said, "With excellent joy, with delight cast looks on me. I am a fair free woman, I surrender to you of my own will, command me anything."

Rama tied Sita's wedding pearl-leaf back in her hair and unbound her braid. "Now you're mine again, with Fire for the witness."

The Fire God was happy. Indra shook his head. He had lived a long long time, but now he had come face to face with something older, some power immeasurably old, from before . . . Indra looked helpless. He said to Sita, "We all serve you," and both gods vanished. And Vibhishana the demon also told Sita, "I too will always protect you wherever you are!"

Sita held Rama. *I am near to you.* She ran her fingers down his face and shut her eyes and slightly parted her lips. *Oh my love, my lover—Oh!*

Still all the kneeling figures on that plain did not look up or move or rise. Vibhishana looked away and the love of Sita washed over Rama. *I love you. Oh, it's all summer, and all roses—it's all gold and all you* . . . . She wept.

Vibhishana said, "Rama, Lakshmana made you a house downhill."

"Let's go," said Sita.

Rama smiled in a daze. "What? Oh!"

Sita put Rama's wide gold ring that Hanuman had brought her back on his finger. She whispered more words like honey in his ear, and at midmorning they walked away down the hill hand in hand, and Rama soon dropped Sita's hand and held her round her waist close to him as they went.

They reached a leafy cabin built by Lakshmana, and Sita sat and put Rama's head on her lap, and saw that he had hurt his leg fighting for her.

❦

On what had been the battleground the animals and Lakshmana stirred at last, and got to their feet smiling. Hanuman asked Vibhishana the Demon King, "Why are the Rakshasas so quick to burn their dead or cast them undersea? Why do your weapons rust so soon?"

"Come, Hanuman," answered Vibhishana. "Come with me."

Vibhishana led Hanuman into Lanka, along the empty yellow brick streets to the royal palace where they entered. They went through a small side door in a plain room and descended many narrow stairs. For a way their path was lighted only by cut jewels set gleaming in the walls; then at the bottom of the stairs candles burned in branching silver trees, and they walked again along a level hall that widened and heightened and grew bright.

They stopped where the hallway ended at a storeroom door. There were locks holding it closed, locks strange and ornate and curious, and of those locks there were ten thousand and one. And though the keyholes were all of different shapes, Vibhishana opened them all with the same key,

366

sweeping his hands to touch them and they opened to him. The demon pushed back the door and they came into a huge well-lit room with no other entrance to be seen.

On golden chains from the ceiling hung globes of glass that held lights within them. The air was fresh and sweet, and scented with musky perfumes. The whole room was cut out smoothly from the heartstone of Trikuta Hill. On the far wall Hanuman could read written in letters of gold inlaid on blue lapis stone—*Please yourself. Tell the truth and be tranquil.*

"Miraculous!" Hanuman saw shelves and racks all over holding cool fine linens of every color; beautiful patterned silks and folded skins of tigers and leopards and lions and silver wolves; rows of magical books and love potions and secret treasure maps and formulas and ore samples and delicious recipes; books of numbers and dictionaries of languages and stars.

There were perfumes and jewels and musical manuscripts and medicines to heal illness and sorrow and all wounds. On the walls were paintings in plaster and on hides; there were bins of irreplaceable wines and unknown scrolls, piles of gold and silver, and on the floor priceless musical instruments sat perfectly tuned in long rows; and over the vaults of the ceiling and on the upper walls were polished copper balls and silver stars, brass suns and bronze faces, golden leaves and moons of ivory and flowers of cold dark iron and blue steel.

Vibhishana pointed to the far wall. "That's the motto of Viswakarman the Architect of Heaven, who first gave beings their names and created them, who built Beautiful Lanka for the race of demons long ago. You are the only outside person who will ever see this room. These are the ancient timeless treasures of our race.

"Narayana drove us out of Lanka and Vaishravana the Lord of Wealth lived here but he never knew of this room. The bird Garuda watched sharp-eyed lest we return in those old days, but from here unseen doors lead down and down underground and we are ever careful of our possessions. We don't throw things away or lose them or forget. We Rakshasas

367

protect many good things. We know a lot. We are strong." Vibhishana smiled with his long fangs. "Hanuman, by the good Dharma law, the Rakshasa knowledge may not perish. My friend, there are such powers of protection over this room that no thief would ever survive if he were but told all their names! These are the powers we draw on as guardians! But for you—if you need anything here, anytime, for anyone help yourself."

"Why will you do this for me?" asked Hanuman.

"You are my first and best friend of another race," replied Vibhishana. "You are faithful and very wise, when you stop to think. You put your whole heart into what you do; and you don't think twice when you've made up your mind, nor seek for any gain, so I call you my friend."

"I am."

"I know you are! In these vaults lies all the lore of old, gathered here since Time began again. People meet in this life and pass by each other like pieces of driftwood afloat on the wild and stormy sea, touching seldom, and once meeting, gone and parted again. Therefore a friend is also a treasure. Now you and Rama and all your armies will go from here. I am immortal; I will rule Lanka forever, and the Rakshasas will one day return who have now hidden themselves beyond your sight. I will cover Lanka and make her invisible from this time on, but you are always welcome here. For you I will reveal whatever you want to see, here on this island amid the great Ocean.

"And so," said Vibhishana, "if you find a friend hold him if you may. And giving gifts, giving to the poor and to others, that is always right; or else, what you save is spent to buy a homesite for you in Hell. So here's a present."

Vibhishana went to a shelf and took down a dusty book covered with the shastra marks of the Law, long shiny palm-leaves tied at the sides with faded string between wood covers. He opened it carefully. "By throwing them into the sea and by swift burning we have set our own war dead beyond the reach of life and death, of which they had grown weary. We long endure while we wish to, or we may sometimes escape life's wheel—and then our weapons rust! Here, learn this verse. Speak it correctly aloud on the hillsides where the dead animals lie, and they will again revive as they did before when you brought that Medicine Hill."

Hanuman learned those Mantras of Compassion and Vibhishana replaced the book where it had been. They locked the treasure room and retraced their steps. Hanuman stood on Earth outside Lanka and said the words, and brought back to life all the dead monkeys and apes and bears. And from then on, wherever any of those animals lived, no matter what the season the trees would flower and unveil before them and the land bear ripe fruit and all springs give water, full and clear.

Whoever was in Rama's army has all benefits and mercies. This is true because with Rama there is no fear, and no defeat, but instead great kindliness and victory.

However they had died, burnt or broken or cut or crushed to die, all the animals awoke from death unhurt, and they asked in great wonder, "What blessing is this? How are we restored?"

> *Once more!*
> *Live and grow, live and grow:*
> *Let me see my friends, my many friends,*
> *Let me look on you again.*
> *You left your homes behind for me,*
> *You cared nothing for Death,*
> *You lie pale and slain.*
> *I remember you,*
> *I remember all of you;*
> *I want you,*
> *I want you whole and strong!*
> *Once more!*

❧

In the rainy summertime, the men and women of Fair Ayodhya light many candles outside the temple doors, big brass bowls filled with sand where a hundred candles may burn. And then the rain may fall and drench the Earth, and the wind may blow strongly. But the candle flames won't go out; they'll sputter and burn right on through the storm and the night. *Fill me and fulfill me, body and soul!*

The next morning there was Rama in the camp of his huge and famous army, and Sita was there, and he had unbound her braid, her sleek dark hair was combed out, free and scented, and her skin was again like warm gold.

Rama looked into the faces of all his animals, over and over. He said to Vibhishana, "Soon it will be springtime and the fourteen years of my exile will be full. If I am late my brother Bharata will enter a fire and die. Lanka King, have you any way for us to return to our homes that seem so far away and hard to reach?"

"Good fortune to you," said Vibhishana, "take the stolen chariot Pushpaka. But stay here as my guest for a few days."

"You must consider that already done. We will rest onboard that car, and go easily flying home."

"Then wait here," smiled Vibhishana. He entered Lanka and returned walking on foot with that vast and flowery car following along behind him; Pushpaka of a thousand wheels, like a small city, lightly riding just off the ground except when he rose all by himself to clear the golden wall.

Pushpaka came over the hill slopes. There he was, that grand and glorious chariot glittering with gold and silver, made by Viswakarman the heavenly builder, adorned with clear sapphires and golden rooms, with blue blossoms and red flowers and silver pavilions and nets of pink pearls, with his flags all flying and his wind-bells softly ringing. He was the immense mind-driven chariot taken from Vaishravana the Treasure King, easily able to carry any number of riders anywhere they would go. There were the great rainbows tied into beautiful colored knots and smoothed to make Pushpaka's frame, and bathing Vibhishana in colors and lights as he walked in the shadow below the car.

Pushpaka was painted in colors with trees and swarms of birds and stars and pictures of rivers; he had saffron canopies and lotus flowers strung over summerhouses of carved wood and wooden hills planted with grass and latticed windows; he had altars and upper rooms and dining halls and white flagstaffs, set in crystal bases; he had benches and beds and coverlets and good things to eat and drink.

Vibhishana arrived with that aerial chariot like a hill and said, "Climb on, it's here, what more shall I do?"

Hanuman flew onto the chariot and untied Pushpaka's many ladders and steps and let them down. Soon the animals were standing among the flowers and along the railings, lining the galleries and paths, running through the parks and cool fountains. With the sunlight pouring through his golden fur, Prince Angada leaned over and let down a big basket on a rope, and drew up Rama holding Sita. Then came Lakshmana carrying all Rama's weapons and his own.

Rama looked over the edge. "Vibhishana, give me your permission to go, Majesty."

Vibhishana replied, "There's lots of room on that thing. It's a fine large carriage. I want to see you made King of the Earth; take me along with my four ministers."

Rama heard something thumping next to him. He turned and saw Hanuman switching his tail against the wooden walkway floor, with his arm round Jambavan the bear. Hanuman smiled, "King Rama, we want to stop at Kishkindhya for our families, and then we all of us want to see all the people from the strange lands at the limits of the world, who will gather to see you made the Ayodhya King. We'll greet your mothers and bow to your friends and go through all your royal forests and gardens."

"Yes," said Rama. He looked back down. "Climb to Fair Ayodhya, Rakshasas."

When everyone was aboard, that huge chariot arose with a

. . . and drew up Rama holding Sita . . .

great noise like fireworks and waterfalls; then silently high in the sky he turned north in a wide climbing curve, carrying Sita who had been lost and found again, and two mortal men, and five demons and twenty-three million monkeys and bears sitting there at their pleasure in the free-flying gardens, facing the fresh morning wind as if they owned the world.

the wonderful return

On the hillside in the Sun,
The King is home, his war is done.
The fountains play and I can hear
The Master of the Revels cheer,
And singing soft and music clear.

The flowers in their colors there
Are falling down beside the stair,
And Fair Ayodhya at my feet,
And all along her silver street
My friends I find, my loves I meet.

And this is how my world shall be;
My days are bright, my ways are free.

Rama rode with Sita. He said, "Look down, there are the heavenly flowers marking where we fought and won you; there is the shore and our bridge thrown across the sea; there is Ocean, seeming endless with no farther shore, and that bridge seems to go off into the sky over the edge of Earth."

Vibhishana approached them. "Lord, free the sea as my gift." Rama smiled, and as they watched, the waters stopped holding up the bridge stones. The long bridge broke and sank; it was gone. The waves danced, leaping unbounded.

Pushpaka went on flying, and Rama continued, "There you can see gleams of gold far underwater, coming from Mainaka Hill who still has his wings, the golden-winged Friend of the Wind; now there is the northern seashore—see how far Hanuman can jump! Smell the sandalwood scent of the Malaya Hills; they look blue from here, and those lakes look green.

There, through that spreading countryside below we marched from Kishkindhya; it will be an early spring this year. I think your mother Earth rejoices, and doesn't count the time."

Pushpaka started to descend. "There is the mouth of the cave city Kishkindhya, and there is Prasravana the Hill of Springs where I spent the rains, and I didn't even move out of the way when snakes crawled over me, I was so lost without you, and in that garden I killed Vali."

Sita said, "You are my Rama. Whatever you do is right."

Hanuman and Sugriva and King Jambavan were listening to Rama together. Hanuman sighed and said, "I wish I hadn't!"

"Hadn't what?" asked the Bear King.

"I wish *we* hadn't drunk up all Sugriva's wild honey wine."

The two Animal Lords smiled at each other. Pushpaka came in for a landing. Sugriva said, "Just get ready, monkey!"

"You mean? Where is it?"

Jambavan gave him a swat. "That monkey!! I don't see how we ever made it!"

"And it's not easy being a king," said Sugriva. "Remember that the next time you call me names."

Pushpaka caressed the Earth and was still and solid. All the monkey and bear children ran out of Kishkindhya cave as fast as they could. "What a car; can we ride?!"

Swiftly the animal wives and mothers and sisters dressed in all their best clothes and came to meet their men. Animal people were flying and running and jumping all over each other. Rama said, "We'll stay here overnight."

Hanuman was yelling, "You can ride tomorrow, all the way to Ayodhya!"

"There's Queen Ruma," said Jambavan. "Sugriva, go to her."

"Beautiful," said Sugriva. He turned to Rama. "Come inside with us until tomorrow."

Rama looked at Sita. Sugriva was turning his ears like an animal to hear where every sound came from. Down on the ground bears sat playing with their own children and holding baby monkeys. Kishkindhya monkey people were leaping

375

and raising dust from the green forest trees. The whole world had gone out of its mind.

Jambavan gave a roar from deep in his throat and threw himself into the air. Hanuman plunged over the railing.

Sugriva started to twitch his tail but our Lady Sita buried her fingers in the thick golden winter's ruff round his neck.

Sita laughed like an angel. "We'd love to!"

❧

Then on the next day they all flew to Ayodhya. Rama told Sita, "I'll show you; see, there is Rishyamukha Hill where we met that Hanuman; there is desolate Dandaka Forest, now free from harm, and there is where we burned the Vulture King Jatayu. Here come the Vindhya Hills and Agastya's hermitage. There is Chitrakuta—"

"Chitrakuta Hill in springtime!" Sita laid her head on Rama's shoulder. "Remember? And the birds all singing!"

"There flows the Yamuna river."

"From way up here the trees are like a carpet and the rivers are small as threads! How wonderful!"

Rama said, "By the grinding rapids of Yamuna and Ganga is Bharadwaja's retreat. Let me invite him to Fair Ayodhya to repay the feast he gave Bharata."

Pushpaka landed where Yamuna meets the Ganges. Rama met Bharadwaja and asked, "How is Bharata?"

Bharadwaja embraced Rama and smelled the crown of his head. "He is fine. But send him word you are safe."

"I will. Ride with us and be our guest; let us return the welcome, the feast that you gave."

"Oh Rama, a good dinner is as much a duty as fasting and not eating could ever be. Blessings, Majesty! I must be here where the two rivers change their colors and join—white Ganga and deep dark Yamuna! Blessed be you, Rama; blessed be!" Bharadwaja knelt before Rama. "I know all that has happened to you and all that you did. Now you must stay at home and live among your friends with Sita. Do as I say."

"Yes, I understand." Rama summoned Hanuman. "Go to Bharata and tell him we're coming home. I'll take the chariot to the Secret Forest of Guha the king of hunters for the night. Read Bharata's expression and his looks, and if he wants to keep Kosala as his own he may have her."

"He'll be the same," said Hanuman, and flew away.

Pushpaka chariot left Bharadwaja's hermitage and soon landed in a clearing in the Kingdom of the Far Forest, near the Ganges. Wherever he flew, there was always space there for Pushpaka to land when he arrived.

Rama and Sita and Lakshmana got down and walked through the forest trees. They heard whistling like a bird, then Guha came running at them. He fell on Rama and threw his arms around him. He looked as weird and outrageous as ever. He squeezed Lakshmana. He smiled his white smile at Sita. "Freedom! Freedom to you, my friends!" There he was again, the king of the wild, painted with yellow and green and red and blue all over his brown skin, wearing feathers long and waving in his curly hair.

"You'll stay for supper," said Guha. "Where did you get that flying city?"

"It's a magic chariot," said Sita. "Can the King of Lanka eat with us too? Our animal friends have their own food on the car, and . . . ."

"Yes, we're hunters, it's true. Vibhishana is welcome." Guha whistled and a forest man came bringing a new feather cloak for Sita, green and gold, just like the one he had given her fourteen years before. "Welcome to your tribe, princess. You are still my daughter, I'm glad you wear my necklace."

"It helped to save me," smiled Sita.

Guha said, "I sometimes take wild fruit to Bharadwaja the holy man. He often sent his students invisibly by air to the south, and from him I know most all you've done. Before, I didn't like to see you three enter the forest alone. But now the demons who ate unarmed men are gone from the woods as if they had never been. Oh, that was well done! Was that Hanuman we saw fly past?"

"Yes," answered Sita. "We have an army of monkeys and bears."

"An animal army. Yes, they're good fighters," said Guha.

"Then that is the chariot stolen from the King of Wealth. It's all true!"

"Come to Ayodhya with us tomorrow," said Rama.

"No, I have the wild forest in me, I can't go into a walled-up city. I ran there once and came right back," said Guha. "Sumantra the Charioteer and the three Queens are well. Get Vibhishana, and come and eat now under that same big nut tree."

Vibhishana joined them and those five—the demon, and Rama and Lakshmana, and Sita holding Guha's hand—walked along the river to that old tree, and the silent dark hunters appeared to serve them.

It was evening. The running lamps on Pushpaka were lit, and he was like a city suddenly appearing complete amidst the forest. Shadows fell under the trees and Guha's men came out with torches. Rama and Lakshmana and Sita washed in the river. Then on blankets round a fire, under the ancient tree where they had been fourteen years before they ate with Guha, and with them Vibhishana first tasted the delicious wilderness cooking and ate a savage forest feast.

❧

Hanuman flew over Kosala. He saw the roads coming to Ayodhya from many countries, the fields and farms, the flag-flying temples and holy bathing places along the rivers, the great white-walled city of Ayodhya seeming empty—and an earshot beyond, the little village of Nandigrama crowded with people.

Bharata sat there dressed in barkcloth at the foot of the red and gold Ayodhya throne, and on the throne were Rama's two wooden sandals painted with flowers. Every royal officer looked like a hermit all dressed in bark or skins, his hair matted into knots, his armor hidden as Rama's had been. Satrughna sat nearby on the grass. In all Kosala no man wore good clothes or any color, but the women dressed as they would, because Sita did not leave her robes and ornaments behind to go into the forest.

378

Hanuman dropped from the sky like a bouncing ball. He bowed first to Rama's sandals and then to Bharata. "Rama sends me to greet you. I am Hanuman the Son of the Wind. Is your kingdom well? Is there Dharma and Justice in Kosala? I hope lovers are not kept parted and young men respect the old, and do the rich not ignore the poor?"

Tears of happiness ran down Bharata's face. "Rama's land of Kosala is well; Fair Ayodhya is waiting. I give you a thousand cows and a hundred villages, and sixteen wives of noble birth, young and beautiful with skin like gold."

Hanuman laughed. "I touch them and give them back." He looked at Bharata with all the playful insanity of a cat. "What are you doing here like this? Rama and Lakshmana washed their hair out days ago! He'll meet you tomorrow by the city."

Bharata having truth for prowess said, "Set the signal fires to the villages and all the countryside." Satrughna set wine and fruit down by Hanuman. Everyone was smiling.

The priest Vasishtha approached and said, "The fourteen years are full. The trees are in blossom."

The Kosala men were changing clothes and bathing, lighting fires and trimming their hair and beards. Hanuman had a drink and ate three peaches. Bharata sent runners to Ayodhya to say—*Tomorrow*, and evening fell on the little village. In the reflecting firelight silver and gold, armor and rich silk were shining.

"Will you stay?" asked Bharata.

Hanuman said, "Surely."

Sumantra the old charioteer came, and many people sat circled round Hanuman and Bharata and Satrughna. Cooks brought fine food, a real dinner after fourteen years of eating hermit's food, fourteen centuries of grass and plain water it seemed.

Hanuman feasted on fruit and nuts, and Bharata said, "If we can hear it, unfold to us all that happened these many years to Rama."

"Well," said Hanuman, "Ravana stole Sita and—"

"What!" said Sumantra. "How did that happen?"

379

"We saved her. We fought a war and won."

"Ah," said Bharata. "The animals . . . bless them all . . . ."

"Now Ravana is dead," said Hanuman, "and Rama is tonight in Guha's kingdom."

Satrughna said, "Hanuman, we saw you fly over holding a red-hot mountain a few nights ago."

"We've heard this and that," said Bharata, "and we waited for Rama's call to aid him. You must tell us everything. After a long time our desires are fulfilled."

Hanuman settled back contentedly and the people grew still. "I will tell you Rama's story, fillled with loneliness and love, romance and glamor . . . . Listen, Prince—I am Hanuman, the son of the far-going Wind, and one day on a hilltop . . . ."

Let all cares be forgotten,
Let your worries fly away:
For the Master of the Revels
Will rule the land this day!

It was early morning. The Revels Master stood up and slowly brushed fourteen years of dust and ashes and sand out of his old clothes. He found the wine-key he'd thrown away still on its chain; he found his vests and ribbons and his fur hat. The royal palace had been astir all night. He opened the king's wine-vaults and broke the seal on a tall dusty crock, and poured himself a cheerful cordial drink. The Master of the Revels smiled again.

In Ayodhya the gay silk pennons and streamers were unfurled. Musicians restrung their silent lutes; drivers put the wheels back on the Kosala chariots. They dressed and painted the royal white elephant, and Fair Ayodhya threw open her gates and waited for her Lord Rama.

Behold! Fair Ayodhya! the city of my dreams; Ayodhya of many dreams and gardens. No war was there; the war-songs were made into dances, and the marches were for parades for the children. In Ayodhya you could walk anywhere, anytime, free and unafraid. You could love openly, and couples embraced in daylight in the gardens.

380

She was in the low hills, the breathing hills of home, and she was the most beautiful city ever made by man, with her hanging stairway gardens and her sprays of flowers. Her homes were my dream houses; I knew that when I first saw them in the bright clear sunlight. Purple petals fell on the green barefoot grasses by the stairs outside, and vines of spicy sweet flowers seemed growing from her housetop roofs, and her flowering trees in blossom scented the air. The colored flower gardens fell down her slopes, holding ferns and green things and small tame wild animals. Her side streets were like long green tunnels overarched by old trees touching from each side. The leafy trees swayed in the gentle breeze of the Kosala hills, and I walked below through spotted sunlight and moving shade.

Hearts are young in Fair Ayodhya, and all's forgiven now. Her streets are sprinkled with sandalwood water. She has fishponds and splashing fountains lovely to hear, where flights of white birds play, graceful and happy. Bushes of ripe blackberries look like bees swarming. Her gardens are the flowery shelters of my childhood. Fair Ayodhya—won't you be mine, till the end of Time?

There's nothing I have to do, I've done it all. It's time to relax, time to have a good dinner, and to be peaceful. From peace in my own heart peace will go out to my courtyard, to my city, my kingdom, to all the world . . . .

The wine flows free, the music calls;
I smile within the dancing halls . . . .

I spend my days with my friends doing nothing. Sometimes the grey river mist comes in off the slow Sarayu river where I swim, and the tops of the tall trees are lost in the cool fog. It makes the trees like low clouds themselves; it is wet under them and nowhere else; and I hear the boatmen calling out on the river.

Fair Ayodhya, my old home; the city I love, my own free city; you are very dear to me. You are the home of friendship and alive, gleaming with lamps at night. You are where the great roads cross, and people traveling often stay here and go no farther. Fair Ayodhya, my love to you where the food is good and no man poor.

She was my city; I loved all of her, by day or night, and all her people. They were my family and my friends, where I belonged—good words and loving homes—cozy and warm, or easy and cool, just as I wanted. She was my Innocent City. Everything was all right there.

> *Beyond the end of every Time*
> *You'll find Valmiki makes a rhyme;*
> *The blue Sarayu's flowing by,*
> *And butterflies like flying flowers*
> *Pass me by,*
> *I lie in bowers.*
> *Oh Rama!*

Ayodhya was dancing, shining with decorations; and in the palace, men gathered the coronation supplies and women went in rustling dresses wearing gold. Shrill pipes and horns played in the street and shell-trumpets sounded from the temples. Royal musicians and courtiers smiled, and the dancing girls caught their breath.

People lined the wide streets and the rolling hills. Children were eating candy from gold-paper wrappings. The houses and doorways were all white and there were flowers in the streets. Rama had already spent a night awake in silence thinking of all those years before, and that when he came home now, he would be king without waiting.

Bharata and Satrughna and Hanuman, followed by the whole village of Nandigrama, went to a field outside the city with Rama's sandals on the white elephant's back beneath a white umbrella. Out from Ayodhya rode the Kosala warriors on a thousand horses with jingling rings and chains, carrying shining spears and long lances.

Then Pushpaka came, flying with colored banners in the sun. He landed in that field and his riders crowded to the rails high above. The ladders came down, and Bharata led the

elephant over, and took the sandals from him. He was pulled up onto the chariot and fell into Rama's arms. And while all Ayodhya watched, Bharata knelt and swiftly tied the shoes back on Rama's feet.

Bharata stood and smiled, looking level into Rama's eyes. He ran his hand through his red hair and said, "Majesty! I return to you all your kingdom left in my care—how good to see you!" He faced Lakshmana. "Blessed is my birth since today I may see all of you safe at home."

Bharata told King Sugriva, "You are our brothers. Friendship grows from kindness and giving help, not from close ties of blood."

He told Jambavan, "Lord of Bears, I am your servant." He said to Vibhishana, "Lord, take the freedom of Fair Ayodhya as our guest forever; you have made this possible."

The animals and the five demons descending from Pushpaka were met by Kosala men and women and welcomed and led to houses and lodgings all over Ayodhya. The stories about a faraway animal city were true, Hanuman's story was true—it was all true!

Then Rama stood on the ground and the four brothers embraced, and Vasishtha led Sita to Sumantra's car to be driven to see her three mothers.

At arms' length Bharata put his hands on Rama's shoulders and said, "A child cannot easily pick up and carry the burden set down by a man. We have survived only by the power of your sandals. Take this land back, my king; take her back from me!"

"In a moment," smiled Rama. "Let's walk into town. I'm not used to all this."

❦

At last Dasaratha's four sons were walking together, through Fair Ayodhya to the white royal palace on a hill, and the Kosalas stood quiet along the roads waiting to know what Rama would do. Rama and Lakshmana entered alone to see the Queens. They were combing Sita's hair with silver combs and Rama's mother Kausalya said—*We are well; by good fortune we see you again with all your enemies dead.* Then she hugged him.

Vasishtha came in. He said to Kaikeyi the youngest Queen, "By your doing were the worlds saved from tyranny."

He told Queen Sumitra, "Your son Lakshmana is the silent support of Rama; Satrughna is Bharata's quiet companion; you are yourself the good friend of these two Queens."

He said to Kausalya, "We have lived to see this day!"

And he told Rama, "Rule as long as the world endures, as far as the world extends."

"Yes," said Rama.

Vasishtha said, "These hours and days are fortunate." He went to a window and shouted, "He will!"

A Kosala lion-roar came back from the street. The palace trembled with noise, incredibly loud. The first Ayodhya festival in fourteen years began, and the best celebration she had ever known. The people were dancing again, and men and

384

monkeys and bears all jammed into the wineshops shoulder to shoulder, trading drinks and stories and lots of loose talk.

"I'll get ready," said Vasishtha, "and make you King tomorrow."

Sugriva found Hanuman wearing flower garlands piled round his shoulders up to his ears. The Monkey King gave Hanuman a golden jar and said, "For a present to Rama, fill this with water from each of Earth's five hundred rivers."

"Say no more!" said Hanuman.

"And don't try to fool me with well-water, because I know the taste of every sea and stream."

"Well, they won't let a monkey taste the Ayodhya King's waterjars!" laughed Hanuman.

"And if you see any fair or beautiful thing that may be brought, bring it."

The Kosalas gave the animals and demons new clothes and fine ornaments, and when Bharata served free food from the royal kitchens Ayodhya maidens carried tasty treats to monkeys and bears lying on soft beds or on grass in the parks. For Fair Ayodhya, all the sorrow in the world was used up. People poured into town from the countryside; they danced and heard music and gambled and watched tumblers and plays on the street corners.

The holy trees were hung with ribbons and brahmanas blessed everyone. In the early evening countless candles burned outdoors like blossoms of light and incense rose into the air. Lanterns glistened and torchlight burned. The night was warm and the stars were clear.

Then late at night Sita sat by a fountain in the palace while Rama slept on a bed in an open room nearby, and Manthara the hunchback came to her. Manthara knelt, "Forgive me for remembering those two wishes."

Sita was beautiful. She answered, "Not only men, but even the gods have been freed from fear of Ravana. Death had surrendered to the Demon King; the Moon and Sun were his subjects; and Indra King of heaven was a captive."

385

"Lord!" said Manthara.

Sita said, "Rama killed Ravana only because of what you did."

Manthara smiled, and sat beside Sita. "Queen Sita, I am always your faithful servant."

"Yes," said Sita.

After fourteen years awake and watching over Rama every night, Lakshmana slept, held fast in sleep beside his loving wife.

❧

The night passed quickly by. Soon the sky grew light and the morning Sun rose red for Rama to see him. Bharata had brought the Ayodhya throne from Nandigrama village to the royal park by the palace so everyone could see Rama made king.

Rama came out, like a lion coming out of his cave, and girls tossed fragrant flowers from windows and rooftops. He walked to the park with Lakshmana holding a seven-tiered white parasol over him. White cows were tied all along the way. Bharata and Sugriva the monkey King stood behind the throne holding white yaktail fans. Rama sat on the throne facing east, and Sita sat on a lower chair beside him, on a deerskin cover trimmed in gold. The animals and demons and men gathered there sat down on the grass.

Virgin maids brought spotless white cattle with gold-plated horns, and unthreshed heads of grain for Rama to touch. Then Vasishtha entered the park holding a hollow horn wrapped in silver wire and a little dipper. First the priest stopped by Hanuman and dipped some of the river water of all the world into the horn. Four brahmanas unsealed four brimful stone jars of seawater. Four Ayodhya girls set before Rama a handful of jewels and one of seed, a handful of herbs and one of sea pearls.

Vasishtha put some of the waters of the Eastern Sea in his horn from the first stone jar. Four more girls came forward and

386

put before Rama a jar of honey, parched grain dyed with saffron, a bowl of milk and some incense unlit.

Vasishtha dipped water out of the Western Sea, whose waters smell like camphor. Four more beautiful maidens brought Rama turquoise and blue water flowers, a lump of silver and a dish of curds.

Vasishtha added the black seawater of the cold North Sea; and the last four maidens set down by Rama's throne a fresh-loomed cloth unbordered, and corals, and beautiful seashells and white garlands. Then Vasishtha took water from the Southern Sea waterjar.

Finally at noon Vasishtha stood by Rama and emptied the water over his head, and made him King and Lord of Earth; the Solar King of Fair Ayodhya, the Kosala Lord, and Sita was his one Queen with him.

Rama gave many presents—horses and cows, earrings and bracelets, rings and bells and a silver crest for Sugriva, and round Sita's neck he fastened a smooth pearl necklace. Sita held the strands in her hand and looked at them, and looked at Rama, and looked at the animals.

Rama said, "Give those pearls to whom you please!"

Lotus-eyed Sita gave them to Hanuman. He knelt before her and she put the pearls around his neck and smiled at him. The necklace seemed to glow like little moons nestled in his white fur. "This gift is for your courage and strength, your valor and bravery and skill, and for your faithful service."

Rama said to all his people, "I am pleased that you have gathered here to welcome me."

They cheered back—*King Rama! Rule forever!*

❦

The Ayodhya throne, all red and gold, was carried into the King's palace, and the coronation was over. All afternoon the animals and men ate their way through hills of food and drank up lakes of Rama's wines, and there was not one person without some gift. Evening came and the Sun set as Ayodhya sang her twilight prayers. Then Night veiled the worlds as Rama went into the inner rooms with Sita.

So passed the first day of Rama's long reign of eleven thousand years. Rama could discover the truth of things, and men resorted to him from all over Earth, as the rivers of the world all flow to the sea. Rama was well-honored and well-loved. His presence filled the heart.

Rama was strong enough to support all men, and gentle as the new Moon's beams. Fame and Wealth never left him. When he was king men were long in life, and lived surrounded by their children and grandchildren and all their families. The old never had to make funerals for the young. There was rain and fertile Earth; indeed, the Earth became bountiful.

Peace and Rama ruled as friends together, and bad things did not happen. Men grew kind and fearless. Everyone had about him a certain air and look of good fortune.

A King like Rama was never seen before and nowhere remembered from the past in any kingdom, nor did any like him ever follow in the later ages of this world.

§

THE END OF THE BOOK OF THE BATTLES.
HERE BEGINS THE SEVENTH AND FINAL BOOK,
THE UTTARA KANDA, THE LAST BOOK.

§

in what dream?

At the end hear the first words . . . .

After a month in Ayodhya, early one morning before it was light, while the Kosalas still slept with closed eyes, Vibhishana and Sugriva met Rama in the palace gardens, and the Monkey King said, "Majesty, we have all seen you, now we shall go home to our deep forest and far countries."

"Blessed are friends like you," answered Rama.

"Farewell," said Vibhishana. He bowed his head, then with his four knights he flew away to Lanka, going swiftly through the sky with a sound of thunders and gleam of lightnings.

Rama went outside the palace courtyard and looked out at the monkeys and the dark bears all gathered in the streets. He embraced Hanuman. "It seems you have been here but a moment."

"Farewell, Lord of Earth." And then with all desired things given them by Rama, the animals of the greenwood returned to dwell in their homes, blinking their eyes and half unwilling to leave Fair Ayodhya.

It was still very early, and as Rama walked alone back to his palace, through a grove of trees with fair new leaves in the morning, he heard a voice call from above him—*Rama, Rama, Rama*—and he found he stood in a long wide shadow.

Rama looked up. There were the giant rainbows over his head. "I am Pushpaka chariot, the spring flower car. By your leave I will return to Vaishravana the Treasure Lord. Give me permission to live on Kailasa Hill, and I will come back to you if ever you need me, whenever you want me."

Rama said, "Welcome to you, best of chariots. Go where

389

you will. Be not sorry for our separation. May your ways be smooth and good forever." Then Pushpaka rose and flew north to the silver hill Kailasa from where Ravana had stolen him.

Indeed, when Rama was King many creatures and created things could speak to men sometimes. When deer ate the crops the Kosalas would speak with the deer kings in good-will, and those kings would withdraw their people to the wild grasslands. If one wished to hear stories of past times he could speak with an old sword about ancient battles, or hear the old tales told by the trees and stones.

❧

Rama ruled from Fair Ayodhya and all the world saluted him, and time went by until his reign lacked only twelve years and a few months of being ten thousand years long, when one winter evening Rama met Sita wearing a beautiful robe, and saw that she was with child. Knowing of the strange longings of pregnant women he asked her, "Is there some wish of yours I may give?"

Sita smiled. "I want to go again to the retreats along the Ganges, just for a day or two, to eat the fresh wild food and sleep once more on grasses. And as we first went away from Ayodhya, thousands of years ago I promised Ganga to visit her . . . let me go now, my Lord . . . ."

Rama said, "Go tomorrow if you want to," and he embraced his Queen with great love and happiness.

And with those kind and innocent words sorrow again came into Rama's life.

We look at man's life and we cannot untangle this song.
Rings and knots of joy and grief, all interlaced and locking.

Later that night Rama met with some of his ministers and in passing he asked lightly, "What do my people say of me?"

"Majesty," answered the minister Bhadra, "they speak good of you as King, and in their homes tell stories of your war against Ravana long ago."

390

"The king is the refuge of those who have no shelter, so I must be without fault. People tread in their king's footsteps, so I must avoid even the report of any wrong. Hide nothing from me," said Rama.

Bhadra joined his hands. "They say—*today men stand at a ruined pier hung with colored rags on the far south shores and dream of a bridge a hundred leagues long across the dancing sea, where the ocean breaks in luminous waves. Rama did a deed unheard of. Ravana was unconquerable. No man ever brought the wild animals of the wood into his armies before*—and so they talk of many things."

"What else?"

"Majesty, Kings must hear good news and not think on mistakes. Don't seek wisdom from coarse common people, but forget their talk; pity them their ignorance and trust in things to turn out right."

Rama said, "Those who live uneventfully at home with their wives and families may alone really know life. No king can ignore what his folk say of him . . . do not refuse to tell me."

Bhadra said, "Rama, we must obey you. They also say—*The King desires Sita although Ravana touched her. How could he forget she lived with another? And the Queen must also remember the Demon King*—so speak the lowest men."

And the other ministers of Kosala lowered their eyes and sadly said, "Lately this is true."

Rama left them there without a word, and sent a message to Lakshmana—*Come to me at once.*

Lakshmana and Rama met in a private room of the palace. Rama stood alone by a window. His face was pale, his hands trembled like leaves in a wind, the lights of his eyes were gone as though clouded over.

Lakshmana frowned. He looked and saw no enemy; he felt no threat. Lakshmana harshly threw the end of his robe back over his shoulder, and knelt and asked, "Who dares?"

"Arise," said Rama. "Promise to obey me."

Lakshmana walked back and forth. "The threads of that design! Who told you?"

"A king must be blameless."

"Such words pierce my heart," said Lakshmana. "Fire himself proved her innocent. She is fired gold, poured into golden fire!"

Rama said, "Lakshmana, consider what is a king. Kings cannot afford blame. Ill fame is evil to kings; they above all men must be beyond reproach . . . see, into what a chasm of sorrow a King may fall . . . ."

Lakshmana said, "Gradually everything seems to change again, and even an Emperor must pay his way through life."

Rama faced his brother. "It must be! It's all the same, can't you see? Where there is growth there is decay; where there is prosperity there is ruin; and where there is birth there is death."

Lakshmana sighed hopelessly. "Well, what will you do?"

"Sita expects to go to the forests tomorrow. Let Sumantra the Charioteer drive you both there, and when you arrive by the river Ganga abandon her."

"She will die. Your child will die!"

"No," said Rama. "I command you! Not a word to anyone."

Lakshmana said, "Surely a king is remote and lonely, and very far from reason. We cannot speak to you . . . ."

Rama said, "Each person can be told what he will understand of the nature of the world, and no more than that—for the rest, take my word."

"I'll take it," answered Lakshmana. "Just . . . leave her there, alone?"

"Yes."

Lakshmana looked around the room. "Rama, since we were young children I have followed you; now I will still serve you. For right and wrong are very subtle and hard to tell apart, and the Dharma Law is difficult to know—*and, it is inconceivable to me, that I should ever willingly disobey you, Rama.*"

✧

The next morning Sita took some little presents for the hermits' wives of the forest, tied them in a silk cloth, and got on Sumantra's chariot with Lakshmana. Sumantra's four red horses went out of Fair Ayodhya and down along the Tamasa riverside, through plumes of morning fog.

They stayed that night in the woods meeting no one, and continued their way the next day. It was cloudy; the Sun had fled from having to see Sita betrayed. They came to the mouth of the dark Tamasa where she meets Ganga, and Sumantra found an ancient abandoned fisher-boat drawn up onshore and said, "Come across Ganga and we may meet someone."

At that instant, in the city of Lanka, Vibhishana the King felt danger to Sita. He went outside and looked far in every direction to see what was amiss. His far-seeing blue eyes gleamed and his black face darkened. He wrapped himself in a blue cloak and flew to heaven.

By the peaceful stream of the heavenly branch of the holy Ganga river he saw the sage Narada leaning back against a tree with his eyes closed. Vibhishana gently knelt on the ground of heaven and touched Narada's shoulder. "Wake up. Get moving!"

Narada opened his eyes, saw Vibhishana's face with his long fangs and decided he had a bad dream. He shut his eyes again. But King Vibhishana gripped Narada hard as steel and said—*For the protection of Sita, the Demon King calls on any power! Awake this instant, she is in danger! Get up! Do right!*

"Sita!" Narada was on his feet. "Where?"

Vibhishana said, "Down on Earth, oh Minstrel, across from where Tamasa flows into Ganga below, where inside an anthill sits the lone hermit Valmiki."

❦

Sumantra and Lakshmana took Sita across Ganga in that old boat and helped her out on the other side. Then Lakshmana looked at her and wept.

"What's wrong?" asked Sita.

Lakshmana could not answer her, and Sumantra the Charioteer replied, "We see bad signs, Earth to us is sad, we are restless and empty of happiness."

Sita said, "You miss Rama, but when we see what hermits we will find and give them my gifts we may all go back home."

Sumantra sighed and bent low his head, and looking down he said, "This is the work of destiny that cannot be overcome. I was angry when Dasaratha banished Rama, but this time I made no protest, for this is fate. This was foretold, and I overheard it long ago."

"What?" asked Sita. "What are you talking about?"

Lakshmana replied, "In fear of scandal, like a coward Rama now uses this journey as the pretext to abandon you here in the woods." He turned to Sumantra. "This is clearly unjust. I cannot understand, what can we gain by doing wrong to please a fool?"

"Then suspend your reason and get a glimpse of Eternity." Sumantra looked at Ganga's waters flowing by. "This is in part ancient history beyond men's knowing, and in part what I have heard was to happen. Rama will live alone from now on, apart from you."

Sita wept, "Oh why?"

"My Lady," said Sumantra, "all the universe is but a sign to be read rightly; colors and forms are only put here to speak to us; and all is spirit, there is nothing else in existence. War and peace, love and separation are hidden gateways to other worlds and other times. Let us not grow old still believing that truth is what the most people see around them . . . Oh Lakshmi of the Lotus, Daughter of Videha, we are fit objects of blame for all men by leaving you. But banish your sorrow over what must be."

Sumantra silently spoke a spell that all forest creatures might protect Sita, and as he began to speak aloud again, the dark blue clouds settled lower on the hills around them.

Sumantra said, "Dasaratha and I knew part of our future, and I have never told this story. Now I am an old man, and I remember long times ago, and I break secrecy to tell you how it was, that Kaikeyi won her two wishes."

❧

Listen, my children—

It was in the olden time, long before your births, when your

394

father Dasaratha and I were young men . . . it seems now to have been in another age of this world. Little remembering your father as an old man, little looking at me now can you see the brave young prince and the lucky charioteer of those days, who fought on the side of the gods themselves against the Asuras of drought. With Indra and others, and helped by Jatayu the young vulture prince who made our friendship then, we tried to unlock the clouds where all the rain was imprisoned.

Then I fought alone as a warrior and did not drive Dasaratha's car that flew through the air by grace of Lord Indra's spell, pulled by the same four red horses I have used all these years since. There was a better driver than I to take your father against the demon strongholds in the black clouds—there was Princess Kaikeyi, nine years old and unafraid.

The demons armed the clouds with artillery and turned them into fortress cities. They shot many of our warriors from the sky. We never saw the Sun. It was hot and stifling. At night lights flashed overhead as gods and demons fought; by day we saw the shadowy giant warriors and heard the charge of horse and chariot and the clash of arms. Indra's white elephant called and trumpeted; he threw down the demon walls and many black stones fell on Earth. They broke our lands and the fields lay parched. That was dread fatal war; we faced famine.

Those days gone by seemed brighter and of more glory than today, or darker with more sorrow. In the countryside our cattle shifted and lowed; the deer burst running through the forest like horses driven from a battlefield. The clouds were black, and dry, and rimmed with red; the world was dark; all daylight was gone. There was forever confusion in heaven, and our warriors who returned from flights above the clouds at night told us how the stars and planets swerved and could not hold their paths from fright, but went in fearful uncertainty blocking heaven's ways, striking against each other, a terror to mind and sight. Flames burst like blood from the stricken stars.

Your grandfather Aja was King. He helped Indra, and we

fought back against the demons guided by our flares and fires high in the windy sky. We battled the drought demons with Indra's thunderbolts. I have myself thrown many brilliant thunders, made by Viswakarman for Indra, and for that we wore a thick glove of wet green leaves, and bits of fires scarred our arms.

Kaikeyi never failed Dasaratha. She could feel an enemy's shortcomings; she felt when to draw near, when to stay and when to turn away. She ran her four red horses through the celestial skies and ruled them by some miraculous power of friendship. Behind her was a seven-layered white umbrella with slender ribs of silver over the warrior's station on her chariot, and to each side of it a chowrie fan, gold on the right, silver on the left, and there stood your father fighting for rain.

One night high in the air, the demons attacked that car with conjurations on a hundred sides. Your father was sadly wounded. Part of a comet tore through his side, and a flying fragment of his shattered armor cut Kaikeyi's hand deeply. And at the same moment a demon arrow snapped the bolt-end off the right axle and the wheel started to slip off.

Dasaratha was unconscious and saved from falling to death by Kaikeyi. She drove the chariot so it did not overturn in the air, and kept that wheel on, and brought her horses and the car softly down to Earth.

Kaikeyi wore shimmering armor made from green silk threads and fine steel interwoven, a green cloak like winter's grass. It was strong, but she loved your father and tore away a strip of it to bandage Dasaratha's wounds, and her hand bled, their blood mingled. She nursed him for many days as he recovered slowly, and he told her—*You restored my life that my enemies had taken from me . . . ask me twice for anything in return.*

Then one night Indra came to Ayodhya. We met him as comrades, we drank from the same cup. He healed Dasaratha completely, and would have taken the scar from Kaikeyi's hand but she refused him. We went to a field outside the city, and there were all the gods of heaven, and they thanked us for

396

our help. The gods were cheerful; they had just received the promise of aid from Lord Narayana.

We heard it. Out in the night, from far far away came the call of Narayana's battle-shell. We felt the first winds of Garuda's approaching flight. Our torches were blown out; the shrill winds screamed around us. There was a great loud sound as of many old trees straining and creaking in the Wind, and that was the drawing back of Narayana's bow. There was a hum and rattle and groan of metal, and that was the razor-edged, diamond-naved discus whirling madly on its pole. There was a terrific loud snap, and the bowstring of Narayana was loosed and spoke death to the drought-demons. We grown men shielded our eyes and covered our ears from the wind and noise, but young Kaikeyi stood looking up into heaven, standing beside Lord Indra, holding his hand and smiling, a child fearless beside heaven's Lord.

The rain spilled down onto the land, and fell spraying into our rivers. It came down on the mountains and fell into the seas. And with the rain fell down demons covered with red arrows and mangled.

Then through the night dark forms ran past us into Ayodhya. They were demons and we followed armed, but they were not invading; they sought refuge from Narayana. They came to an old brahmana's house and his wife gave them shelter. That old couple had never taken life, and always saved others when they could; and now they accepted the demons' surrender in the name of King Aja, and sent word to the royal palace.

Running to Ayodhya, we were thrown down and Garuda swept past us screaming like a thousand eagles, flying low between the high towers of Ayodhya, shearing our city gates and his claws tearing through our treetops. Riding on his back we saw Narayana enraged. His dark blue skin gleamed and his yellow robes flew. He killed that brahmana's wife when she faced him, without letting her speak, and in terrible anger he broke that sanctuary and beheaded the helpless demons.

There was great turmoil. Down the street came King Aja, furious at the Lord's treason, that his protection and name had been ignored. The old brahmana wept over his wife's body. Then standing a little apart I overheard Vasishtha the priest speak an unbearable curse on Narayana the Lord. In hot anger Vasishtha threw down his staff and cursed Narayana to be born on Earth, in a royal family rich and wise, a family most honored and kind, and once born to be parted from his wife as he had broken that brahmana's marriage. Vasishtha said—*So will it be! He is a man of ours you harmed!*

King Aja drew the royal Ayodhya sword and spoke defiance and threats to Narayana and ordered him from our kingdom, but Narayana was departing as he spoke. Aja approached us, men and gods, and told us, "Can't you kill fairly, or must you enlist the aid of giant cowards? By heaven fight fair next time!"

We put away our lances and spears, our lightnings and swords. The Asuras that lock away rain were defeated; it rained for days, and then we saw the Sun again.

Vasishtha was appalled that he had cursed Narayana. But the words of a holy saint prove adamant—and we knew what must happen. All is destiny, all is change and what endures?

Vasishtha told me, "Be silent about this. But remember: Lord Narayana will never take man's life without accepting it all. He will have the adventure; he will take all the gain and all the loss."

For days Vasishtha sat alone in seclusion. When he left his meditation he said, "*Her large eyes are tearful and her ringlets are dark . . .* I can discover no more; we must wait."

◈ ◈ ◈

"No one knew what that meant until now," said Sumantra. "Sita, I'm a chariot driver, a good guide, and you'll get back to Rama only by entering this forest now. Try to remember us well. This world's life is like vapor from breath blown on a mirror, it does not last, therefore summon patience. We'll tell no one where you are."

398

Sita said, "Goodbye, Sumantra. You have touched my heart."

Sumantra said, "Farewell, Sita. The light of our lives is gone, and this ends all that we've known. May I see you again."

"Goodbye, Lakshmana."

Lakshmana said, "I cannot go, this is a lonely wood and Rama is not here."

But even as he said that, Lakshmana was going. Sumantra led him back to their boat and they recrossed Ganga, and drove away in the chariot looking back many times.

❧

It was noon. The Sun came out and Ganga flowed sparkling by. Sita stayed by the riverside, all alone with her small gifts of needles and thread and combs and mirrors and perfumes on the ground in a package beside her, and all the wood was silent but for the cries of peacocks far away.

Ganga the beautiful river goddess spoke softly from within her moving waters—*What price, what price? Let life go with love and not outlive it, cut the bonds when happiness goes . . . .*

Ganga whispered, "There is a home for you now. I am the curtain to pass through, beyond me golden rooms are yours forever. *Come home, come home, dive into me . . . .*"

Sita was entranced. She stared at the shimmering water. Then four hermit boys appeared from out of the forest, and saw her, and ran off. Then a wild shaggy man ran to her, covered with dust from an anthill, with hair and beard long as eternity.

"I am Valmiki. Make my hermitage your home."

Sita looked at him bewildered and Valmiki said again, "Make this your home, stay here." He smiled, and many hermit wives led Sita away. And so a hermit who became the first poet led the Queen of Ayodhya to safety.

The women took Sita to a quiet glen, into a new house of leaves in Valmiki's retreat that had just been created by one of Narada's songs. She stayed there, and when her time was

Sita was entranced.

come, there her twin sons were born. It was at night in the summer, and midwives awoke Valmiki and said, "Poet, protect the newborn."

Valmiki grabbed an armful of shiny fresh-cut kusa grass, the pale long grassblades used for sacrifice and ceremonies. He went to where Sita lay and rubbed her twin newborn sons with it. He rubbed the firstborn with the grass tips and named him Kusa. He rubbed his brother with the cut grass ends and named him Lava.

For twelve years Sita and her sons lived with Valmiki while he composed this *Ramayana*. He taught Kusa and Lava every verse over the years and they learned to sing this story to the music of a lute and drum.

❦

When Kusa and Lava were twelve years old, Rama had ruled in Fair Ayodhya for ten thousand years, and once on a summer night that was neither hot nor cold he spoke with Lakshmana, and said, "I will declare a great public festival, a happy gathering somewhere in the countryside, a peaceful celebration that will be long remembered and a year's giving of gifts to all the world."

"A King's wife must be present," said Lakshmana.

"Happiness I want now," said Rama. "My heart must no longer hurt. I have made a golden statue of Sita that will stand beside me. We'll have food and music. We'll make it a thanksgiving for what good fortune we have, a long and excellent ceremony where all will be well-received, and let it begin next month. We will invite everyone. In Naimisha Forest, along the river."

Rama sent Kosala riders to Kekaya to invite Bharata's uncle and to Videha to invite King Janaka, and to all the kings of the world. Some went to Kishkindhya to invite the monkeys and bears, and from there Hanuman carried them to invisible Lanka, and Vibhishana was asked to come. And everyone that these horsemen met was told of Rama's festival.

Rama sent his brother Satrughna into the forests to invite

the holy saints and hermits dwelling apart from men. Satrughna rode a black horse with a red mouth and the first person he met was Guha the hunter. He and his savage people accepted the invitation, for that yearlong festival would not be held inside any city.

Satrughna's last stop was at Valmiki's hermitage, and he knew nothing of Sita's living there or of her two sons.

Valmiki was all smiles. "Prince, welcome to you! By the Gods, that was a deed well done by Rama, when he killed Ravana! He freed all the worlds . . . ." Valmiki embraced Satrughna and smelled the crown of his head. "Rest here with your men, take whatever you want as some small gift from my love for all of you . . . ." And Valmiki in his old, holy hermitage talked with great gratitude of the battle of Lanka, as if it had happened just before his eyes, and not ten thousand years before.

"I invite you and all your people to Rama's festival," said Satrughna.

"I accept, we'll be there."

❧

Late that evening Satrughna lay half asleep with his companions in one of the huts of Valmiki's retreat. And there in the night, from somewhere among the dark forest trees around him, he heard verses and parts of a musical song—

> . . . Only the starbeams showed it then;
> Rama the refuge of the world,
> And all my hopes . . . .

Satrughna heard Earth's first poetry, two high voices singing a true song telling everything just as it had been. Kusa and Lava were running through pieces of Rama's story in the dark wood, and Satrughna lay still and listened until they stopped.

> In the land of King Janaka
> Is Shiva's bow no man can bend,
> Even in a dream . . .

402

Then they changed—

Out from the land, out from the land,
There goes Hanuman swift as the Wind
Racing to Lanka over the Sea,
And Rama's ring gleams gold in his hand.

Satrughna closed his eyes. The voices sang, and he saw
Naga serpents with jewels shining in their heads at night, saw
the Demon King and a golden deer, heard the screams of
Jatayu the Vulture . . . was the past happening again before his
eyes? Is this really Dandaka Forest again?

When silence returned the Kosalas were stunned and quiet
a long time. They had tears in their eyes, they were breathing
fast. Then they said, "We hear in song the past of long ago
made alive again, as though happening right now. An excel-
lent song, we see it all around us. It is a wonder, a precious
treasure! Words like these were never heard before. Where
are we, in what dream?"

They asked Satrughna, "Find Valmiki, discover whose song
this is."

But Satrughna said, "After a long time the old memories
return to my mind. It is wrong to pry into a saint's life. There
are many mysteries here, and it is not for us to speak of them
at all."

In the clear bright morning Satrughna departed. Once more
returned to Fair Ayodhya he walked with Rama outside by the
palace, under the falling blossom petals like white snow, and
said, "I went far away and came back. Majesty, I will never
more travel away from you."

farewell again,
my lady and my king

*Rama, only you deserve the gift of this
first poem.*

Valmiki the Morning Star of Song!

And so it was, Saunaka, that in this very Naimisha Forest
where we are now, Rama gave a celebration and festival one
age of the world ago. The Kosalas cleared a great field by the
river, long and wide, and built guesthouses of brick. All work
was begun at the right hours on the right days, and in a month
a fairground stood complete.

It was less than a day from the city, but it was in the fair
countryside among the wild roses, among the flowering trees
of gold and red like smokeless fires, and the honeysuckle
vines, and lotus ponds of red and white and blue where
weeping trees bent trailing their leaves.

Rama's guests arrived through welcome archways and gifts
were given. Brahmanas remembered the rules to make things
right in other worlds, and for this one, there were everywhere
hearty feasts and a wonderful hospitality. There were salons
for beautiful courtesans and homes for ascetics, taverns and
baths, stables and theatres. And at dawn, at the end of a warm
night under the stars, King Rama and Prince Lakshmana rode
from Ayodhya to Naimisha Forest and opened the festival
park.

They found Vasishtha the brahmana and Rama said, "Let it
begin; let no barrier block my thanksgiving; let no flaw occur."

404

"Majesty, follow me." Vasishtha led Rama apart and the King bathed at sunrise and spent the morning alone. He bathed again at noon and all over the forest ground the fires were lit and fed with butter, and brahmanas called the gods to take their shares and offerings. Then Rama entered and stood by his royal forest pavilion and rooms receiving people, and beside him as his partner in the merit of that feast and sacrifice was a golden image of Sita, dressed in gold cloth and wearing gold flowers.

❧

Sita's father King Janaka came from Mithila; Viswamitra the brahmana came down from his hills; Guha the hunter king and his people came from the Secret Forest; Vibhishana and the old Rakshasi Trijata and many demons came from Lanka; King Aswapati with thundering running horses came from high Kekeya; Sugriva and Hanuman and Jambavan the bear and all the animals were there; the vulture king Sampati came from ruling Dandaka Forest; Sumantra and Bharata and Satrughna and the three Queen Mothers arrived; eighty thousand Kings came from every land in wonderful pomp and splendor, riding slowly through the smiling people; and the Poet Valmiki with his household also came, and in a solitary corner of Rama's clearing they all made little cottages of vines and boughs and lived in them, away from crowds and near the water.

Peace and good fortune be unto brahmanas and cows! First King Rama gave away all the world to the brahmanas, and Vasishtha spoke for them, "We cannot rule Earth's four quarters, Lord. We have no time away from our lonely thought and study." And Rama bought back the world from them and gave out her price in gold and cattle. King Janaka the husband of Earth looked on smiling to see land bought and sold by mortal men.

There in Naimisha everything good was gathered. Monkeys and demons gave out gifts. Everyone had a good time —the old, right, good-time ways! The world was all nice, for a change. Rama and the Kosalas—they were indeed great men.

At that celebration no one was judged and need was provided for and loud words softly answered. Men were transported by wine and carried away by women; the women were clothed in excitement and bright new robes. People sat by lovely easy stairways on the riverside, feasting under umbrellas and fans. Village girls danced with the dread royal warriors no longer grave and serious, and Hanuman and Jambavan chased animal children through the trees and streets, and they almost caught them eight hundred and thirty-seven times, and the celebration really started.

King Sugriva stood in the kitchens among the meats and spices and steaming savory sauces along with Vibhishana and many monkeys and bears and demons. The two kings said, "Receive and serve our friends and please them. Be peaceful and be generous. Cherish our guests. Don't be careless, don't throw presents and shove food at people. You will be pouring out the treasures of Ayodhya, and beware lest their mere touch make you greedy."

When all had arrived Rama thanked them for coming and housed them, and brahmanas blessed him by a three-sided brick fire-altar. Then throughout the clearing priests set up twenty-one ornamental stakes carved of fine woods, each taller than a man, with eight sides and hung with bright strips of colored cloth and flowers and jewels like stars.

Among those stakes strutted the proud and powerful Kings and Emperors of the world drinking from winejars and talking. They said,"Rama never came to us to fight Ravana, or it would have been over just like that! Just right! That's the whole truth—lucky for the demons!"

Hanuman was stuffed with apricots and apples and he heard them from where he sat with Jambavan the bear against a tree. He finished some wine and strolled grinning into their midst, and bowed low to the Great King of the East and to the Lord of the Western Tribes. Then he looked up at them with a really silly smile and answered, "Oh Lords don't think you're

406

useless—we were but the blind instruments of Ravana's death . . . he was really killed by your fatal strength of tongue!" And Hanuman rolled laughing and laughing in the dust, till the towering bear king came and gently picked him up and carried him away in his furry arms still laughing and kicking his feet in the air. And old Jambavan smiled and growled, "Why in the old days . . . ."

And also later on that first day of Rama's festival, we two began to sing this song *Ramayana*, and everyone grew still and quiet around us, and the King came to listen.

❧

Now we have done this every day, for the year of this festival here in Naimisha Forest. And today is the last day of your celebration, Majesty.

These will be the last verses of this song of our teacher Valmiki.

Oh Rama, well done! We are delighted to see you and to meet your courtesy. After walking over Earth of many fields and ways we arrived here with some people of our hermitage, and came along aisles of food and wines. Your demons scared us a little, for though we have often sung of them yet we had never seen one beside us.

Lion among Kings, we have spoken with the wise men of the forest who see all things as Brahma. They have seen the gods come here each day in the smoke of offerings and return much brightened to their heavens. You have given away a whole year's gifts and your treasury is still full. This is how things truly are, Rama. There is in you some grace that warms the hearts of all who know you, and without knowing why, men find that their lives and fortunes are good, when they are by you.

A year ago when we came here, Valmiki the first Poet in the world brought with us a basket of ripe mangoes from a hilltop by our hermitage. He poured them out on our small cottage floor and said, "Eat these right now, and your voices cannot fail, your memory cannot stray for the rest of your lives. Both

407

of you, sing my *Ramayana* to the King. Today after bathing, go to an open place near Rama and start to sing. He will hear his name and come; sing well for him as you have done for me. Sing in parts, a little every day. Take no reward for it; of what use are riches to hermits living in the wild, eating roots and wearing skins? If Rama soon asks of you your names, say that you are my disciples. But each day before you start, first bow to the King as to a father, for he is the father of all the living people in his land."

"Indeed," said Kusa and Lava, "now the time is the present and we have finished all the sections of *Ramayana.*"

Then, Saunaka, the two boys stopped singing, and Kusa held straight out his open hand and turned it over, saying— *This is all my story.*

Sauti the storyteller said, "But a thousand years later Valmiki composed the last part of *Ramayana.*"

Saunaka who lived in the forest said, "Then there is more!"

Sauti smiled. "At Rama's festival this would have been a song of the future. Rama never heard these last verses, and they tell of the rest of his life."

Listen, my friend—

After Rama's great departure, and a thousand years after his festival here in Naimisha Forest, those after years of Rama's life were revealed to Valmiki as before. He taught his later verses to Kusa and Lava and they first sang them as grown men, there in Valmiki's hermitage to a forest audience.

Kusa and Lava welcomed the poem with great joy, and when they had learned it they tuned the lute and tightened the drum. Under the blue skies of many mornings they sang a little every day. Their voices were deep but they had lost no skill nor art. Kusa and Lava began to sing and many listeners gathered round them and Valmiki smiled. All the forest animals were hushed and still, and birds flew to hear.

They sang, "Be at your ease, free your mind from ill-will and all unkindness. Let go of anger and hear us ever without malice. Now hear the end—We sing a song of kingly fame, Oh Listen . . . ."

◈   ◈   ◈

Now oh Father you begin to know who we were there singing to you, and why you have looked at us thinking to know us and wondering who we were . . . .

When Kusa and Lava sang Valmiki's song to King Rama every day for a year at his feast in the forest, people gathered round in a circle from every nation all over the world. The desert men and the people from beyond the hills, the silk-merchants and men from the Land of Gold all listened. Rakshasas and monkeys and bears listened, many figures, all still. At other times there was mirth and merry cheer, men were tired with elaborate pleasures, or did their jobs and followed their crafts. But when those two boys sang they stopped to hear.

There were gathered the King, old men of science and young mothers holding their children, actors and palm readers and fat cooks, grim philosophers who could answer every question but the one, and young warriors fearless of harm from all men's armies. Their hair stood on end, their hearts were ravished, each one was drawn into the music and story of Rama's Way as though it were the tale of his own life, unrolling there before him in great beauty and with great praise.

The audience were breathtaken and delighted with the charms of those verses of Valmiki; they were entranced and spellbound in rapture, surprised and wonderstruck; they laughed and cried aloud. Every day when Kusa and Lava quit singing, ascetics snapped their fingers and waved their upper garments in the air and shook their waterjars, and noble kings threw their heavy bracelets into the circle. But Kusa and Lava would let all such treasures lie and touched none of them.

Ramayana is a fabulous and wonderful tale, an old well-loved story of the younger age of the world. And now it ends with this farthest last-following part. It will be the inspiration and give themes to poets of the future, for this story of Rama will endure forever in this world.

Ramayana will gain the hearer long life, health and strength and a good and beautiful wife, every merit and profit and success and skill. He will have children and riches and good friends, and all his desires will be won. He will get over every trouble and have good crops. The gods will be delighted with him.

This book frees a house from evil spirits. May good betide you. In our bodies, there is inside the heart a spirit living quietly, and if a man will be victorious let him be tuned and at one with this quiet person, and that brings happiness to the gods and good to himself.

> *I am Valmiki's song;*
> *Valmiki made me:*
> *Ever true;*
> *Just for you.*

❧

The greatest excellence, the one thing that made Rama's festival so wonderful was the singing of Kusa and Lava, their good music and fine words. Those two young boys sang *Ramayana* to a silver-stringed lute and a two-headed drum. They sang in unison or at intervals. The drum beat along swift as rainfall or lingered in silence. The lute sang; it cried and warned. It fought through perils, through chance and sorrow; it triumphed and rejoiced.

On the last day of the festival Kusa and Lava ended all Valmiki's verses of that time, and Vibhishana the demon said, "Wonderful it is, after a long time the old recollections come again to my mind. All you have said is true."

410

Sugriva the Monkey King told them, "Sunlight and glory, song and wine! We must always feed the storytellers and give them presents."

But Kusa and Lava took up their lute and drum and set out for their cottage as they did after every day's singing. And Rama looked after them and thought, "They are just like me, boys just as I was then."

Rama told Lakshmana, "The longer I hear those two boys sing the more I love to listen; the longer I look on them the more I want to see them. Go follow them and give them whatever they want."

Lakshmana caught up to Kusa and Lava and said, "We are never satisfied hearing your song. Blessings and long life to you. Blessed be you, blessed be! Beautiful is Valmiki's story, beautifully have you sung and ended it. The King offers you—"

"No, no," answered Kusa and Lava. "Thank the King, and we must go to our master Valmiki."

Lakshmana returned to Rama, "They refuse all reward for that tale whose words are touched by song."

"Those twin brothers are my two sons," said Rama. He called Hanuman and said, "Son of the Wind, find Sita in Valmiki's house. Here and now this very day will I take her back home with me before all my people."

Hanuman soon returned with the Poet Valmiki. Valmiki said, "Majesty, good fortune to you. A husband is a wife's lord, and Sita will come to you."

"She is here!"

"Rama, I will bring her to you. Those two boys are your sons Kusa and Lava. They were born in my retreat."

"I know." Rama smiled and put his hand on Valmiki's shoulder. "You have brought verse in to the world, and now anyone can start a poem, but you have brought yours to a blazing wonderful finish. You've brought it all together; you did it right!"

Valmiki asked, "Did you like it, Rama?"

"It is excellent, Valmiki, I say it is excellent. I shall never forget those verses."

"Oh Lord!"

"Poet, you have brought happiness to us all . . . I loved it well. Surely you knew I liked it?"

"No, I didn't . . . if you don't tell me, how will I know? You have to say." Valmiki smiled.

And Rama said, "See how the world flowers! All good things have come to men."

Then Valmiki waved his arms. "Lord Rama like the Moon, you are a mortal man. She loves you. The bounty of Earth is not your doing, Majesty." Valmiki knelt down. "For ten thousand years you lived with her, and for twelve she's been away. The ten thousand years were the rich ones. King, with you permission Sita will meet you this day."

Tears flowed down Rama's face from his green eyes. "Rise, Poet."

❧

That afternoon everyone at the festival assembled outside, sitting motionless in a circle around the Ayodhya throne in the clearing where Rama's sons had sung his story, holding their breaths, not talking. Rama sat on his throne and the people left wide room around him. The golden statue of Sita had been carried away.

Then the crowd parted and Sita came there following Valmiki. She was beautiful; she walked looking down, but glancing up at Rama many times. Valmiki stopped, and Sita stood alone by Rama within that circle of people, dressed in bright gold and scarlet.

Then into that circle stepped King Janaka, Sita's father the Videha lord. Janaka had swift wide wisdom like a sharp keen blade; he opened locked doors, he found treasure and the True. In his youth Janaka fought a hundred battles. He took hard blows and gave harder. But then he changed. He was Earth's husband, and never more put his heart away behind armor.

Earth's forests and furrows confused his enemies and his kingdom was safe in the foothills. Janaka took all men for

412

brothers; he ever watched for a stray life to save. Passing pleasures called him, in forms quite beautiful, but Janaka did what he knew was right and forgot the people who said he was wrong. And being free, having nothing to hide however small, he found the far sweetest pleasure of speaking out his mind to any man. He wed the Earth and loved her.

Janaka thought it all out for himself, and fought for Dharma. He warred on the loss of love through unkindness and the fetters of wrong desire; he fought for freedom by blasting off the chains of attachment; he killed deceptions with words that released the spirit. It was a hard fight, and Janaka told his warriors—*I give up owning the world's gear. I give up thirst for things to find true love, that never fades.* And his best guard of warriors answered—*We'll keep your word, we'll obey our King. We put down our swords and take the robes of harmless men. What?! Shall we have faced all our wars together and not go into this fight beside you?*

Janaka said to Rama, "There is no blame for this."

Rama answered, "Forgive me, and forgive us all." The people pressed forward around that circle.

Janaka raised his voice, "Ring this circle!" And his unarmed warriors stepped forward from the crowd, wayfarers to the True, and they joined their strong hands and arms like iron, and formed an inner wall that held everyone back.

Janaka said, "King Rama, I'll give you ten million pieces of gold if you will abandon your throne, and use your strength in my service."

Rama was startled. "I can't do that, Janaka."

"Then I offer you nine million pieces."

"But I cannot, it is wrong," said Rama.

"But I'll give you five million in gold."

"No."

"One million then," said Janaka.

"No."

"A thousand to serve me!"

"Janaka, what are you doing?" asked Rama. "In the world of men one offers more and more of money for what he cannot get at first, but you have swiftly lowered the price."

413

Janaka answered, "So quickly does your life pass by! Now men may live many thousand years, but what do you think? Is that long to put off what must be done?"

"It seems but a short while to me also."

"How long might it truly be then?"

Rama replied, "It is really but the time of one day. A whole lifetime may seem to have been very short as it closes, like a morning and an afternoon spent in the sunlight as Night comes."

"No," said Janaka.

"It is but an hour," said Rama.

"No, not even an hour."

"A lifetime, that is the time it takes to fill a waterjar at the riverside."

"You have not understood me."

Rama said, "All our life is but the blink of an eye."

"Yes," said Janaka, "now you understand. Make haste to follow the good Dharma law; hurry to do right while you can, before it's too late." Janaka embraced his daughter Sita. "I sowed seed in Earth and tended her, and she bore you to me from a plowed field. I've loved you all your life, though I let you marry and go."

Janaka left Sita alone with Rama, surrounded by spectators. Sita looked at Rama and smiled. She looked out at the people, and smiled at Sumantra the Charioteer, and at Trijata the old Rakshasi, and at Lakshmana. Then her smile widened bright; she saw Hanuman the monkey there in his best clothes, wearing the pearls she had given him, his white hair finely brushed like a halo round his head.

Hanuman smiled happily back at her, and when he did a scented cool wind blew lightly through Naimisha Forest. That was heaven's wind, come down to Earth as a witness. Vayu the Wind Lord threw gladness and joy over all of them there, like a wealthy king scattering jewels and flowers with abandon on all his friends. As when the world was newfound, when Earth was young, a springtime wind blew again once more through heaven and Earth and sky, all one.

414

Sita was forever beautiful. Wearing her ornaments she turned slowly around and looked at every person there. "Rama, let me prove my innocence, here before everyone."

"I give my permission," said Rama.

Then Sita stepped a little away from him and said, "Mother Earth, if I have been faithful to Rama take me home, hide me!"

Earth rolled and moved beneath our feet. With a great rumbling noise the ground broke apart near Sita and a deep chasm opened, lighted from below with bright lights like lightning flashes, from the castles of the Naga serpent kings.

From underground rose four tall Nagas, like great cobras, the treasure guardians of Earth's riches; their hoods were flat out; they were hissing and weaving, swaying and spitting fire, turning their red eyes at the people; they were all dressed in jewels and rippling silver scales like moonlight on the ocean's waves at night. That opening widened, the serpents were one at each corner, and from below rose up a throne carved of stones, and wrought of roots and set with diamonds.

On that throne sat Mother Earth. Earth was not old, she was fair to look on, she was not sad but smiling. She wore flowers and a girdle of seas. Earth supports all life, but she feels no burden in all that. She is patient. She was patient then, under the Sun and Moon and through the rainfalls of countless years. She was patient with seasons and with kings and farmers; she endured all things and bore no line of care from it.

But this was the end of her long patience with Rama. Earth looked at her husband Janaka and smiled. Then she stretched out her arms and took her only child Sita on her lap. She folded her beautiful arms around her daughter and laid Sita's head softly against her shoulder as a mother would. Earth stroked her hair with her fair hands, and Sita closed her eyes like a little girl.

The throne sank back underground and they all were gone; the Nagas dove beneath the ground and the crevice closed gently over them, forever.

The gods spoke, "Well done, Oh Sita. Praise to you." And

... "took her only child ...

every person watching Sita's descent into Earth, and all living creatures in the world were very happy. For a moment the whole Universe was everywhere equal. Happiness and great delight spread over the three worlds. Men cried aloud in joy; or were silent and held still by their happiness, unable to move. The wild animals of Naimisha Forest watched motionless from the trees as flowers fell from heaven above—yellow and red, blue and white and orange gold . . . .

Rama smiled. "I am King and Lord of Earth, but she has taken my wife away before my very eyes. I will never meet Sita again while I live as a man." Rama sighed, and still he was smiling. He turned to King Janaka. "Indeed, it is a brief life given to Man—but the Dream, the Dream!"

❦

That festival and sacrifice was finished. It was excellent; it destroyed big and little sins, it brought heaven to everyone there. The guests departed, the foreign kings went home, and the ground shook with the tread of elephants and horses and the chariot wheels.

After the others had departed, Janaka and Rama, Lakshmana and Hanuman sat on the bare ground and drank wine in the afternoon. After one cup Lakshmana held his head and covered his eyes and fell over asleep. After a second round Hanuman dropped off. Janaka and Rama drank a third cup and Rama rubbed his eyes.

"What drink is this?"

"Varuni, the Goddess of Spirits, made this palm wine to bring sleep. Overcome her, drink her down."

Rama leaned back against a tree. "Janaka, why am I here? What am I doing here? Can you tell me why?"

"Whatever you have done, you did it to serve the good Dharma Law." Janaka filled the winecups and once more they both drank deep, sitting in the cool shade. "Rama, may you have love for us so we may find some place in your heart."

"I have."

"The honors you have given and the good words, these are

417

natural to you. You are Rama, you are my safe refuge. We do not know what more to say to you. Lord, we have gone far, and we find you there still farther beyond us." Rama slept, and Janaka got to his feet and walked away.

Viswamitra, who had first taken Rama from Ayodhya as a boy, and King Janaka walked together back to Mithila city in the Videha land, just the two of them going by back roads and woodland trails. After a few days they began to climb into the foothills, and they could see Janaka's city.

They walked across the rich fields of Videha, through the new-plowed dirt, and Vishwamitra said, "Remember them? They were sixteen, and everyone loved Rama even then."

"See those trees?" asked Janaka. "They grow from fragments of Shiva's bow, thrown under Earth when Rama broke it."

"With one pull, after all the world had failed!" Viswamitra the friend of all stood leaning on his mendicant's staff. "Rama is a heart-winning man. He freed Ahalya the Beautiful, and she pressed beauty into him with her hand."

Janaka said, "There's no other person as brave as Rama."

Viswamitra answered, "There's Sita."

"There is no one else, only Rama! If you tell such lies get out of my ancestral kingdom."

Viswamitra smiled. "I obey. Where is your kingdom? Where do your lands end? What are the limits of your realm, and where is the dominion of another king?"

Janaka looked around, this way and that. "Well, my kingdom is not these fields, it might be the city."

"Where?"

"No, I see nothing of mine there. Surely then, my own body must be my kingdom, and I will look . . . ."

"What do you find?" asked Viswamitra.

"You may go or stay anywhere as long as you like," smiled Janaka. "Even this body is not mine, this I am not. It is no part of me. Or else—I rule all space, for I do not hold onto the sounds that enter these ears; I rule all land, for I desire no scents but let them come and go; I rule the waters for I do not

418

grasp at any taste; my eye does not cling to lights and colors and so I rule all fire; I care not for any touch, nor do I avoid it, and so I rule the air and winds . . . ."

Viswamitra said, "Janaka, no craving nor thirst have you. You have found the everlasting Dharma wheel and truly set it turning, set it rolling out of the hills and past the reach of Death and beyond the rule of Time; beyond rebirth; beyond old age, beyond sickness, beyond death again—the glorious Wheel of the Good Law, the Dharma Law a man may win for himself as he wins a battle, with a lion-roar of victory and a shout of great joy!"

Janaka reached down and held the rich dark Earth in his hands. "Dissolution is the end of all things compounded out of the elements and each man fares according to his deeds." He crumbled the soil and let it fall through his fingers. "Sita has died to this world. May all beings everywhere be happy and safe! May all creatures born or seeking to be born have happy minds, may none wish another ill! May loving kindness wash over the worlds!"

❧

Naimisha Forest was deserted and the jungle quickly grew back over Rama's clearing. Kusa and Lava and the poet Valmiki returned to their forest home. Rama ruled in Fair Ayodhya for a thousand years more, alone without Sita, keeping her golden statue by him in her palace rooms.

After a long time Queen Kausalya died looking on Rama's face. Then Sumitra and Kaikeyi followed her to the peaceful land of the dead, then to the Moon, and then wearing robes of light to heaven where they were all three reunited with King Dasaratha, and where no one is old.

Then one spring morning, after those thousand years were full, Time in the guise of a hermit came quietly to the Ayodhya palace door and told Lakshmana, "A powerful King sends me as an ambassador to Rama."

Lakshmana led the hermit inside to a private room and brought Rama. Rama asked, "Whose message do you bear?"

419

"Maharaja," said Time, "let us talk alone. Lion among Kings, good fortune to you. Oh King of the World and Lord of Men, Oh Rama order the door to this room closed while I am here with you, and promise me that anyone who shall see us together or overhear our words shall die."

"I promise. Lakshmana, shut the door and stand yourself outside, and prevent anyone from entering."

When they were alone Rama said, "Speak freely. Who sends you here to me?"

The hermit faced him. "Father, I am Kala, I am Time. I bring Brahma's words. But to speak first for myself, you stand always beyond me, you are forever older than I, and so I call you Father. Whatever goes beyond me, you make it go. But even for you strength and youth pass away, and I flow as a river with no obstacle in her bed and nothing to hold her back, once gone by never to return. Spend me or waste me as you will, I can nevermore turn back to you."

Rama said, "Your end is your beginning, you start when you finish. Long since, my child, did the Sun and Moon and stars appear, and Time began to run again. You are my own dear son and my good true servant. You open the spring flowers and unite lovers. You forgive all; you hurt, then you heal. Time will always tell. Sooner or later you reveal all secrets, and you are wise, all the lore of all worlds knowing."

Time said, "I bring love, I marry men and women, I keep the little babies alive. I make the moon rise and I give food and wealth. Do you speak? . . . I let you. Do you do good? . . . My hand guides yours. When you meet a great new day . . . I made it come. It is all one, Rama, all the time that ever was or will be is all one . . . end and beginning are hard to see and they are one, Rama . . . ." Time smiled. "And oh, I lie a lot, Rama . . . I must admit . . . ."

Rama answered, "Time, you have taken dear parts of my life and put them beyond my reach. I have lived through so many cold winters and scented springtimes, so many days and nights that I cannot believe there will not always be more and more of them."

"Ah," said Time, "there you overreach me, I know nothing of poetry."

"What are Brahma's words?"

"Listen. The Grandfather of the worlds tells you—

You killed Ravana. Your promised time is full. Oh Narayana, Lakshmi awaits you, so have I heard. I send Time to remind you. Return to yourself, my friend, we have not seen you for a moment in heaven.

Rama replied, "Those are good words, I am pleased with your coming. I've not forgotten. I remember all of you . . . ."

❦

And as Rama and Time were talking a while, the short-tempered brahmana Durvasas, a grim self-denying ascetic, a sky-clad hermit walked quickly up to Lakshmana at the door and said, "My time is passing! I need food, take me in there first to see the King."

"Great saint, Rama is busy," said Lakshmana. "Command me what to do and I will serve you."

Durvasas wiped some ashes from his brow. "I've just finished my fast and after many years the King must feed me! Admit me to him, I am impatient. Or I will curse all Kosala to burn if you do not announce me this instant."

"Those are dreadful words."

"Every soul will die. My anger is rising, I cannot restrain my growing wrath!"

"Forsake your ill will. My own death is better." Lakshmana pulled open the door. Time's iron staff fell from his hand and clanged on the stone floor, and that noise rang in Lakshmana's ears like the pealing of bells.

Lakshmana went in. "Durvasas needs to see you, Rama."

Rama said, "Lakshmana, you must die for entering here."

Time and Lakshmana looked at each other, and Lakshmana said, "Yes. Great halls are silent after Time has visited them, and dark and hidden is this person's course."

Time said, "Say not so, Lakshmana, say not so. I know the old deeds dimly remembered, the youthful deeds of past

421

lives." Time looked into Lakshmana's blue eyes, blue as wild-flowers, and backed away toward the door. "Oh people all like to abuse me, but I always politely wait my turn, I never crowd in. Rama's heart is boundless, above, below, and all around him. I take away, I take away all the things I've given, but no more than that. You four brothers have all the same nature. You will only go home first. Just as you are, you have won! Well, I must be moving on, Lakshmana, I can never stand still . . . ."

Rama said, "Kala, go, I dismiss you."

Oh, the Dharma Wheel, like a rolling golden Sun!

❦

Then Rama fed the recluse Durvasas, until after a hundred dishes he was full, and without a word that brahmana turned his back on the king and went away into the forests some-where.

Rama looked at Lakshmana. "Farewell, my brother."

Lakshmana made no answer. He walked three times around Rama, and left the palace. He went half a league to where the Sarayu river swiftly flowed.

Lakshmana sat by the running river. With open eyes he looked around him and saw all things as Rama, thought of them as Rama. He rinsed his mouth with the clear water and stopped his breathing. The luminous person within Lakshma-na's heart, the soul no bigger than a thumb made ready to leave this world behind. The life-centers stopped spinning and went out, and Lakshmana's energy, the fourth part of Lord Nara-yana, rose step by step up along his backbone, seeking flight out the crown of his head where the skull bones join their seams.

Lakshmana shut his eyes and watched the lights of his life slowly die. The lights of war long ago, the lights of his first love and marriage . . . the lights of his childhood . . . . And he thought," . . . it's like—something that I made once . . . all of us . . . ."

In heaven, Lord Indra heard empty stone vault doors closing

422

one after another in echoes. Sight was closing, hearing closing, mind turning away. Spirit was rising and leaving empty rooms. The ether space within the heart was empty, fires and lamps turned off, locks and threads snapped and untied, and all released.

Indra swept across Kosala invisibly. He took Lakshmana's soul into his own heart and flew to heaven carrying him and bearing light. Indra the bright King of the Sky took him away. Lakshmana's body fell into the water and was gone.

❦

Shiva the great god divided this romance into three parts, one for heaven, one for Earth, and one for the underworlds. He had one section left, and divided that into three. He had one verse left, and divided that as well. Shiva had one word left, that he kept for himself—the word *Rama*—as being the essence and heart of the whole thing.

One who sees Rama even for a moment gains heaven. He is Narayana, identical with the souls of all creatures. He is the Ocean and the forests and the air I breathe. He is more subtle than an atom. He goes everywhere by illusion, without beginning or end, unchangeable, unconquerable, holding a shell trumpet and a wheel, a mace and a lotus flower. So let us remember him when we are in any difficulty, from inside or out.

Tomorrow won't always be like today. Now, while there is time, today take this *Ramayana* to your home before the great world ends for you. Tune your senses to Dharma, say *Rama* while you have a chance, and make your heart a loving holy place, lighten it, clear it of good and evil, or high and low.

> *Very happy, or near to tears;*
> *So keep this book, and live your years.*
> *Oh Rama!*

Thunders rolled over Ayodhya although the sky was clear. The white houses rocked and Earth shook. The brahmana Vasishtha was with Rama, and Rama said, "Where is my life

423

and where am I? I'm going all the way on through to my own home now, I'm going back around by going forward, and I'll be again as I was before being born into this world . . . ."

Vasishtha said, "Look out at your city. The people kneel outside their homes; they lower their heads and do not move, or lie like corpses."

Goodbye, Rama; goodbye Father, goodbye, goodbye . . . .

Bharata and Satrughna entered, and Bharata said, "Fair Ayodhya is ended as we have known her."

Vasishtha said, "Majesty, I'll leave you now. I'll go alive to heaven for awhile, and rest and tend the cow of wishes in her peaceful pasture." And he left them there.

I think the Fair Ayodhya that Rama knew must now be sought for elsewhere than on this Earth. Those were other days. But though I must dream or die to do it—I've been to Fair Ayodhya and I'll go back there again.

Rama asked his brothers, "What can I do?"

"Don't forsake us, don't leave us behind," said Bharata.

"That's all we ask," said Satrughna. "Now all of us will follow the Well-Farer."

Rama asked, "Why will you go with me?"

"Near you is ever all my happiness."

"Whoever will, let them come. Then go and send the Kosalas who wish to stay behind on Earth to places far from here. Give them wealth and chariots and elephants; let them leave me and go into the woods or to the seas, or into the snowy hills."

❧

Then learning somehow of Rama's great departure, that very day to Ayodhya came the monkeys and dark bears of the forest, and the Lanka king Vibhishana from over the sea. They spoke among themselves, "Now the waiting's done, now the day has come. Who would not be ready to follow you? . . ." The animals stood along the streets beside Kosala men and Gandharvas of heaven, beside Nagas from the underworld and hermits from the empty wood, all still and silent, waiting by the palace walls and gates, and along the roads to the Sarayu River.

The Kosalas told them, "Lakshmana is lost for a flawless promise. Dasaratha's four sons are dead. We follow Rama."

Vibhishana the dark demon said, "Set out the great brilliant umbrellas along the northern high road to the riverside."

Hanuman said, "That will look well, but if you want a high road to heaven, just say *Rama*."

Rama came walking on the streets. He wore thin green silk and held in his right fingers a sheaf of grass. He turned to the north, humming some of the song Kusa and Lava had sung a thousand years before. Our Lady Lakshmi of the Lotus walked on his right; Mother Earth went patiently on his left. And behind him walked many weapons in human forms, sharp spears and arrows and huge bows, merciless swords and heavy-set maces and the howling knives of war, and many tears of blood ran from their hard eyes.

First Vibhishana wearing gold approached Rama and said, "Let me also go through the open gates."

Rama replied, "Lanka King, you are immortal. Death will never touch you, while my memory lives. As long as the Moon and Sun and Earth shall exist, as long as the mountains and rivers continue on Earth's face, as long as the sea beats with his eternal waves against the solid land, so long shall my wonderful story of *Ramayana* remain in the world."

Then Sugriva the Monkey King came to Rama. "I give Kishkindhya to Angada. I will go with you."

Rama said, "Yes."

Jambavan the bear bowed to Rama. He did not speak, only a low growl came from his throat. Rama blessed the Bear King and said, "You will live while Valmiki's *Ramayana* is heard on Earth." He bent close and gave Jambavan a charm, a present, something precious. "And Hanuman also will live so long, where is he now?"

Hanuman came bounding down from the sky. He hit the ground with a thud like a thunderstone. He was right close to Rama, smiling at him, laughing and gay.

"Oh Hanuman!"

"My King!" Hanuman knelt before Rama.

Rama said, "As long as men shall speak of you, you will live on Earth. No one can equal you. Your heart is true; your arms are strong; you have the energy to do anything. You have served me faithfully and done things for me that couldn't be done."

"It's nothing," said Hanuman. "I am your friend, that's all."

Rama wore a rare golden bracelet set with gemstones on his right arm, a costly irreplaceable ornament inherited from among the wealth of the Solar Kings from ancient days. He said, "Best of Monkeys, take this as my gift," and gave it to Hanuman.

Hanuman snatched the bracelet from Rama and started to turn it over and around in his white furry paws, looking closely at it. Then he bent and broke it; he twisted the gold and pulled out the jewels, and put them between his hard teeth. He bit down on the priceless gems and broke them like nuts, and carefully searched over the pieces, looking everywhere for something.

Rama asked him, "Monkey, at a time like this why are you still difficult?"

Hanuman answered, "Lord, though this bracelet looked expensive it was really worthless, for nowhere on it did it bear your name. I have no need of it, Rama. What do I want with anything plain?"

Vibhishana sniffed at that. "Then I can't see what value life has to you. Why don't you destroy your body as well?"

Then with his sharp fingernails Hanuman tore open his breast and pulled back the flesh. And see! There was written again and again on every bone, in fine little letters—*Rama Rama Rama Rama Rama . . . .*

Rama put down the grass he held, and with his two hands he pressed together Hanuman's parted flesh, and the wound over his beating heart came together leaving no scar at all, not even one big as a grain of dust, or the tip of a hair. Rama drew off his hand his broad gleaming gold ring that said *Rama*, the ring

426

that Hanuman had carried to Sita. He put it into Hanuman's wet bloodstained paw and gently closed the monkey fingers over it.

Who is this monkey Hanuman? Rama has let him loose in the world. He knows Rama and Rama knows him. Hanuman can break in or break out of anywhere. He cannot be stopped, like the free wind in flight.

Hanuman can spot a tyrant, he looks at deeds not words, and he'll go and pull his beard. Disguises and words of talk cannot confuse a mere wild animal. Hanuman's rescue of brave poets in any peril may be had for their asking, and that monkey will break the handsome masks of evil kings.

Hanuman will take your sad tune and use it to make a happy dance. We have seen that white monkey. Strong is his guard. Especially take warning, never harm a free Poet.

The Son of the Wind. The warm dry night wind, and all the trees swaying! I don't care for love or death or loneliness— here comes the high Wind, and what am I . . . ?

❦

Vibhishana and Hanuman and Jambavan the bear flew away. Rama stood speechless and bright and brilliant, like the lighted Sun.

Rama walked on to the Sarayu River, and whoever saw him pass followed him. Many stones wept that they had to stay behind, leaving streaks and marks one can still see. The tall trees swayed and bent creaking after him, and water ran along beside Rama's road. Some birds called out to him—*Stay right there, stay right there*—while others said—*Go far, go fast! Go fast! We'll follow you, you.*

The deer came crashing noisily up through the brush and onto the road. Dumb beasts were walking along beside great-minded men. Little animals never seen in the city were going with Rama. Whoever breathed tried to follow him . . . children skipped and ran, and women walked together, talking to monkeys and bears.

It was just afternoon, and they all passed between colored

. . . first in through the water.

rows of Ayodhya umbrellas. Death was watching. Death wept with joy to see those beautiful colors, all like a glorious sunrise.

Oh Rama, nobody knows all of you. But here by Sarayu's water, we will step through, Lord.

By the river, in the saffron shade of the last umbrella stood Guha the hunter king, and Sumantra the old charioteer beaming in joy. Sumantra had freed the four royal red horses, but they followed him and stood there. Wild hunters wearing skins and feathers knelt barefoot and waited, resting their long bamboo spears pointing up to the sky.

Animal and human people touched and reached out to each other up and down that riverside then. A green hand and a red one, a bear paw, deer's hoof, little birds' wings, black skin and gold and brown, all touching, and the water flowing by like Time. Bharata gave Rama his birthfire and his brothers' all mixed, and Rama threw them into Sarayu. The fires stopped burning and were peaceful.

Trust the True! The King took a broad jump and went first in through the water. He went on through to the other side, winning all time past and all to come . . . .

The four red horses leapt. Wild birds flew out of their trees and dove down through the river, men and animals and women followed, the timid forest deer threw themselves out from the riverbank and went in shooting curves under the water swift-flowing to the sea with rising waves.

Chitraratha the five-crested Gandharva King stood by heaven's open massive gate, singing the old true songs. He looked out at the sky. It was the evening of a day in heaven. The air was velvet dark below, and the stars of spring hung swaying on their ropes of wind. Sparkling souls were coming up from Earth along the distant sky-paths, and drawing near were flights of heaven's songbirds soaring over the oceans of space, and the innocent heavenly deer were leaping, brilliant as gods.

❖ ❖ ❖

Kusa and Lava sang, "This ends our Father's Way, the tale is done at last."

429

All the twenty-four thousand verses were finished, sung in their melody and measure. This story has been told for a very long time, it will be told long into the future. All life is pleased, and well pleased with you for hearing it now.

Hearing or reading *Ramayana* you will get from Rama what you wish for, so be aware! Don't ask too little. Good fortune to you all. This is the world's first best poem.

In the first age of the world men crossed the ocean of existence by their spirit alone. In the second age sacrifice and ritual began, and then Rama lived, and by giving their every act to him men lived well their ways. Now in our age what is there to do but worship Rama's feet? But my friend, the last age of this world shall be the best. For then no act has any worth, all is useless . . . except only to say *Rama*. The future will read this. Therefore I tell them, when all is in ruin around you, just say *Rama*.

We have gone from the spiritual to the passionate. Next will come ignorance. Universal war. Say *Rama* and win! Your time cannot touch you!

Remember Indrajit. Guard yourself—against the real things. Everything counts, and so be kind. Do not dare to lie politely with casual unmeant promises, for Indrajit always believes that you will mean what you say to him.

Narayana was back in his heaven, with Lakshmi an instant later. The four dark hands picked up again the shell and the lotus, the discus and the mace . . . .

Sauti the storyteller said, "Rama's name alone brings victory. Oh Saunaka my friend, whoever tells *Ramayana* to others becomes free and does not have to labor painfully for his food."

Sauti sat facing Saunaka in Naimisha Forest, by Saunaka's woodland home. Sauti continued, "I carry the name *Rama* sealed within an amulet when I travel over the world, and I keep it in my house when I am home. It lets me go in peace and return safely to those who love me.

430

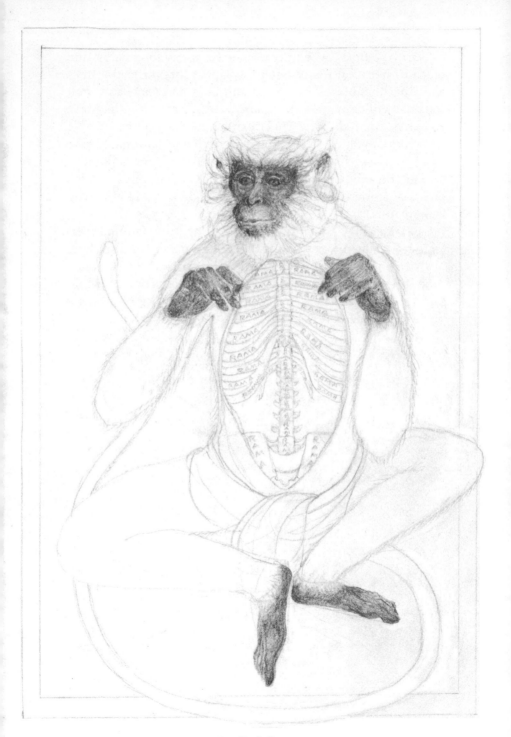

. . . in fine little letters . . .

"Fair Ayodhya was empty of men for many long years, and much of her wealth and beauty was lost forever to the trees and vines that buried her. Kusa and Lava had sons, and their sons had children,and later there were Kosala kings again in Ayodhya. But today she is a city much like any other.

"Still today, high in the pine forests lives Hanuman," said Sauti. "He will always be listening wherever Rama's name is spoken; he will listen endlessly to his old adventures and his own true stories. So take care, he is here. Now you know who Hanuman is."

Saunaka said, "Imagine that!" Then he saw Hanuman listening, a white monkey sitting there behind Sauti and smiling. "What you say is all true!" He looked into Hanuman's eyes.

Sauti turned to Hanuman, then back to his friend. "I told you so. Valmiki was seeking the True before he ever was a poet, and when it all was done he sang—

> I'm still myself, I'm me.
> Here is the True, have no fear;
> This is for you, for you are dear
> To me; I'm still myself."

Sauti said, "Here we close our story, good fortune to you! Rama! Rama! Rama!"

> Again the Players come.
> Love to all men.

❖ ❖ ❖

HERE ENDS THE RAMAYANA

432